# FROM WONDER TO WISDOM

Introductory Readings in Philosophy

# FROM WONDER TO WISDOM

## Introductory Readings in Philosophy

EDITED BY Fidel A. Arnecillo Jr.

*California State University—San Bernardino*

cognella® | ACADEMIC PUBLISHING

Bassim Hamadeh, CEO and Publisher
Mieka Porter, Senior Field Acquisitions Editor
Tony Paese, Project Editor
Alia Bales, Production Editor
Jess Estrella, Senior Graphic Designer
Danielle Gradisher, Licensing Associate
Don Kesner, Interior Designer
Natalie Piccotti, Director of Marketing
Kassie Graves, Vice President of Editorial
Jamie Giganti, Director of Academic Publishing



Printed in the United States of America.

ISBN: 978-1-5165-3174-5 (pbk) / 978-1-5165-3175-2 (br)

cognella® | ACADEMIC PUBLISHING

# CONTENTS

# PREFACE

This is an anthology for an introductory course in philosophy. Its focus is mainly on classic readings in Western philosophy. A classic work in philosophy should be one that stood the test of time. These readings have been critically analyzed and evaluated for numerous years, but somehow they manage to stay relevant. That should count for something. These readings were, of course, conditioned by intellectual cultures with their distinct ways of life and thinking. Some intellectual cultures appear to be much more conducive to philosophically sophisticated discourses. For example, I assume that a well-developed language, as opposed to a poorly developed one, makes such discourses possible. In addition, the cultures in more affluent societies generally provide some people the luxuries of thinking about problems that do not seem to have immediate practical relevance. This condition allows some people to engage in a painstakingly slow mastication of ideas. So, a sophisticated language and a particular set of social conditions partly, but significantly, contribute to making a society ripe for fruitful philosophical inquiries. Great civilizations in the world paved the way for the intellectual developments that significantly involved philosophy. We see such developments in China, India, Greece, Rome, Persia, and Japan in the ancient and medieval world, and Italy, France, England, Scotland, Germany, the US, Canada, Australia, and Russia in the modern and contemporary world. In the West at least, it appears that the Christian religion played an important role in shaping its intellectual history. According to some philosophers,[1] Christianity shaped natural philosophy in such a way that made the Scientific Revolution possible. In addition, Jurgen Habermas,[2] a prominent contemporary German philosopher, even claims that its enduring legacy made the development of major democratic values possible.

Considering the scope of what this anthology covers, we can naturally expect that mostly males of European descent must have been the ones who were responsible for writing these texts. I am not in any way denying the contributions of women and non-Europeans in the development of philosophy. I think that the criticism that this anthology preserves a narrative that implicitly treats European males as having intellectual dominance is arguably fair. However, I think that it is unfair to downplay the contributions of classic philosophers just because they are European males. It will be a stretch to think that philosophers such as Descartes, Locke, and Kant, for example, did not significantly shape the narrative about the history of philosophy in the West. Whether we like it or not, they were ones of the many European males who are primarily responsible for what we now call as Western philosophy. Philosophy in the West developed through their works. That's undeniable. Of course, it ought not to be that way. But, it developed in the way that it did. Furthermore, we cannot deny the fact that, unfortunately even today, philosophy remains to be dominated by males of European descent.[3] I, of course, do not want it to be that way. But it remains to be that way. History is far from being ideal, but we don't get to fully choose what transpires in history. Many contributing factors are surely beyond our control. So, by focusing on the philosophical classics, I remain true to what transpired in Western philosophy, despite its obviously flawed history. As a merely foundational course, introductory philosophy courses must cover the classics, although philosophy should not get stuck there. There are more women now in philosophy than in the past. They have proven themselves to be capable of producing quality works in philosophy. We now have Ruth Barcan Marcus, Judith Jarvis Thomson, Susan Haack, Patricia Churchland, Martha Nussbaum, Laurie Paul, and many more. In addition, some prominent philosophers today are non-white, such as Cornel West, Kenneth Taylor, Jaegwon Kim, Ernest Sosa, and others. But, despite their non-whiteness or non-maleness, they generally do philosophy in ways that are indistinguishable from their white or male counterparts. That, I think, shows that philosophy can be done objectively. A reasonable stance is discoverable through methodologies that are not merely distinctively used by white and male philosophers. Reason is no respecter of person. When you follow where it leads

1 For example, see Stephen Gaukroger, *The Emergence of a Scientific Culture: Science and the Shaping of Modernity 1210–1685* (New York: Oxford University Press, 2006).

2 See Jurgen Habermas, *Time of Transitions* (Cambridge, UK: Polity Press, 2006), 150–151.

3 See Myisha Cherry and Eric Schwitzgebel, "Like the Oscar's, #PhilosophySoWhite," *Los Angeles Times*, http://www.latimes.com/opinion/op-ed/la-oe-0306-schwitzgebel-cherry-philosophy-so-white-20160306-story.html

through the guidance of evidences, intuitions, or sound inferences, you should end up in roughly the same spot as other rational inquirers. You do not necessarily get to the truth. But, you get to somewhere within the range of what can be plausibly true. That should suffice for now.

For this anthology, I specifically selected philosophical issues that I find to be interesting to the philosophically uninitiated. After teaching college-level philosophy for almost twenty years, I seem to have the relevant competency to weigh in on which issue is a hit in my classes. Questions about God, mind, knowledge, and morality seem to be the ones that students find appealing. So, I settle with these four topics. But, keep in mind that philosophy is much larger than what this anthology covers. It will barely scratch the surface. I want students to have the impression that philosophy matters to them. Its questions are not fully detached from the students' intellectual or even practical concerns. Philosophical matters don't need to be relegated to mere abstractions. Questions of philosophy are essentially the questions that we ask as humans. Thinking hard about such questions can provide us with deeper perspectives on all sorts of issues. When we think hard about the possibility and scope of human knowledge, we begin to have a deeper understanding of the nature and extent of science. When we think hard about the nature of morality, we begin to have a deeper understanding of the plausible status of our moral judgments. Deeper understanding of profound issues deeply enriches our discussions or conversations about the things that matter dearly to us as humans.

I want to thank the very friendly and very professional staff members of Cognella Academic Publishing, especially Mieka Portier, for making the process of editing an anthology go as smoothly as possible. I also want to thank thousands of students and many philosophical colleagues who gave me the wonderful opportunities to hone my teaching skills. Among my colleagues, I benefited a lot from the teaching evaluations that I received from Matthew Davidson, Tony Roy, Chris Naticchia, Susan Finsen, Lawry Finsen, and William Vanderburgh. Lastly, I want to thank my wife and my son for their love and support.

# INTRODUCTION

"How charming is divine philosophy!
Not harsh and crabbed as dull fools suppose
But musical as is Apollo's lute
And a perpetual feast of nectared sweets"

**—John Milton**

## The Journey from Wonder to Wisdom

Those who have found wisdom after being consumed by wonder must have earned the positions of serving as guides for the perplexed. There's no doubt that Plato and Aristotle can serve as such guides. Philosophers, since the ancient times, positively associate wonder with philosophy. According to Plato (427–347 BCE) in *Theaetetus,* "Wonder is the feeling of the philosopher, and philosophy begins in wonder."[1] For some of them at least, wonder is an emotion that motivates a philosopher to philosophize. A philosopher finds himself or herself astonished by a profound issue. Despite not having any clear resolution for it, he or she nonetheless considers it as important due to its profundity. That should initially trigger a curiosity that can incrementally be satisfied through the deepening of our understanding of the issue, although ultimately such curiosity may end up being endlessly insatiable. So, the lack of clear resolution does not necessarily spell doom for the value of philosophical inquiries. Rather, it should push us to think hard about how we can potentially have a clear resolution and what is that resolution. The process of thinking hard about it should, if done intelligently, makes it possible to consider plausible resolutions. Of course, among plausible resolutions, the actual resolution can likely be found.[2]

Wonder will hopefully lead to wisdom or knowledge. That appears to be what the study of philosophy envisions. Aristotle (384–322 BCE) appears to make a similar claim:

### ARISTOTLE, *METAPHYSICS* 1, 982B

"It is through wonder that men now begin and originally began to philosophize; wondering in the first place at obvious perplexities, and then by gradual progression raising questions about the greater matters too, e.g. about the changes of the moon and of the sun, about the stars and about the origin of the universe. Now he who wonders and is perplexed feels that he is ignorant ... therefore if it was to escape ignorance that men studied philosophy, it is obvious that they pursued science for the sake of knowledge, and not for any practical utility. The actual course of events bears witness to this; for speculation of this kind began with a view to recreation and pastime, at a time when practically all the necessities of life were already supplied. Clearly then it is for no extrinsic advantage that we seek this knowledge; for just as we call a man independent who exists for himself and not for another, so we call this the only independent science, since it alone exists for itself.

For this reason its acquisition might justly be supposed to be beyond human power, since in many respects human nature is servile; in which case, as Simonides says, 'God alone can have this privilege,' and man should only seek the knowledge which is within his reach."

1 See Benjamin Jowett's English translation of Plato's *Theaetetus* 155d

2 I am not claiming here that all philosophers agree with the ancient philosophers in equating wonder with curiosity or viewing wonder as the origin of philosophy. For example, Martin Heidegger (1889–1976), a German philosopher, distinguishes wonder from curiosity and considers curiosity as "a weak and pitiful determination" of philosophy's origin. See Heidegger, *Basic Question of Philosophy* (Bloomington: Indiana University Press, 1994).

In this passage,[3] Aristotle is concerned with the formation of human knowledge. Here's an enumeration of the steps of knowledge formation, as Aristotle understood it:

- Perplexities cause us to wonder.
- Wonder causes us to ask questions.
- Questions lead us to recognize our ignorance.
- Philosophy helps us escape our ignorance.
- Philosophical inquiries aim for knowledge.

**PERPLEXITIES → WONDER → QUESTIONS → IGNORANCE → PHILOSOPHY → KNOWLEDGE**

Humans, as finite entities, inevitably become perplexed about certain issues. Considering that humans have certain cognitive abilities, they wonder about the issues that they find perplexing. An issue that is deeply perplexing can make us feel that we can't help but wonder about it.[4] For example, suppose you are perplexed about the existence of an immaterial mind. It likely strikes you as true that there is such a thing, but perplexity ensues after you find out that the majority of scientists and philosophers deny its existence. So, you begin to wonder. But, wonder inevitably leads to questions. At least in philosophy, the aim is to raise well-thought-out questions, since the right sorts of questions are essential for knowledge formation. In intellectual history, it's not hard to find instances where the one who figures out a better question to ask cracks the code for a deeper understanding of an issue. Some philosophers, such as Justin Weinberg from the *Daily Nous*,[5] even argue that the creation of questions is the intellectual achievement of philosophers. The act of asking questions implies the ignorance of the questioner. In the questions, the questioner recognizes his or her lack of knowledge. That leads to the beginning of a philosophical inquiry. One can at least hope that philosophical inquiries will eventually lead to wisdom or knowledge.

The role of philosophy as an academic discipline in the pursuit of wisdom or knowledge is often ignored or minimized by some people. They might appreciate the important contributions that philosophers made in giving birth to all sorts of academic disciplines, but they are skeptical of the enduring relevance of philosophy as a substantive partner of the sciences in the pursuit of knowledge. It is widely recognized that physics, psychology, linguistics, economics, sociology, political science, anthropology, etc. branched out from philosophy. Biology, chemistry, and mathematics, for instance, have philosophy as a part of their histories. The continuities between philosophical questions and scientific questions should at least indicate that philosophers in the past did not waste their time in inquiring about certain questions. The quests for knowledge began with the philosophers in wonderment, but sciences and mathematics usually get the credit for all sorts of knowledge. But, even if we grant that philosophy does not substantively and directly contribute in the formation of scientific knowledge, or any knowledge for that matter, philosophizing can at least lead to wisdom. As a matter of fact, etymologically, philosophy is the love of wisdom. A brief account of the distinctions between knowledge and wisdom seems necessary here.

What does it mean when someone says that he or she knows something? He or she has a belief about a certain state of affairs or a fact about reality.[6] Suppose one says that he or she knows that there is a bottle on top of the

3 The quote is taken from the English version of Aristotle's *Metaphysics* in Tufts University's Perseus Digital Library with Gregory R. Crane as the editor-in-chief. See http://www.perseus.tufts.edu/

4 I am hesitant to claim that humans are the only ones who are capable of wondering. I assume that wonder is closely associated with curiosity. Some animals at least exhibit a capacity for curiosity. In addition, machines will probably learn how to be curious. As a matter of fact, there are computer scientists who are now coding curiosity into machines. See John Pavlus, "Clever Machines Learn How to Be Curious," *Quanta Magazine*, September 9, 2017, https://www.quantamagazine.org/clever-machines-learn-how-to-be-curious-20170919/

5 See his blog post, entitled "The Intellectual Achievement of Creating Questions," on August 23, 2017 in dailynous.com.

6 My use of "state of affairs" as almost synonymous to the term "fact" appears to be similar to D. M. Armstrong's use of "state of affairs." See D. M. Armstrong, "A World of States of Affairs," *Philosophical Perspectives* 7(1993): 429–440.

table. At least two things are involved here: the belief that there is a bottle on top of the table and a state of affairs where a specific bottle is on top of a specific table. A mere belief does not automatically count as knowledge. People can believe certain beliefs that do not even correspond to certain states of affairs. One who believes that there is a unicorn cannot properly say that he or she knows that there is really such a being. First, he or she cannot say that he or she knows it, since an existential claim (i.e., "x exists" or "There is x") is justifiable as long as what is claimed to exist is within the scope of his or her perceptual experience and he or she has no perceptual experience of an existing unicorn. So, justifiability of a belief, in addition to it being true, seems necessary for what we can legitimately call *knowledge*. It should be noticed here that, by describing knowledge in such a way, it makes it closer to the goal of scientific inquiries. Science attempts to describe a world of states of affairs or facts. It has been clearly successful since its advent in the early modern period. On the other hand, philosophy is not primarily concerned with describing such a world. In a way, philosophers address issues that are much more elusive than the scientific issues. Philosophers wonder about much more fundamental issues. For example, they wonder about what exactly it is that science describes. Does it merely describe the states of affairs as constructed by our distinctive cognitive faculties? Do our senses have access to such a world that they try to represent? There are no easy answers to these questions. One must think hard with the hope of cracking the code for having a glimpse of some insights.

Wisdom, at least in the way that it is used here, has more to do with at least one the following descriptions:

- Qualitatively deeper understanding of the world than what factual knowledge provides
- Qualitatively deeper understanding of the art of living well than the kind of life that is simply informed by factual information about the world
- Qualitatively deeper understanding of how the facts about the world hang together
- Qualitatively deeper understanding of appropriate attitudinal postures in relation to what one deeply understands about the world

Wisdom, of course, can involve some factual knowledge. However, factual knowledge is neither necessary nor sufficient for wisdom. A farmer can make intuitively wise decisions, even if he or she does not fully know all the facts about farming. Wisdom has to do with qualitatively deeper understanding of something, while knowledge has to do with quantitatively robust understanding of the world. What is "qualitatively deeper understanding"? Wisdom is an understanding of something that puts into play all sorts of information and intuitions to have bearing on what one tries to understand. Knowledge is concerned with what can be observed and measured. Wisdom goes beyond what can be observed and measured. A philosopher in performing the tasks of philosophical inquiries invites the insights of past philosophical giants into the conversations, considers historical contingencies that shape the process of understanding, incorporates sensible intuitions, imagines all sorts of possibilities (even the ones beyond physical possibilities), uses logical tools rigorously, takes into account all sorts of scientific claims, disambiguates or clarifies concepts and ideas, challenges well-established norms of all sorts, etc.

Philosophers are not just concerned with the external world as an object of understanding. They are also concerned with how one ought to live his or her life. What is the ideal life? We all know that humans do not live by bread alone, since humans do not just live through what they can put inside their mouths. People with enough resources to buy all sorts of bread are not necessarily satisfied with their lives. So, bread will not suffice as the only thing that matters in life. There are other things in the world that make life satisfying. Philosophers reflect about the things that make life satisfying. By reflecting on such matters, they address issues that have to do with how an individual ought to live and how a political community ought to be structured or designed. Should we treat other people fairly? What is fairness? Should a community be racially diverse? Is it ever justifiable to disobey the laws? What makes the act of killing wrong? How can one justify his or her moral judgment? Should rights be extended to animals? Of course, many more questions can be asked.

Let me now introduce each part of this anthology.

# Part One: Socrates—A Philosopher in Action

The anthology starts with Socrates, who is widely known as the "father" of Western philosophy. We don't really know much about the historical Socrates, since he did not write a book about any of his teachings. **Plato** (429–347 BCE), in his dialogues that highlight the positive intellectual traits of Socrates, gives us the Socrates who embodied the virtues (intellectual and moral) that were admired by many in the ancient world. Socrates, as portrayed by Plato as the major character in his dialogues, somewhat exemplified for us a classic way of doing philosophy. A philosopher, as he or she inquires, engages in meticulous and rigorous intellectual activities. He or she identifies the dilemma or misconception, challenges the traditional and culturally conditioned ways of resolving the dilemma or untangling the misconception, shows the inadequacies in the common responses, shatters the ungrounded confidences of her conversation partners, captures some insights in the process, and points to the roads less traveled. But, in the end, nothing but tension-filled philosophical conundrums await. In the midst of such mental disruptions, the mind begins to reveal philosophical dead-ends and suggests, even in subtle ways, plausible answers. The conversation that transpired in Plato's *Euthyphro* illustrates such a process as Socrates and Euthyphro talk about the nature of piety.

# Part Two: God's Existence

The first issue has to do with God's existence. That's not to say that philosophers primarily care about God. As a matter of fact, a large majority of philosophers do not believe in God.[7] So, many of them probably do not care about issues pertaining to God's existence. But, that of course does not mean that conversations about God's existence have no philosophical value. They are valuable. According to John Polkinghorne, formerly a Cambridge physicist, "The question of the existence of God is the single most important question we face about the nature of reality."[8] At least for Polkinghorne, it appears that God's existence (or non-existence) has bearing on the theoretical framework that one uses in understanding the nature of reality. I assume that a world without God will be understood differently than a world with God. One who assumes a world with God will be concerned with the plausible roles of God in the beginning, orchestration, and sustenance of the universe. However, one who assumes a world without God will settle with purely naturalistic accounts of its beginning, design, and operations.

Peter Kreeft, a philosopher from Boston College, identified twenty arguments for God's existence.[9] This anthology covers four of them: ontological, cosmological, teleological, and Pascal's Wager. Let me briefly describe each argument. I will start with the ontological proof. **Anselm of Canterbury** (1033–1109 CE) was the first one to formulate this argument. It is commonly known as an a priori proof for God's existence, (i.e., a proof that does not utilize the data from sense experiences). It begins with a particular concept of God, namely God as that being than which nothing greater can be conceived. If existence is greater than nonexistence, then God as that being than which nothing greater can be conceived has to exist. Suppose that God does not exist. It implies that other things must be greater than God, since anything that exists must be greater than God. If other things are greater than God, then God cannot be that being than which nothing greater can be conceived. In addition, according to Anselm, since necessary existence (an attribute of one that cannot fail to exist) is greater than contingent existence (an attribute of one that can fail to exist or could have failed to exist), God must necessarily exist if God even exists at all. If God only exists contingently, then another thing that can be conceived as necessarily existing is greater than God. If that argument sounds like mere play on words for you, then you are in good company. Arthur Schopenhauer, a nineteenth-century German philosopher, has been known to describe it as a "sleight of hand trick" and "a charming joke." Anselm's argument immediately found a detractor.

7 According to the PhilPapers Surveys (see https://philpapers.org/surveys/results.pl), 72.8 percent of philosophers who participated in the surveys accept or lean toward atheism.

8 John Polkinghorne, *The Faith of a Physicist: Reflections of a Bottom-Up Thinker* (Princeton: Princeton University Press, 1994), p. 52.

9 Peter Kreeft, "20 Arguments for the Existence of God," http://www.peterkreeft.com/topics-more/20_arguments-gods-existence.htm.

**Gaunilo of Marmoutiers**, a fellow monk of Anselm, provided a classic response to Anselm's ontological proof. Gaunilo played the devil's advocate by supposedly putting himself in the shoes of Anselm's imaginary opponent (i.e., the fool who claims that there's no God). Instead of directly challenging any of Anselm's premises, Gaunilo identified a false claim that Anselm allegedly assumed as true. For Gaunilo, Anselm assumed that conceivability of x implies the actual existence of x. The mere fact that one can conceive of the most excellent car, for instance, does not imply that the most excellent car exists. So, in the same way, the mere fact that one can conceive of God as that being than which nothing greater can be conceived does not imply that such God exists. In response to Gaunilo, Anselm pointed out that there is at least one significant difference between the most excellent car and God. So, the mere fact that there is no positive connection between conceivability and existence with regards to the most excellent car does not mean that such positive connection does not obtain with regards to God. Even if one does not find Anselm's proof as compelling, one should at least recognize that it is a well-thought-out argument.

Two arguments for God's existence that are commonly considered as a posteriori proofs (i.e., proofs that utilize the data from sense experiences) are cosmological and teleological proofs. **Thomas Aquinas** (1225–1274 CE), who is possibly the greatest medieval thinker, popularized the cosmological proofs. His versions of them, at least, attempted to reconcile Christian theology with Aristotelian science. In my general summary of such proofs, I will not directly appeal to the specific contributions of Aristotelian science to Aquinas's argument. In addition, I will set aside the distinctive aspects of each version of such proofs. Cosmological proofs generally appeal to the origin or causation of the universe. They aim to address the necessary precondition that makes the universe possible. They assume the truth of what appear to be intuitively true claims. For example, something cannot come out of nothing. So, the mere fact that the universe exists indicates that something or someone else must have caused its existence, unless it is simply uncaused. But, every single existent physical thing could have failed to exist. The universe as a mere aggregate of all such things could have also failed to exist. Anything that could have failed to exist, as far as one can tell, did not exist prior to its existence. Hence, there must be someone or something that exists to cause the existence of the universe. Such cause as the ultimate cause of all things that exists is God. The teleological proofs, on the other hand, highlight the seeming complexities of the designs or purposes of all sorts of things in the universe. For thinkers, such as **William Paley** (1743–1805), complex designs imply designers or creators. For Paley, the universe exhibits complex designs that are analogous to the complex designs of human artifacts (e.g., watches). So, the universe must have a designer, who is commonly identified as God. These proofs assume that there are sufficient similarities between human artifacts and the universe that legitimize the claim about their analogical relations. The teleological proofs are now formulated with far more intellectual sophistications than what we find in the work of Paley. Contemporary versions of such proofs contain much more compelling examples of complex designs in the universe than the kinds of examples that Paley had in mind. Some people believe that the teleological proofs as they are now formulated are probably the most compelling proof for God's existence.

**David Hume** (1711–1776) was a Scottish philosopher. He is known as one of the greatest critics of religion. He gave classic objections to each of the theistic proofs presented, but this anthology includes Hume's objections against the analogical version of the teleological proof (e.g., Paley's teleological proof). His objections do not necessarily argue for atheism. They simply point out the failures of the teleological proof to prove God's existence. He gave four objections. First, the analogy between natural machines and human-made machines is a bad one, considering the significant dissimilarities between the two. Second, a naturalistic explanation for the design in the universe is much more preferable than a super-naturalistic one, since the latter explanation involves many things that are beyond our comprehension. But, the analogical version of the teleological proof favors the latter explanation. Third, the proportionality of the effect to its cause should imply that the imperfect universe demands an imperfect creator. Religious people are of course uncomfortable with the claim that God is imperfect. Fourth, the universe is more comparable to animal bodies or vegetation than human artifacts. In the same way that animal bodies or vegetation naturally come about, the universe could have come about naturalistically. But, the teleological proof mistakenly assumes a greater degree of comparability between the universe and human artifacts.

Not all theists (i.e., people who believe in God's existence) like theistic proofs. Some theists do not like them. Some at least claim that, since there is an infinite cognitive gap between humans and God, God should be infinitely incomprehensible from the standpoint of humans. That means that reason (theoretical) must be incapable of discovering anything about God, including God's existence. Since theistic proofs are based on reason, they are doomed to fail in saying anything substantive about God. They might be able to say something about a god that is conceived in a particular way. But that cannot say anything about the actual God, assuming that God exists. **Blaise Pascal** (1623–1662), a French mathematician, seemed to adhere to such view. In response to the problem of knowing anything about God, Pascal devised a way to persuade those who are reluctant to believe due to the absence of any substantive evidences and arguments for God's existence. He is well known for giving us what is popularly known as "the Wager." The Wager puts one in a hypothetical situation, where he or she is asked to bet everything that he or she owns once and for all. So, the stake is significant, considering that there is a possibility that one can lose everything. But, the act of betting, here, is not optional, since either one believes in God's existence or one does not believe in God's existence. There is no other option. Before one makes a bet, he or she has no clue how things will exactly pan out (i.e., whether the outcome will be favorable or unfavorable relative to his or her choice). In the case of the Wager, one cannot know anything about God's existence. The believer is assumed to win eternal life, if he or she happens to be correct. The unbeliever, on the other hand, is assumed to receive eternal damnation, if he or she happens to be wrong. Pascal concludes that it is prudent for one to favor a safer bet. It can be the one that avoids eternal damnation. Therefore, it is wiser to believe in God's existence than not to believe in God's existence. Once the wiser choice is established through the Wager, one should recognize that it is wiser to believe than not believe. However, if he or she is still having a hard time believing due to the lack of evidences or arguments, he or she should simply set aside such concerns for evidences or arguments. An effective way to make one's self believe that which has been determined as wiser to believe, at least according to Pascal, is the conditioning of oneself to believe by initially faking it (i.e., acting as if he or she believes it) until he or she believes it. For Pascal, the belief-formation process is generally involuntary. The kinds of things that persuade the heart to form a particular belief is not the same as the things that persuade the mind. But, since one already determines that it is better to believe in God's existence than not believe, he or she just needs to do what can effectively make him or her believe in God's existence.

Now, let's turn to atheism (the belief that God does not exist). As an argument for it, I use the problem of evil. The problem of evil does not need to show that God does not exist. It can simply show that God as traditionally conceived does not exist. But, if one assumes that only God as traditionally conceived qualifies as God, then the problem of evil has to be viewed as an argument for atheism. Cases of gratuitous evil (i.e., sufferings that do not lead to a greater good or that are lacking in morally sufficient reasons) count against the existence of God, assuming that God is at least omnipotent, omniscient, and omnibenevolent. It is conceivable that such God is capable of creating a world without evil. Such God must also hate all cases of gratuitous evil. So, there shouldn't be gratuitous evil at all in the world. There are cases of gratuitous evil, even if it remains possible that God has morally sufficient reasons for them. The gratuitousness is contingent on how evil the events or situations appear to humans. **David Hume** (1711–1776) aptly described the implications of evil on an evidentially coherent conception of God. For example, for Hume, in the absence of any innate idea of God, one must rely on what he or she can observe in the world to formulate a concept of God. The pervasiveness of seemingly gratuitous evil should be sufficient to prevent one from thinking that God is omnipotent, omniscient, and omnibenevolent. Such God is supposed to do away with things that make evil possible. It can be expected that there were all sorts of conceivable worlds that were available to God before creating the actual world. An omnipotent God must have been capable of creating any of the conceivable worlds. An omniscient God must have been capable of knowing the extent of evil in the conceivable world that had been eventually actualized. An omnibenevolent God must deeply abhor anything that is evil, especially the gratuitous ones. But, the actual world does not reflect any such attributes. So, if God exists, God cannot be a being who has all such attributes. On the other hand, **John Hick** (1922–2012) provided a Christian-inspired response to the problem of evil that is relevant to Hume's argument. For Hick, God could have created a world where sufferings are purposefully used by God to bring about a greater good, such as gaining mature perspectives or the soul-making process. Hick's theodicy (i.e., a possible explanation for why God allows evil) incorporates the theory of evolution. It is not just the physical reality that is going through that process of evolution. The soul is also undergoing a process of evolution that allows humans to reach their goal of becoming children of God. This process is supposed to continue even after one's death, in order to fully realize the goal of the process of being perfected.

# Part Three: Mind-Body Problem

Mind-body problem is a topic that caught the attention of philosophers in the past and the present. It recently became a pertinent topic in science. In a 2005 issue of *Science* (magazine), it is second on the list of "25 Big Questions Facing Science over the Next Quarter-Century."[10] There is no reason to set it aside as another irrelevant philosophical topic. It has to do with the following question: "What is the biological basis of consciousness?" Even Eric R. Kandel, a Nobel Prize winner from Columbia University, considers the attempt to understand consciousness as "by far the most challenging task confronting science."[11] Paul Bloom, a Yale psychologist, is known for saying that humans are natural-born dualists. We naturally see a distinction between mind (immaterial or nonphysical) and body (material or physical). It also seems to strike us as intuitive that there are two-way causal interactions between the two. The mind appears to causally interact with the body (e.g., my thought of ghosts causes me to have goose bumps). The body also appears to causally interact with the mind (e.g., one who steps on a nail is caused to have sensation of pain). But the claim that an immaterial mind causally interacts with a material body appears to be incompatible with the conservation of energy (i.e., first law of thermodynamics). Considering that the conservation of energy denies the possibility of creating or destroying energy, it must presuppose that the universe is a closed or isolated system. The mind as immaterial must be outside of such a system. Its interactions with the body will create energy. That violates the first law of thermodynamics.

**Rene Descartes** (1596–1650 CE), who presented a dualistic view in *Meditations on First Philosophy* (1641), received similar objection from his student, Princess Elizabeth of Bohemia (1618–1680). There are different interpretations of Descartes's view, but I'll stick to the standard textbook account of it, which is controversial among Descartes's scholars. In Descartes's dualism (commonly known as Cartesian dualism), mind and body causally interact with one another. It does not just affirm bottom-up interaction (body → mind), but it also affirms top-down interaction (mind → body). In Cartesian dualism, mind and body are considered to be independent of each other. It implies the possibility of a disembodied mind that is causally efficacious in the physical world. It causally interacts with the brain through the pineal gland as "the principal seat of the soul," according to Descartes. Being near the center of the brain and the midpoint between the brain's hemispheres, Descartes's account should have struck seventeenth-century thinkers as initially plausible. But, despite his mistaken view on the pineal gland, his point that the interactions between nonphysical mind and physical body take place in the brain maintains some level of plausibility. As a matter of fact, William Lycan, a prominent philosopher of mind who rejects dualism, still claims that standard objections to dualism failed.[12] But, Princess Elisabeth considered it as problematic to think that a nonphysical mind has causal powers in the natural world.

Descartes had a legitimate worry that made it inescapable for him to assume the mind's existence. Unlike many artificial intelligence experts today, Descartes thought that matter or purely physical things couldn't think. So, the mere fact that humans think means that there must be more to humans than just simply physical bodies. For Descartes, there is something incorrigible about the claim that I exist. In the moment that I doubt my very own existence, it readily indicates my own existence, since I must exist as the one who doubts. Doubt is a form of thinking. So, the incorrigibility of the claim about my own existence assumes my capacity to think. Since the possibility of thought grounds the possibility of doubt and the possibility of doubt grounds the possibility of conclusively affirming my existence, I should not be able to doubt that I am a being who thinks. It cannot be my physical body that is doing the thinking. So, for Descartes, the mind whose principal attribute is thought must exist as the thinking thing. Descartes also offered an argument for the existence of the body, which is external to the mind and extended in space. For him, the fact that I involuntarily perceive an object implies that it is not merely a construct of my mind, since I don't get to decide on the objects of my perception. So, the ideas (e.g., colors, shapes, sizes, etc.) that my senses perceive must be coming from somewhere other than my mind. But, one cannot readily assume that the ideas come from a body. There are, of course, other possibilities. Considering the possibility that there is no actually and independently existing external world, it remains a possibility that the ideas that I perceive are not dependent on my mind and not

---

10 https://www.sciencemag.org/site/feature/misc/webfeat/125th/

11 Eric R. Kandel, *In Search of Memory: The Emergence of a New Science of Mind* (New York: W. W. Norton and Company, 2006), p. 377.

12 See William Lycan, "Giving Dualism Its Due," *Australasian Journal of Philosophy* 87, no. 4 (2009): 551–563.

coming from a body. They can be ideas that come from God or, let's say, an evil genius, as someone who directly feeds me these ideas. But, Descartes seemed to think that, after he established the existence of God as the most perfect of all beings, the possibility that God is a deceiver can already be ruled out. Deception is an imperfection; so, the most perfect of all beings cannot be a deceiver. It means that God would not create a world where God made it to appear that there was an external world, which in fact did not exist at all. So, God would not create a world with an evil genius that would bring about deception of the grandest scale. By process of elimination, Descartes concluded that the ideas that I perceive must come from an external and extended body.

But, due to the difficulties in plausibly accounting for the two-way interaction between the mind and body, the popularity of the so-called Cartesian dualism would wane, despite its intuitive appeal. So, another theory must take its place. Materialism was up to the task. It appears that, based on the *PhilPapers Surveys*, 55 percent or more of philosophers today are materialists of some sorts. It should also be fair to say that the majority of scientists are materialists. It denies the existence of an immaterial or a nonphysical mind, since it affirms that all things must be reducible to things that are material or physical. So, for it, any of the allegedly mental or nonphysical states or things should have a neural correlate or biological basis. A quote from the opening of Francis Crick's *The Astonishing Hypothesis* captures the essence of materialism:

> The astonishing hypothesis is that you, your joys and your sorrows, your memories and ambitions, your sense of personal identity and free will, are in fact no more than the behavior of a vast assembly of nerve cells and their associated molecules. As Lewis Caroll's Alice might have phrased it, 'You're nothing but a pack of neurons.'[13]

One of the most popular arguments for materialism is the one given by **David Papineau**, a contemporary philosopher from King's College London. Papineau argues that, since every physical effect can be fully explained by appealing to its physical cause, there is no need to assume that there are mental causes. It is a case of over-determination to think that two distinct causes independently bring about the same physical effect. If one of the two distinct causes can adequately explain the physical effect, then there is no need for the other cause. The explanation that makes the least amount of assumptions should be preferred. Considering that one needs more assumptions in the explanations that involve mental causes than the ones that simply appeal to physical causes, the explanations that simply appeal to physical causes should be preferred. His argument concludes by affirming the identity between mental and physical causes. **Frank Jackson**, another contemporary philosopher from Australian National University, presented a classic objection to materialism. He thought that there are at least some things that are irreducible to physical things. So, materialism must be false. There are things about subjective experiences (e.g., hurtfulness of pain, itchiness of itches, etc.) that seem to be unaccounted for in the process of exhaustively identifying the corresponding neural correlates for all sorts of mental states. He referred to the felt qualities of such experiences as epiphenomenal qualia. The term *epiphenomenal* has to do with qualia being byproducts of brain activities and not having any causal powers in relation to the brain. These epiphenomenal qualia are distinct qualities of certain feelings or experiences. My experience of seeing a certain color, for example, comes about through certain brain activities, but there is no amount of empirical studies of such activities that will capture the distinct qualities of such experience. The experience is only accessible to the experiencer. The observer from the outside will never know the experiencer's experience of a certain color.

## Part Four: Human Knowledge

Standard sources of knowledge (e.g. sciences, mainstream media, etc.) have been treated as suspect, at least in the US. There are many people who reject the consensuses among almost all scientists and scientific organizations in the world regarding the significant roles of human activities in causing threatening changes on the earth's climate. There are many people who think that the vaccinations of children are extremely harmful to children, while most medical doctors consider them to be extremely safe and deeply needed medical interventions in suppressing the

13 Francis Crick, *The Astonishing Hypothesis: Scientific Search for the Soul* (New York: Touchstone, 1995).

spread of threatening human illnesses. There are many people who buy the political propagandas that are designed to maliciously delegitimize reliable sources of information. So, it is a pressing task for people to reflect about reliable sources of knowledge. By discounting expertise, for example, we'll likely hasten the destructions of our planet or endanger the lives of children. By mistakenly labeling reliable news sources as fake news, we'll miss out on reliable and important information that might be essential to our decision-making processes in all areas of our lives. So, it is an important question to ask about reliable sources of knowledge.

This anthology focuses its attention on some of the epistemological discourses in seventeenth- to eighteenth-century Western philosophy. They seem to capture the birth of the scientific revolution that somehow made modern science possible. Standard narrative of this period in the history of philosophy, which is not necessarily an accurate one (but useful for introductory philosophy courses nonetheless), highlights the debates between the so-called *rationalists* and the so-called *empiricists.* These labels should be taken with a grain of salt, since the classification of philosophers as if they were members of a group can be misleading. They don't necessarily have exactly the same position on every single issue. Such classification ignores the different nuances in their views. It is merely based on rough resemblances in the views of different philosophers. Nevertheless, it is a useful pedagogical tool. Rationalism is generally described as the view that considers reason or intellectual intuition as primarily the most, but not necessarily the only, reliable source of knowledge. The process by which we arrive at mathematical knowledge seems to illustrate the most reliable knowledge-acquisition process that rationalists had in mind. Mathematical knowledge is more certain than sense knowledge. Rationalists, such as Plato and Descartes, are generally suspicious of sense knowledge. They even claim that some of our knowledge is independent of sense experiences. For example, in Descartes's argument for the existence of the "I" or self as the thinking thing, he inferred that there is at least one thing that we cannot doubt by going through a series of logical inferences, independent of any appeal to sense experiences. After weeding out all things that could be conceivably doubted from beliefs that are acquired from the senses to basic arithmetical claims, Descartes concluded that he could not doubt his own existence, since the very moment he doubted it would automatically imply his own existence as the doubter. That process of discovery was devoid of any appeal to the senses, while, at the same time, Descartes, at least, viewed it as successful in getting at the most certain of all knowledge.

For rationalists, some of our knowledge is at least innate or natural. They are not acquired or derived from sensible experiences. For example, some basic moral principles strike us as intuitively true. It seems natural for us to recognize basic ideas of justice or goodness. So, at least some rationalists treat such ideas or principles as innate. In addition to the innateness of certain aspects of morality, innateness can also be found in other places, such as certain aspects of mathematics, metaphysics, aesthetics, linguistics, psychology, biology, etc. Empiricists, on the other hand, reject the view that there's even anything innate. For them, knowledge must be ultimately derived from the senses. We all start from scratch, since our minds are blank slates prior to the use of the senses. It means that ideas somehow originated from the senses. Like the other empiricists, **John Locke** (1632–1704), a British philosopher, rejected the view that there are innate ideas. For Locke, rationalists think that there are innate ideas, since there are certain principles that are objects of universal agreement. But, Locke denied the premise by claiming that there are no such principles. If children or idiots, according to Locke, would not recognize the truth of such principles, then such principles must not be innate. Rather, they must have been acquired. Locke anticipated the following rejoinder from rationalists: Once children or idiots learn the use of reason, they should begin to recognize that such principles are true. However, for Locke, the use of reason presupposes sense experiences. Particular ideas are perceived by the senses. They are somehow stored in the mind. That should make it possible for me to recognize such ideas as they are embodied in different objects. My constant encounters with the same objects with certain qualities allow me to have general conceptions of different qualities that can be attributed to all sorts of objects. After seeing many objects that I eventually and individually identify with the term "bag," I begin to have an idea of a bag and use the term "bag" to refer to each and every bag. After seeing many objects with a particular color that I eventually identify with the term "blue," I begin to have an idea of blueness and use the term "blue" to refer to each and every instantiation of it in all sorts of objects. The use of reason, for Locke, seems to be involved in the process of forming judgments, such as "The bag is blue." But that presupposes the particular ideas (such as the idea of a bag and blueness) that have been acquired from the senses. So, the use of reason presupposes sense experiences. It means that sense experiences precede the use of reason.

**Immanuel Kant** (1724–1804), a German philosopher, offered a way to reconcile rationalism and empiricism. He thought that human cognition is a byproduct of what we perceive through our senses and some mental apparatuses that allow us to understand, in a humanly distinctive way, the data that our senses provide. Both are indispensable elements of that process of cognition. Without the senses, there's nothing to know. Without such mental apparatuses, there's no understanding that can take place. These mental apparatuses involve certain a priori categories that allow us to organize, put together, put in temporal order, etc. our experiences of the world. Due to them, we have a coherent understanding of the world from a finite human perspective.

# Part Five: Morality

Humans find themselves inevitably making moral judgments. For example, one generally condemns the behavior of his or her partner who has been cheating on him or her behind his or her back. In addition, humans also seem to share common intuitions about moral matters. For example, humans generally recognize the wrongness of unnecessarily lying to other people or unnecessarily killing innocent people. Even if such act is not in fact wrong, it remains true that humans generally recognize such an act as wrong. There seem to be rational constraints to moral thinking. It's natural for philosophers to wonder about the very nature of human judgment about the wrongness (or rightness) of certain acts. There are different, and even competing, ways of understanding their nature. For some, moral judgments are based on social conventions or agreements among members of a particular group of people. For others, moral judgments are based on the will, nature, or commandments of the supreme moral lawgiver (e.g., God). It is also possible that morality has to do with certain principles or laws that are conducive to the establishment of sustainable societies and discoverable through the utilizations of our rational faculties.

While basic concepts of morality, such as justice, rights, equality, etc., are essential grounds of coherent and justifiable laws of the land, the debates about the grounds of morality are much more intractable. **Thomas Aquinas**, for example, considered moral laws as deeply embedded parts of our universe, in the same way as the laws of nature being deeply embedded parts of our world. Humans, who have the natural light of reason, are tasked with discovering such laws. So, rational inquiries can give us access to such laws. On the other hand, **Thomas Hobbes** (1588–1679), a British philosopher, rejected any metaphysical basis for morality. Rather, for him, morality has a purely political basis. It has to do with the establishment of order in a political world for the purpose of survival and the attainment of the common good. Self-interested people want to survive. Without any rules of conduct that can facilitate social cooperation among humans, one's survival is surely threatened, but humans, as rational creatures, can, of course, figure out effective ways to achieve the peace that everyone desires. So, for their own benefits, they have no choice but to enter into pacts with other people. Through social agreements, they can establish the needed laws. That's what he calls the social contract, where each member of such pacts mutually gives up certain rights for the purpose of cooperatively pursuing the common good. **David Hume** gave a different account of the foundation of morality. For Hume, emotion is the foundation of morality. A moral judgment is a judgment about how one feels about a particular act. It has to do with whether a moral agent likes or dislikes a certain act. One considers an act as good if he or she has feeling of approbation in relation to such act. Of course, the bad act corresponds to feeling of disapprobation. For Hume, reason only has two objects: logical relations and empirical facts. But, morality is neither about logical relations nor about empirical facts. One does not recognize the truth in the claim "Lying is wrong" in the same way he or she recognizes the truth in the claim that "All bachelors are unmarried males." Based on the meanings of "bachelors" and "unmarried males," one should readily recognize the necessary logical connections between the two. However, that's not the case with the claim "Lying is wrong." There is no necessary logical connection between "lying" and "wrongness." One also does not recognize the claim "Lying is wrong" in the same way he or she recognizes the truth in the claim "The bottle is on top of the table." Based on the empirical facts that one can observe, he or she recognizes the truth in the claim "The bottle is on top of the table." But, there are no empirical facts that correspond to the claim "Lying is wrong." So, if morality has nothing to do with reason, then it has something to do with emotion.

Another important issue in the study of morality has to do with the ontological status of morality. In other words, it has to do with the nature of the existence of morality or moral laws, principles, concepts, and rules. Is morality a byproduct of cultural conventions? Is it a byproduct of one's own subjective valuation of a particular act? Does it have an existence independent of our cultural conventions or social agreements? Is it even objective in the same way that some people consider the laws of nature as objective? It's important to find some sort of answers to these questions, considering that we inevitably make moral judgments and it makes sense to make moral judgments if they are somehow objective. But, there are reasons for thinking that morality is relative (i.e., dependent on the preferences, biases, or desires of a particular moral agent or a group of moral agents). **Ruth Benedict** (1887–1948), an American anthropologist, gave many accounts of the radical differences among different societies. An abnormal behavior in one society seems normal in another society. The determination of abnormality or normality of moral behaviors seems to be dependent on factors that are relative to the contexts of a particular society (e.g., its historical, cultural, environmental, or social conditions).

Lastly, this textbook covers some readings on classic ethical theories. It includes readings on virtue ethics, utilitarian ethics, and Kantian ethics. Classical ethical theories address questions about important considerations in determining the rightness or wrongness of an act. For some virtue ethicists, such as **Aristotle** (384–322 BCE), ethics should not be about do's and don'ts. Rather, it should be about the cultivation of a virtuous character. The virtuous person is one who can be expected to exhibit all sorts of virtues, such as courage, generosity, temperance, etc., as if it is second nature to him or her to exhibit them. He or she is a person who comes to a point, after enough practice, where he or she finds it pleasurable to live virtuously. A virtuous life is one that is lived in moderation. For example, a virtuous person avoids the two extremes by finding that which is the mean relative to him or her. Instead of living stingily or extravagantly, he or she lives generously in a way that fits his or her resources. A virtuous person is one who can figure out the right thing to do at the right time and at the right place. So, a virtuous act in one particular situation is not necessarily a virtuous act in another. The right act is the act that a virtuous person chooses to do in a particular moral situation.

Utilitarian ethicists in general think that the consequence of an act has something to do with its moral status. Favorable consequences can provide some sort of justifications for the act's rightness, while unfavorable ones can render it a wrong act. So, nothing is inherently right or wrong. Rather, right or wrong has to do with whether the means are conducive to some desired ends. **Jeremy Bentham** (1748–1832), a British philosopher, thought that goodness could be quantified. For him, pleasure is the one that matters, so pain should be avoided. The maximization of pleasure and minimization of pain for the greater number of people become the goals of moral decision making. Several factors need to be considered in strengthening the likelihood of maximizing pleasure and minimizing pain: intensity of pleasure and pain, duration of pleasure and pain, number of people who will find the consequences as favorable, etc. **John Stuart Mill** (1806–1873), another British utilitarian, objects to Bentham's emphasis on the quantity of pleasures. Rather, for Mill, the quality of the pleasures is the one that should matter, since the quality of the pleasures is the one that matters for happiness. Higher-order pleasures, which are keys to a happy life, are the ones that need to be maximized. Humans, not animals, are the ones who can enjoy this kind of pleasure (e.g., intellectual, aesthetic, moral, etc.) As a matter of fact, for Mill, humans generally prefer such pleasures more than lower-order ones (e.g., eating, drinking, sex, etc.). Finally, the last reading in the textbook is a reading from **Immanuel Kant**. He offered an ethical theory that can easily be contrasted with utilitarian ethics. Unlike utilitarian ethicists, Kant thought that motives, not consequences, are the things that matter in determining the moral status of an act, since for Kant the end does not justify the means. Humans as rational beings have intrinsic worth, rather than merely instrumental worth. So, a moral agent in his or her morally relevant act must treat humanity as an end in itself, not merely as a means to an end. So, the right act for Kant is one that is done solely out of respect for what morality demands (e.g., treating humans as ends in themselves or performing an act that one can reasonably deem as a universal law).

It is my hope that the students who will use this textbook will enjoy their journeys from wonder to wisdom. I hope that, like the philosophers, they will also become lovers of wisdom.

CHAPTER I

# Socrates: A Philosopher in Action

# EUTHRYPHRO

**BY Plato, translated by G. M. A. Grube and John M. Cooper**

*Euthyphro is surprised to meet Socrates near the king-archon's court, for Socrates is not the kind of man to have business with courts of justice. Socrates explains that he is under indictment by one Meletus for corrupting the young and for not believing in the gods in whom the city believes. After a brief discussion of this, Socrates inquires about Euthyphro's business at court and is told that he is prosecuting his own father for the murder of a laborer who is himself a murderer. His family and friends believe his course of action to be impious, but Euthyphro explains that in this they are mistaken and reveal their ignorance of the nature of piety. This naturally leads Socrates to ask, What is piety? And the rest of the dialogue is devoted to a search for a definition of piety, illustrating the Socratic search for universal definitions of ethical terms, to which a number of early Platonic dialogues are devoted. As usual, no definition is found that satisfies Socrates.*

*The Greek term hosion means, in the first instance, the knowledge of the proper ritual in prayer and sacrifice and of course its performance (as Euthyphro himself defines it in 14b). But obviously Euthyphro uses it in the much wider sense of pious conduct generally (e.g., his own), and in that sense the word is practically equivalent to righteousness (the justice of the* Republic*), the transition being by way of conduct pleasing to the gods.*

*Besides being an excellent example of the early, so-called Socratic dialogues,* Euthyphro *contains several passages with important philosophical implications. These include those in which Socrates speaks of the one Form, presented by all the actions that we call pious (5d), as well as the one in which we are told that the gods love what is pious because it is pious; it is not pious because the gods love it (10d). Another passage clarifies the difference between genus and species (11e–12d).*

*—G.M.A. Grube*

EUTHYPHRO:[1] What's new, Socrates, to make you leave your usual haunts in the Lyceum and spend your time here by the king-archon's court?[2] Surely you are not prosecuting anyone before the king-archon as I am?

SOCRATES: The Athenians do not call this a prosecution but an indictment, Euthyphro.

EUTHYPHRO: What is this you say? Someone must have indicted you, for you are not going to tell me that you have indicted someone else.

SOCRATES: No indeed.

EUTHYPHRO: But someone else has indicted you?

SOCRATES: Quite so.

EUTHYPHRO: Who is he?

1 We know nothing about Euthyphro except what we can gather from this dialogue. He is obviously a professional priest who considers himself an expert on ritual and on piety generally and, it seems, is generally so considered. One Euthyphro is mentioned in Plato's *Cratylus* (396d) who is given to *enthousiasmos*, inspiration or possession, but we cannot be sure that it is the same person.

2 The Lyceum was an outdoor gymnasium, just outside the walls of Athens, where teenage young men engaged in exercises and athletic competitions. Socrates and other intellectuals carried on discussions with them there and exhibited their skills. See the beginnings of Plato's *Euthydemus* and *Lysis*, and the last paragraph of *Symposium*. The king-archon, one of the nine principal magistrates of Athens, had the responsibility to oversee religious rituals and purifications, and as such had oversight of legal cases involving alleged offenses against the Olympian gods, whose worship was a civic function—it was regarded as a serious offense to offend them.

SOCRATES: I do not really know him myself, Euthyphro. He is apparently young and unknown. They call him Meletus, I believe. He belongs to the Pitthean deme,[3] if you know anyone from that deme called Meletus, with long hair, not much of a beard, and a rather aquiline nose.

EUTHYPHRO: I don't know him, Socrates. What charge does he bring against you?

SOCRATES: What charge? A not ignoble one I think, for it is no small thing for a young man to have knowledge of such an important subject. He says he knows how our young men are corrupted and who corrupts them. He is likely to be wise, and when he sees my ignorance corrupting his contemporaries, he proceeds to accuse me to the city as to their mother. I think he is the only one of our public men to start out the right way, for it is right to care first that the young should be as good as possible, just as a good farmer is likely to take care of the young plants first, and of the others later. So, too, Meletus first gets rid of us who corrupt the young shoots, as he says, and then afterwards he will obviously take care of the older ones and become a source of great blessings for the city, as seems likely to happen to one who started out this way.

EUTHYPHRO: I could wish this were true, Socrates, but I fear the opposite may happen. He seems to me to start out by harming the very heart of the city by attempting to wrong you. Tell me, what does he say you do to corrupt the young?

SOCRATES: Strange things, to hear him tell it, for he says that I am a maker of gods, and on the ground that I create new gods while not believing in the old gods, he has indicted me for their sake, as he puts it.

EUTHYPHRO: I understand, Socrates. This is because you say that the divine sign keeps coming to you.[4] So he has written this indictment against you as one who makes innovations in religious matters, and he comes to court to slander you, knowing that such things are easily misrepresented to the crowd. The same is true in my case. Whenever I speak of divine matters in the assembly[5] and foretell the future, they laugh me down as if I were crazy; and yet I have foretold nothing that did not happen. Nevertheless, they envy all of us who do this. One need not worry about them, but meet them head-on.

SOCRATES: My dear Euthyphro, to be laughed at does not matter perhaps, for the Athenians do not mind anyone they think clever, as long as he does not teach his own wisdom, but if they think that he makes others to be like himself they get angry, whether through envy, as you say, or for some other reason.

EUTHYPHRO: I have certainly no desire to test their feelings towards me in this matter.

SOCRATES: Perhaps you seem to make yourself but rarely available, and not be willing to teach your own wisdom, but I'm afraid that my liking for people makes them think that I pour out to anybody anything I have to say, not only without charging a fee but even glad to reward anyone who is willing to listen. If then they were intending to laugh at me, as you say they laugh at you, there would be nothing unpleasant in their spending their time in court laughing and jesting, but if they are going to be serious, the outcome is not clear except to you prophets.

EUTHYPHRO: Perhaps it will come to nothing, Socrates, and you will fight your case as you think best, as I think I will mine.

SOCRATES: What is your case, Euthyphro? Are you the defendant or the prosecutor?

EUTHYPHRO: The prosecutor.

SOCRATES: Whom do you prosecute?

EUTHYPHRO: One whom I am thought crazy to prosecute.

SOCRATES: Are you pursuing someone who will easily escape you?

EUTHYPHRO: Far from it, for he is quite old.

SOCRATES: Who is it?

EUTHYPHRO: My father.

SOCRATES: My dear sir! Your own father?

EUTHYPHRO: Certainly.

---

3 A deme was, in effect, one of the constituent villages of Attica, the territory whose center was the city of Athens (though Athens itself was divided into demes, too). Athenian citizens had first of all to be enrolled and recognized as citizens in their demes.

4 In Plato, Socrates always speaks of his divine sign or voice as intervening to prevent him from doing or saying something (e.g., *Apology* 31d), but never positively. The popular view was that it enabled him to foretell the future, and Euthyphro here represents that view. Note, however, that Socrates dissociates himself from "you prophets" (3e).

5 The assembly was the final decision-making body of the Athenian democracy. All adult males could attend and vote.

SOCRATES: What is the charge? What is the case about?

EUTHYPHRO: Murder, Socrates.

SOCRATES: Good heavens! Certainly, Euthyphro, most men would not know how they could do this and be right. It is not the part of anyone to do this, but of one who is far advanced in wisdom.

EUTHYPHRO: Yes, by Zeus, Socrates, that is so.

SOCRATES: Is then the man your father killed one of your relatives? Or is that obvious, for you would not prosecute your father for the murder of a stranger.

EUTHYPHRO: It is ridiculous, Socrates, for you to think that it makes any difference whether the victim is a stranger or a relative. One should only watch whether the killer acted justly or not; if he acted justly, let him go, but if not, one should prosecute, if, that is to say, the killer shares your hearth and table. The pollution is the same if you knowingly keep company with such a man and do not cleanse yourself and him by bringing him to justice. The victim was a dependent of mine, and when we were farming in Naxos he was a servant of ours.[6] He killed one of our household slaves in drunken anger, so my father bound him hand and foot and threw him in a ditch, then sent a man here to inquire from the priest what should be done. During that time he gave no thought or care to the bound man, as being a killer, and it was no matter if he died, which he did. Hunger and cold and his bonds caused his death before the messenger came back from the seer. Both my father and my other relatives are angry that I am prosecuting my father for murder on behalf of a murderer when he hadn't even killed him, they say, and even if he had, the dead man does not deserve a thought, since he was a killer. For, they say, it is impious for a son to prosecute his father for murder. But their ideas of the divine attitude to piety and impiety are wrong, Socrates.

SOCRATES: Whereas, by Zeus, Euthyphro, you think that your knowledge of the divine, and of piety and impiety, is so accurate that, when those things happened as you say, you have no fear of having acted impiously in bringing your father to trial?

EUTHYPHRO: I should be of no use, Socrates, and Euthyphro would not be superior to the majority of men, if I did not have accurate knowledge of all such things.

SOCRATES: It is indeed most important, my admirable Euthyphro, that I should become your pupil, and as regards this indictment, challenge Meletus about these very things and say to him: that in the past too I considered knowledge about the divine to be most important, and that now that he says that I am guilty of improvising and innovating about the gods I have become your pupil. I would say to him: "If, Meletus, you agree that Euthyphro is wise in these matters, consider me, too, to have the right beliefs and do not bring me to trial. If you do not think so, then prosecute that teacher of mine, not me, for corrupting the older men, me and his own father, by teaching me and by exhorting and punishing him." If he is not convinced, and does not discharge me or indict you instead of me, I shall repeat the same challenge in court.

EUTHYPHRO: Yes, by Zeus, Socrates, and, if he should try to indict me, I think I would find his weak spots and the talk in court would be about him rather than about me.

SOCRATES: It is because I realize this that I am eager to become your pupil, my dear friend. I know that other people as well as this Meletus do not even seem to notice you, whereas he sees me so sharply and clearly that he indicts me for ungodliness. So tell me now, by Zeus, what you just now maintained you clearly knew: what kind of thing do you say that godliness and ungodliness are, both as regards murder and other things; or is the pious not the same and alike in every action, and the impious the opposite of all that is pious and like itself, and everything that is to be impious presents us with one form[7] or appearance insofar as it is impious?

EUTHYPHRO: Most certainly, Socrates.

SOCRATES: Tell me then, what is the pious, and what the impious, do you say?

---

6 Naxos is a large island in the Aegean Sea southeast of Athens, where Athens had appropriated land and settled many of its citizens under its imperial rule in the mid-fifth century B.C.

7 This is the kind of passage that makes it easier for us to follow the transition from Socrates' universal definitions to the Platonic theory of separately existent eternal universal Forms. The words *eidos* and *idea*, the technical terms for the Platonic Forms, commonly mean physical stature or bodily appearance. As we apply a common epithet, in this case pious, to different actions or things, these must have a common characteristic, present a common appearance or form, to justify the use of the same term, but in the early dialogues, as here, it seems to be thought of as immanent in the particulars and without separate existence. The same is true of 6d where the word "form" is also used.

EUTHYPHRO: I say that the pious is to do what I am doing now, to prosecute the wrongdoer, be it about murder or temple robbery or anything else, whether the wrongdoer is your father or your mother or anyone else; not to prosecute is impious. And observe, Socrates, that I can cite powerful evidence that the law is so. I have already said to others that such actions are right, not to favor the ungodly, whoever they are. These people themselves believe that Zeus is the best and most just of the gods, yet they agree that he bound his father because he unjustly swallowed his sons, and that he in turn castrated his father for similar reasons. But they are angry with me because I am prosecuting my father for his wrongdoing. They contradict themselves in what they say about the gods and about me.

SOCRATES: Indeed, Euthyphro, this is the reason why I am a defendant in the case, because I find it hard to accept things like that being said about the gods, and it is likely to be the reason why I shall be told I do wrong. Now, however, if you, who have full knowledge of such things, share their opinions, then we must agree with them, too, it would seem. For what are we to say, we who agree that we ourselves have no knowledge of them? Tell me, by the god of friendship, do you really believe these things are true?

EUTHYPHRO: Yes, Socrates, and so are even more surprising things, of which the majority has no knowledge.

SOCRATES: And do you believe that there really is war among the gods, and terrible enmities and battles, and other such things as are told by the poets, and other sacred stories such as are embroidered by good writers and by representations of which the robe of the goddess is adorned when it is carried up to the Acropolis?[8] Are we to say these things are true, Euthyphro?

EUTHYPHRO: Not only these, Socrates, but, as I was saying just now, I will, if you wish, relate many other things about the gods which I know will amaze you.

SOCRATES: I should not be surprised, but you will tell me these at leisure some other time. For now, try to tell me more clearly what I was asking just now, for, my friend, you did not teach me adequately when I asked you what the pious was, but you told me that what you are doing now, in prosecuting your father for murder, is pious.

EUTHYPHRO: And I told the truth, Socrates.

SOCRATES: Perhaps. You agree, however, that there are many other pious actions.

EUTHYPHRO: There are.

SOCRATES: Bear in mind then that I did not bid you tell me one or two of the many pious actions but that form itself that makes all pious actions pious, for you agreed that all impious actions are impious and all pious actions pious through one form, or don't you remember?

EUTHYPHRO: I do.

SOCRATES: Tell me then what this form itself is, so that I may look upon it and, using it as a model, say that any action of yours or another's that is of that kind is pious, and if it is not that it is not.

EUTHYPHRO: If that is how you want it, Socrates, that is how I will tell you.

SOCRATES: That is what I want.

EUTHYPHRO: Well then, what is dear to the gods is pious, what is not is impious.

SOCRATES: Splendid, Euthyphro! You have now answered in the way I wanted. Whether your answer is true I do not know yet, but you will obviously show me that what you say is true.

EUTHYPHRO: Certainly.

SOCRATES: Come then, let us examine what we mean. An action or a man dear to the gods is pious, but an action or a man hated by the gods is impious. They are not the same, but quite opposite, the pious and the impious. Is that not so?

EUTHYPHRO: It is indeed.

SOCRATES: And that seems to be a good statement?

EUTHYPHRO: I think so, Socrates.

SOCRATES: We have also stated that the gods are in a state of discord, that they are at odds with each other, Euthyphro, and that they are at enmity with each other. Has that, too, been said?

EUTHYPHRO: It has.

---

8 The Acropolis is the huge rocky outcropping in the center of Athens that served as the citadel for Attica, and also the center of its religious life. Major temples to the gods were there, including the Parthenon, the temple of Athena, the city's protectress. Every four years in an elaborate festival in her honor maidens brought up the ceremonial robe referred to here, in which to clothe her statue.

SOCRATES: What are the subjects of difference that cause hatred and anger? Let us look at it this way. If you and I were to differ about numbers as to which is the greater, would this difference make us enemies and angry with each other, or would we proceed to count and soon resolve our difference about this?

EUTHYPHRO: We would certainly do so.

SOCRATES: Again, if we differed about the larger and the smaller, we would turn to measurement and soon cease to differ.

EUTHYPHRO: That is so.

SOCRATES: And about the heavier and the lighter, we would resort to weighing and be reconciled.

EUTHYPHRO: Of course.

SOCRATES: What subject of difference would make us angry and hostile to each other if we were unable to come to a decision? Perhaps you do not have an answer ready, but examine as I tell you whether these subjects are the just and the unjust, the beautiful and the ugly, the good and the bad. Are these not the subjects of difference about which, when we are unable to come to a satisfactory decision, you and I and other men become hostile to each other whenever we do?

EUTHYPHRO: That is the difference, Socrates, about those subjects.

SOCRATES: What about the gods, Euthyphro? If indeed they have differences, will it not be about these same subjects?

EUTHYPHRO: It certainly must be so.

SOCRATES: Then according to your argument, my good Euthyphro, different gods consider different things to be just, beautiful, ugly, good, and bad, for they would not be at odds with one another unless they differed about these subjects, would they?

EUTHYPHRO: You are right.

SOCRATES: And they like what each of them considers beautiful, good, and just, and hate the opposites of these?

EUTHYPHRO: Certainly.

SOCRATES: But you say that the same things are considered just by some gods and unjust by others, and as they dispute about these things they are at odds and at war with each other. Is that not so?

EUTHYPHRO: It is.

SOCRATES: The same things then are loved by the gods and hated by the gods, and would be both god-loved and god-hated.

EUTHYPHRO: It seems likely.

SOCRATES: And the same things would be both pious and impious, according to this argument?

EUTHYPHRO: I'm afraid so.

SOCRATES: So you did not answer my question, you surprising man. I did not ask you what same thing is both pious and impious, and it appears that what is loved by the gods is also hated by them. So it is in no way surprising if your present action, namely punishing your father, may be pleasing to Zeus but displeasing to Cronus and Uranus,[9] pleasing to Hephaestus but displeasing to Hera, and so with any other gods who differ from each other on this subject.

EUTHYPHRO: I think, Socrates, that on this subject no gods would differ from one another, that whoever has killed anyone unjustly should pay the penalty.

SOCRATES: Well now, Euthyphro, have you ever heard any man maintaining that one who has killed or done anything else unjustly should not pay the penalty?

EUTHYPHRO: They never cease to dispute on this subject, both elsewhere and in the courts, for when they have committed many wrongs they do and say anything to avoid the penalty.

SOCRATES: Do they agree they have done wrong, Euthyphro, and in spite of so agreeing do they nevertheless say they should not be punished?

EUTHYPHRO: No, they do not agree on that point.

---

9 Zeus' father, whom he fought and defeated (see 6a), was Cronus; Cronus, in turn, had castrated his own father Uranus. The story of Hephaestus and his mother Hera, mentioned next, similarly involves a son punishing his parent.

SOCRATES: So they do not say or do just anything. For they do not venture to say this, or dispute that they must not pay the penalty if they have done wrong, but I think they deny doing wrong. Is that not so?

EUTHYPHRO: That is true.

SOCRATES: Then they do not dispute that the wrongdoer must be punished, but they may disagree as to who the wrongdoer is, what he did, and when.

EUTHYPHRO: You are right.

SOCRATES: Do not the gods have the same experience, if indeed they are at odds with each other about the just and the unjust, as your argument maintains? Some assert that they wrong one another, while others deny it, but no one among gods or men ventures to say that the wrongdoer must not be punished.

EUTHYPHRO: Yes, that is true, Socrates, as to the main point.

SOCRATES: And those who disagree, whether men or gods, dispute about each action, if indeed the gods disagree. Some say it is done justly, others unjustly. Is that not so?

EUTHYPHRO: Yes, indeed.

SOCRATES: Come now, my dear Euthyphro, tell me, too, that I may become wiser, what proof you have that all the gods consider that man to have been killed unjustly who became a murderer while in your service, was bound by the master of his victim, and died in his bonds before the one who bound him found out from the seers what was to be done with him, and that it is right for a son to denounce and to prosecute his father on behalf of such a man. Come, try to show me a clear sign that all the gods definitely believe this action to be right. If you can give me adequate proof of this, I shall never cease to extol your wisdom.

EUTHYPHRO: This is perhaps no light task, Socrates, though I could show you very clearly.

SOCRATES: I understand that you think me more dull-witted than the jury, as you will obviously show them that these actions were unjust and that all the gods hate such actions.

EUTHYPHRO: I will show it to them clearly, Socrates, if only they will listen to me.

SOCRATES: They will listen if they think you show them well. But this thought came to me as you were speaking, and I am examining it, saying to myself: "If Euthyphro shows me conclusively that all the gods consider such a death unjust, to what greater extent have I learned from him the nature of piety and impiety? This action would then, it seems, be hated by the gods, but the pious and the impious were not thereby now defined, for what is hated by the gods has also been shown to be loved by them." So I will not insist on this point; let us assume, if you wish, that all the gods consider this unjust and that they all hate it. However, is this the correction we are making in our discussion, that what all the gods hate is impious, and what they all love is pious, and that what some gods love and others hate is neither or both? Is that how you now wish us to define piety and impiety?

EUTHYPHRO: What prevents us from doing so, Socrates?

SOCRATES: For my part nothing, Euthyphro, but you look whether on your part this proposal will enable you to teach me most easily what you promised.

EUTHYPHRO: I would certainly say that the pious is what all the gods love, and the opposite, what all the gods hate, is the impious.

SOCRATES: Then let us again examine whether that is a sound statement, or do we let it pass, and if one of us, or someone else, merely says that something is so, do we accept that it is so? Or should we examine what the speaker means?

EUTHYPHRO: We must examine it, but I certainly think that this is now a fine statement.

SOCRATES: We shall soon know better whether it is. Consider this: Is the pious being loved by the gods because it is pious, or is it pious because it is being loved by the gods?

EUTHYPHRO: I don't know what you mean, Socrates.

SOCRATES: I shall try to explain more clearly: we speak of something carried and something carrying, of something led and something leading, of something seen and something seeing, and you understand that these things are all different from one another and how they differ?

EUTHYPHRO: I think I do.

SOCRATES: So there is also something loved and—a different thing—something loving.

EUTHYPHRO: Of course.

SOCRATES: Tell me then whether the thing carried is a carried thing because it is being carried, or for some other reason?

EUTHYPHRO: No, that is the reason.

SOCRATES: And the thing led is so because it is being led, and the thing seen because it is being seen?

EUTHYPHRO: Certainly.

SOCRATES: It is not being seen because it is a thing seen but on the contrary it is a thing seen because it is being seen; nor is it because it is something led that it is being led but because it is being led that it is something led; nor is something being carried because it is something carried, but it is something carried because it is being carried. Is what I want to say clear, Euthyphro? I want to say this, namely, that if anything is being changed or is being affected in any way, it is not being changed because it is something changed, but rather it is something changed because it is being changed; nor is it being affected because it is something affected, but it is something affected because it is being affected.[10] Or do you not agree?

EUTHYPHRO: I do.

SOCRATES: Is something loved either something changed or something affected by something?

EUTHYPHRO: Certainly.

SOCRATES: So it is in the same case as the things just mentioned; it is not being loved by those who love it because it is something loved, but it is something loved because it is being loved by them?

EUTHYPHRO: Necessarily.

SOCRATES: What then do we say about the pious, Euthyphro? Surely that it is being loved by all the gods, according to what you say?

EUTHYPHRO: Yes.

SOCRATES: Is it being loved because it is pious, or for some other reason?

EUTHYPHRO: For no other reason.

SOCRATES: It is being loved then because it is pious, but it is not pious because it is being loved?

EUTHYPHRO: Apparently.

SOCRATES: And yet it is something loved and god-loved because it is being loved by the gods?

EUTHYPHRO: Of course.

SOCRATES: Then the god-loved is not the same as the pious, Euthyphro, nor the pious the same as the god-loved, as you say it is, but one differs from the other.

EUTHYPHRO: How so, Socrates?

SOCRATES: Because we agree that the pious is being loved for this reason, that it is pious, but it is not pious because it is being loved. Is that not so?

EUTHYPHRO: Yes.

SOCRATES: And that the god-loved, on the other hand, is so because it is being loved by the gods, by the very fact of being loved, but it is not being loved because it is god-loved.

EUTHYPHRO: True.

SOCRATES: But if the god-loved and the pious were the same, my dear Euthyphro, then if the pious was being loved because it was pious, the god-loved would also be being loved because it was god-loved; and if the god-loved was god-loved because it was being loved by the gods, then the pious would also be pious because it was being loved by the gods. But now you see that they are in opposite cases as being altogether different from each other: the one is such as to be loved because it is being loved, the other is being loved because it is such as to be loved. I'm afraid, Euthyphro, that when you were asked what piety is, you did not wish to make its nature clear to me, but you told me an affect or a quality of it, that the pious has the quality of being loved by all the gods, but you have not yet told me what the pious is. Now, if you will, do not hide things from me but tell me again from the beginning what piety is,

10 Here Socrates gives the general principle under which, he says, the specific cases already examined—those of leading, carrying, and seeing—all fall. It is by being changed by something that changes *it* (e.g., by carrying it somewhere) that anything is a changed thing—not vice versa: it is not by something's being a changed thing that something *else* then changes it so that it comes to be being changed (e.g., by carrying it somewhere). Likewise for "affections" such as being seen by someone: it is by being "affected" by something that "affects" it that anything is an "affected" thing, not vice versa. It is not by being an "affected" thing (e.g., a thing seen) that something else then "affects" it.

whether being loved by the gods or having some other quality—we shall not quarrel about that—but be keen to tell me what the pious and the impious are.

EUTHYPHRO: But Socrates, I have no way of telling you what I have in mind, for whatever proposition we put forward goes around and refuses to stay put where we establish it.

SOCRATES: Your statements, Euthyphro, seem to belong to my ancestor, Daedalus.[11] If I were stating them and putting them forward, you would perhaps be making fun of me and say that because of my kinship with him my conclusions in discussion run away and will not stay where one puts them. As these propositions are yours, however, we need some other jest, for they will not stay put for you, as you say yourself.

EUTHYPHRO: I think the same jest will do for our discussion, Socrates, for I am not the one who makes them go around and not remain in the same place; it is you who are the Daedalus; for as far as I am concerned they would remain as they were.

SOCRATES: It looks as if I was cleverer than Daedalus in using my skill, my friend, insofar as he could only cause to move the things he made himself, but I can make other people's things move as well as my own. And the smartest part of my skill is that I am clever without wanting to be, for I would rather have your statements to me remain unmoved than possess the wealth of Tantalus as well as the cleverness of Daedalus. But enough of this. Since I think you are making unnecessary difficulties, I am as eager as you are to find a way to teach me about piety, and do not give up before you do. See whether you think all that is pious is of necessity just.

EUTHYPHRO: I think so.

SOCRATES: And is then all that is just pious? Or is all that is pious just, but not all that is just pious, but some of it is and some is not?

EUTHYPHRO: I do not follow what you are saying, Socrates.

SOCRATES: Yet you are younger than I by as much as you are wiser. As I say, you are making difficulties because of your wealth of wisdom. Pull yourself together, my dear sir, what I am saying is not difficult to grasp. I am saying the opposite of what the poet said who wrote:

> You do not wish to name Zeus, who had done it, and who made all things grow, for where there is fear there is also shame.[12]

I disagree with the poet. Shall I tell you why?

EUTHYPHRO: Please do.

SOCRATES: I do not think that "where there is fear there is also shame," for I think that many people who fear disease and poverty and many other such things feel fear, but are not ashamed of the things they fear. Do you not think so?

EUTHYPHRO: I do indeed.

SOCRATES: But where there is shame there is also fear. For is there anyone who, in feeling shame and embarrassment at anything, does not also at the same time fear and dread a reputation for wickedness?

EUTHYPHRO: He is certainly afraid.

SOCRATES: It is then not right to say "where there is fear there is also shame," but that where there is shame there is also fear, for fear covers a larger area than shame. Shame is a part of fear just as odd is a part of number, with the result that it is not true that where there is number there is also oddness, but that where there is oddness there is also number. Do you follow me now?

EUTHYPHRO: Surely.

SOCRATES: This is the kind of thing I was asking before, whether where there is piety there is also justice, but where there is justice there is not always piety, for the pious is a part of justice. Shall we say that, or do you think otherwise?

EUTHYPHRO: No, but like that, for what you say appears to be right.

---

11 Socrates may have been a stonemason, as his father was. In Greek mythology Daedalus' statues (made of wood) could move themselves.

12 Author unknown.

SOCRATES: See what comes next: if the pious is a part of the just, we must, it seems, find out what part of the just it is. Now if you asked me something of what we mentioned just now, such as what part of number is the even, and what number that is, I would say it is the number that is divisible into two equal, not unequal, parts. Or do you not think so?

EUTHYPHRO: I do.

SOCRATES: Try in this way to tell me what part of the just the pious is, in order to tell Meletus not to wrong us any more and not to indict me for ungodliness, since I have learned from you sufficiently what is godly and pious and what is not.

EUTHYPHRO: I think, Socrates, that the godly and pious is the part of the just that is concerned with the care of the gods, while that concerned with the care of men is the remaining part of justice.

SOCRATES: You seem to me to put that very well, but I still need a bit of information. I do not know yet what you mean by care, for you do not mean the care of the gods in the same sense as the care of other things, as, for example, we say, don't we, that not everyone knows how to care for horses, but the horse breeder does.

EUTHYPHRO: Yes, I do mean it that way.

SOCRATES: So horse breeding is the care of horses.

EUTHYPHRO: Yes.

SOCRATES: Nor does everyone know how to care for dogs, but the hunter does.

EUTHYPHRO: That is so.

SOCRATES: So hunting is the care of dogs.

EUTHYPHRO: Yes.

SOCRATES: And cattle raising is the care of cattle.

EUTHYPHRO: Quite so.

SOCRATES: While piety and godliness is the care of the gods, Euthyphro. Is that what you mean?

EUTHYPHRO: It is.

SOCRATES: Now care in each case has the same effect; it aims at the good and the benefit of the object cared for, as you can see that horses cared for by horse breeders are benefited and become better. Or do you not think so?

EUTHYPHRO: I do.

SOCRATES: So dogs are benefited by dog breeding, cattle by cattle raising, and so with all the others. Or do you think that care aims to harm the object of its care?

EUTHYPHRO: By Zeus, no.

SOCRATES: It aims to benefit the object of its care?

EUTHYPHRO: Of course.

SOCRATES: Is piety then, which is the care of the gods, also to benefit the gods and make them better? Would you agree that when you do something pious you make some one of the gods better?

EUTHYPHRO: By Zeus, no.

SOCRATES: Nor do I think that this is what you mean—far from it—but that is why I asked you what you meant by the care of gods, because I did not believe you meant this kind of care.

EUTHYPHRO: Quite right, Socrates, that is not the kind of care I mean.

SOCRATES: Very well, but what kind of care of the gods would piety be?

EUTHYPHRO: The kind of care, Socrates, that slaves take of their masters.

SOCRATES: I understand. It is likely to be a kind of service of the gods.

EUTHYPHRO: Quite so.

SOCRATES: Could you tell me to the achievement of what goal service to doctors tends? Is it not, do you think, to achieving health?

EUTHYPHRO: I think so.

SOCRATES: What about service to shipbuilders? To what achievement is it directed?

EUTHYPHRO: Clearly, Socrates, to the building of a ship.

SOCRATES: And service to housebuilders to the building of a house?

EUTHYPHRO: Yes.

SOCRATES: Tell me then, my good sir, to the achievement of what aim does service to the gods tend? You obviously know since you say that you, of all men, have the best knowledge of the divine.

EUTHYPHRO: And I am telling the truth, Socrates.

SOCRATES: Tell me then, by Zeus, what is that excellent aim that the gods achieve, using us as their servants?

EUTHYPHRO: Many fine things, Socrates.

SOCRATES: So do generals, my friend. Nevertheless you could easily tell me their main concern, which is to achieve victory in war, is it not?

EUTHYPHRO: Of course.

SOCRATES: The farmers, too, I think, achieve many fine things, but the main point of their efforts is to produce food from the earth.

EUTHYPHRO: Quite so.

SOCRATES: Well then, how would you sum up the many fine things that the gods achieve?

EUTHYPHRO: I told you a short while ago, Socrates, that it is a considerable task to acquire any precise knowledge of these things, but, to put it simply, I say that if a man knows how to say and do what is pleasing to the gods at prayer and sacrifice, those are pious actions such as preserve both private houses and public affairs of state. The opposite of these pleasing actions are impious and overturn and destroy everything.

SOCRATES: You could tell me in far fewer words, if you were willing, the sum of what I asked, Euthyphro, but you are not keen to teach me, that is clear. You were on the point of doing so, but you turned away. If you had given that answer, I should now have acquired from you sufficient knowledge of the nature of piety. As it is, the lover of inquiry must follow his beloved wherever it may lead him. Once more then, what do you say that piety and the pious are? Are they a knowledge of how to sacrifice and pray?

EUTHYPHRO: They are.

SOCRATES: To sacrifice is to make a gift to the gods, whereas to pray is to beg from the gods?

EUTHYPHRO: Definitely, Socrates.

SOCRATES: It would follow from this statement that piety would be a knowledge of how to give to, and beg from, the gods.

EUTHYPHRO: You understood what I said very well, Socrates.

SOCRATES: That is because I am so desirous of your wisdom, and I concentrate my mind on it, so that no word of yours may fall to the ground. But tell me, what is this service to the gods? You say it is to beg from them and to give to them?

EUTHYPHRO: I do.

SOCRATES: And to beg correctly would be to ask from them things that we need?

EUTHYPHRO: What else?

SOCRATES: And to give correctly is to give them what they need from us, for it would not be skillful to bring gifts to anyone that are in no way needed.

EUTHYPHRO: True, Socrates.

SOCRATES: Piety would then be a sort of trading skill between gods and men?

EUTHYPHRO: Trading yes, if you prefer to call it that.

SOCRATES: I prefer nothing, unless it is true. But tell me, what benefit do the gods derive from the gifts they receive from us? What they give us is obvious to all. There is for us no good that we do not receive from them, but how are they benefited by what they receive from us? Or do we have such an advantage over them in the trade that we receive all our blessings from them and they receive nothing from us?

EUTHYPHRO: Do you suppose, Socrates, that the gods are benefited by what they receive from us?

SOCRATES: What could those gifts from us to the gods be, Euthyphro?

EUTHYPHRO: What else, do you think, than honor, reverence, and what I mentioned just now, to please them?

SOCRATES: The pious is then, Euthyphro, pleasing to the gods, but not beneficial or dear to them?

EUTHYPHRO: I think it is of all things most dear to them.

SOCRATES: So the pious is once again what is dear to the gods.

EUTHYPHRO: Most certainly.

SOCRATES: When you say this, will you be surprised if your arguments seem to move about instead of staying put? And will you accuse me of being Daedalus who makes them move, though you are yourself much more skillful than Daedalus and make them go around in a circle? Or do you not realize that our argument has moved around and come again to the same place? You surely remember that earlier the pious and the god-loved were shown not to be the same but different from each other. Or do you not remember?

EUTHYPHRO: I do.

SOCRATES: Do you then not realize now that you are saying that what is dear to the gods is the pious? Is this not the same as the god-loved? Or is it not?

EUTHYPHRO: It certainly is.

SOCRATES: Either we were wrong when we agreed before, or, if we were right then, we are wrong now.

EUTHYPHRO: That seems to be so.

SOCRATES: So we must investigate again from the beginning what piety is, as I shall not willingly give up before I learn this. Do not think me unworthy, but concentrate your attention and tell the truth. For you know it, if any man does, and I must not let you go, like Proteus,[13] before you tell me. If you had no clear knowledge of piety and impiety you would never have ventured to prosecute your old father for murder on behalf of a servant. For fear of the gods you would have been afraid to take the risk lest you should not be acting rightly, and would have been ashamed before men, but now I know well that you believe you have clear knowledge of piety and impiety. So tell me, my good Euthyphro, and do not hide what you think it is.

EUTHYPHRO: Some other time, Socrates, for I am in a hurry now, and it is time for me to go.

SOCRATES: What a thing to do, my friend! By going you have cast me down from a great hope I had, that I would learn from you the nature of the pious and the impious and so escape Meletus' indictment by showing him that I had acquired wisdom in divine matters from Euthyphro, and my ignorance would no longer cause me to be careless and inventive about such things, and that I would be better for the rest of my life.

---

13 In Greek mythology Proteus was a sort of old man of the sea, who could keep on changing his form and so escape being questioned. See Homer, *Odyssey* iv.382 ff.

CHAPTER II

# God's Existence

# THE ONTOLOGICAL PROOF

BY Anselm, translated by David Burr

## CHAPTER 1: ENCOURAGING THE MIND TO CONTEMPLATE GOD

Come on now little man, get away from your worldly occupations for a while, escape from your tumultuous thoughts. Lay aside your burdensome cares and put off your laborious exertions. Give yourself over to God for a little while, and rest for a while in Him. Enter into the cell of your mind, shut out everything except God and whatever helps you to seek Him once the door is shut. Speak now, my heart, and say to God, "I seek your face; your face, Lord, I seek."

Come on then, my Lord God, teach my heart where and how to seek you, where and how to find you. Lord, if you are not here, where shall I find you? If, however, you are everywhere, why do I not see you here? But certainly you dwell in inaccessible light. And where is that inaccessible light? Or how do I reach it? Or who will lead me to it and into it, so that I can see you in it? And then by what signs, under what face shall I seek you? I have never seen you, my Lord God, or known your face. What shall I do, Highest Lord, what shall this exile do, banished far from you as he is? What should your servant do, desperate as he is for your love yet cast away from your face? He longs to see you, and yet your face is too far away from him. He wants to come to you, and yet your dwelling place is unreachable. He yearns to discover you, and he does not know where you are. He craves to seek you, and does not know how to recognize you. Lord, you are my Lord and my God, and I have never seen you. You have made me and nurtured me, given me every good thing I have ever received, and I still do not know you. I was created for the purpose of seeing you, and I still have not done the thing I was made to do.

Oh, how miserable man's lot is when he has lost what he was made for! Oh how hard and dire was that downfall! Alas, what did he lose and what did he find? What was taken away and what remains? He has lost beatitude for which he was made, and he has found misery for which he was not made. That without which he cannot be happy has been taken away, and that remains which in itself can only make him miserable. Back then man ate the bread of angels for which he now hungers, and now he eats the bread of griefs which he did not even know back then. Alas for the common grief of man, the universal lamentation of Adam's sons! He belched in his satiety, while we sigh in our want. He was rich, we are beggars. He happily possessed and miserably abandoned, we unhappily lack and miserably desire, yet alas, we remain empty. Why, since it would have been easy for him, did he not keep what we so disastrously lack? Why did he deprive us of light, and cover us with darkness instead? Why did he take life away from us and inflict death instead? From what have we poor wretches been expelled, and toward what are we being driven? From what have we been cast down, in what buried? From our fatherland into exile, from the vision of God into blindness. From the happiness of immortality into the bitterness and horror of death. What a miserable transformation! From so much good into so much evil! A heavy injury, a heavy, heavy grief.

I have come to you as a poor man to a rich one, as a poor rich to a merciful giver. May I not return empty and rejected! And if "I sigh before I eat" (Job 3:4), once I have sighed give me something to eat. Lord, turned in (incurvatus) as I am I can only look down, so raise me up so that I can look up. "My iniquities heaped on my head" cover me over and weigh me down "like a heavy toad" (Ps. 37:5). Dig me out and set me free before "the pit" created by them "shuts its jaws over me" (Ps. 67:16). Let me see your light, even if I see it from afar or from the depths. Teach me to seek you, and reveal yourself to this seeker. For I cannot seek you unless you teach me how, nor can I find you unless you show yourself to me. Let me seek you in desiring you, and desire you in seeking you. Let me find you in loving you and love you in finding you.

I acknowledge, Lord, and I give thanks that you have created in me this your image, so that I can remember you, think about you and love you. But it is so worn away by sins, so smudged over by the smoke of sins, that it cannot do what it was created to do unless you renew and reform it. I do not even try, Lord, to rise up to your heights, because my intellect does not measure up to that task; but I do want to understand in some small measure your truth, which my heart believes in and loved. Nor do I seek to understand so that I can believe, but rather I believe so that I can understand. For I believe this too, that "unless I believe I shall not understand" (Isa. 7:9).

## CHAPTER 2: THAT GOD REALLY EXISTS

Therefore, Lord, you who give knowledge of the faith, give me as much knowledge as you know to be fitting for me, because you are as we believe and that which we believe. And indeed we believe you are something greater than which cannot be thought. Or is there no such kind of thing, for "the fool said in his heart, 'there is no God'" (Ps. 13:1, 52:1)? But certainly that same fool, having heard what I just said, "something greater than which cannot be thought," understands what he heard, and what he understands is in his thought, even if he does not think it exists. For it is one thing for something to exist in a person's thought and quite another for the person to think that thing exists. For when a painter thinks ahead to what he will paint, he has that picture in his thought, but he does not yet think it exists, because he has not done it yet. Once he has painted it he has it in his thought and thinks it exists because he has done it. Thus even the fool is compelled to grant that something greater than which cannot be thought exists in thought, because he understands what he hears, and whatever is understood exists in thought. And certainly that greater than which cannot be understood cannot exist only in thought, for if it exists only in thought it could also be thought of as existing in reality as well, which is greater. If, therefore, that than which greater cannot be thought exists in thought alone, then that than which greater cannot be thought turns out to be that than which something greater actually can be thought, but that is obviously impossible. Therefore something than which greater cannot be thought undoubtedly exists both in thought and in reality.

## CHAPTER 3: THAT GOD CANNOT BE THOUGHT NOT TO EXIST

In fact, it so undoubtedly exists that it cannot be thought of as not existing. For one can think there exists something that cannot be thought of as not existing, and that would be greater than something which can be thought of as not existing. For if that greater than which cannot be thought can be thought of as not existing, then that greater than which cannot be thought is not that greater than which cannot be thought, which does not make sense. Thus that than which nothing can be thought so undoubtedly exists that it cannot even be thought of as not existing.

And you, Lord God, are this being. You exist so undoubtedly, my Lord God, that you cannot even be thought of as not existing. And deservedly, for if some mind could think of something greater than you, that creature would rise above the creator and could pass judgment on the creator, which is absurd. And indeed whatever exists except you alone can be thought of as not existing. You alone of all things most truly exists and thus enjoy existence to the fullest degree of all things, because nothing else exists so undoubtedly, and thus everything else enjoys being in a lesser degree. Why therefore did the foot say in his heart "there is no God, "since it is so evident to any rational mind that you above all things exist? Why indeed, except precisely because he is stupid and foolish?

## CHAPTER 4: HOW THE FOOL MANAGED TO SAY IN HIS HEART THAT WHICH CANNOT BE THOUGHT

How in the world could he have said in his heart what he could not think? Or how indeed could he not have thought what he said in his heart, since saying it in his heart is the same as thinking it? But if he really thought it because he said it in his heart, and did not say it in his heart because he could not possibly have thought it—and that seems to be precisely what happened—then there must be more than one way in which something can be said in one's heart or thought. For a thing is thought in one way when the words signifying it are thought, and it is thought in quite another way when the thing signified is understood. God can be thought not to exist in the first way but not in the second. For no one who understands what God is can think that he does not exist. Even though he may say those words in his heart he will give them some other meaning or no meaning at all. For God is that greater than which cannot be thought. Whoever understands this also understands that God exists in such a way that one cannot even think of him as not existing.

Thank you, my good God, thank you, because what I believed earlier through your gift I now understand through your illumination in such a way that I would be unable not to understand it even if I did not want to believe you existed.

# ON BEHALF OF THE FOOL

BY Gaunilo, translated by David Burr

To one who questions whether (or simply denies that) there exists something of such a nature that nothing greater can be imagined, it is said that its existence is proved in the first place by the fact that anyone denying it already has it in his thought, since upon hearing it said he understands what is said; and in the second place by the fact that what he understands necessarily exists not only in the mind but in reality as well. Thus its existence is proved, because it is a greater thing to exist in reality as well than to exist in the mind alone, and if it exists only in the mind, then what exists in reality as well will be greater, and thus that which is greater than all else will be less than something else and not greater than all else, which is nonsense. Thus what is greater than all else must necessarily exist, not only in the mind (which has already been acknowledge to be the case), in reality as well, or else it could not be greater than all else.

But perhaps the fool could reply that this thing is said to exist in my mind only in the sense that I understand what is said. For could I not say that all sorts of false and completely nonexistent things exist in my mind since when someone speaks of them I understand what is said? Unless perhaps what is being said here is that one entertains this particular thing in the mind in a completely different way than one thinks of false or doubtful things, and thus what is being said is that having heard this particular thing I do not merely think it but understand it, for I cannot think of this thing in any other way except by understanding it, and that means understanding with certainty that it actually exists. But if this is true, then in the first place there will be no difference between first entertaining that thing in the mind and then understanding that it exists. Imagine the case of that picture which is first in the painter's mind, then exists in reality. It seems unthinkable that, once such an object was spoken of the words heard, the object could not be thought not to exist in the same way God can be thought not to exist. For if God cannot be thought not to exist, then what is the point of launching this whole argument against someone who might deny that something of such a nature actually exists? And in the second place, this basic notion—that God is such that, as soon as he is thought of, he must be perceived by the mind as unquestionably existing—this notion, I say, must be proved to me by some unquestionable argument, but not by the one offered here, namely that this must be in my understanding because I understand what I'm hearing. For as far as I am concerned one might say the same thing about other things that are certain or even false, things about which I might be deceived (as I believe I often am).

Thus the example of the painter who already has in his mind the picture he is about to produce cannot be made to support this argument. For that picture, before it comes into being, exists in the art of the painter, and such a thing existing in the art of some painter is nothing other than a certain part of his understanding; for as Saint Augustine says, "If a craftsman is going to make a box, he first has it in his art. The box he actually produces is not life, but that in his art is life, because the artisan's soul, in which all such things exist before they are brought forth, is alive. And how are these things alive in the living soul of the artisan unless because are nothing other than the knowledge or understanding of the soul itself? But leaving aside those things which are known to belong to the nature of the mind itself, in the case of those things which are perceived as true by the mind through hearing or thought, in this case there is a difference between the thing itself and the mind which grasps it. Thus even if it should be true that there is something greater than which cannot be thought, this thing, whether heard or understood, would not be like the as-yet-unmade picture in the painter's mind.

Moreover, there is the point already suggested earlier, namely that when hear of something greater than all other things which can be thought of—and that something can be nothing other than God himself—I can no more entertain a thought of this being in terms of species or genera familiar to me than I can entertain such a thought

Gaunilo, "Gaunilo: How Someone Writing on Behalf of the Fool Might Reply to All This," *Anselm on God's Existence*, trans. David Burr. 

of God himself, and for this reason I am able to think he does not exist. For I have not known the thing itself and I cannot form a similitude of it from other things. For if I hear about some man completely unknown to me, whom I do not even know exists, I could at least think about him through that specific and generic knowledge by which I know what a man is or what men are like Yet it could be true that, because the speaker was lying, the man I thought about actually did not exist at all, even though I had thought of him as an existing thing, my idea of him being based, not on knowledge of this particular man, but on knowledge of man in general. But when I hear someone say "God" or "something greater than everything else" I cannot think of it as I thought of that nonexistent man, for I was able to think of the latter in terms of some truly existing thing known to me, while in the former case I can think only of the bare words, and on this basis alone one can seldom or never gain any true knowledge. For when one thinks in this way, one thinks not so much of the word itself—which, insofar as it is the sound of letters or syllables is itself a real thing, but of what is signified by the sound heard. But a phrase like "that which is greater than everything else" is not thought of as one thinks about words when one knows what they mean. It is not thought of, that is, as one thinks about something he knows is true either in reality or in thought alone. It is thought of, instead, as one does when he does not really know what the words mean, but thinks of it only in terms of an affection produced by the words within his soul, yet tries to imagine what the words mean. On this basis, though, it would be amazing if he was ever able to penetrate to the truth of the thing. It is in this way and only in this way that this being is in my mind when I hear and understand someone saying there is something greater than everything else that can be thought of. So much for the claim that the supreme nature already exists in my mind.

Nevertheless, that this being must exist not only in my mind but in reality as well is proved to me by the following argument: If it did not, then whatever did exist in reality would be greater, and thus the thing which has already been proved to exist in my mind will not be greater than everything else. If it is said that this being, which cannot be conceived of in terms of any existing thing, exists in the mind, I do not deny that it exists in mine. But through this alone it can hardly be said to attain existence in reality. I will not concede that much to it unless convinced by some indubitable argument. For whoever says that it must exist because otherwise that which is greater than all other beings will not be greater than all other beings, that person isn't paying careful enough attention to what he says. For I do not yet grant, in fact I deny it or at least question it, that the thing existing in my mind is greater than any real thing. Nor do I concede that it exists in any way except this: the sort of existence (if you can call it such) a thing has when the mind attempts to form some image of a thing unknown to it on the basis of nothing more than some words the person has heard. How then is it demonstrated to me that the thing exists in reality merely because it is said to be greater than everything else? For I continue to deny and doubt that this is established, since I continue to question whether this greater thing is in my mind or thought even in the way that many doubtful or unreal things are. It would first have to be proved to me that this greater thing really exists somewhere. Only then will we be able to infer from the fact that is greater than everything else that it also subsists in itself.

For example, they say there is in the ocean somewhere an island which, due to the difficulty (or rather the impossibility) of finding what does not actually exist, is called "the lost island." And they say that this island has all manner of riches and delights, even more of them than the Isles of the Blest, and having no owner or inhabitant it is superior in the abundance of its riches to all other lands which are inhabited by men. If someone should tell me that such is the case, I will find it easy to understand what he says, since there is nothing difficult about it. But suppose he then adds, as if he were stating a logical consequence, "Well then, you can no longer doubt that this island more excellent than all other lands really exists somewhere, since you do not doubt that it is in your mind; and since it is more excellent to exist not only in the mind but in reality as well, this island must necessarily exist, because if it didn't, any other island really existing would be more excellent than it, and thus that island now thought of by you as more excellent will not be such. "If, I say, someone tries to convince me though this argument that the island really exists and there should be no more doubt about it, I will either think he is joking or I will have a hard time deciding who is the bigger fool, me if I believe him or him if he thinks he has proved its existence without having first convinced me that this excellence is something undoubtedly existing in reality and not just something false or uncertain existing in my mind.

In the meantime, this is how the fool answers. If it is asserted in the first place that this being is so great that its nonbeing is logically inconceivable (this in turn being proved by nothing except that otherwise it would not be greater than all other beings), then the fool can answer, "When did I say that such a being, namely one greater than all others, actually exists, thus allowing you to proceed from there to argue that it so really exists that its very nonexistence is inconceivable?" It should first be proved conclusively that some being superior to (that is, greater and better than) all others exists, so that on this basis we can go on to prove the attributes such a greater and better being must possess. When, however, it is said that this highest being cannot be thought of as not existing, perhaps it would have been better to say that its nonbeing or the possibility of its nonbeing is unintelligible. For strictly speaking false things are unintelligible even though they can be thought of in the same way the fool thought God did not exist. I am absolutely certain that I exist, although I nevertheless know that my nonexistence is possible. And I understand without doubting it that the highest thing there is, namely God, exists and cannot not exist. I do not know, however, whether I can think of myself as nonexistant when I know for certain that I exist. If it turns out that I can do so in this case, why should I not be able to do the same concerning other things I know with equal certainty? If I cannot, though, the impossibility of doing so will not be something peculiar to thinking about God.

The other parts of that book are argued with such veracity, brilliance and splendor, and filled with such value, such an intimate fragrance of devout and holy feeling, that they should in no way be condemned because of those things which, at the beginning" it also prove that he exists are rightly intuited but less firmly argued. Rather those things should be argued more robustly and the entire work thus received with great respect and praise.

# THE COSMOLOGICAL PROOF

BY Thomas Aquinas, translated by Fathers of the English Dominican Province

## THIRD ARTICLE [I, Q. 2, ART. 3]

### Whether God Exists?

OBJECTION 1: It seems that God does not exist; because if one of two contraries be infinite, the other would be altogether destroyed. But the word "God" means that He is infinite goodness. If, therefore, God existed, there would be no evil discoverable; but there is evil in the world. Therefore God does not exist.

OBJ. 2: Further, it is superfluous to suppose that what can be accounted for by a few principles has been produced by many. But it seems that everything we see in the world can be accounted for by other principles, supposing God did not exist. For all natural things can be reduced to one principle which is nature; and all voluntary things can be reduced to one principle which is human reason, or will. Therefore there is no need to suppose God's existence.

*On the contrary,* It is said in the person of God: "I am Who am." (Ex. 3:14)

*I answer that,* The existence of God can be proved in five ways.

The first and more manifest way is the argument from motion. It is certain, and evident to our senses, that in the world some things are in motion. Now whatever is in motion is put in motion by another, for nothing can be in motion except it is in potentiality to that towards which it is in motion; whereas a thing moves inasmuch as it is in act. For motion is nothing else than the reduction of something from potentiality to actuality. But nothing can be reduced from potentiality to actuality, except by something in a state of actuality. Thus that which is actually hot, as fire, makes wood, which is potentially hot, to be actually hot, and thereby moves and changes it. Now it is not possible that the same thing should be at once in actuality and potentiality in the same respect, but only in different respects. For what is actually hot cannot simultaneously be potentially hot; but it is simultaneously potentially cold. It is therefore impossible that in the same respect and in the same way a thing should be both mover and moved, i.e. that it should move itself. Therefore, whatever is in motion must be put in motion by another. If that by which it is put in motion be itself put in motion, then this also must needs be put in motion by another, and that by another again. But this cannot go on to infinity, because then there would be no first mover, and, consequently, no other mover; seeing that subsequent movers move only inasmuch as they are put in motion by the first mover; as the staff moves only because it is put in motion by the hand. Therefore it is necessary to arrive at a first mover, put in motion by no other; and this everyone understands to be God.

The second way is from the nature of the efficient cause. In the world of sense we find there is an order of efficient causes. There is no case known (neither is it, indeed, possible) in which a thing is found to be the efficient cause of itself; for so it would be prior to itself, which is impossible. Now in efficient causes it is not possible to go on to infinity, because in all efficient causes following in order, the first is the cause of the intermediate cause, and the intermediate is the cause of the ultimate cause, whether the intermediate cause be several, or only one. Now to take away the cause is to take away the effect. Therefore, if there be no first cause among efficient causes, there will be no ultimate, nor any intermediate cause. But if in efficient causes it is possible to go on to infinity, there will be no first efficient cause, neither will there be an ultimate effect, nor any intermediate efficient causes; all of which is plainly false. Therefore it is necessary to admit a first efficient cause, to which everyone gives the name of God.

The third way is taken from possibility and necessity, and runs thus. We find in nature things that are possible to be and not to be, since they are found to be generated, and to corrupt, and consequently, they are possible to be

St. Thomas Aquinas, "The Existence of God (In Three Articles)," trans. Fathers of the English Dominican Province, Summa Theologica.

and not to be. But it is impossible for these always to exist, for that which is possible not to be at some time is not. Therefore, if everything is possible not to be, then at one time there could have been nothing in existence. Now if this were true, even now there would be nothing in existence, because that which does not exist only begins to exist by something already existing. Therefore, if at one time nothing was in existence, it would have been impossible for anything to have begun to exist; and thus even now nothing would be in existence—which is absurd. Therefore, not all beings are merely possible, but there must exist something the existence of which is necessary. But every necessary thing either has its necessity caused by another, or not. Now it is impossible to go on to infinity in necessary things which have their necessity caused by another, as has been already proved in regard to efficient causes. Therefore we cannot but postulate the existence of some being having of itself its own necessity, and not receiving it from another, but rather causing in others their necessity. This all men speak of as God.

The fourth way is taken from the gradation to be found in things. Among beings there are some more and some less good, true, noble and the like. But *more* and *less* are predicated of different things, according as they resemble in their different ways something which is the maximum, as a thing is said to be hotter according as it more nearly resembles that which is hottest; so that there is something which is truest, something best, something noblest and, consequently, something which is uttermost being; for those things that are greatest in truth are greatest in being, as it is written in *Metaph.* ii. Now the maximum in any genus is the cause of all in that genus; as fire, which is the maximum heat, is the cause of all hot things. Therefore there must also be something which is to all beings the cause of their being, goodness, and every other perfection; and this we call God.

The fifth way is taken from the governance of the world. We see that things which lack intelligence, such as natural bodies, act for an end, and this is evident from their acting always, or nearly always, in the same way, so as to obtain the best result. Hence it is plain that not fortuitously, but designedly, do they achieve their end. Now whatever lacks intelligence cannot move towards an end, unless it be directed by some being endowed with knowledge and intelligence; as the arrow is shot to its mark by the archer. Therefore some intelligent being exists by whom all natural things are directed to their end; and this being we call God.

REPLY OBJ. 1: As Augustine says (Enchiridion xi): "Since God is the highest good, He would not allow any evil to exist in His works, unless His omnipotence and goodness were such as to bring good even out of evil." This is part of the infinite goodness of God, that He should allow evil to exist, and out of it produce good.

REPLY OBJ. 2: Since nature works for a determinate end under the direction of a higher agent, whatever is done by nature must needs be traced back to God, as to its first cause. So also whatever is done voluntarily must also be traced back to some higher cause other than human reason or will, since these can change or fail; for all things that are changeable and capable of defect must be traced back to an immovable and self-necessary first principle, as was shown in the body of the Article.

# THE TELEOLOGICAL PROOF

BY **William Paley**

## STATE OF THE ARGUMSENT

In crossing a heath, suppose I pitched my foot against a *stone,* and were asked how the stone came to be there; I might possibly answer, that, for anything I knew to the contrary, it had lain there forever: nor would it perhaps be very easy to show the absurdity of this answer. But suppose I had found a *watch* upon the ground, and it should be inquired how the watch happened to be in that place; I should hardly think of the answer which I had before given, that, for anything I knew, the watch might have always been there. Yet why should not this answer serve for the watch as well as for the stone? Why is it not as admissible in the second case, as in the first? For this reason, and for no other, viz. that, when we come to inspect the watch, we perceive (what we could not discover in the stone) that its several parts are framed and put together for a purpose, *e. g.* that they are so formed and adjusted as to produce motion, and that motion so regulated as to point out the hour of the day; that if the different parts had been differently shaped from what they are, of a different size from what they are, or placed after any other manner, or in any other order, than that in which they are placed, either no motion at all would have been carried on in the machine, or none which would have answered the use that is now served by it. To reckon up a few of the plainest of these parts, and of their offices, all tending to one result: [See Plate I.]—We see a cylindrical box containing a coiled elastic spring, which, by its endeavor to relax itself, turns round the box. We next observe a flexible chain (artificially wrought for the sake of flexure) communicating the action of the spring from the box to the fusee. We then find a series of wheels, the teeth of which catch in, and apply to each other, conducting the motion from the fusee to the balance, and from the balance to the pointer; and at the same time, by the size and shape of those wheels, so regulating that motion, as to terminate in causing an index, by an equable and measured progression, to pass over a given space in a given time. We take notice that the wheels are made of brass in order to keep them from rust; the springs of steel, no other metal being so elastic; that over the face of the watch there is placed a glass, a material employed in no other part of the work; but in the room of which, if there had been any other than a transparent substance, the hour could not be seen without opening the case. This mechanism being observed (it requires indeed an examination of the instrument, and perhaps some previous knowledge of the subject, to perceive and understand it; but being once, as we have said, observed and understood,) the inference, we think, is inevitable; that the watch must have had a maker; that there must have existed, at sometime, and at some place or other, an artificer or artificers, who formed it for the purpose which we find it actually to answer; who comprehended its construction, and designed its use.

I. Nor would it, I apprehend, weaken the conclusion, that we had never seen a watch made: that we had never known an artist capable of making one; that we were altogether incapable of executing such a piece of workmanship ourselves, or of understanding in what manner it was performed; all this being no more than what is true of some exquisite remains of ancient art, of some lost arts, and, to the generality of mankind, of the more curious productions of modern manufacture. Does one man in a million know how oval frames are turned? Ignorance of this kind exalts our opinion of the unseen and unknown artist's skill, if he be unseen and unknown, but raises no doubt in our minds of the existence and agency of such an artist, at some former time, and in some place or other. Nor can I perceive that it varies at all the inference, whether the question arise concerning a human agent, or concerning an agent of a different species, or an agent possessing, in some respects, a different nature.

II. Neither, secondly, would it invalidate our conclusion, that the watch sometimes went wrong, or that it seldom went exactly right. The purpose of the machinery, the design and the designer, might be evident, and in the case supposed would be evident, in whatever way we accounted for the irregularity of the movement, or whether we

William Paley, "State of the Argument and Application of the Argument," *Natural Theology, Or: Evidences of the Existence and Attributes of the Deity Collected from the Appearances of Nature*, pp. 5-8, 13.

could account for it or not. It is not necessary that a machine be perfect, in order to show with what design it was made: still less necessary, where the only question is, whether it were made with any design at all.

III. Nor, thirdly, would it bring any uncertainty into the argument, if there were a few parts of the watch, concerning which we could not discover, or had not yet discovered, in what manner they conduced to the general effect; or even some parts, concerning which we could not ascertain whether they conduced to that effect in any manner whatever. For, as to the first branch of the case; if by the loss, or disorder, or decay of the parts in question, the movement of the watch were found in fact to be stopped, or disturbed, or retarded, no doubt would remain in our minds as to the utility or intention of these parts, although we should be unable to investigate the manner according to which, or the connexion by which, the ultimate effect depended upon their action or assistance; and the more complex is the machine, the more likely is this obscurity to arise. Then, as to the second thing supposed, namely, that there were parts which might be spared, without prejudice to the movement of the watch, and that we had proved this by experiment—these superfluous parts, even if we were completely assured that they were such, would not vacate the reasoning which we had instituted concerning other parts. The indication of contrivance remained, with respect to them, nearly as it was before.

IV. Nor, fourthly, would any man in his senses think the existence of the watch, with its various machinery, accounted for, by being told that it was one out of possible combinations of material forms; that whatever he had found in the place where he found the watch, must have contained some internal configuration or other; and that this configuration might be the structure now exhibited, viz. of the works of a watch, as well as a different structure.

V. Nor, fifthly, would it yield his inquiry more satisfaction to be answered, that there existed in things a principle of order, which had disposed the parts of the watch into their present form and situation. He never knew a watch made by the principle of order; nor can he even form to himself an idea of what is meant by a principle of order distinct from the intelligence of the watchmaker.

VI. Sixthly, he would be surprised to hear that the mechanism of the watch was no proof of contrivance, only a motive to induce the mind to think so.

VII. And not less surprised to be informed, that the watch in his hand was nothing more than the result of the laws of *metallic* nature. It is a perversion of language to assign any law as the efficient, operative cause of anything. A law presupposes an agent; for it is only the mode according to which an agent proceeds: it implies a power; for it is the order, according to which that power acts. Without this agent, without this power, which are both distinct from itself, the *law* does nothing; is nothing. The expression, "the law of metallic nature," may sound strange and harsh to a philosophic ear; but it seems quite as justifiable as some others which are more familiar to him, such as "the law of vegetable nature," "the law of animal nature," or indeed as "the law of nature" in general, when assigned as the cause of phenomena, in exclusion of agency and power; or when it is substituted into the place of these.

VIII. Neither, lastly, would our observer be driven out of his conclusion, or from his confidence in its truth, by being told that he knew nothing at all about the matter. He knows enough for his argument. He knows the utility of the end: he knows the subserviency and adaptation of the means to the end. These points being known, his ignorance of other points, his doubts concerning other points, affect not the certainty of his reasoning. The consciousness of knowing little need not beget a distrust of that which he does know.

## APPLICATION OF THE ARGUMENT

This is atheism: for every indication of contrivance, every manifestation of design, which existed in the watch, exists in the works of nature; with the difference, on the side of nature, of being greater and more, and that in a degree which exceeds all computation. I mean, that the contrivances of nature surpass the contrivances of art, in the complexity, subtilty, and curiosity of the mechanism; and still more, if possible, do they go beyond them in number and variety: yet, in a multitude of cases, are not less evidently mechanical, not less evidently contrivances, not less evidently accommodated to their end, or suited to their office, than are the most perfect productions of human ingenuity.

# OBJECTIONS TO THE TELEOLOGICAL PROOF

BY **David Hume**

## PART 2

I must own, CLEANTHES, said DEMEA, that nothing can more surprise me, than the light in which you have all along put this argument. By the whole tenor of your discourse, one would imagine that you were maintaining the Being of a God, against the cavils of Atheists and Infidels; and were necessitated to become a champion for that fundamental principle of all religion. But this, I hope, is not by any means a question among us. No man, no man at least of common sense, I am persuaded, ever entertained a serious doubt with regard to a truth so certain and self-evident. The question is not concerning the being, but the nature of God. This, I affirm, from the infirmities of human understanding, to be altogether incomprehensible and unknown to us. The essence of that supreme Mind, his attributes, the manner of his existence, the very nature of his duration; these, and every particular which regards so divine a Being, are mysterious to men. Finite, weak, and blind creatures, we ought to humble ourselves in his august presence; and, conscious of our frailties, adore in silence his infinite perfections, which eye hath not seen, ear hath not heard, neither hath it entered into the heart of man to conceive. They are covered in a deep cloud from human curiosity. It is profaneness to attempt penetrating through these sacred obscurities. And, next to the impiety of denying his existence, is the temerity of prying into his nature and essence, decrees and attributes.

But lest you should think that my piety has here got the better of my philosophy, I shall support my opinion, if it needs any support, by a very great authority. I might cite all the divines, almost, from the foundation of Christianity, who have ever treated of this or any other theological subject: But I shall confine myself, at present, to one equally celebrated for piety and philosophy. It is Father MALEBRANCHE, who, I remember, thus expresses himself [Recherche de la Verite. Liv. 3. Chap.9]. "One ought not so much," says he, "to call God a spirit, in order to express positively what he is, as in order to signify that he is not matter. He is a Being infinitely perfect: Of this we cannot doubt. But in the same manner as we ought not to imagine, even supposing him corporeal, that he is clothed with a human body, as the ANTHROPOMORPHITES asserted, under colour that that figure was the most perfect of any; so, neither ought we to imagine that the spirit of God has human ideas, or bears any resemblance to our spirit, under colour that we know nothing more perfect than a human mind. We ought rather to believe, that as he comprehends the perfections of matter without being material. ... he comprehends also the perfections of created spirits without being spirit, in the manner we conceive spirit: That his true name is, He that is; or, in other words, Being without restriction, All Being, the Being infinite and universal."

After so great an authority, DEMEA, replied PHILO, as that which you have produced, and a thousand more which you might produce, it would appear ridiculous in me to add my sentiment, or express my approbation of your doctrine. But surely, where reasonable men treat these subjects, the question can never be concerning the Being, but only the Nature, of the Deity. The former truth, as you well observe, is unquestionable and self-evident. Nothing exists without a cause; and the original cause of this universe (whatever it be) we call God; and piously ascribe to him every species of perfection. Whoever scruples this fundamental truth, deserves every punishment which can be inflicted among philosophers, to wit, the greatest ridicule, contempt, and disapprobation. But as all perfection is entirely relative, we ought never to imagine that we comprehend the attributes of this divine Being, or to suppose that his perfections have any analogy or likeness to the perfections of a human creature. Wisdom, Thought, Design, Knowledge; these we justly ascribe to him; because these words are honourable among men, and we have no

David Hume, "The Problem of Evil," *Dialogues Concerning Natural Religion.*

other language or other conceptions by which we can express our adoration of him. But let us beware, lest we think that our ideas anywise correspond to his perfections, or that his attributes have any resemblance to these qualities among men. He is infinitely superior to our limited view and comprehension; and is more the object of worship in the temple, than of disputation in the schools.

In reality, CLEANTHES, continued he, there is no need of having recourse to that affected scepticism so displeasing to you, in order to come at this determination. Our ideas reach no further than our experience. We have no experience of divine attributes and operations. I need not conclude my syllogism. You can draw the inference yourself. And it is a pleasure to me (and I hope to you too) that just reasoning and sound piety here concur in the same conclusion, and both of them establish the adorably mysterious and incomprehensible nature of the Supreme Being.

Not to lose any time in circumlocutions, said CLEANTHES, addressing himself to DEMEA, much less in replying to the pious declamations of PHILO; I shall briefly explain how I conceive this matter. Look round the world: contemplate the whole and every part of it: You will find it to be nothing but one great machine, subdivided into an infinite number of lesser machines, which again admit of subdivisions to a degree beyond what human senses and faculties can trace and explain. All these various machines, and even their most minute parts, are adjusted to each other with an accuracy which ravishes into admiration all men who have ever contemplated them. The curious adapting of means to ends, throughout all nature, resembles exactly, though it much exceeds, the productions of human contrivance; of human designs, thought, wisdom, and intelligence. Since, therefore, the effects resemble each other, we are led to infer, by all the rules of analogy, that the causes also resemble; and that the Author of Nature is somewhat similar to the mind of man, though possessed of much larger faculties, proportioned to the grandeur of the work which he has executed. By this argument a posteriori, and by this argument alone, do we prove at once the existence of a Deity, and his similarity to human mind and intelligence.

I shall be so free, CLEANTHES, said DEMEA, as to tell you, that from the beginning, I could not approve of your conclusion concerning the similarity of the Deity to men; still less can I approve of the mediums by which you endeavour to establish it. What! No demonstration of the Being of God! No abstract arguments! No proofs a priori! Are these, which have hitherto been so much insisted on by philosophers, all fallacy, all sophism? Can we reach no further in this subject than experience and probability? I will not say that this is betraying the cause of a Deity: But surely, by this affected candour, you give advantages to Atheists, which they never could obtain by the mere dint of argument and reasoning.

What I chiefly scruple in this subject, said PHILO, is not so much that all religious arguments are by CLEANTHES reduced to experience, as that they appear not to be even the most certain and irrefragable of that inferior kind. That a stone will fall, that fire will burn, that the earth has solidity, we have observed a thousand and a thousand times; and when any new instance of this nature is presented, we draw without hesitation the accustomed inference. The exact similarity of the cases gives us a perfect assurance of a similar event; and a stronger evidence is never desired nor sought after. But wherever you depart, in the least, from the similarity of the cases, you diminish proportionably the evidence; and may at last bring it to a very weak analogy, which is confessedly liable to error and uncertainty. After having experienced the circulation of the blood in human creatures, we make no doubt that it takes place in TITIUS and MAEVIUS. But from its circulation in frogs and fishes, it is only a presumption, though a strong one, from analogy, that it takes place in men and other animals. The analogical reasoning is much weaker, when we infer the circulation of the sap in vegetables from our experience that the blood circulates in animals; and those, who hastily followed that imperfect analogy, are found, by more accurate experiments, to have been mistaken.

If we see a house, CLEANTHES, we conclude, with the greatest certainty, that it had an architect or builder; because this is precisely that species of effect which we have experienced to proceed from that species of cause. But surely you will not affirm, that the universe bears such a resemblance to a house, that we can with the same certainty infer a similar cause, or that the analogy is here entire and perfect. The dissimilitude is so striking, that the utmost you can here pretend to is a guess, a conjecture, a presumption concerning a similar cause; and how that pretension will be received in the world, I leave you to consider.

It would surely be very ill received, replied CLEANTHES; and I should be deservedly blamed and detested, did I allow, that the proofs of a Deity amounted to no more than a guess or conjecture. But is the whole adjustment of means to ends in a house and in the universe so slight a resemblance? The economy of final causes? The order, proportion, and arrangement of every part? Steps of a stair are plainly contrived, that human legs may use them in mounting; and this inference is certain and infallible. Human legs are also contrived for walking and mounting; and this inference, I allow, is not altogether so certain, because of the dissimilarity which you remark; but does it, therefore, deserve the name only of presumption or conjecture?

Good God! cried DEMEA, interrupting him, where are we? Zealous defenders of religion allow, that the proofs of a Deity fall short of perfect evidence! And you, PHILO, on whose assistance I depended in proving the adorable mysteriousness of the Divine Nature, do you assent to all these extravagant opinions of CLEANTHES? For what other name can I give them? or, why spare my censure, when such principles are advanced, supported by such an authority, before so young a man as PAMPHILUS?

You seem not to apprehend, replied PHILO, that I argue with CLEANTHES in his own way; and, by showing him the dangerous consequences of his tenets, hope at last to reduce him to our opinion. But what sticks most with you, I observe, is the representation which CLEANTHES has made of the argument a posteriori; and finding that that argument is likely to escape your hold and vanish into air, you think it so disguised, that you can scarcely believe it to be set in its true light. Now, however much I may dissent, in other respects, from the dangerous principles of CLEANTHES, I must allow that he has fairly represented that argument; and I shall endeavour so to state the matter to you, that you will entertain no further scruples with regard to it.

Were a man to abstract from every thing which he knows or has seen, he would be altogether incapable, merely from his own ideas, to determine what kind of scene the universe must be, or to give the preference to one state or situation of things above another. For as nothing which he clearly conceives could be esteemed impossible or implying a contradiction, every chimera of his fancy would be upon an equal footing; nor could he assign any just reason why he adheres to one idea or system, and rejects the others which are equally possible.

Again; after he opens his eyes, and contemplates the world as it really is, it would be impossible for him at first to assign the cause of any one event, much less of the whole of things, or of the universe. He might set his fancy a rambling; and she might bring him in an infinite variety of reports and representations. These would all be possible; but being all equally possible, he would never of himself give a satisfactory account for his preferring one of them to the rest. Experience alone can point out to him the true cause of any phenomenon.

Now, according to this method of reasoning, DEMEA, it follows, (and is, indeed, tacitly allowed by CLEANTHES himself,) that order, arrangement, or the adjustment of final causes, is not of itself any proof of design; but only so for as it has been experienced to proceed from that principle. For aught we can know a priori, matter may contain the source or spring of order originally within itself, as well as mind does; and there is no more difficulty in conceiving, that the several elements, from an internal unknown cause, may fall into the most exquisite arrangement, than to conceive that their ideas, in the great universal mind, from a like internal unknown cause, fall into that arrangement. The equal possibility of both these suppositions is allowed. But, by experience, we find, (according to CLEANTHES), that there is a difference between them. Throw several pieces of steel together, without shape or form; they will never arrange themselves so as to compose a watch. Stone, and mortar, and wood, without an architect, never erect a house. But the ideas in a human mind, we see, by an unknown, inexplicable economy, arrange themselves so as to form the plan of a watch or house. Experience, therefore, proves, that there is an original principle of order in mind, not in matter. From similar effects we infer similar causes. The adjustment of means to ends is alike in the universe, as in a machine of human contrivance. The causes, therefore, must be resembling.

I was from the beginning scandalised, I must own, with this resemblance, which is asserted, between the Deity and human creatures; and must conceive it to imply such a degradation of the Supreme Being as no sound Theist could endure. With your assistance, therefore, DEMEA, I shall endeavour to defend what you justly call the adorable mysteriousness of the Divine Nature, and shall refute this reasoning of CLEANTHES, provided he allows that I have made a fair representation of it.

When CLEANTHES had assented, PHILO, after a short pause, proceeded in the following manner.

That all inferences, CLEANTHES, concerning fact, are founded on experience; and that all experimental reasonings are founded on the supposition that similar causes prove similar effects, and similar effects similar causes; I shall not at present much dispute with you. But observe, I entreat you, with what extreme caution all just reasoners proceed in the transferring of experiments to similar cases. Unless the cases be exactly similar, they repose no perfect confidence in applying their past observation to any particular phenomenon. Every alteration of circumstances occasions a doubt concerning the event; and it requires new experiments to prove certainly, that the new circumstances are of no moment or importance. A change in bulk, situation, arrangement, age, disposition of the air, or surrounding bodies; any of these particulars may be attended with the most unexpected consequences: And unless the objects be quite familiar to us, it is the highest temerity to expect with assurance, after any of these changes, an event similar to that which before fell under our observation. The slow and deliberate steps of philosophers here, if any where, are distinguished from the precipitate march of the vulgar, who, hurried on by the smallest similitude, are incapable of all discernment or consideration.

But can you think, CLEANTHES, that your usual phlegm and philosophy have been preserved in so wide a step as you have taken, when you compared to the universe houses, ships, furniture, machines, and, from their similarity in some circumstances, inferred a similarity in their causes? Thought, design, intelligence, such as we discover in men and other animals, is no more than one of the springs and principles of the universe, as well as heat or cold, attraction or repulsion, and a hundred others, which fall under daily observation. It is an active cause, by which some particular parts of nature, we find, produce alterations on other parts. But can a conclusion, with any propriety, be transferred from parts to the whole? Does not the great disproportion bar all comparison and inference? From observing the growth of a hair, can we learn any thing concerning the generation of a man? Would the manner of a leaf's blowing, even though perfectly known, afford us any instruction concerning the vegetation of a tree?

But, allowing that we were to take the operations of one part of nature upon another, for the foundation of our judgement concerning the origin of the whole, (which never can be admitted,) yet why select so minute, so weak, so bounded a principle, as the reason and design of animals is found to be upon this planet? What peculiar privilege has this little agitation of the brain which we call thought, that we must thus make it the model of the whole universe? Our partiality in our own favour does indeed present it on all occasions; but sound philosophy ought carefully to guard against so natural an illusion.

So far from admitting, continued PHILO, that the operations of a part can afford us any just conclusion concerning the origin of the whole, I will not allow any one part to form a rule for another part, if the latter be very remote from the former. Is there any reasonable ground to conclude, that the inhabitants of other planets possess thought, intelligence, reason, or any thing similar to these faculties in men? When nature has so extremely diversified her manner of operation in this small globe, can we imagine that she incessantly copies herself throughout so immense a universe? And if thought, as we may well suppose, be confined merely to this narrow corner, and has even there so limited a sphere of action, with what propriety can we assign it for the original cause of all things? The narrow views of a peasant, who makes his domestic economy the rule for the government of kingdoms, is in comparison a pardonable sophism.

But were we ever so much assured, that a thought and reason, resembling the human, were to be found throughout the whole universe, and were its activity elsewhere vastly greater and more commanding than it appears in this globe; yet I cannot see, why the operations of a world constituted, arranged, adjusted, can with any propriety be extended to a world which is in its embryo state, and is advancing towards that constitution and arrangement. By observation, we know somewhat of the economy, action, and nourishment of a finished animal; but we must transfer with great caution that observation to the growth of a foetus in the womb, and still more to the formation of an animalcule in the loins of its male parent. Nature, we find, even from our limited experience, possesses an infinite number of springs and principles, which incessantly discover themselves on every change of her position and situation. And what new and unknown principles would actuate her in so new and unknown a situation as that of the formation of a universe, we cannot, without the utmost temerity, pretend to determine.

A very small part of this great system, during a very short time, is very imperfectly discovered to us; and do we thence pronounce decisively concerning the origin of the whole?

Admirable conclusion! Stone, wood, brick, iron, brass, have not, at this time, in this minute globe of earth, an order or arrangement without human art and contrivance; therefore the universe could not originally attain its order and arrangement, without something similar to human art. But is a part of nature a rule for another part very wide of the former? Is it a rule for the whole? Is a very small part a rule for the universe? Is nature in one situation, a certain rule for nature in another situation vastly different from the former?

And can you blame me, CLEANTHES, if I here imitate the prudent reserve of SIMONIDES, who, according to the noted story, being asked by HIERO, What God was? desired a day to think of it, and then two days more; and after that manner continually prolonged the term, without ever bringing in his definition or description? Could you even blame me, if I had answered at first, that I did not know, and was sensible that this subject lay vastly beyond the reach of my faculties? You might cry out sceptic and railler, as much as you pleased: but having found, in so many other subjects much more familiar, the imperfections and even contradictions of human reason, I never should expect any success from its feeble conjectures, in a subject so sublime, and so remote from the sphere of our observation. When two species of objects have always been observed to be conjoined together, I can infer, by custom, the existence of one wherever I see the existence of the other; and this I call an argument from experience. But how this argument can have place, where the objects, as in the present case, are single, individual, without parallel, or specific resemblance, may be difficult to explain. And will any man tell me with a serious countenance, that an orderly universe must arise from some thought and art like the human, because we have experience of it? To ascertain this reasoning, it were requisite that we had experience of the origin of worlds; and it is not sufficient, surely, that we have seen ships and cities arise from human art and contrivance . . .

PHILO was proceeding in this vehement manner, somewhat between jest and earnest, as it appeared to me, when he observed some signs of impatience in CLEANTHES, and then immediately stopped short. What I had to suggest, said CLEANTHES, is only that you would not abuse terms, or make use of popular expressions to subvert philosophical reasonings. You know, that the vulgar often distinguish reason from experience, even where the question relates only to matter of fact and existence; though it is found, where that reason is properly analysed, that it is nothing but a species of experience. To prove by experience the origin of the universe from mind, is not more contrary to common speech, than to prove the motion of the earth from the same principle. And a caviller might raise all the same objections to the Copernican system, which you have urged against my reasonings. Have you other earths, might he say, which you have seen to move? Have . . .

Yes! cried PHILO, interrupting him, we have other earths. Is not the moon another earth, which we see to turn round its centre? Is not Venus another earth, where we observe the same phenomenon? Are not the revolutions of the sun also a confirmation, from analogy, of the same theory? All the planets, are they not earths, which revolve about the sun? Are not the satellites moons, which move round Jupiter and Saturn, and along with these primary planets round the sun? These analogies and resemblances, with others which I have not mentioned, are the sole proofs of the COPERNICAN system; and to you it belongs to consider, whether you have any analogies of the same kind to support your theory.

In reality, CLEANTHES, continued he, the modern system of astronomy is now so much received by all inquirers, and has become so essential a part even of our earliest education, that we are not commonly very scrupulous in examining the reasons upon which it is founded. It is now become a matter of mere curiosity to study the first writers on that subject, who had the full force of prejudice to encounter, and were obliged to turn their arguments on every side in order to render them popular and convincing. But if we peruse GALILEO's famous Dialogues concerning the system of the world, we shall find, that that great genius, one of the sublimest that ever existed, first bent all his endeavours to prove, that there was no foundation for the distinction commonly made between elementary and celestial substances. The schools, proceeding from the illusions of sense, had carried this distinction very far; and had established the latter substances to be ingenerable, incorruptible, unalterable, impassable; and had assigned all the opposite qualities to the former. But GALILEO, beginning with the moon, proved its similarity in every particular to the earth; its convex figure, its natural darkness when not illuminated, its density, its distinction into solid and liquid, the variations of its phases, the mutual illuminations of the earth and moon, their mutual eclipses, the inequalities of the lunar surface, &c. After many instances of this kind, with regard to all the planets, men plainly saw that these bodies became proper objects of experience; and that the similarity of their nature enabled us to extend the same arguments and phenomena from one to the other.

In this cautious proceeding of the astronomers, you may read your own condemnation, CLEANTHES; or rather may see, that the subject in which you are engaged exceeds all human reason and inquiry. Can you pretend to show any such similarity between the fabric of a house, and the generation of a universe? Have you ever seen nature in any such situation as resembles the first arrangement of the elements? Have worlds ever been formed under your eye; and have you had leisure to observe the whole progress of the phenomenon, from the first appearance of order to its final consummation? If you have, then cite your experience, and deliver your theory.

## PART 4

It seems strange to me, said CLEANTHES, that you, DEMEA, who are so sincere in the cause of religion, should still maintain the mysterious, incomprehensible nature of the Deity, and should insist so strenuously that he has no manner of likeness or resemblance to human creatures. The Deity, I can readily allow, possesses many powers and attributes of which we can have no comprehension: But if our ideas, so far as they go, be not just, and adequate, and correspondent to his real nature, I know not what there is in this subject worth insisting on. Is the name, without any meaning, of such mighty importance? Or how do you mystics, who maintain the absolute incomprehensibility of the Deity, differ from Sceptics or Atheists, who assert, that the first cause of all is unknown and unintelligible? Their temerity must be very great, if, after rejecting the production by a mind, I mean a mind resembling the human, (for I know of no other,) they pretend to assign, with certainty, any other specific intelligible cause: And their conscience must be very scrupulous indeed, if they refuse to call the universal unknown cause a God or Deity; and to bestow on him as many sublime eulogies and unmeaning epithets as you shall please to require of them.

Who could imagine, replied DEMEA, that CLEANTHES, the calm philosophical CLEANTHES, would attempt to refute his antagonists by affixing a nickname to them; and, like the common bigots and inquisitors of the age, have recourse to invective and declamation, instead of reasoning? Or does he not perceive, that these topics are easily retorted, and that Anthropomorphite is an appellation as invidious, and implies as dangerous consequences, as the epithet of Mystic, with which he has honoured us? In reality, CLEANTHES, consider what it is you assert when you represent the Deity as similar to a human mind and understanding. What is the soul of man? A composition of various faculties, passions, sentiments, ideas; united, indeed, into one self or person, but still distinct from each other. When it reasons, the ideas, which are the parts of its discourse, arrange themselves in a certain form or order; which is not preserved entire for a moment, but immediately gives place to another arrangement. New opinions, new passions, new affections, new feelings arise, which continually diversify the mental scene, and produce in it the greatest variety and most rapid succession imaginable. How is this compatible with that perfect immutability and simplicity which all true Theists ascribe to the Deity? By the same act, say they, he sees past, present, and future: His love and hatred, his mercy and justice, are one individual operation: He is entire in every point of space; and complete in every instant of duration. No succession, no change, no acquisition, no diminution. What he is implies not in it any shadow of distinction or diversity. And what he is this moment he ever has been, and ever will be, without any new judgement, sentiment, or operation. He stands fixed in one simple, perfect state: nor can you ever say, with any propriety, that this act of his is different from that other; or that this judgement or idea has been lately formed, and will give place, by succession, to any different judgement or idea.

I can readily allow, said CLEANTHES, that those who maintain the perfect simplicity of the Supreme Being, to the extent in which you have explained it, are complete Mystics, and chargeable with all the consequences which I have drawn from their opinion. They are, in a word, Atheists, without knowing it. For though it be allowed, that the Deity possesses attributes of which we have no comprehension, yet ought we never to ascribe to him any attributes which are absolutely incompatible with that intelligent nature essential to him. A mind, whose acts and sentiments and ideas are not distinct and successive; one, that is wholly simple, and totally immutable, is a mind which has no thought, no reason, no will, no sentiment, no love, no hatred; or, in a word, is no mind at all. It is an abuse of terms to give it that appellation; and we may as well speak of limited extension without figure, or of number without composition.

Pray consider, said PHILO, whom you are at present inveighing against. You are honouring with the appellation of Atheist all the sound, orthodox divines, almost, who have treated of this subject; and you will at last be, yourself, found, according to your reckoning, the only sound Theist in the world. But if idolaters be Atheists, as, I think, may justly be asserted, and Christian Theologians the same, what becomes of the argument, so much celebrated, derived from the universal consent of mankind?

But because I know you are not much swayed by names and authorities, I shall endeavour to show you, a little more distinctly, the inconveniences of that Anthropomorphism, which you have embraced; and shall prove, that there is no ground to suppose a plan of the world to be formed in the Divine mind, consisting of distinct ideas, differently arranged, in the same manner as an architect forms in his head the plan of a house which he intends to execute.

It is not easy, I own, to see what is gained by this supposition, whether we judge of the matter by Reason or by Experience. We are still obliged to mount higher, in order to find the cause of this cause, which you had assigned as satisfactory and conclusive.

If Reason (I mean abstract reason, derived from inquiries a priori) be not alike mute with regard to all questions concerning cause and effect, this sentence at least it will venture to pronounce, That a mental world, or universe of ideas, requires a cause as much, as does a material world, or universe of objects; and, if similar in its arrangement, must require a similar cause. For what is there in this subject, which should occasion a different conclusion or inference? In an abstract view, they are entirely alike; and no difficulty attends the one supposition, which is not common to both of them.

Again, when we will needs force Experience to pronounce some sentence, even on these subjects which lie beyond her sphere, neither can she perceive any material difference in this particular, between these two kinds of worlds; but finds them to be governed by similar principles, and to depend upon an equal variety of causes in their operations. We have specimens in miniature of both of them. Our own mind resembles the one; a vegetable or animal body the other. Let experience, therefore, judge from these samples. Nothing seems more delicate, with regard to its causes, than thought; and as these causes never operate in two persons after the same manner, so we never find two persons who think exactly alike. Nor indeed does the same person think exactly alike at any two different periods of time. A difference of age, of the disposition of his body, of weather, of food, of company, of books, of passions; any of these particulars, or others more minute, are sufficient to alter the curious machinery of thought, and communicate to it very different movements and operations. As far as we can judge, vegetables and animal bodies are not more delicate in their motions, nor depend upon a greater variety or more curious adjustment of springs and principles.

How, therefore, shall we satisfy ourselves concerning the cause of that Being whom you suppose the Author of Nature, or, according to your system of Anthropomorphism, the ideal world, into which you trace the material? Have we not the same reason to trace that ideal world into another ideal world, or new intelligent principle? But if we stop, and go no further, why go so far? why not stop at the material world? How can we satisfy ourselves without going on in infinitum? And, after all, what satisfaction is there in that infinite progression? Let us remember the story of the Indian philosopher and his elephant. It was never more applicable than to the present subject. If the material world rests upon a similar ideal world, this ideal world must rest upon some other; and so on, without end. It were better, therefore, never to look beyond the present material world. By supposing it to contain the principle of its order within itself, we really assert it to be God; and the sooner we arrive at that Divine Being, so much the better. When you go one step beyond the mundane system, you only excite an inquisitive humour which it is impossible ever to satisfy.

To say, that the different ideas which compose the reason of the Supreme Being, fall into order of themselves, and by their own nature, is really to talk without any precise meaning. If it has a meaning, I would fain know, why it is not as good sense to say, that the parts of the material world fall into order of themselves and by their own nature. Can the one opinion be intelligible, while the other is not so?

We have, indeed, experience of ideas which fall into order of themselves, and without any known cause. But, I am sure, we have a much larger experience of matter which does the same; as, in all instances of generation and vegetation, where the accurate analysis of the cause exceeds all human comprehension. We have also experience of particular systems of thought and of matter which have no order; of the first in madness, of the second in corruption. Why, then, should we think, that order is more essential to one than the other? And if it requires a cause in both, what do we gain by your system, in tracing the universe of objects into a similar universe of ideas? The first step which we make leads us on for ever. It were, therefore, wise in us to limit all our inquiries to the present world, without looking further. No satisfaction can ever be attained by these speculations, which so far exceed the narrow bounds of human understanding.

It was usual with the PERIPATETICS, you know, CLEANTHES, when the cause of any phenomenon was demanded, to have recourse to their faculties or occult qualities; and to say, for instance, that bread nourished by its nutritive faculty, and senna purged by its purgative. But it has been discovered, that this subterfuge was nothing but the disguise of ignorance; and that these philosophers, though less ingenuous, really said the same thing with the sceptics or the vulgar, who fairly confessed that they knew not the cause of these phenomena. In like manner, when it is asked, what cause produces order in the ideas of the Supreme Being; can any other reason be assigned by you, Anthropomorphites, than that it is a rational faculty, and that such is the nature of the Deity? But why a similar answer will not be equally satisfactory in accounting for the order of the world, without having recourse to any such intelligent creator as you insist on, may be difficult to determine. It is only to say, that such is the nature of material objects, and that they are all originally possessed of a faculty of order and proportion. These are only more learned and elaborate ways of confessing our ignorance; nor has the one hypothesis any real advantage above the other, except in its greater conformity to vulgar prejudices.

You have displayed this argument with great emphasis, replied CLEANTHES: You seem not sensible how easy it is to answer it. Even in common life, if I assign a cause for any event, is it any objection, PHILO, that I cannot assign the cause of that cause, and answer every new question which may incessantly be started? And what philosophers could possibly submit to so rigid a rule? philosophers, who confess ultimate causes to be totally unknown; and are sensible, that the most refined principles into which they trace the phenomena, are still to them as inexplicable as these phenomena themselves are to the vulgar. The order and arrangement of nature, the curious adjustment of final causes, the plain use and intention of every part and organ; all these bespeak in the clearest language an intelligent cause or author. The heavens and the earth join in the same testimony: The whole chorus of Nature raises one hymn to the praises of its Creator. You alone, or almost alone, disturb this general harmony. You start abstruse doubts, cavils, and objections: You ask me, what is the cause of this cause? I know not; I care not; that concerns not me. I have found a Deity; and here I stop my inquiry. Let those go further, who are wiser or more enterprising.

I pretend to be neither, replied PHILO: And for that very reason, I should never perhaps have attempted to go so far; especially when I am sensible, that I must at last be contented to sit down with the same answer, which, without further trouble, might have satisfied me from the beginning. If I am still to remain in utter ignorance of causes, and can absolutely give an explication of nothing, I shall never esteem it any advantage to shove off for a moment a difficulty, which, you acknowledge, must immediately, in its full force, recur upon me. Naturalists indeed very justly explain particular effects by more general causes, though these general causes themselves should remain in the end totally inexplicable; but they never surely thought it satisfactory to explain a particular effect by a particular cause, which was no more to be accounted for than the effect itself. An ideal system, arranged of itself, without a precedent design, is not a whit more explicable than a material one, which attains its order in a like manner; nor is there any more difficulty in the latter supposition than in the former.

## PART 5

But to show you still more inconveniences, continued PHILO, in your Anthropomorphism, please to take a new survey of your principles. Like effects prove like causes. This is the experimental argument; and this, you say too, is the sole theological argument. Now, it is certain, that the liker the effects are which are seen, and the liker the causes which are inferred, the stronger is the argument. Every departure on either side diminishes the probability, and renders the experiment less conclusive. You cannot doubt of the principle; neither ought you to reject its consequences.

All the new discoveries in astronomy, which prove the immense grandeur and magnificence of the works of Nature, are so many additional arguments for a Deity, according to the true system of Theism; but, according to your hypothesis of experimental Theism, they become so many objections, by removing the effect still further from all resemblance to the effects of human art and contrivance. For, if LUCRETIUS[Lib. II 1094], even following the old system of the world, could exclaim,

> Quis regere immensi summam, quis habere profundi
> Indu manu validas potis est moderanter habenas?
> Quis pariter coelos omnes convertere? et omnes
> Ignibus aetheriis terras suffire feraces?
> Omnibus inque locis esse omni tempore praesto?

If TULLY [De. nat. Deor. Lib. I] esteemed this reasoning so natural, as to put it into the mouth of his EPICUREAN:

"Quibus enim oculis animi intueri potuit vester Plato fabricam illam tanti operis, qua construi a Deo atque aedificari mundum facit? quae molitio? quae ferramenta? qui vectes? quae machinae? qui ministri tanti muneris fuerunt? quemadmodum autem obedire et parere voluntati architecti aer, ignis, aqua, terra potuerunt?"

If this argument, I say, had any force in former ages, how much greater must it have at present, when the bounds of Nature are so infinitely enlarged, and such a magnificent scene is opened to us? It is still more unreasonable to form our idea of so unlimited a cause from our experience of the narrow productions of human design and invention.

The discoveries by microscopes, as they open a new universe in miniature, are still objections, according to you, arguments, according to me. The further we push our researches of this kind, we are still led to infer the universal cause of all to be vastly different from mankind, or from any object of human experience and observation.

And what say you to the discoveries in anatomy, chemistry, botany? ... These surely are no objections, replied CLEANTHES; they only discover new instances of art and contrivance. It is still the image of mind reflected on us from innumerable objects. Add, a mind like the human, said PHILO. I know of no other, replied CLEANTHES. And the liker the better, insisted PHILO. To be sure, said CLEANTHES.

Now, CLEANTHES, said PHILO, with an air of alacrity and triumph, mark the consequences. First, By this method of reasoning, you renounce all claim to infinity in any of the attributes of the Deity. For, as the cause ought only to be proportioned to the effect, and the effect, so far as it falls under our cognisance, is not infinite; what pretensions have we, upon your suppositions, to ascribe that attribute to the Divine Being? You will still insist, that, by removing him so much from all similarity to human creatures, we give in to the most arbitrary hypothesis, and at the same time weaken all proofs of his existence.

Secondly, You have no reason, on your theory, for ascribing perfection to the Deity, even in his finite capacity, or for supposing him free from every error, mistake, or incoherence, in his undertakings. There are many inexplicable difficulties in the works of Nature, which, if we allow a perfect author to be proved a priori, are easily solved, and become only seeming difficulties, from the narrow capacity of man, who cannot trace infinite relations. But according to your method of reasoning, these difficulties become all real; and perhaps will be insisted on, as new instances of likeness to human art and contrivance. At least, you must acknowledge, that it is impossible for us to tell, from our limited views, whether this system contains any great faults, or deserves any considerable praise, if compared to other possible, and even real systems. Could a peasant, if the Aeneid were read to him, pronounce that poem to be absolutely faultless, or even assign to it its proper rank among the productions of human wit, he, who had never seen any other production?

But were this world ever so perfect a production, it must still remain uncertain, whether all the excellences of the work can justly be ascribed to the workman. If we survey a ship, what an exalted idea must we form of the ingenuity of the carpenter who framed so complicated, useful, and beautiful a machine? And what surprise must we feel, when we find him a stupid mechanic, who imitated others, and copied an art, which, through a long succession of ages, after multiplied trials, mistakes, corrections, deliberations, and controversies, had been gradually improving? Many worlds might have been botched and bungled, throughout an eternity, ere this system was struck out; much labour lost, many fruitless trials made; and a slow, but continued improvement carried on during infinite ages in the art of world-making. In such subjects, who can determine, where the truth; nay, who can conjecture where the probability lies, amidst a great number of hypotheses which may be proposed, and a still greater which may be imagined?

And what shadow of an argument, continued PHILO, can you produce, from your hypothesis, to prove the unity of the Deity? A great number of men join in building a house or ship, in rearing a city, in framing a commonwealth; why may not several deities combine in contriving and framing a world? This is only so much greater similarity to human affairs. By sharing the work among several, we may so much further limit the attributes of each, and get rid of that extensive power and knowledge, which must be supposed in one deity, and which, according to you, can only serve to weaken the proof of his existence. And if such foolish, such vicious creatures as man, can yet often unite in framing and executing one plan, how much more those deities or demons, whom we may suppose several degrees more perfect!

To multiply causes without necessity, is indeed contrary to true philosophy: but this principle applies not to the present case. Were one deity antecedently proved by your theory, who were possessed of every attribute requisite to the production of the universe; it would be needless, I own, (though not absurd,) to suppose any other deity existent. But while it is still a question, Whether all these attributes are united in one subject, or dispersed among several independent beings, by what phenomena in nature can we pretend to decide the controversy? Where we see a body raised in a scale, we are sure that there is in the opposite scale, however concealed from sight, some counterpoising weight equal to it; but it is still allowed to doubt, whether that weight be an aggregate of several distinct bodies, or one uniform united mass. And if the weight requisite very much exceeds any thing which we have ever seen conjoined in any single body, the former supposition becomes still more probable and natural. An intelligent being of such vast power and capacity as is necessary to produce the universe, or, to speak in the language of ancient philosophy, so prodigious an animal exceeds all analogy, and even comprehension.

But further, CLEANTHES: men are mortal, and renew their species by generation; and this is common to all living creatures. The two great sexes of male and female, says MILTON, animate the world. Why must this circumstance, so universal, so essential, be excluded from those numerous and limited deities? Behold, then, the theogony of ancient times brought back upon us.

And why not become a perfect Anthropomorphite? Why not assert the deity or deities to be corporeal, and to have eyes, a nose, mouth, ears, &c.? EPICURUS maintained, that no man had ever seen reason but in a human figure; therefore the gods must have a human figure. And this argument, which is deservedly so much ridiculed by CICERO, becomes, according to you, solid and philosophical.

In a word, CLEANTHES, a man who follows your hypothesis is able perhaps to assert, or conjecture, that the universe, sometime, arose from something like design: but beyond that position he cannot ascertain one single circumstance; and is left afterwards to fix every point of his theology by the utmost license of fancy and hypothesis. This world, for aught he knows, is very faulty and imperfect, compared to a superior standard; and was only the first rude essay of some infant deity, who afterwards abandoned it, ashamed of his lame performance: it is the work only of some dependent, inferior deity; and is the object of derision to his superiors: it is the production of old age and dotage in some superannuated deity; and ever since his death, has run on at adventures, from the first impulse and active force which it received from him. You justly give signs of horror, DEMEA, at these strange suppositions; but these, and a thousand more of the same kind, are CLEANTHES's suppositions, not mine. From the moment the attributes of the Deity are supposed finite, all these have place. And I cannot, for my part, think that so wild and unsettled a system of theology is, in any respect, preferable to none at all.

These suppositions I absolutely disown, cried CLEANTHES: they strike me, however, with no horror, especially when proposed in that rambling way in which they drop from you. On the contrary, they give me pleasure, when I see, that, by the utmost indulgence of your imagination, you never get rid of the hypothesis of design in the universe, but are obliged at every turn to have recourse to it. To this concession I adhere steadily; and this I regard as a sufficient foundation for religion.

## PART 7

But here, continued PHILO, in examining the ancient system of the soul of the world, there strikes me, all on a sudden, a new idea, which, if just, must go near to subvert all your reasoning, and destroy even your first inferences, on which you repose such confidence. If the universe bears a greater likeness to animal bodies and to vegetables, than to the works of human art, it is more probable that its cause resembles the cause of the former than that of the latter, and its origin ought rather to be ascribed to generation or vegetation, than to reason or design. Your conclusion, even according to your own principles, is therefore lame and defective.

Pray open up this argument a little further, said DEMEA, for I do not rightly apprehend it in that concise manner in which you have expressed it.

Our friend CLEANTHES, replied PHILO, as you have heard, asserts, that since no question of fact can be proved otherwise than by experience, the existence of a Deity admits not of proof from any other medium. The world, says he, resembles the works of human contrivance; therefore its cause must also resemble that of the other. Here we may remark, that the operation of one very small part of nature, to wit man, upon another very small part, to wit that inanimate matter lying within his reach, is the rule by which CLEANTHES judges of the origin of the whole; and he measures objects, so widely disproportioned, by the same individual standard. But to waive all objections drawn from this topic, I affirm, that there are other parts of the universe (besides the machines of human invention) which bear still a greater resemblance to the fabric of the world, and which, therefore, afford a better conjecture concerning the universal origin of this system. These parts are animals and vegetables. The world plainly resembles more an animal or a vegetable, than it does a watch or a knitting-loom. Its cause, therefore, it is more probable, resembles the cause of the former. The cause of the former is generation or vegetation. The cause, therefore, of the world, we may infer to be something similar or analogous to generation or vegetation.

But how is it conceivable, said DEMEA, that the world can arise from any thing similar to vegetation or generation?

Very easily, replied PHILO. In like manner as a tree sheds its seed into the neighbouring fields, and produces other trees; so the great vegetable, the world, or this planetary system, produces within itself certain seeds, which, being scattered into the surrounding chaos, vegetate into new worlds. A comet, for instance, is the seed of a world; and after it has been fully ripened, by passing from sun to sun, and star to star, it is at last tossed into the unformed elements which every where surround this universe, and immediately sprouts up into a new system.

Or if, for the sake of variety ( for I see no other advantage), we should suppose this world to be an animal; a comet is the egg of this animal: and in like manner as an ostrich lays its egg in the sand, which, without any further care, hatches the egg, and produces a new animal; so . . .

I understand you, says DEMEA: But what wild, arbitrary suppositions are these! What data have you for such extraordinary conclusions? And is the slight, imaginary resemblance of the world to a vegetable or an animal sufficient to establish the same inference with regard to both? Objects, which are in general so widely different, ought they to be a standard for each other?

Right, cries PHILO: This is the topic on which I have all along insisted. I have still asserted, that we have no data to establish any system of cosmogony. Our experience, so imperfect in itself, and so limited both in extent and duration, can afford us no probable conjecture concerning the whole of things. But if we must needs fix on some hypothesis; by what rule, pray, ought we to determine our choice? Is there any other rule than the greater similarity of the objects compared? And does not a plant or an animal, which springs from vegetation or generation, bear a stronger resemblance to the world, than does any artificial machine, which arises from reason and design?

But what is this vegetation and generation of which you talk? said DEMEA. Can you explain their operations, and anatomise that fine internal structure on which they depend?

As much, at least, replied PHILO, as CLEANTHES can explain the operations of reason, or anatomise that internal structure on which it depends. But without any such elaborate disquisitions, when I see an animal, I infer, that it sprang from generation; and that with as great certainty as you conclude a house to have been reared by design. These words, generation, reason, mark only certain powers and energies in nature, whose effects are known, but whose essence is incomprehensible; and one of these principles, more than the other, has no privilege for being made a standard to the whole of nature.

In reality, DEMEA, it may reasonably be expected, that the laiger the views are which we take of things, the better will they conduct us in our conclusions concerning such extraordinary and such magnificent subjects. In this little corner of the world alone, there are four principles, reason, instinct, generation, vegetation, which are similar to each other, and are the causes of similar effects. What a number of other principles may we naturally suppose in the immense extent and variety of the universe, could we travel from planet to planet, and from system to system, in order to examine each part of this mighty fabric? Any one of these four principles above mentioned, (and a hundred others which lie open to our conjecture,) may afford us a theory by which to judge of the origin of the world; and it is a palpable and egregious partiality to confine our view entirely to that principle by which our own minds operate. Were this principle more intelligible on that account, such a partiality might be somewhat excusable: But reason, in its internal fabric and structure, is really as little known to us as instinct or vegetation; and, perhaps, even that vague, indeterminate word, Nature, to which the vulgar refer every thing, is not at the bottom more inexplicable. The effects of these principles are all known to us from experience; but the principles themselves, and their manner of operation, are totally unknown; nor is it less intelligible, or less conformable to experience, to say, that the world arose by vegetation, from a seed shed by another world, than to say that it arose from a divine reason or contrivance, according to the sense in which CLEANTHES understands it.

But methinks, said DEMEA, if the world had a vegetative quality, and could sow the seeds of new worlds into the infinite chaos, this power would be still an additional argument for design in its author. For whence could arise so wonderful a faculty but from design? Or how can order spring from any thing which perceives not that order which it bestows?

You need only look around you, replied PHILO, to satisfy yourself with regard to this question. A tree bestows order and organisation on that tree which springs from it, without knowing the order; an animal in the same manner on its offspring; a bird on its nest; and instances of this kind are even more frequent in the world than those of order, which arise from reason and contrivance. To say, that all this order in animals and vegetables proceeds ultimately from design, is begging the question; nor can that great point be ascertained otherwise than by proving, a priori, both that order is, from its nature, inseparably attached to thought; and that it can never of itself, or from original unknown principles, belong to matter.

But further, DEMEA; this objection which you urge can never be made use of by CLEANTHES, without renouncing a defence which he has already made against one of my objections. When I inquired concerning the cause of that supreme reason and intelligence into which he resolves every thing; he told me, that the impossibility of satisfying such inquiries could never be admitted as an objection in any species of philosophy. "We must stop somewhere", says he; "nor is it ever within the reach of human capacity to explain ultimate causes, or show the last connections of any objects. It is sufficient, if any steps, so far as we go, are supported by experience and observation." Now, that vegetation and generation, as well as reason, are experienced to be principles of order in nature, is undeniable. If I rest my system of cosmogony on the former, preferably to the latter, it is at my choice. The matter seems entirely arbitrary. And when CLEANTHES asks me what is the cause of my great vegetative or generative faculty, I am equally entitled to ask him the cause of his great reasoning principle. These questions we have agreed to forbear on both sides; and it is chiefly his interest on the present occasion to stick to this agreement. Judging by our limited and imperfect experience, generation has some privileges above reason: for we see every day the latter arise from the former, never the former from the latter.

Compare, I beseech you, the consequences on both sides. The world, say I, resembles an animal; therefore it is an animal, therefore it arose from generation. The steps, I confess, are wide; yet there is some small appearance of analogy in each step. The world, says CLEANTHES, resembles a machine; therefore it is a machine, therefore it arose from design. The steps are here equally wide, and the analogy less striking. And if he pretends to carry on my hypothesis a step further, and to infer design or reason from the great principle of generation, on which I insist; I may, with better authority, use the same freedom to push further his hypothesis, and infer a divine generation or theogony from his principle of reason. I have at least some faint shadow of experience, which is the utmost that can ever be attained in the present subject. Reason, in innumerable instances, is observed to arise from the principle of generation, and never to arise from any other principle.

HESIOD, and all the ancient mythologists, were so struck with this analogy, that they universally explained the origin of nature from an animal birth, and copulation. PLATO too, so far as he is intelligible, seems to have adopted some such notion in his TIMAEUS.

The BRAHMINS assert, that the world arose from an infinite spider, who spun this whole complicated mass from his bowels, and annihilates afterwards the whole or any part of it, by absorbing it again, and resolving it into his own essence. Here is a species of cosmogony, which appears to us ridiculous; because a spider is a little contemptible animal, whose operations we are never likely to take for a model of the whole universe. But still here is a new species of analogy, even in our globe. And were there a planet wholly inhabited by spiders, (which is very possible,) this inference would there appear as natural and irrefragable as that which in our planet ascribes the origin of all things to design and intelligence, as explained by CLEANTHES. Why an orderly system may not be spun from the belly as well as from the brain, it will be difficult for him to give a satisfactory reason.

I must confess, PHILO, replied CLEANTHES, that of all men living, the task which you have undertaken, of raising doubts and objections, suits you best, and seems, in a manner, natural and unavoidable to you. So great is your fertility of invention, that I am not ashamed to acknowledge myself unable, on a sudden, to solve regularly such out-of-the-way difficulties as you incessantly start upon me: though I clearly see, in general, their fallacy and error. And I question not, but you are yourself, at present, in the same case, and have not the solution so ready as the objection: while you must be sensible, that common sense and reason are entirely against you; and that such whimsies as you have delivered, may puzzle, but never can convince us.

# SELECTIONS FROM *PENSÉES*

BY **Blaise Pascal**

## 233

*Infinite—nothing.*—Our soul is cast into a body, where it finds number, time, dimension. Thereupon it reasons, and calls this nature, necessity, and can believe nothing else.

Unity joined to infinity adds nothing to it, no more than one foot to an infinite measure. The finite is annihilated in the presence of the infinite, and becomes a pure nothing. So our spirit before God, so our justice before divine justice. There is not so great a disproportion between our justice and that of God, as between unity and infinity.

The justice of God must be vast like His compassion. Now justice to the outcast is less vast, and ought less to offend our feelings than mercy towards the elect.

We know that there is an infinite, and are ignorant of its nature. As we know it to be false that numbers are finite, it is therefore true that there is an infinity in number. But we do not know what it is. It is false that it is even, it is false that it is odd; for the addition of a unit can make no change in its nature. Yet it is a number, and every number is odd or even (this is certainly true of every finite number). So we may well know that there is a God without knowing what He is. Is there not one substantial truth, seeing there are so many things which are not the truth itself?

We know then the existence and nature of the finite, because we also are finite and have extension. We know the existence of the infinite, and are ignorant of its nature, because it has extension like us, but not limits like us. But we know neither the existence nor the nature of God, because He has neither extension nor limits.

But by faith we know His existence; in glory we shall know His nature. Now, I have already shown that we may well know the existence of a thing, without knowing its nature.

Let us now speak according to natural lights.

If there is a God, He is infinitely incomprehensible, since, having neither parts nor limits, He has no affinity to us. We are then incapable of knowing either what He is or if He is. This being so, who will dare to undertake the decision of the question? Not we, who have no affinity to Him.

Who then will blame Christians for not being able to give a reason for their belief, since they profess a religion for which they cannot give a reason? They declare, in expounding it to the world, that it is a foolishness, *stultitiam*; and then you complain that they do not prove it! If they proved it, they would not keep their word; it is in lacking proofs, that they are not lacking in sense. "Yes, but although this excuses those who offer it as such, and takes away from them the blame of putting it forward without reason, it does not excuse those who receive it." Let us then examine this point, and say, "God is, or He is not." But to which side shall we incline? Reason can decide nothing here. There is an infinite chaos which separated us. A game is being played at the extremity of this infinite distance where heads or tails will turn up. What will you wager? According to reason, you can do neither the one thing nor the other; according to reason, you can defend neither of the propositions.

Do not then reprove for error those who have made a choice; for you know nothing about it. "No, but I blame them for having made, not this choice, but a choice; for again both he who chooses heads and he who chooses tails are equally at fault, they are both in the wrong. The true course is not to wager at all."

Yes; but you must wager. It is not optional. You are embarked. Which will you choose then? Let us see. Since you must choose, let us see which interests you least. You have two things to lose, the true and the good; and two things to stake, your reason and your will, your knowledge and your happiness; and your nature has two things to shun, error and misery. Your reason is no more shocked in choosing one rather than the other, since you must of necessity choose. This is one point settled. But your happiness? Let us weigh the gain and the loss in wagering that

Blaise Pascal, Pascal's Pensées.

God is. Let us estimate these two chances. If you gain, you gain all; if you lose, you lose nothing. Wager, then, without hesitation that He is.—"That is very fine. Yes, I must wager; but I may perhaps wager too much."—Let us see. Since there is an equal risk of gain and of loss, if you had only to gain two lives, instead of one, you might still wager. But if there were three lives to gain, you would have to play (since you are under the necessity of playing), and you would be imprudent, when you are forced to play, not to chance your life to gain three at a game where there is an equal risk of loss and gain. But there is an eternity of life and happiness. And this being so, if there were an infinity of chances, of which one only would be for you, you would still be right in wagering one to win two, and you would act stupidly, being obliged to play, by refusing to stake one life against three at a game in which out of an infinity of chances there is one for you, if there were an infinity of an infinitely happy life to gain. But there is here an infinity of an infinitely happy life to gain, a chance of gain against a finite number of chances of loss, and what you stake is finite. It is all divided; wherever the infinite is and there is not an infinity of chances of loss against that of gain, there is no time to hesitate, you must give all. And thus, when one is forced to play, he must renounce reason to preserve his life, rather than risk it for infinite gain, as likely to happen as the loss of nothingness.

For it is no use to say it is uncertain if we will gain, and it is certain that we risk, and that the infinite distance between the *certainty* of what is staked and the *uncertainty* of what will he gained, equals the finite good which is certainly staked against the uncertain infinite. It is not so, as every player stakes a certainly to gain an uncertainty, and yet he stakes a finite certainty to gain a finite uncertainty, without transgressing against reason. There is not an infinite distance between the certainty staked and the uncertainty of the gain; that is untrue. In truth, there is an infinity between the certainty of gain and the certainty of loss. But the uncertainty of the gain is proportioned to the certainty of the stake according to the proportion of the glances of gain and loss. Hence it comes that, if there are as many risks on one side as on the other, the course is to play even; and then the certainty of the stake is equal to the uncertainty of the gain, so far is it from fact that there is an infinite distance between them. And so our proposition is of infinite force, when there is the finite to stake in a game where there are equal risks of gain and of loss, and the infinite to gain. This is demonstrable; and if men are capable of any truths, this is one.

"I confess it, I admit it. But, still, is there no means of seeing the faces of the cards?"—Yes, Scripture and the rest, etc. "Yes, but I have my hands tied and my mouth closed; I am forced to wager, and am not free. I am not released, and am so made that I cannot believe. What, then, would you have me do?"

True. But at least learn your inability to believe, since reason brings you to this, and yet you cannot believe. Endeavour then to convince yourself, not by increase of proofs of God, but by the abatement of your passions. You would like to attain faith, and do not know the way; you would like to cure yourself of unbelief, and ask the remedy for it. Learn of those who have been bound like you, and who now stake all their possessions. These are people who know the way which you would follow, and who are cured of an ill of which you would be cured. Follow the way by which they began; by acting as if they believed, taking the holy water, having masses said, etc. Even this will naturally make you believe, and deaden your acuteness.—"But this is what I am afraid of."—And why? What have you to lose?

But to show you that this leads you there, it is this which will lessen the passions, which are your stumbling—blocks.

*The end of this discourse.*—Now, what harm will befall you in taking this side? You will be faithful, honest, humble, grateful, generous, a sincere friend, truthful. Certainly you will not have those poisonous pleasures, glory and luxury; but will you not have others? I will tell you that you will thereby gain in this life, and that, at each step you take on this road, you will see so great certainty of gain, so much nothingness in what you risk, that you will at last recognise that you have wagered for something certain and infinite, for which you have given nothing.

"Ah! This discourse transports me, charms me," etc.

If this discourse pleases you and seems impressive, know that it is made by a man who has knelt, both before and after it, in prayer to that Being, infinite and without parts, before whom he lays all he has, for you also to lay before Him all you have for your own good and for His glory, that so strength may be given to lowliness.

## 234

If we must not act save on a certainty, we ought not to act on religion, for it is not certain. But how many things we do on an uncertainty, sea voyages, battles! I say then we must do nothing at all, for nothing is certain, and that there is more certainty in religion than there is as to whether we may see to-morrow; for it is not certain that we may see to-morrow, and it is certainly possible that we may not see it. We cannot say as much about religion. It is not certain that it is; but who will venture to say that it is certainly possible that it is not? Now when we work for to-morrow, and so on an uncertainty, we act reasonably; for we ought to work for an uncertainty according to the doctrine of chance which was demonstrated above.

Saint Augustine has seen that we work for an uncertainty, on sea, in battle, etc. But he has not seen the doctrine of chance which proves that we should do so. Montaigne has seen that we are shocked at a fool, and that habit is all-powerful; but he has not seen the reason of this effect.

All these persons have seen the effects, but they have not seen the causes. They are, in comparison with those who have discovered the causes, as those who have only eyes are in comparison with those who have intellect. For the effects are perceptible by sense, and the causes are visible only to the intellect. And although these effects are seen by the mind, this mind is, in comparison with the mind which sees the causes, as the bodily senses are in comparison with the intellect.

### 252

For we must not misunderstand ourselves; we are as much automatic as intellectual; and hence it comes that the instrument by which conviction is attained is not demonstrated alone. How few things are demonstrated? Proofs only convince the mind. Custom is the source of our strongest and most believed proofs. It bends the automaton, which persuades the mind without its thinking about the matter. Who has demonstrated that there will be a tomorrow, and that we shall die? And what is more believed? It is, then, custom which persuades us of it; it is custom that makes so many men Christians; custom that makes them Turks, heathens, artisans, soldiers, etc. (Faith in baptism is more received among Christians than among Turks.) Finally, we must have recourse to it when once the mind has seen where the truth is, in order to quench our thirst, and steep ourselves in that belief, which escapes us at every hour; for always to have proofs ready is too much trouble. We must get an easier belief, which is that of custom, which, without violence, without art, without argument, makes us believe things, and inclines all our powers to this belief, so that out soul falls naturally into it. It is not enough to believe only by force of conviction, when the automaton is inclined to believe the contrary. Both our parts must be made to believe, the mind by reasons which it is sufficient to have seen once in a lifetime, and the automaton by custom, and by not allowing it to incline to the contrary. *Inclina cor meum, Deus*

The reason acts slowly, with so many examinations, and on so many principles, which must be always present, that at every hour it falls asleep, or wanders, through want of having all its principles present. Feeling does not act thus; it acts in a moment, and is always ready to act. We must then put our faith in feeling; otherwise it will be always vacillating.

### 277

The heart has its reasons, which reason does not know. We feel it in a thousand things. I say that the heart naturally loves the Universal Being, and also itself naturally, according as it gives itself to them; and it hardens itself against one or the other at its will. You have rejected the one, and kept the other. Is it by reason that you love yourself?

### 347

Man is but a reed, the most feeble thing in nature; but he is a thinking reed. The entire universe need not arm itself to crush him. A vapour, a drop of water suffices to kill him. But, if the universe were to crush him, man would still be more noble than that which killed him, because he knows that he dies and the advantage which the universe has over him; the universe knows nothing of this.

All our dignity consists, then, in thought. By it we must elevate ourselves, and not by space and time which we cannot fill. Let us endeavour, then, to think well; this is the principle of morality.

### 356

The nourishment of the body is little by little. Fullness of nourishment and smallness of substance.

# THE PROBLEM OF EVIL

BY **David Hume**

## PART 11

I scruple not to allow, said CLEANTHES, that I have been apt to suspect the frequent repetition of the word infinite, which we meet with in all theological writers, to savour more of panegyric than of philosophy; and that any purposes of reasoning, and even of religion, would be better served, were we to rest contented with more accurate and more moderate expressions. The terms, admirable, excellent, superlatively great, wise, and holy; these sufficiently fill the imaginations of men; and any thing beyond, besides that it leads into absurdities, has no influence on the affections or sentiments. Thus, in the present subject, if we abandon all human analogy, as seems your intention, DEMEA, I am afraid we abandon all religion, and retain no conception of the great object of our adoration. If we preserve human analogy, we must for ever find it impossible to reconcile any mixture of evil in the universe with infinite attributes; much less can we ever prove the latter from the former. But supposing the Author of Nature to be finitely perfect, though far exceeding mankind, a satisfactory account may then be given of natural and moral evil, and every untoward phenomenon be explained and adjusted. A less evil may then be chosen, in order to avoid a greater; inconveniences be submitted to, in order to reach a desirable end; and in a word, benevolence, regulated by wisdom, and limited by necessity, may produce just such a world as the present. You, PHILO, who are so prompt at starting views, and reflections, and analogies, I would gladly hear, at length, without interruption, your opinion of this new theory; and if it deserve our attention, we may afterwards, at more leisure, reduce it into form.

My sentiments, replied PHILO, are not worth being made a mystery of; and therefore, without any ceremony, I shall deliver what occurs to me with regard to the present subject. It must, I think, be allowed, that if a very limited intelligence, whom we shall suppose utterly unacquainted with the universe, were assured, that it were the production of a very good, wise, and powerful Being, however finite, he would, from his conjectures, form beforehand a different notion of it from what we find it to be by experience; nor would he ever imagine, merely from these attributes of the cause, of which he is informed, that the effect could be so full of vice and misery and disorder, as it appears in this life. Supposing now, that this person were brought into the world, still assured that it was the workmanship of such a sublime and benevolent Being; he might, perhaps, be surprised at the disappointment; but would never retract his former belief, if founded on any very solid argument; since such a limited intelligence must be sensible of his own blindness and ignorance, and must allow, that there may be many solutions of those phenomena, which will for ever escape his comprehension. But supposing, which is the real case with regard to man, that this creature is not antecedently convinced of a supreme intelligence, benevolent, and powerful, but is left to gather such a belief from the appearances of things; this entirely alters the case, nor will he ever find any reason for such a conclusion. He may be fully convinced of the narrow limits of his understanding; but this will not help him in forming an inference concerning the goodness of superior powers, since he must form that inference from what he knows, not from what he is ignorant of. The more you exaggerate his weakness and ignorance, the more diffident you render him, and give him the greater suspicion that such subjects are beyond the reach of his faculties. You are obliged, therefore, to reason with him merely from the known phenomena, and to drop every arbitrary supposition or conjecture.

Did I show you a house or palace, where there was not one apartment convenient or agreeable; where the windows, doors, fires, passages, stairs, and the whole economy of the building, were the source of noise, confusion, fatigue, darkness, and the extremes of heat and cold; you would certainly blame the contrivance, without any further examination. The architect would in vain display his subtlety, and prove to you, that if this door or that window were altered, greater ills would ensue. What he says may be strictly true: The alteration of one particular, while the other parts of the building remain, may only augment the inconveniences. But still you would assert in general, that, if the architect had had skill and good intentions, he might have formed such a plan of the whole, and might have adjusted the parts in such a manner, as would have remedied all or most of these inconveniences. His ignorance, or even your own ignorance of such a plan, will never convince you of the impossibility of it. If you find any inconveniences and deformities in the building, you will always, without entering into any detail, condemn the architect.

In short, I repeat the question: Is the world, considered in general, and as it appears to us in this life, different from what a man, or such a limited being, would, beforehand, expect from a very powerful, wise, and benevolent Deity? It must be strange prejudice to assert the contrary. And from thence I conclude, that however consistent the world may be, allowing certain suppositions and conjectures, with the idea of such a Deity, it can never afford us an inference concerning his existence. The consistence is not absolutely denied, only the inference. Conjectures, especially where infinity is excluded from the Divine attributes, may perhaps be sufficient to prove a consistence, but can never be foundations for any inference.

There seem to be four circumstances, on which depend all, or the greatest part of the ills, that molest sensible creatures; and it is not impossible but all these circumstances may be necessary and unavoidable. We know so little beyond common life, or even of common life, that, with regard to the economy of a universe, there is no conjecture, however wild, which may not be just; nor any one, however plausible, which may not be erroneous. All that belongs to human understanding, in this deep ignorance and obscurity, is to be sceptical, or at least cautious, and not to admit of any hypothesis whatever, much less of any which is supported by no appearance of probability. Now, this I assert to be the case with regard to all the causes of evil, and the circumstances on which it depends. None of them appear to human reason in the least degree necessary or unavoidable; nor can we suppose them such, without the utmost license of imagination.

The first circumstance which introduces evil, is that contrivance or economy of the animal creation, by which pains, as well as pleasures, are employed to excite all creatures to action, and make them vigilant in the great work of self-preservation. Now pleasure alone, in its various degrees, seems to human understanding sufficient for this purpose. All animals might be constantly in a state of enjoyment: but when urged by any of the necessities of nature, such as thirst, hunger, weariness; instead of pain, they might feel a diminution of pleasure, by which they might be prompted to seek that object which is necessary to their subsistence. Men pursue pleasure as eagerly as they avoid pain; at least they might have been so constituted. It seems, therefore, plainly possible to carry on the business of life without any pain. Why then is any animal ever rendered susceptible of such a sensation? If animals can be free from it an hour, they might enjoy a perpetual exemption from it; and it required as particular a contrivance of their organs to produce that feeling, as to endow them with sight, hearing, or any of the senses. Shall we conjecture, that such a contrivance was necessary, without any appearance of reason? and shall we build on that conjecture as on the most certain truth?

But a capacity of pain would not alone produce pain, were it not for the second circumstance, viz. the conducting of the world by general laws; and this seems nowise necessary to a very perfect Being. It is true, if everything were conducted by particular volitions, the course of nature would be perpetually broken, and no man could employ his reason in the conduct of life. But might not other particular volitions remedy this inconvenience? In short, might not the Deity exterminate all ill, wherever it were to be found; and produce all good, without any preparation, or long progress of causes and effects?

Besides, we must consider, that, according to the present economy of the world, the course of nature, though supposed exactly regular, yet to us appears not so, and many events are uncertain, and many disappoint our expectations. Health and sickness, calm and tempest, with an infinite number of other accidents, whose causes are unknown and variable, have a great influence both on the fortunes of particular persons and on the prosperity of public societies; and indeed all human life, in a manner, depends on such accidents. A being, therefore, who knows the secret springs of the universe, might easily, by particular volitions, turn all these accidents to the good of mankind, and render the whole world happy, without discovering himself in any operation. A fleet, whose purposes were salutary to society, might always meet with a fair wind. Good princes enjoy sound health and long life. Persons born to power and authority, be framed with good tempers and virtuous dispositions. A few such events as these, regularly and wisely conducted, would change the face of the world; and yet would no more seem to disturb the course of nature, or confound human conduct, than the present economy of things, where the causes are secret, and variable, and compounded. Some small touches given to CALIGULA's brain in his infancy, might have converted him into a TRAJAN. One wave, a little higher than the rest, by burying CAESAR and his fortune in the bottom of the ocean, might have restored liberty to a considerable part of mankind. There may, for aught we know, be good reasons why Providence interposes not in this manner; but they are unknown to us; and though the mere supposition, that such reasons exist, may be sufficient to save the conclusion concerning the Divine attributes, yet surely it can never be sufficient to establish that conclusion.

If every thing in the universe be conducted by general laws, and if animals be rendered susceptible of pain, it scarcely seems possible but some ill must arise in the various shocks of matter, and the various concurrence and opposition of general laws; but this ill would be very rare, were it not for the third circumstance, which I proposed to mention, viz. the great frugality with which all powers and faculties are distributed to every particular being. So well adjusted are the organs and capacities of all animals, and so well fitted to their preservation, that, as far as history or tradition reaches, there appears not to be any single species which has yet been extinguished in the universe. Every animal has the requisite endowments; but these endowments are bestowed with so scrupulous an economy, that any considerable diminution must entirely destroy the creature. Wherever one power is increased, there is a proportional abatement in the others. Animals which excel in swiftness are commonly defective in force. Those which possess both are either imperfect in some of their senses, or are oppressed with the most craving wants. The human species, whose chief excellency is reason and sagacity, is of all others the most necessitous, and the most deficient in bodily advantages; without clothes, without arms, without food, without lodging, without any convenience of life, except what they owe to their own skill and industry. In short, nature seems to have formed an exact calculation of the necessities of her creatures; and, like a rigid master, has afforded them little more powers or endowments than what are strictly sufficient to supply those necessities. An indulgent parent would have bestowed a large stock, in order to guard against accidents, and secure the happiness and welfare of the creature in the most unfortunate concurrence of circumstances. Every course of life would not have been so surrounded with precipices, that the least departure from the true path, by mistake or necessity, must involve us in misery and ruin. Some reserve, some fund, would have been provided to ensure happiness; nor would the powers and the necessities have been adjusted with so rigid an economy. The Author of Nature is inconceivably powerful: his force is supposed great, if not altogether inexhaustible: nor is there any reason, as far as we can judge, to make him observe this strict frugality in his dealings with his creatures. It would have been better, were his power extremely limited, to have created fewer animals, and to have endowed these with more faculties for their happiness and preservation. A builder is never esteemed prudent, who undertakes a plan beyond what his stock will enable him to finish.

In order to cure most of the ills of human life, I require not that man should have the wings of the eagle, the swiftness of the stag, the force of the ox, the arms of the lion, the scales of the crocodile or rhinoceros; much less do I demand the sagacity of an angel or cherubim. I am contented to take an increase in one single power or faculty of his soul. Let him be endowed with a greater propensity to industry and labour; a more vigorous spring and activity of mind; a more constant bent to business and application. Let the whole species possess naturally an equal diligence with that which many individuals are able to attain by habit and reflection; and the most beneficial consequences, without any allay of ill, is the immediate and necessary result of this endowment. Almost all the moral, as well as natural evils of human life, arise from idleness; and were our species, by the original constitution of their frame, exempt from this vice or infirmity, the perfect cultivation of land, the improvement of arts and manufactures, the exact execution of every office and duty, immediately follow; and men at once may fully reach that state of society, which is so imperfectly attained by the best regulated government. But as industry is a power, and the most valuable of any, Nature seems determined, suitably to her usual maxims, to bestow it on men with a very sparing hand; and rather to punish him severely for his deficiency in it, than to reward him for his attainments. She has so contrived his frame, that nothing but the most violent necessity can oblige him to labour; and she employs all his other wants to overcome, at least in part, the want of diligence, and to endow him with some share of a faculty of which she has thought fit naturally to bereave him. Here our demands may be allowed very humble, and therefore the more reasonable. If we required the endowments of superior penetration and judgement, of a more delicate taste of beauty, of a nicer sensibility to benevolence and friendship; we might be told, that we impiously pretend to break the order of Nature; that we want to exalt ourselves into a higher rank of being; that the presents which we require, not being suitable to our state and condition, would only be pernicious to us. But it is hard; I dare to repeat it, it is hard, that being placed in a world so full of wants and necessities, where almost every being and element is either our foe or refuses its assistance ... we should also have our own temper to struggle with, and should be deprived of that faculty which can alone fence against these multiplied evils.

The fourth circumstance, whence arises the misery and ill of the universe, is the inaccurate workmanship of all the springs and principles of the great machine of nature. It must be acknowledged, that there are few parts of the universe, which seem not to serve some purpose, and whose removal would not produce a visible defect and disorder in the whole. The parts hang all together; nor can one be touched without affecting the rest, in a greater or less degree. But at the same time, it must be observed, that none of these parts or principles, however useful, are so accurately adjusted, as to keep precisely within those bounds in which their utility consists; but they are, all of them, apt, on every occasion, to run into the one extreme or the other. One would imagine, that this grand production had not received the last hand of the maker; so little finished is every part, and so coarse are the strokes with which it is executed. Thus, the winds are requisite to convey the vapours along the surface of the globe, and to assist men in navigation: but how oft, rising up to tempests and hurricanes, do they become pernicious? Rains are necessary to nourish all the plants and animals of the earth: but how often are they defective? how often excessive? Heat is requisite to all life and vegetation; but is not always found in the due proportion. On the mixture and secretion of the humours and juices of the body depend the health and prosperity of the animal: but the parts perform not regularly their proper function. What more useful than all the passions of the mind, ambition, vanity, love, anger? But how oft do they break their bounds, and cause the greatest convulsions in society? There is nothing so advantageous in the universe, but what frequently becomes pernicious, by its excess or defect; nor has Nature guarded, with the requisite accuracy, against all disorder or confusion. The irregularity is never perhaps so great as to destroy any species; but is often sufficient to involve the individuals in ruin and misery.

On the concurrence, then, of these four circumstances, does all or the greatest part of natural evil depend. Were all living creatures incapable of pain, or were the world administered by particular volitions, evil never could have found access into the universe: and were animals endowed with a large stock of powers and faculties, beyond what strict necessity requires; or were the several springs and principles of the universe so accurately framed as to preserve always the just temperament and medium; there must have been very little ill in comparison of what we feel at present. What then shall we pronounce on this occasion? Shall we say that these circumstances are not necessary, and that they might easily have been altered in the contrivance of the universe? This decision seems too presumptuous for creatures so blind and ignorant. Let us be more modest in our conclusions. Let us allow, that, if the goodness of the Deity (I mean a goodness like the human) could be established on any tolerable reasons a priori, these phenomena, however untoward, would not be sufficient to subvert that principle; but might easily, in some unknown manner, be reconcilable to it. But let us still assert, that as this goodness is not antecedently established, but must be inferred from the phenomena, there can be no grounds for such an inference, while there are so many ills in the universe, and while these ills might so easily have been remedied, as far as human understanding can be allowed to judge on such a subject. I am Sceptic enough to allow, that the bad appearances, notwithstanding all my reasonings, may be compatible with such attributes as you suppose; but surely they can never prove these attributes. Such a conclusion cannot result from Scepticism, but must arise from the phenomena, and from our confidence in the reasonings which we deduce from these phenomena.

Look round this universe. What an immense profusion of beings, animated and organised, sensible and active! You admire this prodigious variety and fecundity. But inspect a little more narrowly these living existences, the only beings worth regarding. How hostile and destructive to each other! How insufficient all of them for their own happiness! How contemptible or odious to the spectator! The whole presents nothing but the idea of a blind Nature, impregnated by a great vivifying principle, and pouring forth from her lap, without discernment or parental care, her maimed and abortive children!

Here the MANICHAEAN system occurs as a proper hypothesis to solve the difficulty: and no doubt, in some respects, it is very specious, and has more probability than the common hypothesis, by giving a plausible account of the strange mixture of good and ill which appears in life. But if we consider, on the other hand, the perfect uniformity and agreement of the parts of the universe, we shall not discover in it any marks of the combat of a malevolent with a benevolent being. There is indeed an opposition of pains and pleasures in the feelings of sensible creatures: but are not all the operations of Nature carried on by an opposition of principles, of hot and cold, moist and dry, light and heavy? The true conclusion is, that the original Source of all things is entirely indifferent to all these principles; and has no more regard to good above ill, than to heat above cold, or to drought above moisture, or to light above heavy.

There may four hypotheses be framed concerning the first causes of the universe: that they are endowed with perfect goodness; that they have perfect malice; that they are opposite, and have both goodness and malice; that they have neither goodness nor malice. Mixed phenomena can never prove the two former unmixed principles; and the uniformity and steadiness of general laws seem to oppose the third. The fourth, therefore, seems by far the most probable.

What I have said concerning natural evil will apply to moral, with little or no variation; and we have no more reason to infer, that the rectitude of the Supreme Being resembles human rectitude, than that his benevolence resembles the human. Nay, it will be thought, that we have still greater cause to exclude from him moral sentiments, such as we feel them; since moral evil, in the opinion of many, is much more predominant above moral good than natural evil above natural good.

But even though this should not be allowed, and though the virtue which is in mankind should be acknowledged much superior to the vice, yet so long as there is any vice at all in the universe, it will very much puzzle you Anthropomorphites, how to account for it. You must assign a cause for it, without having recourse to the first cause. But as every effect must have a cause, and that cause another, you must either carry on the progression in infinitum, or rest on that original principle, who is the ultimate cause of all things . . .

Hold! hold! cried DEMEA: Whither does your imagination hurry you? I joined in alliance with you, in order to prove the incomprehensible nature of the Divine Being, and refute the principles of CLEANTHES, who would measure every thing by human rule and standard. But I now find you running into all the topics of the greatest libertines and infidels, and betraying that holy cause which you seemingly espoused. Are you secretly, then, a more dangerous enemy than CLEANTHES himself?

And are you so late in perceiving it? replied CLEANTHES. Believe me, DEMEA, your friend PHILO, from the beginning, has been amusing himself at both our expense; and it must be confessed, that the injudicious reasoning of our vulgar theology has given him but too just a handle of ridicule. The total infirmity of human reason, the absolute incomprehensibility of the Divine Nature, the great and universal misery, and still greater wickedness of men; these are strange topics, surely, to be so fondly cherished by orthodox divines and doctors. In ages of stupidity and ignorance, indeed, these principles may safely be espoused; and perhaps no views of things are more proper to promote superstition, than such as encourage the blind amazement, the diffidence, and melancholy of mankind. But at present . . .

Blame not so much, interposed PHILO, the ignorance of these reverend gentlemen. They know how to change their style with the times. Formerly it was a most popular theological topic to maintain, that human life was vanity and misery, and to exaggerate all the ills and pains which are incident to men. But of late years, divines, we find, begin to retract this position; and maintain, though still with some hesitation, that there are more goods than evils, more pleasures than pains, even in this life. When religion stood entirely upon temper and education, it was thought proper to encourage melancholy; as indeed mankind never have recourse to superior powers so readily as in that disposition. But as men have now learned to form principles, and to draw consequences, it is necessary to change the batteries, and to make use of such arguments as will endure at least some scrutiny and examination. This variation is the same (and from the same causes) with that which I formerly remarked with regard to Scepticism.

Thus PHILO continued to the last his spirit of opposition, and his censure of established opinions. But I could observe that DEMEA did not at all relish the latter part of the discourse; and he took occasion soon after, on some pretence or other, to leave the company.

# THE 'VALE OF SOUL-MAKING' THEODICY

**BY John Hick**

Fortunately there is another and better way. As well as the 'majority report' of the Augustinian tradition, which has dominated Western Christendom, both Catholic and Protestant, since the time of Augustine himself, there is the 'minority report' of the Irenaean tradition. This latter is both older and newer than the other, for it goes back to St. Irenaeus and others of the early Hellenistic Fathers of the Church in the two centuries prior to St. Augustine, and it has flourished again in more developed forms during the last hundred years.

Instead of regarding man as having been created by God in a finished state, as a finitely perfect being fulfilling the divine intention for our human level of existence, and then falling disastrously away from this, the minority report sees man as still in process of creation. Irenaeus himself expressed the point in terms of the (exegetically dubious) distinction between the 'image' and the 'likeness' of God referred to in Genesis i. 26: 'Then God said, Let us make man in our image, after our likeness.'[1] His view was that man as a personal and moral being already exists in the image, but has not yet been formed into the finite likeness of God. By this 'likeness' Irenaeus means something more than personal existence as such; he means a certain valuable quality of personal life which reflects finitely the divine life. This represents the perfecting of man, the fulfilment of God's purpose for humanity, the 'bringing of many sons to glory',[2] the creating of 'children of God' who are 'fellow heirs with Christ' of his glory.[3]

And so man, created as a personal being in the image of God, is only the raw material for a further and more difficult stage of God's creative work. This is the leading of men as relatively free and autonomous persons, through their own dealings with life in the world in which He has placed them, towards that quality of personal existence that is the finite likeness of God. The features of this likeness are revealed in the person of Christ, and the process of man's creation into it is the work of the Holy Spirit. In St. Paul's words, 'And we all, with unveiled faces, beholding the glory of the Lord, are being changed into his likeness (εἰκών) from one degree of glory to another; for this comes from the Lord who is the Spirit';[4] or again, 'For God knew his own before ever they were, and also ordained that they should be shaped to the likeness (εἰκών) of his Son.'[5] In Johannine terms, the movement from the image to the likeness is a transition from one level of existence, that of animal life (*Bios*), to another and higher level, that of eternal life (*Zoe*), which includes but transcends the first. And the fall of man was seen by Irenaeus as a failure within the second phase of this creative process, a failure that has multiplied the perils and complicated the route of the journey in which God is seeking to lead mankind.

In the light of modern anthropological knowledge some form of two-stage conception of the creation of man has become an almost unavoidable Christian tenet. At the very least we must acknowledge as two distinguishable stages the fashioning of *homo sapiens* as a product of the long evolutionary process, and his sudden or gradual spiritualization as a child of God. But we may well extend the first stage to include the development of man as a rational and responsible person capable of personal relationship with the personal Infinite who has created him. This first stage of the creative process was, to our anthropomorphic imaginations, easy for divine omnipotence. By an exercise of creative power God caused the physical universe to exist, and in the course of countless ages to bring

1 *A.H.* v. vi. 1. Cf. pp. 211 f. above.

2 Hebrews ii 10.

3 Romans viii. 17.

4 II Corinthians iii. 18.

5 Romans viii. 29. Other New Testament passages expressing a view of mar as undergoing a process of spiritual growth within God's purpose, are: Ephesians ii. 21; iii. 16; Colossians ii. 19; I John iii. 2; II Corinthians iv. 16.

forth within it organic life, and finally to produce out of organic life personal life; and when man had thus emerged out of the evolution of the forms of organic life, a creature had been made who has the possibility of existing in conscious fellowship with God. But the second stage of the creative process is of a different kind altogether. It cannot be performed by omnipotent power as such. For personal life is essentially free and self-directing. It cannot be perfected by divine fiat, but only through the uncompelled responses and willing co-operation of human individuals in their actions and reactions in the world in which God has placed them. Men may eventually become the perfected persons whom the New Testament calls 'children of God', but they cannot be created ready-made as this.

The value-judgement that is implicitly being invoked here is that one who has attained to goodness by meeting and eventually mastering temptations, and thus by rightly making responsible choices in concrete situations, is good in a richer and more valuable sense than would be one created *ab initio* in a state either of innocence or of virtue. In the former case, which is that of the actual moral achievements of mankind, the individual's goodness has within it the strength of temptations overcome, a stability based upon an accumulation of right choices, and a positive and responsible character that comes from the investment of costly personal effort. I suggest, then, that it is an ethically reasonable judgement, even though in the nature of the case not one that is capable of demonstrative proof, that human goodness slowly built up through personal histories of moral effort has a value in the eyes of the Creator which justifies even the long travail of the soul-making process.

The picture with which we are working is thus developmental and teleological. Man is in process of becoming the perfected being whom God is seeking to create. However, this is not taking place—it is important to add—by a natural and inevitable evolution, but through a hazardous adventure in individual freedom. Because this is a pilgrimage within the life of each individual, rather than a racial evolution, the progressive fulfilment of God's purpose does not entail any corresponding progressive improvement in the moral state of the world. There is no doubt a development in man's ethical situation from generation to generation through the building of individual choices into public institutions, but this involves an accumulation of evil as well as of good.[6] It is thus probable that human life was lived on much the same moral plane two thousand years ago or four thousand years ago as it is today. But nevertheless during this period uncounted millions of souls have been through the experience of earthly life, and God's purpose has gradually moved towards its fulfilment within each one of them, rather than within a human aggregate composed of different units in different generations.

If, then, God's aim in making the world is 'the bringing of many sons to glory',[7] that aim will naturally determine the kind of world that He has created. Antitheistic writers almost invariably assume a conception of the divine purpose which is contrary to the Christian conception. They assume that the purpose of a loving God must be to create a hedonistic paradise; and therefore to the extent that the world is other than this, it proves to them that God is either not loving enough or not powerful enough to create such a world. They think of God's relation to the earth on the model of a human being building a cage for a pet animal to dwell in. If he is humane he will naturally make his pet's quarters as pleasant and healthful as he can. Any respect in which the cage falls short of the veterinarian's ideal, and contains possibilities of accident or disease, is evidence of either limited benevolence or limited means, or both. Those who use the problem of evil as an argument against belief in God almost invariably think of the world in this kind of way. David Hume, for example, speaks of an architect who is trying to plan a house that is to be as comfortable and convenient as possible. If we find that 'the windows, doors, fires, passages, stairs, and the whole economy of the building were the source of noise, confusion, fatigue, darkness, and the extremes of heat and cold' we should have no hesitation in blaming the architect. It would be in vain for him to prove that if this or that defect were corrected greater ills would result: 'still you would assert in general, that, if the architect had had skill and good intentions, he might have formed such a plan of the whole, and might have adjusted the parts in such a manner, as would have remedied all or most of these inconveniences'.[8]

But if we are right in supposing that God's purpose for man is to lead him from human *Bios*, or the biological life of man, to that quality of *Zoe*, or the personal life of eternal worth, which we see in Christ, then the question that

6 This fact is symbolized in early Christian literature both by the figure of the Antichrist, who continually opposes God's purposes in history, and by the expectation of cataclysmic calamity and strife in the last days before the end of the present world order.

7 Hebrews ii. 10.

8 *Dialogues Concerning Natural Religion*, pt. xi. Kemp-Smith's ed. (Oxford: Clarendon Press, 1935), p. 251.

we have to ask is not, Is this the kind of world that an all-powerful and infinitely loving being would create as an environment for his human pets? or, Is the architecture of the world the most pleasant and convenient possible? The question that we have to ask is rather, Is this the kind of world that God might make as an environment in which moral beings may be fashioned, through their own free insights and responses, into 'children of God'?

Such critics as Hume are confusing what heaven ought to be, as an environment for perfected finite beings, with what this world ought to be, as an environment for beings who are in process of becoming perfected. For if our general conception of God's purpose is correct the world is not intended to be a paradise, but rather the scene of a history in which human personality may be formed towards the pattern of Christ. Men are not to be thought of on the analogy of animal pets, whose life is to be made as agreeable as possible, but rather on the analogy of human children, who are to grow to adulthood in an environment whose primary and overriding purpose is not immediate pleasure but the realizing of the most valuable potentialities of human personality.

Needless to say, this characterization of God as the heavenly Father is not a merely random illustration but an analogy that lies at the heart of the Christian faith. Jesus treated the likeness between the attitude of God to man, and the attitude of human parents at their best towards their children, as providing the most adequate way for us to think about God. And so it is altogether relevant to a Christian understanding of this world to ask, How does the best parental love express itself in its influence upon the environment in which children are to grow up? I think it is clear that a parent who loves his children, and wants them to become the best human beings that they are capable of becoming, does not treat pleasure as the sole and supreme value. Certainly we seek pleasure for our children, and take great delight in obtaining it for them; but we do not desire for them unalloyed pleasure at the expense of their growth in such even greater values as moral integrity, unselfishness, compassion, courage, humour, reverence for the truth, and perhaps above all the capacity for love. We do not act on the premise that pleasure is the supreme end of life; and if the development of these other values sometimes clashes with the provision of pleasure, then we are willing to have our children miss a certain amount of this, rather than fail to come to possess and to be possessed by the finer and more precious qualities that are possible to the human personality. A child brought up on the principle that the only or the supreme value is pleasure would not be likely to become an ethically mature adult or an attractive or happy personality. And to most parents it seems more important to try to foster quality and strength of character in their children than to fill their lives at all times with the utmost possible degree of pleasure. If, then, there is any true analogy between God's purpose for his human creatures, and the purpose of loving and wise parents for their children, we have to recognize that the presence of pleasure and the absence of pain cannot be the supreme and overriding end for which the world exists. Rather, this world must be a place of soul-making. And its value is to be judged, not primarily by the quantity of pleasure and pain occurring in it at any particular moment, but by its fitness for its primary purpose, the purpose of soul-making.[9]

In all this we have been speaking about the nature of the world considered simply as the God-given environment of man's life. For it is mainly in this connection that the world has been regarded in Irenaean and in Protestant thought.[10] But such a way of thinking involves a danger of anthropocentrism from which the Augustinian and Catholic tradition has generally been protected by its sense of the relative insignificance of man within the totality of the created universe. Man was dwarfed within the medieval world-view by the innumerable hosts of angels and archangels above him—unfallen rational natures which rejoice in the immediate presence of God, reflecting His glory in the untarnished mirror of their worship. However, this higher creation has in our modern world lost its hold upon the imagination. Its place has been taken, as the minimizer of men, by the immensities of outer space and by the material universe's unlimited complexity transcending our present knowledge. As the spiritual environment envisaged

9 The phrase 'the vale of Soul-making' was coined by the poet John Keats in a letter written to his brother and sister in April 1819. He says, 'The common cognomen of this world among the misguided and superstitious is "a vale of tears" from which we are to be redeemed by a certain arbitrary interposition of God and taken to Heaven—What a little circumscribed straightened notion! Call the world if you Please "The vale of Soul-making".' In this letter he sketches a teleological theodicy. 'Do you not see', he asks, 'how necessary a World of Pains and troubles is to school an Intelligence and make it a Soul?' (*The Letters of John Keats*, ed. by M. B. Forman. London: Oxford University Press, 4th ed., 1952, pp. 334–5.)

10 Thus Irenaeus said that 'the creation is suited to [the wants of] man; for man was not made for its sake, but creation for the sake of man' (*A.H.* v. xxix. 1), and Calvin said that 'because we know that the universe was established especially for the sake of mankind, we ought to look for this purpose in his governance also', (*Inst.* 1. xvi. 6.)

by Western man has shrunk, his physical horizons have correspondingly expanded. Where the human creature was formerly seen as an insignificant appendage to the angelic world, he is now seen as an equally insignificant organic excrescence, enjoying a fleeting moment of consciousness on the surface of one of the planets of a minor star. Thus the truth that was symbolized for former ages by the existence of the angelic hosts is today impressed upon us by the vastness of the physical universe, countering the egoism of our species by making us feel that this immense prodigality of existence can hardly all exist for the sake of man—though, on the other hand, the very realization that it is not all for the sake of man may itself be salutary and beneficial to man!

However, instead of opposing man and nature as rival objects of God's interest, we should perhaps rather stress man's solidarity as an embodied being with the whole natural order in which he is embedded. For man is organic to the world; all his acts and thoughts and imaginations are conditioned by space and time; and in abstraction from nature he would cease to be human. We may, then, say that the beauties and sublimities and powers, the microscopic intricacies and macroscopic vastnesses, the wonders and the terrors of the natural world and of the life that pulses through it, are willed and valued by their Maker in a creative act that embraces man together with nature. By means of matter and living flesh God both builds a path and weaves a veil between Himself and the creature made in His image. Nature thus has permanent significance; for God has set man in a creaturely environment, and the final fulfilment of our nature in relation to God will accordingly take the form of an embodied life within 'a new heaven and a new earth'.[11] And as in the present age man moves slowly towards that fulfilment through the pilgrimage of his earthly life, so also 'the whole creation' is 'groaning in travail', waiting for the time when it will be 'set free from its bondage to decay'.[12]

And yet however fully we thus acknowledge the permanent significance and value of the natural order, we must still insist upon man's special character as a personal creature made in the image of God; and our theodicy must still centre upon the soul-making process that we believe to be taking place within human life.

This, then, is the starting-point from which we propose to try to relate the realities of sin and suffering to the perfect love of an omnipotent Creator. And as will become increasingly apparent, a theodicy that starts in this way must be eschatological in its ultimate bearings. That is to say, instead of looking to the past for its clue to the mystery of evil, it looks to the future, and indeed to that ultimate future to which only faith can look. Given the conception of a divine intention working in and through human time towards a fulfilment that lies in its completeness beyond human time, our theodicy must find the meaning of evil in the part that it is made to play in the eventual outworking of that purpose; and must find the justification of the whole process in the magnitude of the good to which it leads. The good that outshines all ill is not a paradise long since lost but a kingdom which is yet to come in its full glory and permanence.

From this point of view we must speak about moral evil; about pain, including that of the lower animals; about the higher and more distinctively human forms of suffering; and about the relation between all this and the will of God as it has been revealed in Jesus Christ.

11 Revelation xxi. 1.

12 Romans viii. 21–22.

CHAPTER III

# Mind-Body Problem

# CARTESIAN DUALISM

BY **Rene Descartes, translated by Donald A. Cress**

## MEDITATION SIX: CONCERNING THE EXISTENCE OF MATERIAL THINGS, AND THE REAL DISTINCTION BETWEEN MIND AND BODY

It remains for me to examine whether material things exist. Indeed I now know that they can exist, at least insofar as they are the object of pure mathematics, since I clearly and distinctly perceive them. For no doubt God is capable of bringing about everything that I am capable of perceiving in this way. And I have never judged that God was incapable of something, except when it was incompatible with my perceiving it distinctly. Moreover, from the faculty of imagination, which I notice I use while dealing with material things, it seems to follow that they exist. For to anyone paying very close attention to what imagination is, it appears to be simply a certain application of the knowing faculty to a body intimately present to it, and which therefore exists.

To make this clear, I first examine the difference between imagination and pure intellection. So, for example, when I imagine a triangle, I not only understand that it is a figure bounded by three lines, but at the same time I also envisage with the mind's eye those lines as if they were present; and this is what I call "imagining." On the other hand, if I want to think about a chiliagon, I certainly understand that it is a figure consisting of a thousand sides, just as well as I understand that a triangle is a figure consisting of three sides, yet I do not imagine those thousand sides in the same way, or envisage them as if they were present. And although in that case—because of force of habit I always imagine something whenever I think about a corporeal thing—I may perchance represent to myself some figure in a confused fashion, nevertheless this figure is obviously not a chiliagon. For this figure is really no different from the figure I would represent to myself, were I thinking of a myriagon or any other figure with a large number of sides. Nor is this figure of any help in knowing the properties that differentiate a chiliagon from other polygons. But if the figure in question is a pentagon, I surely can understand its figure, just as was the case with the chiliagon, without the help of my imagination. But I can also imagine a pentagon by turning the mind's eye both to its five sides and at the same time to the area bounded by those sides. At this point I am manifestly aware that I am in need of a peculiar sort of effort on the part of the mind in order to imagine, one that I do not employ in order to understand. This new effort on the part of the mind clearly shows the difference between imagination and pure intellection.

Moreover, I consider that this power of imagining that is in me, insofar as it differs from the power of understanding, is not required for my own essence, that is, the essence of my mind. For were I to be lacking this power, I would nevertheless undoubtedly remain the same entity I am now. Thus it seems to follow that the power of imagining depends upon something distinct from me. And I readily understand that, were a body to exist to which a mind is so joined that it may apply itself in order, as it were, to look at it any time it wishes, it could happen that it is by means of this very body that I imagine corporeal things. As a result, this mode of thinking may differ from pure intellection only in the sense that the mind, when it understands, in a sense turns toward itself and looks at one of the ideas that are in it; whereas when it imagines, it turns toward the body, and intuits in the body something that conforms to an idea either understood by the mind or perceived by sense. To be sure, I easily understand that the imagination can be actualized in this way, provided a body does exist. And since I can think of no other way of explaining imagination that is equally appropriate, I make a probable conjecture from this that a body exists. But this is only a probability. And even though I may examine everything carefully, nevertheless I do not yet see how the distinct idea of corporeal nature that I find in my imagination can enable me to develop an argument which necessarily concludes that some body exists.

But I am in the habit of imagining many other things, over and above that corporeal nature which is the object of pure mathematics, such as colors, sounds, tastes, pain, and the like, though not so distinctly. And I perceive these things better by means of the senses, from which, with the aid of the memory, they seem to have arrived at the imagination. Thus I should pay the same degree of attention to the senses, so that I might deal with them more appropriately. I must see whether I can obtain any reliable argument for the existence of corporeal things from those things that are perceived by the mode of thinking that I call "sense."

First of all, to be sure, I will review here all the things I previously believed to be true because I had perceived them by means of the senses and the causes I had for thinking this. Next I will assess the causes why I later called them into doubt. Finally, I will consider what I must now believe about these things.

So first, I sensed that I had a head, hands, feet, and other members that comprised this body which I viewed as part of me, or perhaps even as the whole of me. I sensed that this body was found among many other bodies, by which my body can be affected in various beneficial or harmful ways. I gauged what was opportune by means of a certain sensation of pleasure, and what was inopportune by a sensation of pain. In addition to pain and pleasure, I also sensed within me hunger, thirst, and other such appetites, as well as certain bodily tendencies toward mirth, sadness, anger, and other such affects. And externally, besides the extension, shapes, and motions of bodies, I also sensed their hardness, heat, and other tactile qualities. I also sensed light, colors, odors, tastes, and sounds, on the basis of whose variety I distinguished the sky, the earth, the seas, and the other bodies, one from the other. Now given the ideas of all these qualities that presented themselves to my thought, and which were all that I properly and immediately sensed, still it was surely not without reason that I thought I sensed things that were manifestly different from my thought, namely, the bodies from which these ideas proceeded. For I knew by experience that these ideas came upon me utterly without my consent, to the extent that, wish as I may, I could not sense any object unless it was present to a sense organ. Nor could I fail to sense it when it was present. And since the ideas perceived by sense were much more vivid and explicit and even, in their own way, more distinct than any of those that I deliberately and knowingly formed through meditation or that I found impressed on my memory, it seemed impossible that they came from myself. Thus the remaining alternative was that they came from other things. Since I had no knowledge of such things except from those same ideas themselves, I could not help entertaining the thought that they were similar to those ideas. Moreover, I also recalled that the use of the senses antedated the use of reason. And since I saw that the ideas that I myself fashioned were not as explicit as those that I perceived through the faculty of sense, and were for the most part composed of parts of the latter, I easily convinced myself that I had absolutely no idea in the intellect that I did not have beforehand in the sense faculty. Not without reason did I judge that this body, which by a certain special right I called "mine," belongs more to me than did any other. For I could never be separated from it in the same way I could be from other bodies. I sensed all appetites and feelings in and on behalf of it. Finally, I noticed pain and pleasurable excitement in its parts, but not in other bodies external to it. But why should a certain sadness of spirit arise from some sensation or other of pain, and why should a certain elation arise from a sensation of excitement, or why should that peculiar twitching in the stomach, which I call hunger, warn me to have something to eat, or why should dryness in the throat warn me to take something to drink, and so on? I plainly had no explanation other than that I had been taught this way by nature. For there is no affinity whatsoever, at least none I am aware of, between this twitching in the stomach and the will to have something to eat, or between the sensation of something causing pain and the thought of sadness arising from this sensation. But nature also seems to have taught me everything else as well that I judged concerning the objects of the senses, for I had already convinced myself that this was how things were, prior to my assessing any of the arguments that might prove it.

Afterwards, however, many experiences gradually weakened any faith that I had in the senses. Towers that had seemed round from afar occasionally appeared square at close quarters. Very large statues mounted on their pedestals did not seem large to someone looking at them from ground level. And in countless other such instances I determined that judgments in matters of the external senses were in error. And not just the external senses, but the internal senses as well. For what can be more intimate than pain? But I had sometimes heard it said by people whose leg or arm had been amputated that it seemed to them that they still occasionally sensed pain in the very limb they had lost. Thus, even in my own case it did not seem to be entirely certain that some bodily member was causing me pain, even though I did sense pain in it. To these causes for doubt I recently added two quite general ones. The first was that everything I ever thought I sensed while awake I could believe I also sometimes sensed while asleep, and since I do not believe that what I seem to sense in my dreams comes to me from things external to me, I saw no reason why I should hold this belief about those things I seem to be sensing while awake. The second was that, since I was still ignorant of the author of my origin (or at least pretended to be ignorant of it), I saw nothing to prevent my having been so constituted by nature that I should be mistaken even about what seemed to me most true. As to the arguments that used to convince me of the truth of sensible things, I found no difficulty responding to them. For since I seemed driven by nature toward many things about which reason tried to dissuade me, I did not think that what I was taught by nature deserved much credence. And even though the perceptions of the senses did not depend on my will, I did not think that we must therefore conclude that they came from things distinct from me, since perhaps there is some faculty in me, as yet unknown to me, that produces these perceptions.

But now, having begun to have a better knowledge of myself and the author of my origin, I am of the opinion that I must not rashly admit everything that I seem to derive from the senses; but neither, for that matter, should I call everything into doubt.

First, I know that all the things that I clearly and distinctly understand can be made by God such as I understand them. For this reason, my ability clearly and distinctly to understand one thing without another suffices to make me certain that the one thing is different from the other, since they can be separated from each other, at least by God. The question as to the sort of power that might effect such a separation is not relevant to their being thought to be different. For this reason, from the fact that I know that I exist, and that at the same time I judge that obviously nothing else belongs to my nature or essence except that I am a thinking thing, I rightly conclude that my essence consists entirely in my being a thinking thing. And although perhaps (or rather, as I shall soon say, assuredly) I have a body that is very closely joined to me, nevertheless, because on the one hand I have a clear and distinct idea of myself, insofar as I am merely a thinking thing and not an extended thing, and because on the other hand I have a distinct idea of a body, insofar as it is merely an extended thing and not a thinking thing, it is certain that I am really distinct from my body, and can exist without it.

Moreover, I find in myself faculties for certain special modes of thinking, namely the faculties of imagining and sensing. I can clearly and distinctly understand myself in my entirety without these faculties, but not vice versa: I cannot understand them clearly and distinctly without me, that is, without a substance endowed with understanding in which they inhere, for they include an act of understanding in their formal concept. Thus I perceive them to be distinguished from me as modes from a thing. I also acknowledge that there are certain other faculties, such as those of moving from one place to another, of taking on various shapes, and so on, that, like sensing or imagining, cannot be understood apart from some substance in which they inhere, and hence without which they cannot exist. But it is clear that these faculties, if in fact they exist, must be in a corporeal or extended substance, not in a substance endowed with understanding. For some extension is contained in a clear and distinct concept of them, though certainly not any understanding. Now there clearly is in me a passive faculty of sensing, that is, a faculty for receiving and knowing the ideas of sensible things; but I could not use it unless there also existed, either in me or in something else, a certain active faculty of producing or bringing about these ideas. But this faculty surely cannot be in me, since it clearly presupposes no act of understanding, and these ideas are produced without my cooperation and often even against my will. Therefore the only alternative is that it is in some substance different from me, containing either formally or eminently all the reality that exists objectively in the ideas produced by that faculty, as I have just noted above. Hence this substance is either a body, that is, a corporeal nature, which contains formally all that is contained objectively in the ideas, or else it is God, or some other creature more noble than a body, which contains eminently all that is contained objectively in the ideas. But since God is not a deceiver, it is patently obvious that he does not send me these ideas either immediately by himself, or even through the mediation of some creature that contains the objective reality of these ideas not formally but only eminently. For since God has given me no faculty whatsoever for making this determination, but instead has given me a great inclination to believe that these ideas issue from corporeal things, I fail to see how God could be understood not to be a deceiver, if these ideas were to issue from a source other than corporeal things. And consequently corporeal things exist. Nevertheless, perhaps not all bodies exist exactly as I grasp them by sense, since this sensory grasp is in many cases very obscure and confused. But at least they do contain everything I clearly and distinctly understand—that is, everything, considered in a general sense, that is encompassed in the object of pure mathematics.

As far as the remaining matters are concerned, which are either merely particular (for example, that the sun is of such and such a size or shape, and so on) or less clearly understood (for example, light, sound, pain, and the like), even though these matters are very doubtful and uncertain, nevertheless the fact that God is no deceiver (and thus no falsity can be found in my opinions, unless there is also in me a faculty given me by God for the purpose of rectifying this falsity) offers me a definite hope of reaching the truth even in these matters. And surely there is no doubt that all that I am taught by nature has some truth to it; for by "nature," taken generally, I understand nothing other than God himself or the ordered network of created things which was instituted by God. By my own particular nature I understand nothing other than the combination of all the things bestowed upon me by God.

There is nothing that this nature teaches me more explicitly than that I have a body that is ill-disposed when I feel pain, that needs food and drink when I suffer hunger or thirst, and the like. Therefore, I should not doubt that there is some truth in this.

By means of these sensations of pain, hunger, thirst and so on, nature also teaches that I am present not merely to my body in the way a sailor is present in a ship, but that I am most tightly joined and, so to speak, commingled with it, so much so that I and the body constitute one single thing. For if this were not the case, then I, who am only a thinking thing, would not sense pain when the body is injured; rather, I would perceive the wound by means of the pure intellect, just as a sailor perceives by sight whether anything in his ship is broken. And when the body is in need of food or drink, I should understand this explicitly, instead of having confused sensations of hunger and thirst. For clearly these sensations of thirst, hunger, pain, and so on are nothing but certain confused modes of thinking arising from the union and, as it were, the commingling of the mind with the body.

Moreover, I am also taught by nature that various other bodies exist around my body, some of which are to be pursued, while others are to be avoided. And to be sure, from the fact that I sense a wide variety of colors, sounds, odors, tastes, levels of heat, and grades of roughness, and the like, I rightly conclude that in the bodies from which these different perceptions of the senses proceed there are differences corresponding to the different perceptions—though perhaps the latter do not resemble the former. And from the fact that some of these perceptions are pleasant while others are unpleasant, it is plainly certain that my body, or rather my whole self, insofar as I am comprised of a body and a mind, can be affected by various beneficial and harmful bodies in the vicinity.

Granted, there are many other things that I seem to have been taught by nature; nevertheless it was not really nature that taught them to me but a certain habit of making reckless judgments. And thus it could easily happen that these judgments are false: for example, that any space where there is absolutely nothing happening to move my senses is empty; or that there is something in a hot body that bears an exact likeness to the idea of heat that is in me; or that in a white or green body there is the same whiteness or greenness that I sense; or that in a bitter or sweet body there is the same taste, and so on; or that stars and towers and any other distant bodies have the same size and shape that they present to my senses, and other things of this sort. But to ensure that my perceptions in this matter are sufficiently distinct, I ought to define more precisely what exactly I mean when I say that I am "taught something by nature." For I am taking "nature" here more narrowly than the combination of everything bestowed on me by God. For this combination embraces many things that belong exclusively to my mind, such as my perceiving that what has been done cannot be undone, and everything else that is known by the light of nature. That is not what I am talking about here. There are also many things that belong exclusively to the body, such as that it tends to move downward, and so on. I am not dealing with these either, but only with what God has bestowed on me insofar as I am composed of mind and body. Accordingly, it is this nature that teaches me to avoid things that produce a sensation of pain and to pursue things that produce a sensation of pleasure, and the like. But it does not appear that nature teaches us to conclude anything, besides these things, from these sense perceptions unless the intellect has first conducted its own inquiry regarding things external to us. For it seems to belong exclusively to the mind, [83] and not to the composite of mind and body, to know the truth in these matters. Thus, although a star affects my eye no more than does the flame from a small torch, still there is no real or positive tendency in my eye toward believing that the star is no larger than the flame. Yet, ever since my youth, I have made this judgment without any reason for doing so. And although I feel heat as I draw closer to the fire, and I also feel pain upon drawing too close to it, there is not a single argument that persuades me that there is something in the fire similar to that heat, any more than to that pain. On the contrary, I am convinced only that there is something in the fire that, regardless of what it finally turns out to be, causes in us those sensations of heat or pain. And although there may be nothing in a given space that moves the senses, it does not therefore follow that there is no body in it. But I see that in these and many other instances I have been in the habit of subverting the order of nature. For admittedly I use the perceptions of the senses (which are properly given by nature only for signifying to the mind what things are useful or harmful to the composite of which it is a part, and to that extent they are clear and distinct enough) as reliable rules for immediately discerning what is the essence of bodies located outside us. Yet they signify nothing about that except quite obscurely and confusedly.

I have already examined in sufficient detail how it could happen that my judgments are false, despite the goodness of God. But a new difficulty now arises regarding those very things that nature shows me are either to be sought out or avoided, as well as the internal sensations where I seem to have detected errors, as for example, when someone is deluded by a food's pleasant taste to eat the poison hidden inside it. In this case, however, he is driven by nature only toward desiring the thing in which the pleasurable taste is found, but not toward the poison, of which he obviously is unaware. I can only conclude that this nature is not omniscient. This is not remarkable, since man is a limited thing, and thus only what is of limited perfection befits him.

But we not infrequently err even in those things to which nature impels us. Take, for example, the case of those who are ill and who desire food or drink that will soon afterwards be injurious to them. Perhaps it could be said here that they erred because their nature was corrupt. However, this does not remove our difficulty, for a sick man is no less a creature of God than a healthy one, and thus it seems no less inconsistent that the sick man got a deception-prone nature from God. And a clock made of wheels and counter-weights follows all the laws of nature no less closely when it has been badly constructed and does not tell time accurately than it does when it completely satisfies the wish of its maker. Likewise, I might regard a man's body as a kind of mechanism that is outfitted with and composed of bones, nerves, muscles, veins, blood and skin in such a way that, even if no mind existed in it, the man's body would still exhibit all the same motions that are in it now except for those motions that proceed either from a command of the will or, consequently, from the mind. I easily recognize that it would be natural for this body, were it, say, suffering from dropsy and experiencing dryness in the throat (which typically produces a thirst sensation in the mind), and also so disposed by its nerves and other parts to take something to drink, the result of which would be to exacerbate the illness. This is as natural as for a body without any such illness to be moved by the same dryness in the throat to take something to drink that is useful to it. And given the intended purpose of the clock, I could say that it deviates from its nature when it fails to tell the right time. And similarly, considering the mechanism of the human body in terms of its being equipped for the motions that typically occur in it, I may think that it too is deviating from its nature, if its throat were dry when having something to drink is not beneficial to its conservation. Nevertheless, I am well aware that this last use of "nature" differs greatly from the other. For this latter "nature" is merely a designation dependent on my thought, since it compares a man in poor health and a poorly constructed clock with the ideas of a healthy man and of a well-made clock, a designation extrinsic to the things to which it is applied. But by "nature" taken in the former sense, I understand something that is really in things, and thus is not without some truth.

When we say, then, in the case of the body suffering from dropsy, that its "nature" is corrupt, given the fact that it has a parched throat and yet does not need something to drink, "nature" obviously is merely an extrinsic designation. Nevertheless, in the case of the composite, that is, of a mind joined to such a body, it is not a mere designation, but a true error of nature that this body should be thirsty when having something to drink would be harmful to it. It therefore remains to inquire here how the goodness of God does not prevent "nature," thus considered, from being deceptive.

Now my first observation here is that there is a great difference between a mind and a body in that a body, by its very nature, is always divisible. On the other hand, the mind is utterly indivisible. For when I consider the mind, that is, myself insofar as I am only a thinking thing, I cannot distinguish any parts within me; rather, I understand myself to be manifestly one complete thing. Although the entire mind seems to be united to the entire body, nevertheless, were a foot or an arm or any other bodily part to be amputated, I know that nothing has been taken away from the mind on that account. Nor can the faculties of willing, sensing, understanding, and so on be called "parts" of the mind, since it is one and the same mind that wills, senses, and understands. On the other hand, there is no corporeal or extended thing I can think of that I may not in my thought easily divide into parts; and in this way I understand that it is divisible. This consideration alone would suffice to teach me that the mind is wholly diverse from the body, had I not yet known it well enough in any other way.

My second observation is that my mind is not immediately affected by all the parts of the body, but only by the brain, or perhaps even by just one small part of the brain, namely, by that part where the "common" sense is said to reside. Whenever this part of the brain is disposed in the same manner, it presents the same thing to the mind, even if the other parts of the body are able meanwhile to be related in diverse ways. Countless experiments show this, none of which need be reviewed here.

My next observation is that the nature of the body is such that whenever any of its parts can be moved by another part some distance away, it can also be moved in the same manner by any of the parts that lie between them, even if this more distant part is doing nothing. For example, in the cord ABCD, if the final part D is pulled, the first part A would be moved in exactly the same manner as it could be, if one of the intermediate parts B or C were pulled, while the end part D remained immobile. Likewise, when I feel a pain in my foot, physics teaches me that this sensation took place by means of nerves distributed throughout the foot, like stretched cords extending from the foot all the way to the brain. When these nerves are pulled in the foot, they also pull on the inner parts of the brain to which they extend, and produce a certain motion in them. This motion has been constituted by nature so as to affect the mind with a sensation of pain, as if it occurred in the foot. But because these nerves need to pass through the shin, thigh, loins, back, and neck to get from the foot to the brain, it can happen that even if it is not the part in the foot but merely one of the intermediate parts that is being struck, the very same movement will occur in the brain that would occur were the foot badly injured. The inevitable result will be that the mind feels the same pain. The same opinion should hold for any other sensation.

My final observation is that, since any given motion occurring in that part of the brain immediately affecting the mind produces but one sensation in it, I can think of no better arrangement than that it produces the one sensation that, of all the ones it is able to produce, is most especially and most often conducive to the maintenance of a healthy man. Moreover, experience shows that all the sensations bestowed on us by nature are like this. Hence there is absolutely nothing to be found in them that does not bear witness to God's power and goodness. Thus, for example, when the nerves in the foot are agitated in a violent and unusual manner, this motion of theirs extends through the marrow of the spine to the inner reaches of the brain, where it gives the mind the sign to sense something, namely, the pain as if it is occurring in the foot. This provokes the mind to do its utmost to move away from the cause of the pain, since it is seen as harmful to the foot. But the nature of man could have been so constituted by God that this same motion in the brain might have indicated something else to the mind: for example, either the motion itself as it occurs in the brain, or in the foot, or in some place in between, or something else entirely different. But nothing else would have served so well the maintenance of the body. Similarly, when we need something to drink, a certain dryness arises in the throat that moves the nerves in the throat, and, by means of them, the inner parts of the brain. And this motion affects the mind with a sensation of thirst, because in this entire affair nothing is more useful for us to know than that we need something to drink in order to maintain our health; the same holds in the other cases.

From these considerations it is utterly apparent that, notwithstanding the immense goodness of God, the nature of man, insofar as it is composed of mind and body, cannot help being sometimes mistaken. For if some cause, not in the foot but in some other part through which the nerves extend from the foot to the brain, or perhaps even in the brain itself, were to produce the same motion that would normally be produced by a badly injured foot, the pain will be felt as if it were in the foot, and the senses will naturally be deceived. For since an identical motion in the brain can only bring about an identical sensation in the mind, and it is more frequently the case that this motion is wont to arise on account of a cause that harms the foot than on account of some other thing existing elsewhere, it is reasonable that the motion should always show pain to the mind as something belonging to the foot rather than to some other part. And if dryness in the throat does not arise, as is normal, because taking something to drink contributes to bodily health, but from a contrary cause, as happens in the case of someone with dropsy, then it is far better that it should deceive on that occasion than that it should always be deceptive when the body is in good health. The same holds for the other cases.

This consideration is most helpful, not only for my noticing all the errors to which my nature is liable, but also for enabling me to correct or avoid them without difficulty. To be sure, I know that all the senses set forth what is true more frequently than what is false regarding what concerns the welfare of the body. Moreover, I can nearly always make use of several of them in order to examine the same thing. Furthermore, I can use my memory, which connects current happenings with past ones, and my intellect, which now has examined all the causes of error.

Hence I should no longer fear that those things that are daily shown me by the senses are false. On the contrary, the hyperbolic doubts of the last few days ought to be rejected as ludicrous. This goes especially for the chief reason for doubting, which dealt with my failure to distinguish being asleep from being awake. For I now notice that there is a considerable difference between these two; dreams are never joined by the memory with all the other actions of life, as is the case with those actions that occur when one is awake. For surely, if, while I am awake, someone were suddenly to appear to me and then immediately disappear, as occurs in dreams, so that I see neither where he came from nor where he went, it is not without reason that I would judge him to be a ghost or a phantom conjured up in my brain, rather than a true man. But when these things happen, and I notice distinctly where they come from, where they are now, and when they come to me, and when I connect my perception of them without interruption with the whole rest of my life, I am clearly certain that these perceptions have happened to me not while I was dreaming but while I was awake. Nor ought I have even the least doubt regarding the truth of these things, if, having mustered all the senses, in addition to my memory and my intellect, in order to examine them, nothing is passed on to me by one of these sources that conflicts with the others. For from the fact that God is no deceiver, it follows that I am in no way mistaken in these matters. But because the need to get things done does not always permit us the leisure for such a careful inquiry, we must confess that the life of man is apt to commit errors regarding particular things, and we must acknowledge the infirmity of our nature.

# MATERIALISM

BY **David Papineau**

## INTRODUCTION

Books on consciousness often begin by distinguishing between different kinds of consciousness. We are told about self-consciousness and sentience, creature consciousness and state consciousness, phenomenal consciousness and access consciousness, perceptual consciousness, higher-order consciousness, and so on. I'd rather leave all this until later. Some of these distinctions will become significant in due course, and will be explained when they are needed. Others will not matter to my discussion.

For the moment, all I want to say is that I am concerned with that aspect of consciousness that makes it so philosophically interesting. Namely, that having a conscious experience is *like something*, in Thomas Nagel's striking phrase (1974). It has become standard to use 'phenomenal' or 'subjective' to focus on this feature of consciousness, and I shall adopt these usages in what follows.

The idea is best introduced by examples rather than definitions. ('If you gotta ask, you're never gonna know.') Compare the difference between having your eyes shut and having them open, or between having your teeth drilled with and without an anaesthetic. When your eyes are open, you have a conscious visual experience, and when your teeth are drilled without an anaesthetic, you have a conscious pain. It is like something for you to have these experiences. It is not like that when you close your eyes, or when the anaesthetic takes effect. What you lose in these latter cases are elements of phenomenal or subjective consciousness. From now on, when I say 'conscious', I shall mean this kind of consciousness.

Much of what follows will be concerned with a particular philosophical puzzle about consciousness: namely, the puzzle of how consciousness relates to the physical world. There are other philosophical puzzles about consciousness, but this seems to me the most immediate. We will be ill placed to understand anything about consciousness if we cannot understand its relation to the physical realm.

The puzzle can be posed simply. On the one hand, there is a strong argument for adopting a materialist view of conscious states, for supposing that conscious states must be *part* of the physical world, that they must be *identical* to brain states, or something similar. Yet, on the other hand, there are also strong arguments (and even stronger intuitions) which suggest that conscious states must be *distinct* from any material states. I believe that in the end the materialist argument wins. Conscious states are material states. This is not to belittle the anti-materialist arguments and intuitions. They are deep and important. We will not grasp consciousness properly unless we understand how to answer them. Still, I think that careful analysis will show that they are flawed, and that the right solution is to embrace materialism.

I shall begin by putting the materialist argument on the table. It is worth taking some care about this, for there are a number of different defences of materialism on offer in the contemporary literature, and not all of them are equally compelling. However, I think that there is one definitive argument for materialism. I shall call this 'the causal argument', and the burden of this first chapter will be to develop this argument and distinguish it from some less effective defences of materialism.

There is a further reason for laying out the argument for materialism carefully. Many contemporary philosophers harbour grave suspicions about materialism. Thus some philosophers contend that the whole idea of materialism is somehow empty, on the grounds that there is no proper way of characterizing the 'physical' realm. (Crane and Mellor 1990, Crane 1991, Segal 2000). And others suggest that contemporary materialism about the conscious mind rests on nothing but fashion or prejudice, unsupported by serious argument (Burge 1993, Clark 1996).

I intend to show that these attitudes are mistaken. The question of how to define 'physical' in the context of the mind-brain debate does raise a number of interesting points, but there is no great difficulty about pinning down a sense precise enough for the purposes at hand. It will prove easier do this, however, after we have rehearsed the argument for materialism. Accordingly, I shall not worry about the meaning of 'physical' at this stage, but simply begin by outlining the case for materialism. Once we have seen what is at issue, it will become clearer how materialists can best understand the meaning of 'physical', and I shall return to this issue at the end of the chapter.

There is one terminological point which I do need to address at this point, however. When I do fix a meaning for 'physical' at the end of the chapter, I shall read this term in a relatively strict sense, as standing roughly for the kinds of first-order properties studied by the physical sciences. Under the heading of 'materialism', on the other hand, I shall include not only the doctrine that conscious states are identical with physical states in this strict sense, but also the doctrine that they are identical with 'physically realized functional states', or with some other kind of physically realized but not strictly physical states (these possibilities will be explained further in section 4.6 below). It is true that the causal argument can be read as supporting the stricter identification with physical states, and indeed this is how I shall first present it in the next section. But, as we shall see, the causal argument can also be construed as supporting the less strict identification of conscious states with functional or other physically realized states. Since both the strict and the less strict identifications tie conscious states constitutively to the physical world, few of the arguments in this book will require me to decide between them. So it will be useful to have a term which covers both options, and I have adopted 'materialism' for this purpose. Correspondingly, a 'material' state will mean either a physical state in the strict sense or some functional or other physically realized state.

In addition to suspicions about the meaning of 'physical', there is the further allegation mentioned above, that contemporary materialism is nothing but a modish fad. I take the causal argument to be outlined in this chapter to rebut this allegation. The causal argument may not be conclusive, but it certainly shows that the case for materialism goes beyond mere fashion or prejudice.

Some may think that the charge of modishness is supported by historical considerations. Widespread philosophical materialism is a relatively recent phenomenon, largely a creature of the late twentieth century. This recent provenance may seem to support the accusation that contemporary materialism owes its popularity more to fashion than to any serious argument. 'If the case is so substantial', anti-materialists can ask, 'how come it took so long for philosophers to appreciate it?' I take this to be a good historical question. But I think there is also a good historical answer: namely, that a key premiss in the argument for materialism rests on empirical evidence that only became clear-cut during the course of the twentieth century.

However, I shall not complicate the analysis of this chapter by overlaying it with historical commentary. The issues are complicated enough without the added burden of tracing historical strands. Accordingly, this chapter will focus on the structure of the argument for materialism, not its history. For those who are interested in the historical dimension, the Appendix at the end of this book discusses the history of the causal argument, and in particular the question of why it has become persuasive only recently.

## THE CAUSAL ARGUMENT

Let me now outline what I take to be the canonical argument for materialism. Setting to one side all complications, which can be discussed later, it can be put as follows.

Many effects that we attribute to conscious causes have full physical causes. But it would be absurd to suppose that these effects are caused twice over. So the conscious causes must be identical to some part of those physical causes.

To appreciate the force of this argument, consider some bodily behaviour which we would standardly attribute to conscious causes. For example, I walk to the fridge to get a beer, because I consciously feel thirsty. Now combine this example with the thought that, according to modern physical science, such bodily movements are fully caused by prior physical processes in brains and nerves. The obvious conclusion is that the conscious thirst must be identical with some part of those physical processes.

Let me now lay out the above argument more formally. This will help us to appreciate both its strengths and its weaknesses.

As a first premiss, take:

### Conscious Mental Occurrences Have Physical Effects

As I said, the most obvious examples are cases where our conscious feelings and other mental states cause our behaviour.

Now add in this premiss ('the completeness of physics' henceforth):

### All Physical Effects are Fully Caused by Purely Physical Prior Histories

In particular, this covers the behavioural effects of conscious causes to which our attention is drawn by premiss 1. The thought behind premiss 2 is that such physical behaviour will always be fully caused by physical contractions in your muscles, in turn caused by electrical messages travelling down your nerves, themselves due to physical activity in your motor cortex, in turn caused by physical activity in your sensory cortex, and so on.

At first sight, premisses 1 and 2 seem to suggest that a certain range of physical effects (physical behaviour) will have two distinct causes: one involving a conscious state (your thirst, say), and the other consisting of purely physical states (neuronal firings, say). Now, some events are indeed overdetermined in this way, like the death of a man who is simultaneously shot and struck by lightning. But this seems the wrong model for mental causation. After all, overdetermination implies that even if one cause had been absent, the result would still have occurred because of the other cause (the man would still have died even if he hadn't been shot, or, alternatively, even if he hadn't been struck by lightning). But it seems wrong to say that I would still have walked to the fridge even if I hadn't felt thirsty (because my neurons were firing), or, alternatively, that I would still have gone to the fridge even if my neurons hadn't been firing (because I felt thirsty). So let us add the further premiss:

### The Physical Effects of Conscious Causes Aren't Always Overdetermined by Distinct Causes

Materialism now follows. Premisses 1 and 2 tell us that certain effects have a conscious cause and a physical cause. Premiss 3 tells us that they don't have two distinct causes. The only possibility left is that the conscious occurrences mentioned in (1) must be identical with some part of the physical causes mentioned in (2). This respects both (1) and (2), yet avoids the implication of overdetermination, since (1) and (2) no longer imply *distinct* causes.

## EPIPHENOMENALISM AND PRE-ESTABLISHED HARMONY

All this assumes, however, that the abstract claim does follow from the causal argument. Let us now examine this argument more closely.

As laid out above, the causal argument seems valid. So, to deny the conclusion, we need to deny one of the premisses. All of them can be denied without contradiction. Indeed, all of them have been denied by contemporary philosophers, as we shall see. At the same time, they are all highly plausible, and their denials have various unattractive consequences.

Let me start with premiss 1. This claims that, as a matter of empirical fact, particular conscious states have particular physical effects. This certainly seems plausible. Doesn't my conscious thirst cause me to walk to the fridge? Or, again, when I have a conscious headache, doesn't this cause me to ingest an aspirin?

Still, the possibility of denying this premiss is familiar enough, under the guise of 'epiphenomenalism' or 'pre-established harmony'.

The first philosopher to embrace this option was Leibniz. Unlike most other philosophers prior to the twentieth century, Leibniz was committed to the causal completeness of physics (see Appendix). But he was not prepared to accept the identity of mind with brain. So he opted for a denial of our premiss 1, and concluded that mind and matter cannot really influence each other, and that the appearance of interaction must be due to *pre-established harmony*. By this Leibniz meant that God must have arranged things to make sure that mind and matter always keep in step. In reality, they do not interact, but are like two trains running on separate tracks. But God fixed their starting times and speeds so as to ensure they would always run smoothly alongside each other.

Some contemporary philosophers (for example, Jackson 1982) follow Leibniz in avoiding mind-brain identity by denying premiss 1. But they prefer a rather simpler way of keeping mind and matter in step. They allow causal influences 'upwards' from brain to mind, while denying any 'downwards' causation from mind to brain. This position is known as *epiphenomenalism*. It respects the causal completeness of physics, in that nothing non-physical causally influences the physical brain. But it avoids the theological complications of Leibniz's pre-established harmony, by allowing the brain itself to cause conscious effects.

Epiphenomenalism is not a particularly attractive position. For a start, it would require us to deny many apparently obvious truths, such as that my conscious thirst caused me to fetch a beer, or that my conscious headache caused me to swallow an aspirin. According to epiphenomenalism, my behaviour in both these cases is caused solely at the physical level. These physical causes may be accompanied by conscious thirst or a conscious headache, but these conscious states no more cause resulting behaviour than falling barometers cause rain.

That epiphenomenalism has these odd consequences is not in itself decisive. The theoretical truth can often overturn claims which were previously regarded as the merest common sense. Moreover, there is nothing incoherent about epiphenomenalism. As I shall have occasion to stress in what follows, there is nothing conceptually contradictory in the idea of conscious states which exert no causal powers themselves. Still, epiphenomenalism is surely an empirically implausible position, by comparison with the materialist view that conscious states are simply identical to brain states.

If epiphenomenalism were true, then the relation between mind and brain would be like nothing else in nature. After all, science recognizes no other examples of 'causal danglers', ontologically independent states with causes but no effects. So, given the choice between epiphenomenalism and materialism, standard principles of scientific theory choice would seem to favour materialism. If both views can accommodate the empirical data equally well, then ordinary scientific methodology will advise us to adopt the simple view that unifies mind and brain, rather than the ontologically more profligate story which has the conscious states dangling impotently from the brain states.

There remains the possibility that the anti-materialist arguments to be examined later will show that conscious mind and brain *cannot* be identical. If this is so, then one of the premisses of the causal argument must be false. And in that case premiss 1 seems as likely a candidate as any. Certainly most contemporary philosophers who are persuaded by the anti-materialist arguments have opted for epiphenomenalism and the denial of premiss 1, rather than for any other way out of the causal argument.

But this does not invalidate the criticisms I have levelled against epiphenomenalism. My concern at the moment is not to prejudge the anti-materialist case, but merely to assess the causal argument. And the point remains that, in the absence of further considerations, it seems clearly preferable to identify mind with brain than to condemn conscious states to the status of causal danglers. It may be that further anti-materialist considerations will yet require us to reconsider this verdict, but so far we have seen no reason to deny premiss 1, and good reason to uphold it.

Before leaving the issue of epiphenomenalism, it may be worth addressing some more local worries about premiss 1. Even if the blanket epiphenomenalist refusal to credit *any* conscious states with physical effects is methodologically unattractive, there may be some more specific reasons for doubting whether particular sorts of conscious states have the physical effects they are normally credited with. In particular, I am thinking here of conscious *decisions*, and doubts about their causal efficacy arising from the experimental results associated with Benjamin Libet, and of conscious states which are *representational*, and doubts about their causal efficacy arising from the possibility that they may have 'broad contents'. Let me deal with these in turn.

In a series of well-known experiments, Libet asked subjects to decide spontaneously to move their fingers, and simultaneously to note the precise moment of their decision, as measured by a large stop-watch on the wall. Libet also used scalp electrodes to detect the onset of motor cortical activity initiating the finger movement. Amazingly, he found that this neural activity started a full ⅓ to ½ second *before* the subjects were aware of making any conscious decision (Libet 1993).

At first sight, this certainly suggests that such conscious decisions are epiphenomenal with respect to the actions we normally attribute to them: since the conscious decisions come later, it looks as if they must be effects of, rather than identical with, the brain processes that give rise to the action. But in fact this interpretation is not clear-cut. Libet himself points out that the conscious decisions still have the power to 'endorse' or 'cancel', so to speak, the processes initiated by the earlier cortical activity: no action will result if the action's execution is consciously countermanded. Given this, it seems that the conscious decision is part of the cause of the finger movement after all. The initial cortical activity does not determine the finger movement on its own, but only puts the motor cortex in a state of 'readiness', which leads to action in just those cases where the conscious decision is added. This then allows us to reason, as before, via the causal argument, that conscious decisions could not play a part in so influencing physical movements, were they not themselves physical.

In any case, even if conscious decisions did *not* contribute causally to the actions normally attributed to them, it would not follow that they had no physical effects of any kind. For instance, they will still presumably be causes of the sounds I make, or the marks I put on paper, when I later *report* my earlier conscious decisions. So they will still satisfy premiss 1, which requires only that conscious causes have *some* physical effects, and not that they have all the physical effects with which they are normally credited by common sense. So once more the causal argument will run.

The other worry concerned the possibility of conscious states with 'broad' representational contents. The possession of such 'broad contents' hinges on matters outside subjects' heads. For example, Hilary Putnam suggests that the representational state *thinking about water* hinges on what natural kind is actually water in your environment, and Tyler Burge argues that *thinking about arthritis* hinges on facts about other members of your community (Putnam 1975, Burge 1979, 1982).

Now the worry, in the present context, is that if any conscious states are representational in this broad way, then this will not sit happily with premiss 1's claims about causal efficacy. For how can states which hinge on matters outside your head exert a causal influence on your bodily movements? Surely your bodily movements are causally influenced solely by matters inside your skin, not by how matters are outside you.

The possibility of broadly representational conscious states raises any number of tricky issues, not all of which I can pursue here. However, they seem to me to pose no real threat to the causal argument for materialism. Let me content myself with two comments.

First, I am open to the possibility that some, indeed all, conscious states may be essentially representational (cf. n. **1** above); moreover, it seems plausible that representation in general is a broad matter. Even so, it would seem odd to allow that conscious properties in particular, as opposed to representational properties in general, can depend on broad matters outside the skin. Could two people really be internally physically identical, yet nevertheless *feel* different, because things are different outside them? (Cf. Introduction, n. **2**.) Given this, the natural strategy for those who seek to equate some (or all) conscious properties with representational properties is to shear off some species of narrow representation from the general run of broad representational properties, and to equate representational conscious properties with these narrow representational properties. And then, to return to the matter at hand, there will cease to be any reason to doubt that these conscious properties have physical effects such as bodily movements, however it may be with representational properties in general. Second, even if you do wish to insist that some conscious properties are indeed broadly representational, it will not follow that such broad conscious properties do not cause any physical effects. For they may have physical effects *outside* my body. For example, my consciously thirsting for water might affect *which liquid* I put into a glass, and my consciously worrying about arthritis might affect *where the doctor will poke me* when I complain of it. If this is right, then the causal argument will run as before, and imply that any such broad conscious properties must also be identical with physical properties, if their instantiations are to have such physical effects—though these physical properties will now presumably stretch outside bodies, as well as inside.

## ACCEPTING OVERDETERMINATION

There remain the two other premisses to the causal argument. It will be convenient to relegate the discussion of premiss 2, the completeness of physics, to the last section of this chapter and the Appendix. So let me now briefly consider premiss 3, the one ruling out overdetermination.

To reject this premiss is to accept that the physical effects of mental causes are always overdetermined by distinct causes. This is sometimes called the 'belt and braces' view (make doubly sure you get the effects you want), and is defended by D. H. Mellor (1995: 103–5).

At first sight, this position seems to have the odd consequence that you would still have gone to the fridge for a beer even if you hadn't been thirsty (because your cortical neurons would still have been firing), and that you would still have gone to the fridge even if your cortex hadn't been firing (because you would still have been thirsty). These counterfactual implications seem clearly mistaken.

However, defenders of the belt and braces view maintain that such implications can be avoided. They argue that the distinct mental and physical causes may themselves be strongly counterfactually dependent (that is, they hold that, if you hadn't been thirsty, your sensory neurons wouldn't have fired either, and vice versa).

Still, this then raises the question of *why* such causes should always be so counterfactually dependent, if they are ontologically distinct. Why wouldn't my neurons have fired, even in the absence of my conscious thirst? Similarly, why shouldn't I still have been thirsty, even if my neurons hadn't fired? Now, it is not impossible to imagine mechanisms which would ensure such counterfactual dependence between distinct causes. Perhaps the conscious thirst occurs first, and then invariably causes the cortical activity, with both causes thus available to overdetermine the behaviour. Alternatively, the cortical activity could invariably cause the thirst. Or, again, the conscious decision and the cortical activity might be joint effects of some prior common physical cause. But such mechanisms, though conceptually coherent, seem highly implausible, especially given that they need to ensure that the conscious state and the brain state *always* accompany each other.

The relevant point is analogous to one made in the last section. We don't find any 'belt and braces' mechanisms elsewhere in nature—that is, mechanisms which ensure that certain classes of effects invariably have two distinct causes, each of which would suffice by itself. As with the epiphenomenalist model, a belt and braces model requiring such peculiar brain mechanisms would seem to be ruled out by general principles of scientific theory choice. If the simple picture of mental causation offered by materialism accommodates the empirical data as well as the complex mechanisms required by the belt and braces option, then normal methodological principles would seem to weigh heavily against the belt and braces view.

As with the corresponding argument for epiphenomenalism, this appeal to principles of scientific theory choice is defeasible. Perhaps in the end the anti-materialist arguments will force us to accept mind-brain distinctness. In that case, the belt and braces view might be worth another look. True, it is even more Heath-Robinsonish than epiphenomenalism. On the other hand, it does at least have the virtue of retaining the common-sense view that conscious states characteristically cause behaviour. In any case, my present purpose is not to decide this issue finally, but only to point out that, as things stand so far, we have good reason to uphold premiss 3, and none to deny it.

## WHAT IS 'PHYSICS'?

Let me now address a terminological issue flagged earlier, an issue that may have been worrying readers for some time. How exactly is 'physics' to be understood in this context of the causal argument? An awkward dilemma may seem to face anyone trying to defend the crucial second premiss, the completeness of physics. If we take 'physics' to mean the subject-matter currently studied in departments of physics, discussed in physics journals, and so on, then it seems pretty obvious that physics is not complete. The track record of past attempts to list *all* the fundamental forces and particles responsible for physical effects is not good, and it seems highly likely that future physics will identify new categories of physical cause. On the other hand, if we mean by 'physics' the subject-matter of such future scientific theories, then we seem to be in no position to assess its completeness, since we don't yet know what it is.

This difficulty is more apparent than real. If you want to use the causal argument, it isn't crucial that you know exactly what a complete physics would include. Much more important is to know what it won't include. (Cf. Papineau and Spurrett 1999.)

Suppose, to illustrate the point, that we have a well-defined notion of the *mental* realm, identified via some distinctive way of picking out properties as mental. (Thus we might identify this realm as involving intentionality, say, or intelligence, or indeed as involving consciousness—the precise characterization won't matter for the point I am about to make.) Then one way of understanding 'physical' would simply be as 'non-mentally identifiable'—that is, as standing for properties which can be identified independently of this specifically mental conceptual apparatus. And then, provided we can be confident that the 'physical' in this sense is complete—that is, that every non-mentally identifiable effect is fully determined by *non-mentally identifiable* antecedents—then we can conclude that all mental states must be identical with (or realized by) something non-mentally identifiable (otherwise mental states couldn't have non-mentally identifiable effects).

This understanding of 'physical' as 'non-mentally identifiable' is of course a lot weaker than any normal pre-theoretical understanding, but note that it still generates a conclusion of great philosophical interest: namely, that all mental states, and in particular all conscious states, must be identical with non-mentally identifiable states.

We may not know enough about physics to know exactly what a complete 'physics' might include. But as long as we are confident that, whatever it includes, it will have no ineliminable need for any distinctively mental categorizations, we can be confident that mental properties must be identical with (or realized by) certain non-mentally identifiable properties.

In fact, I shall understand 'physical' in a somewhat tighter sense in what follows, as 'identifiable non-mentally-*and*-non-biologically', or 'inanimate' for short, rather than simply as 'non-mentally identifiable'. This is because it is this realm, the 'inanimate', that is most naturally argued to be complete. When I examine the detailed scientific reasons for believing in the completeness of physics, in the Appendix, it will turn out that the realm which science has in fact shown to be causally sufficient unto itself is the inanimate. What science has actually shown is that any inanimate effect (that is, any effect specifiable in terms of mass, or charge, or chemical structure, or . . . in any non-biological and non-mental way) will have an inanimate cause. So it is this thesis that I propose to plug into the causal argument. Conscious causes have inanimate effects. Inanimate effects always have full inanimate causes. So conscious properties must be identical with (or realized by) inanimate properties.

It might not be immediately obvious why I am being so careful here. Why not simply read 'physical' as non-mentally identifiable, as I suggested initially? If the Appendix succeeds is showing that the inanimate is complete, then won't it *a fortiori* show that the non-mentally identifiable is complete? After all, if something is inanimate, then it is certainly non-mentally identifiable. So, if the inanimate is complete, and there are inanimate causes for all inanimate effects, then those causes will be non-mentally identifiable too. And this would thus seem to ensure the completeness of the non-mentally identifiable.

No. This is too quick. To see why, take an *effect* which is *not* inanimate yet *is* non-mentally identifiable. An *arm* moving would be a good example. I take it that the notion of an arm movement is not a *mental* notion. But the notion of *an arm* is certainly a biological notion. So arm movements are not inanimate, even though they are non-mentally identifiable.

Now, the completeness of the inanimate tells us that all inanimate effects have inanimate causes. But, since *arm* movements aren't inanimate, it doesn't follow that they have inanimate causes, nor, therefore, that they must have non-mentally identifiable causes. Maybe, for all the completeness of the inanimate guarantees, arm movements are always caused by mental states alone, like desires or intentions, without any assistance from further causes at the inanimate level. This thus shows that the completeness of the inanimate doesn't guarantee the completeness of the non-mentally identifiable.

This last point suggests a possible way of resisting the causal argument. Anti-materialists could allow that there is a familiar everyday sense in which conscious states have 'physical' effects, and another good sense in which the 'physical' realm is complete, and yet object that the causal argument fails to go through because the two senses are distinct. (Cf. Sturgeon 1998.) Thus they could allow that conscious causes always have non-mentally identifiable bodily effects like arms moving, and also allow that the seriously inanimate realm of mass and motion is complete, but urge that since arm movements aren't themselves inanimate, it doesn't follow that they must have inanimate causes, nor therefore that their conscious antecedents must be identical with anything inanimately identifiable.

This is a serious enough issue, but it is scarcely conclusive against the materialist side. Materialists need only make sure that their senses of 'physical' line up properly. The version of completeness I take to be defensible, as I said, is the completeness of the inanimate. So all I need to make the causal argument go through is a version of premiss 1 which will ensure that conscious causes do have inanimate effects, in addition to their effects on animate body parts.

One way of arguing for this premiss would be to start with the point that the anti-materialist concedes, namely, that conscious states cause animate effects, like arms moving, and then argue that arm movements should themselves be identified with inanimate occurrences, thus giving the conscious causes inanimate effects, as desired. An obvious strategy here would be to note that arm movements themselves have inanimate effects (such as stones flying through the air, say), and then apply the causal argument once more, to conclude that these arm movements must be identified with the inanimate causes of those inanimate effects, if we are to avoid overdetermination.

But this is a somewhat long way round. If the animate bodily effects of conscious causes have inanimate effects, then we can infer directly that the conscious causes must themselves have those inanimate effects, by transitivity, whether or not the animate bodily movements are identified with inanimate occurrences. (Cf. Witmer 2000.) Thus, if some conscious desire causes my arm to move, and this movement in turn has such inanimate effects as a stone flying through the air, a window shattering, and so forth, then my conscious desire itself will cause these inanimate effects. I take it to be uncontroversial that conscious states standardly[15] have such inanimate effects, and will assume this henceforth.

## THE COMPLETENESS OF PHYSICS

Let me conclude this chapter with a few remarks about the causal argument's second premiss, the completeness of physics. It is one thing to fix a sense of 'physics' which renders this a substantial claim which might be true or false. It is another to show that it is in fact true.

Some readers might feel that this is not a problematic issue. Once we have fixed a definite meaning for 'physical', as equivalent to 'inanimate', say, then is it not just a matter of common sense that all physical effects will have physical causes? In particular, if we take the physical effects in this sense that we normally attribute to conscious causes, then is it not obvious that these effects can always in principle be fully accounted for in terms of uncontroversially physical histories, involving the movement of matter (in arms), molecular processes (in muscles), the action of neurotransmitters (in brains) . . . and so on?

This is certainly how I thought of the issue when I first started working on the causal argument. I realized that this argument involved a number of disputable moves, and was therefore ready for it to be queried on various different grounds. But the one assumption that I did expect to be uncontroversial was the completeness of physics. To my surprise, I discovered that a number of my philosophical colleagues didn't agree. They didn't see why some physical occurrences, in our brains perhaps, shouldn't have irreducibly conscious causes.

My first reaction to this suggestion was that it betrayed an insufficient understanding of modern physics. Surely, I felt, the completeness premiss is simply part of standard physical theory. However, when my objectors pressed me, not unreasonably, to show them where the completeness of physics is written down in the physics textbooks, I found myself in some embarrassment. Once I was forced to defend it, I realized that the completeness of physics is by no means self-evident. Indeed, further research has led me to realize that, far from being self-evident, it is an issue on which the post-Galilean scientific tradition has changed its mind several times. The completeness of physics may seem the merest part of common sense to many of us today, but as recently as 150 years ago most people, including most orthodox scientists, would have thought the idea absurd, taking it to be obvious that there must be some *sui generis* conscious states in the causal history of human behaviour.

So the completeness of physics is a doctrine with a history, and a very interesting history at that. In the Appendix I detail this history. My main purpose in doing this is to show that there is good empirical evidence for the completeness of physics. But the historical story also shows that this evidence is relatively recent, and that prior to the twentieth century the empirical case for the completeness of physics was by no means persuasive. At the beginning of this chapter I raised the question of why philosophical materialism has become popular only in the last fifty years or so. As I pointed out, this historical circumstance lends weight to the suggestion that contemporary materialism is a creature of fashion rather than serious philosophical argument. I take the story I tell in the Appendix to rebut this suggestion. There is indeed a good case for materialism. But it has not always been available to philosophers. This is because its crucial premiss, the completeness of physics, rests on empirical evidence which has emerged only relatively recently.

# EPIPHENOMENAL QUALIA

BY **Frank Jackson**

It is undeniable that the physical, chemical and biological sciences have provided a great deal of information about the world we live in and about ourselves. I will use the label 'physical information' for this kind of information, and also for information that automatically comes along with it. For example, if a medical scientist tells me enough about the processes that go on in my nervous system, and about how they relate to happenings in the world around me, to what has happened in the past and is likely to happen in the future, to what happens to other similar and dissimilar organisms, and the like, he or she tells me—if I am clever enough to fit it together appropriately—about what is often called the functional role of those states in me (and in organisms in general in similar cases). This information, and its kin, I also label 'physical'.

I do not mean these sketchy remarks to constitute a definition of 'physical information', and of the correlative notions of physical property, process, and so on, but to indicate what I have in mind here. It is well known that there are problems with giving a precise definition of these notions, and so of the thesis of Physicalism that all (correct) information is physical information.[1] But—unlike some—I take the question of definition to cut across the central problems I want to discuss in this paper.

I am what is sometimes known as a "qualia freak". I think that there are certain features of the bodily sensations especially, but also of certain perceptual experiences, which no amount of purely physical information includes. Tell me everything physical there is to tell about what is going on in a living brain, the kind of states, their functional role, their relation to what goes on at other times and in other brains, and so on and so forth, and be I as clever as can be in fitting it all together, you won't have told me about the hurtfulness of pains, the itchiness of itches, pangs of jealousy, or about the characteristic experience of tasting a lemon, smelling a rose, hearing a loud noise or seeing the sky.

There are many qualia freaks, and some of them say that their rejection of Physicalism is an unargued intuition.[2] I think that they are being unfair to themselves. They have the following argument. Nothing you could tell of a physical sort captures the smell of a rose, for instance. Therefore, Physicalism is false. By our lights this is a perfectly good argument. It is obviously not to the point to question its validity, and the premise is intuitively obviously true both to them and to me.

I must, however, admit that it is weak from a polemical point of view. There are, unfortunately for us, many who do not find the premise intuitively obvious. The task then is to present an argument whose premises are obvious to all, or at least to as many as possible. This I try to do in §I with what I will call "the Knowledge argument". In §II I contrast the Knowledge argument with the Modal argument and in §III with the "What is it like to be" argument. In §IV I tackle the question of the causal role of qualia. The major factor in stopping people from admitting qualia is the belief that they would have to be given a causal role with respect to the physical world and especially the brain;[3] and it is hard to do this without sounding like someone who believes in fairies. I seek in §IV to turn this objection by arguing that the view that qualia are epiphenomenal is a perfectly possible one.

---

1 See, e.g., D. H. Mellor, "Materialism and Phenomenal Qualities", *Aristotelian Society Supp. Vol.* 47 (1973), 107–19; and J. W. Cornman, *Materialism and Sensations* (New Haven and London, 1971).

2 Particularly in discussion, but see, e.g., Keith Campbell, *Metaphysics* (Belmont, 1976), p. 67.

3 See, e.g., D. C. Dennett, "Current Issues in the Philosophy of Mind", *American Philosophical Quarterly*, 15 (1978), 249–61.

## I. THE KNOWLEDGE ARGUMENT FOR QUALIA

People vary considerably in their ability to discriminate colours. Suppose that in an experiment to catalogue this variation Fred is discovered. Fred has better colour vision than anyone else on record; he makes every discrimination that anyone has ever made, and moreover he makes one that we cannot even begin to make. Show him a batch of ripe tomatoes and he sorts them into two roughly equal groups and does so with complete consistency. That is, if you blindfold him, shuffle the tomatoes up, and then remove the blindfold and ask him to sort them out again, he sorts them into exactly the same two groups.

We ask Fred how he does it. He explains that all ripe tomatoes do not look the same colour to him, and in fact that this is true of a great many objects that we classify together as red. He sees two colours where we see one, and he has in consequence developed for his own use two words '$\text{red}_1$' and '$\text{red}_2$' to mark the difference. Perhaps he tells us that he has often tried to teach the difference between $\text{red}_1$ and $\text{red}_2$ to his friends but has got nowhere and has concluded that the rest of the world is $\text{red}_1$-$\text{red}_2$ colour-blind—or perhaps he has had partial success with his children, it doesn't matter. In any case he explains to us that it would be quite wrong to think that because 'red' appears in both '$\text{red}_1$' and '$\text{red}_2$' that the two colours are shades of the one colour. He only uses the common term 'red' to fit more easily into our restricted usage. To him $\text{red}_1$ and $\text{red}_2$ are as different from each other and all the other colours as yellow is from blue. And his discriminatory behaviour bears this out: he sorts $\text{red}_1$ from $\text{red}_2$ tomatoes with the greatest of ease in a wide variety of viewing circumstances. Moreover, an investigation of the physiological basis of Fred's exceptional ability reveals that Fred's optical system is able to separate out two groups of wave-lengths in the red spectrum as sharply as we are able to sort out yellow from blue.[4]

I think that we should admit that Fred can see, really see, at least one more colour than we can; $\text{red}_1$ is a different colour from $\text{red}_2$. We are to Fred as a totally red-green colour-blind person is to us. H. G. Wells' story "The Country of the Blind" is about a sighted person in a totally blind community.[5] This person never manages to convince them that he can see, that he has an extra sense. They ridicule this sense as quite inconceivable, and treat his capacity to avoid falling into ditches, to win fights and so on as precisely that capacity and nothing more. We would be making their mistake if we refused to allow that Fred can see one more colour than we can.

What kind of experience does Fred have when he sees $\text{red}_1$ and $\text{red}_2$? What is the new colour or colours like? We would dearly like to know but do not; and it seems that no amount of physical information about Fred's brain and optical system tells us. We find out perhaps that Fred's cones respond differentially to certain light waves in the red section of the spectrum that make no difference to ours (or perhaps he has an extra cone) and that this leads in Fred to a wider range of those brain states responsible for visual discriminatory behaviour. But none of this tells us what we really want to know about his colour experience. There is something about it we don't know. But we know, we may suppose, everything about Fred's body, his behaviour and dispositions to behaviour and about his internal physiology, and everything about his history and relation to others that can be given in physical accounts of persons. We have all the physical information. Therefore, knowing all this is *not* knowing everything about Fred. It follows that Physicalism leaves something out.

To reinforce this conclusion, imagine that as a result of our investigations into the internal workings of Fred we find out how to make everyone's physiology like Fred's in the relevant respects; or perhaps Fred donates his body to science and on his death we are able to transplant his optical system into someone else—again the fine detail doesn't matter. The important point is that such a happening would create enormous interest. People would say, "At last we will know what it is like to see the extra colour, at last we will know how Fred has differed from us in the way he has struggled to tell us about for so long". Then it cannot be that we knew all along all about Fred. But *ex hypothesi* we did know all along everything about Fred that features in the physicalist scheme; hence the physicalist scheme leaves something out.

Put it this way. *After* the operation, we will know *more* about Fred and especially about his colour experiences. But beforehand we had all the physical information we could desire about his body and brain, and indeed everything

4 Put this, and similar simplifications below, in terms of Land's theory if you prefer. See, e.g., Edwin H. Land, "Experiments in Color Vision", *Scientific American*, 200 (5 May 1959), 84–99.

5 H. G. Wells, *The Country of the Blind and Other Stories* (London, n.d.).

that has ever featured in physicalist accounts of mind and consciousness. Hence there is more to know than all that. Hence Physicalism is incomplete.

Fred and the new colour(s) are of course essentially rhetorical devices. The same point can be made with normal people and familiar colours. Mary is a brilliant scientist who is, for whatever reason, forced to investigate the world from a black and white room *via* a black and white television monitor. She specialises in the neurophysiology of vision and acquires, let us suppose, all the physical information there is to obtain about what goes on when we see ripe tomatoes, or the sky, and use terms like 'red', 'blue', and so on. She discovers, for example, just which wave-length combinations from the sky stimulate the retina, and exactly how this produces *via* the central nervous system the contraction of the vocal chords and expulsion of air from the lungs that results in the uttering of the sentence 'The sky is blue'. (It can hardly be denied that it is in principle possible to obtain all this physical information from black and white television, otherwise the Open University would of *necessity* need to use colour television.)

What will happen when Mary is released from her black and white room or is given a colour television monitor? Will she *learn* anything or not? It seems just obvious that she will learn something about the world and our visual experience of it. But then it is inescapable that her previous knowledge was incomplete. But she had *all* the physical information. *Ergo* there is more to have than that, and Physicalism is false.

Clearly the same style of Knowledge argument could be deployed for taste, hearing, the bodily sensations and generally speaking for the various mental states which are said to have (as it is variously put) raw feels, phenomenal features or qualia. The conclusion in each case is that the qualia are left out of the physicalist story. And the polemical strength of the Knowledge argument is that it is so hard to deny the central claim that one can have all the physical information without having all the information there is to have.

## II. THE MODAL ARGUMENT

By the Modal Argument I mean an argument of the following style.[6] Sceptics about other minds are not making a mistake in deductive logic, whatever else may be wrong with their position. No amount of physical information about another *logically entails* that he or she is conscious or feels anything at all. Consequently there is a possible world with organisms exactly like us in every physical respect (and remember that includes functional states, physical history, *et al.*) but which differ from us profoundly in that they have no conscious mental life at all. But then what is it that we have and they lack? Not anything physical *ex hypothesi.* In all physical regards we and they are exactly alike. Consequently there is more to us than the purely physical. Thus Physicalism is false.[7]

It is sometimes objected that the Modal argument misconceives Physicalism on the ground that that doctrine is advanced as a *contingent* truth.[8] But to say this is only to say that physicalists restrict their claim to *some* possible worlds, including especially ours; and the Modal argument is only directed against this lesser claim. If we in *our* world, let alone beings in any others, have features additional to those of our physical replicas in other possible worlds, then we have non-physical features or qualia.

The trouble rather with the Modal argument is that it rests on a disputable modal intuition. Disputable because it is disputed. Some sincerely deny that there can be physical replicas of us in other possible worlds which nevertheless lack consciousness. Moreover, at least one person who once had the intuition now has doubts.[9]

Head-counting may seem a poor approach to a discussion of the Modal argument. But frequently we can do no better when modal intuitions are in question, and remember our initial goal was to find the argument with the greatest polemical utility.

Of course, *qua* protagonists of the Knowledge argument we may well accept the modal intuition in question; but this will be a *consequence* of our already having an argument to the conclusion that qualia are left out of the physicalist story, not our ground for that conclusion. Moreover, the matter is complicated by the possibility that the

6 See, e.g., Keith Campbell, *Body and Mind* (New York, 1970); and Robert Kirk, "Sentience and Behaviour", *Mind,* 83 (1974), 43–60.

7 I have presented the argument in an inter-world rather than the more usual intraworld fashion to avoid inessential complications to do with supervenience, causal anomalies and the like.

8 See, e.g., W. G. Lycan, "A New Lilliputian Argument Against Machine Functionalism", *Philosophical Studies, 35* (1979), 279–87, p. 280; and Don Locke, "Zombies, Schizophrenics and Purely Physical Objects", *Mind,* 85 (1976), 97–9.

9 See R. Kirk, "From Physical Explicability to Full-Blooded Materialism", *The Philosophical Quarterly,* 29 (1979), 229–37. See also the arguments against the modal intuition in, e.g., Sydney Shoemaker, "Functionalism and Qualia", *Philosophical Studies,* 27 (1975), 291–315.

connection between matters physical and qualia is like that sometimes held to obtain between aesthetic qualities and natural ones. Two possible worlds which agree in all "natural" respects (including the experiences of sentient creatures) must agree in all aesthetic qualities also, but it is plausibly held that the aesthetic qualities cannot be reduced to the natural.

## III. THE "WHAT IS IT LIKE TO BE" ARGUMENT

In "What is it like to be a bat?" Thomas Nagel argues that no amount of physical information can tell us what it is like to be a bat, and indeed that we, human beings, cannot imagine what it is like to be a bat.[10] His reason is that what this is like can only be understood from a bat's point of view, which is not our point of view and is not something capturable in physical terms which are essentially terms understandable equally from many points of view.

It is important to distinguish this argument from the Knowledge argument. When I complained that all the physical knowledge about Fred was not enough to tell us what his special colour experience was like, I was not complaining that we weren't finding out what it is like to *be* Fred. I was complaining that there is something *about* his experience, a property of it, of which we were left ignorant. And if and when we come to know what this property is we still will not know what it is like to *be* Fred, but we will know more *about* him. No amount of knowledge about Fred, be it physical or not, amounts to knowledge "from the inside" concerning Fred. We are not Fred. There is thus a whole set of items of knowledge expressed by forms of words like 'that it is *I myself* who is . . .' which Fred has and we simply cannot have because we are not him.[11]

When Fred sees the colour he alone can see, one thing he knows is the way his experience of it differs from his experience of seeing red and so on, *another* is that he himself is seeing it. Physicalist and qualia freaks alike should acknowledge that no amount of information of whatever kind that *others* have *about* Fred amounts to knowledge of the second. My complaint though concerned the first and was that the special quality of his experience is certainly a fact about it, and one which Physicalism leaves out because no amount of physical information told us what it is.

Nagel speaks as if the problem he is raising is one of extrapolating from knowledge of one experience to another, of imagining what an unfamiliar experience would be like on the basis of familiar ones. In terms of Hume's example, from knowledge of some shades of blue we can work out what it would be like to see other shades of blue. Nagel argues that the trouble with bats *et al.* is that they are too unlike us. It is hard to see an objection to Physicalism here. Physicalism makes no special claims about the imaginative or extrapolative powers of human beings, and it is hard to see why it need do so.[12]

Anyway, our Knowledge argument makes no assumptions on this point. If Physicalism were true, enough physical information about Fred would obviate any need to extrapolate or to perform special feats of imagination or understanding in order to know all about his special colour experience. *The information would already be in our possession.* But it clearly isn't. That was the nub of the argument.

## IV. THE BOGEY OF EPIPHENOMENALISM

Is there any really *good* reason for refusing to countenance the idea that qualia are causally impotent with respect to the physical world? I will argue for the answer no, but in doing this I will say nothing about two views associated with the classical epiphenomenalist position. The first is that mental *states* are inefficacious with respect to the physical world. All I will be concerned to defend is that it is possible to hold that certain *properties* of certain mental states, namely those I've called qualia, are such that their possession or absence makes no difference to the physical world. The second is that the mental is *totally* causally inefficacious. For all I will say it may be that you have to hold that the instantiation of *qualia* makes a difference to *other mental states* though not to anything physical. Indeed general considerations to do with how you could come to be aware of the instantiation of qualia suggest such a position.[13]

10 *The Philosophical Review*, 83 (1974), 435–50. Two things need to be said about this article. One is that, despite my dissociations to come, I am much indebted to it. The other is that the emphasis changes through the article, and by the end Nagel is objecting not so much to Physicalism as to all extant theories of mind for ignoring points of view, including those that admit (irreducible) qualia.

11 Knowledge *de se* in the terms of David Lewis, "Attitudes De Dicto and De Se", *The Philosophical Review*, 88 (1979), 513–43.

12 See Laurence Nemirow's comments on "What is it . . ." in his review of T. Nagel, *Mortal Questions*, in *The Philosophical Review*, 89 (1980), 473–7. I am indebted here in particular to a discussion with David Lewis.

13 See my review of K. Campbell, *Body and Mind*, in *Australasian Journal of Philosophy*, 50 (1972), 77–80.

Three reasons are standardly given for holding that a quale like the hurtfulness of a pain must be causally efficacious in the physical world, and so, for instance, that its instantiation must sometimes make a difference to what happens in the brain. None, I will argue, has any real force. (I am much indebted to Alec Hyslop and John Lucas for convincing me of this.)

(i) It is supposed to be just obvious that the hurtfulness of pain is partly responsible for the subject seeking to avoid pain, saying 'It hurts' and so on. But, to reverse Hume, anything can fail to cause anything. No matter how often *B* follows *A*, and no matter how initially obvious the causality of the connection seems, the hypothesis that *A* causes *B* can be overturned by an over-arching theory which shows the two as distinct effects of a common underlying causal process.

To the untutored the image on the screen of Lee Marvin's fist moving from left to right immediately followed by the image of John Wayne's head moving in the same general direction looks as causal as anything.[14] And of course throughout countless Westerns images similar to the first are followed by images similar to the second. All this counts for precisely nothing when we know the over-arching theory concerning how the relevant images are both effects of an underlying causal process involving the projector and the film. The epiphenomenalist can say exactly the same about the connection between, for example, hurtfulness and behaviour. It is simply a consequence of the fact that certain happenings in the brain cause both.

(ii) The second objection relates to Darwin's Theory of Evolution. According to natural selection the traits that evolve over time are those conducive to physical survival. We may assume that qualia evolved over time—we have them, the earliest forms of life do not—and so we should expect qualia to be conducive to survival. The objection is that they could hardly help us to survive if they do nothing to the physical world.

The appeal of this argument is undeniable, but there is a good reply to it. Polar bears have particularly thick, warm coats. The Theory of Evolution explains this (we suppose) by pointing out that having a thick, warm coat is conducive to survival in the Arctic. But having a thick coat goes along with having a heavy coat, and having a heavy coat is *not* conducive to survival. It slows the animal down.

Does this mean that we have refuted Darwin because we have found an evolved trait—having a heavy coat—which is not conducive to survival? Clearly not. Having a heavy coat is an unavoidable concomitant of having a warm coat (in the context, modern insulation was not available), and the advantages for survival of having a warm coat outweighed the disadvantages of having a heavy one. The point is that all we can extract from Darwin's theory is that we should expect any evolved characteristic to be *either* conducive to survival *or* a by-product of one that is so conducive. The epiphenomenalist holds that qualia fall into the latter category. They are a by-product of certain brain processes that are highly conducive to survival.

(iii) The third objection is based on a point about how we come to know about other minds. We know about other minds by knowing about other behaviour, at least in part. The nature of the inference is a matter of some controversy, but it is not a matter of controversy that it proceeds from behaviour. That is why we think that stones do not feel and dogs do feel. But, runs the objection, how can a person's behaviour provide any reason for believing he has qualia like mine, or indeed any qualia at all, unless this behaviour can be regarded as the *outcome* of the qualia. Man Friday's footprint was evidence of Man Friday because footprints are causal outcomes of feet attached to people. And an epiphenomenalist cannot regard behaviour, or indeed anything physical, as an outcome of qualia.

But consider my reading in *The Times* that Spurs won. This provides excellent evidence that *The Telegraph* has also reported that Spurs won, despite the fact that (I trust) *The Telegraph* does not get the results from *The Times.* They each send their own reporters to the game. *The Telegraph*'s report is in no sense an outcome of *The Times*', but the latter provides good evidence for the former nevertheless.

The reasoning involved can be reconstructed thus. I read in *The Times* that Spurs won. This gives me reason to think that Spurs won because I know that Spurs' winning is the most likely candidate to be what caused the report in *The Times.* But I also know that Spurs' winning would have had many effects, including almost certainly a report in *The Telegraph.*

I am arguing from one effect back to its cause and out again to another effect. The fact that neither effect causes the other is irrelevant. Now the epiphenomenalist allows that qualia are effects of what goes on in the brain. Qualia

14 Cf. Jean Piaget, "The Child's Conception of Physical Causality", reprinted in *The Essential Piaget* (London, 1977).

cause nothing physical but are caused by something physical. Hence the epiphenomenalist can argue from the behaviour of others to the qualia of others by arguing from the behaviour of others back to its causes in the brains of others and out again to their qualia.

You may well feel for one reason or another that this is a more dubious chain of reasoning than its model in the case of newspaper reports. You are right. The problem of other minds is a major philosophical problem, the problem of other newspaper reports is not. But there is no special problem of Epiphenomenalism as opposed to, say, Interactionism here.

There is a very understandable response to the three replies I have just made. "All right, there is no knockdown refutation of the existence of epiphenomenal qualia. But the fact remains that they are an excrescence. They *do* nothing, they *explain* nothing, they serve merely to soothe the intuitions of dualists, and it is left a total mystery how they fit into the world view of science. In short we do not and cannot understand the how and why of them."

This is perfectly true; but is no objection to qualia, for it rests on an overly optimistic view of the human animal, and its powers. We are the products of Evolution. We understand and sense what we need to understand and sense in order to survive. Epiphenomenal qualia are totally irrelevant to survival. At no stage of our evolution did natural selection favour those who could make sense of how they are caused and the laws governing them, or in fact why they exist at all. And that is why we can't.

It is not sufficiently appreciated that Physicalism is an extremely optimistic view of our powers. If it is true, we have, in very broad outline admittedly, a grasp of our place in the scheme of things. Certain matters of sheer complexity defeat us—there are an awful lot of neurons—but in principle we have it all. But consider the antecedent probability that everything in the Universe be of a kind that is relevant in some way or other to the survival of *homo sapiens*. It is very low surely. But then one must admit that it is very likely that there is a part of the whole scheme of things, maybe a big part, which no amount of evolution will ever bring us near to knowledge about or understanding. For the simple reason that such knowledge and understanding is irrelevant to survival.

Physicalists typically emphasise that we are a part of nature on their view, which is fair enough. But if we are a part of nature, we are as nature has left us after however many years of evolution it is, and each step in that evolutionary progression has been a matter of chance constrained just by the need to preserve or increase survival value. The wonder is that we understand as much as we do, and there is no wonder that there should be matters which fall quite outside our comprehension. Perhaps exactly how epiphenomenal qualia fit into the scheme of things is one such.

This may seem an unduly pessimistic view of our capacity to articulate a truly comprehensive picture of our world and our place in it. But suppose we discovered living on the bottom of the deepest oceans a sort of sea slug which manifested intelligence. Perhaps survival in the conditions required rational powers. Despite their intelligence, these sea slugs have only a very restricted conception of the world by comparison with ours, the explanation for this being the nature of their immediate environment. Nevertheless they have developed sciences which work surprisingly well in these restricted terms. They also have philosophers, called slugists. Some call themselves tough-minded slugists, others confess to being soft-minded slugists.

The tough-minded slugists hold that the restricted terms (or ones pretty like them which may be introduced as their sciences progress) suffice in principle to describe everything without remainder. These tough-minded slugists admit in moments of weakness to a feeling that their theory leaves something out. They resist this feeling and their opponents, the soft-minded slugists, by pointing out—absolutely correctly—that no slugist has ever succeeded in spelling out how this mysterious residue fits into the highly successful view that their sciences have and are developing of how their world works.

Our sea slugs don't exist, but they might. And there might also exist super beings which stand to us as we stand to the sea slugs. We cannot adopt the perspective of these super beings, because we are not them, but the possibility of such a perspective is, I think, an antidote to excessive optimism.[15]

15 I am indebted to Robert Pargetter for a number of comments and, despite his dissent, to §IV of Paul E. Meehl, "The Compleat Autocerebroscopist" in *Mind, Matter, and Method*, ed. Paul Feyerabend and Grover Maxwell (Minneapolis, 1966).

# ARE MENTAL STATES IRREDUCIBLE TO NEUROBIOLOGICAL STATES?

BY **Patricia S. Churchland**

## KNOWING FROM THE INSIDE/HAVING A POINT OF VIEW

For Nagel, there is something special about having an introspective capacity—a capacity to know one's thoughts, feelings, and sensations from the inside, as it were. One's experiences have a certain unmistakable phenomenological character, such as the felt quality of pain or the perceived character of red. One therefore has a subjective point of view. It is the *qualia* or qualitative character of experiences, sensations, feelings, and so forth, to which we have introspective access, and it is this that, in Nagel's view, is not reducible to neural states. These mental states resist reduction because introspective access to them has an essentially different character, yielding essentially different information, than does external access via neuroscience. The argument does exert a powerful attraction, but as stated it is still teasingly vague. In order to see exactly how it works, it is necessary to set out a more precise version.

(A)
(1) The qualia of my sensations are knowable to me by introspection.
(2) The properties of my brain states are *not* knowable to me by introspection.
Therefore:
(3) The qualia of my sensations ≠ the properties of my brain states.

A second argument, complementary to the first, seems also in play:

(B)
(1) The properties of my brain states are knowable by the various external senses.
(2) The qualia of my sensations are *not* knowable by the various external senses.
Therefore:
(3) The qualia of my sensations ≠ the properties of my brain states.

The general form of the argument seems to be this:

(1) $a$ is $F$
(2) $b$ is not $F$
Therefore:
(3) $a \neq b$

Leibniz's law says that $a = b$ if and only if $a$ and $b$ have every property in common. So if $a = b$, then if $a$ is red, $b$ is red, if $a$ weighs ten pounds, then $b$ weighs ten pounds, and so forth. If $a$ is red and $b$ is not, then $a \neq b$. Assuming their premises are true, arguments (A) and (B) appear to establish the nonidentity of brain states and mental states. But are their premises true?

Let us begin with argument (A). There is no quarrel with the first premise (the qualia of my sensations are known-to-me-by-introspection), especially since qualia are defined as those sensory qualities known by introspection, and in any case I have no wish to deny introspective awareness of sensations. In contrast, the second premise (the properties of my brain states are *not* known-to-me-by-introspection) looks decidedly troublesome. Its first problem is that it begs the very question at issue—that is, the question of whether or not mental states are identical to brain states. This is easy to see when we ask what the justification is for thinking that premise true.

The point is this: *if in fact* mental states are identical to brain states, then when I introspect a mental state, I do introspect the brain state with which it is identical. Needless to say, I may not *describe* my mental state as a brain state, but whether I do depends on what information I have about the brain, not upon whether the mental state really is identical to some brain state. The identity can be a fact about the world independently of my knowledge that it is a fact about the world. Similarly, when Jones swallows an aspirin, he thereby swallows acetylsalicylic acid, whether or not he thinks of himself thus; when Oedipus kissed Jocasta, he kissed his mother, whether or not he thought of himself thus. In short, identities may obtain even when we have not discovered that they do. The problem with the second premise is that the only justification for denying that introspective awareness of sensations *could be* introspective awareness of brain states derives from the assumption that mental states are not identical with brain states. And that is precisely what the argument is supposed to prove. Hence the charge of begging the question. (Although I have used (A) as an illustration, the same kind of criticism applies equally to (B).)

Other problems with these arguments are more subtle. One difficulty is best brought out by constructing an argument analogous to (A) or (B) with respect to the character of the properties under discussion and comparing the arguments for adequacy. Consider the following arguments:

(C)
(1) Smith believes Hitler to be a mass murderer.
(2) Smith does not believe Adolf Schicklgruber to be a mass murderer.
Therefore:
(3) Adolf Schicklgruber $\neq$ Adolf Hitler.

As it happens, however, Adolf Schicklgruber = Adolf Hitler, so the argument cannot be right.

Or consider another instance of the general argument form where the property taking the place of *F* is a complex property concerning what John believes or knows:

(D)
(1) Aspirin is *known by John to be a pain reliever.*
(2) Acetylsalicylic acid is *not* known by John to be a pain reliever.
Therefore:
(3) Aspirin $\neq$ acetylsalicylic acid,

And one final example more closely analogous to the arguments at issue:

(E)
(1) Temperature is *directly apprehendable by me as a feature of material objects.*
(2) Mean molecular kinetic energy is *not* directly apprehendable by me as a feature of material objects.
Therefore:
(3) Temperature $\neq$ mean molecular kinetic energy.

These arguments fail because being-recognized-as-a-something or being-believed-to-be-a-something is not a genuine feature of the object itself, but rather is a feature of the object *as apprehended under some description or other* or *as thought about in some manner.* Having a certain mass is a property of the object, but being-thought-by-Smith-to-have-a-certain-mass is not a genuine property of the object. Such queer properties are sometimes called "intentional properties" to reflect their thought-mediated dependency. Notice that in (B) the property is being-knowable-by-the-various-external-senses, and in (A) the property is being-known-by-me-by-introspection. Both are sterling examples of thought-dependent properties.

Now the arguments (C) through (E) are fallacious because they treat intentional properties as though they were genuine properties of the objects, and a mistake of this type is called the *intentional fallacy*. It is evident that the arguments designed to demonstrate the nonidentity of qualia and brain states are analogous to arguments (C) through (E). Consequently, they are equally fallacious, and the nonidentity of mental states and brain states cannot be considered established by arguments such as (A) and (B).[4]

The last difficulty with the arguments is better seen in a slightly different and more compelling version of the argument for the nonidentity of mental states and brain states, which I present and discuss below.

## KNOWING OUR SENSATIONS: JACKSON'S ARGUMENT

The strategy of this second argument once again involves showing that differences between knowing our states via introspection and knowing via nonintrospective means are of such a nature as to constitute grounds for denying the reducibility of psychology to neuroscience. In order to clarify those differences, Frank Jackson (1982) has constructed the following thought-experiment. Suppose that Mary is a neuroscientist who has lived her entire life in a room carefully controlled to display no colors, but only shades of white, gray, and black. Her information about the outside world is transmitted to her by means of a black-and-white television. Suppose further that one way or another she comes to know everything there is to know about the brain and how it works. That is, she comes to understand a completed neuroscience that, among other things, explains the nature of thinking, feeling, and perception, including the perception of colors. (This is all wildly unlikely, of course, but just suppose.)

Now for the argument: despite her knowing everything there is to know about the brain and about the visual system, there would still be something Mary would not know that her cohorts with a more regular childhood would, namely, the nature of the experience of seeing a red tomato. Granted, she knows all about the neural states at work when someone sees a red tomato—after all, she has the utopian neuroscience at hand. What she would not know is *what it is like to see red*—what it is like to have that specific experience. Conclusion: her utopian neuroscience leaves something out. This omission implies that there is something in psychology that is not captured by neuroscience, which in turn implies that psychology cannot be reduced to neuroscience.[5]

More formally and with some simplifications, the argument is this:

(F)
(1) Mary knows everything there is to know about brain states and their properties.
(2) It is not the case that Mary knows everything there is to know about sensations and their properties.
Therefore:
(3) Sensations and their properties ≠ brain states and their properties.

The argument is very interesting, and it gives an unusually clean line to the intuition that mental states are essentially private and have an irreducibly phenomenological character. Nonetheless I am not convinced, and I shall try to explain why.

First, I suspect that the intentional fallacy, which caused problems for arguments (A) and (B), likewise haunts the premises of argument (F). That aside, there are perhaps more revealing criticisms to be made. Paul M. Churchland (1985) and David Lewis (1983) have independently argued that "knows about" is used in different senses in the two premises. As they see it, one sense involves the manipulation of concepts, as when one knows about electromagnetic radiation and can use the concept "electromagnetic radiation" by having been tutored in the theory. The other sense involves a prelinguistic apprehension, as when one knows about electromagnetic radiation by having had one's retina stimulated in the light of day, though one cannot use the expression "electromagnetic radiation." The latter sense may involve innate dispositions to make certain discriminations, for example. If the first premise uses "knows about" in the first sense and the second uses it in the second sense, then the argument founders on the fallacy of equivocation.

The important point is this: if there are two (at least) modes of knowing about the world, then it is entirely possible that what one knows about via one method is identical to what one knows about via a different method. Pregnancy is something one can know about by acquiring the relevant theory from a medical text or by being pregnant. What a childless obstetrician knows about is the very same process as the process known by a pregnant but untutored woman. They both know about pregnancy. By parity of reasoning, the object of Mary's knowledge when she knows the neurophysiology of seeing red might well be the very same state as the state known by her tomato-picking cohort. Just as the obstetrician does not become pregnant by knowing all about pregnancy, so Mary does not have the sensation of redness by knowing all about the neurophysiology of perceiving and experiencing red. Clearly it is no argument in support of nonidentity to say that Mary's knowledge fails to cause the sensation of redness. Whyever suppose that it should?

There is a further reservation about this argument. With the first premise I take no issue, since we are asked to adopt it simply for the sake of argument. The second premise, in contrast, is supposed to be accepted because it is highly credible or perhaps dead obvious. Now although it does have a first blush plausibility, it is the premise on which the argument stands or falls, and closer scrutiny is required.

On a second look, its obviousness dissolves into contentiousness, because the premise asks me to be confident about something that is too far beyond the limits of what I know and understand. How can I assess what Mary will know and understand if she knows *everything* there is to know about the brain? Everything is a lot, and it means, in all likelihood, that Mary has a radically different and deeper understanding of the brain than anything barely conceivable in our wildest flights of fancy.

One might say well, if Mary knew everything about *existing* neuroscience, she would not know what it was like to experience red, and knowing *absolutely* everything will just be more of the same. That is an assumption to which the property dualist is not entitled to help himself. For to know everything about the brain might well be qualitatively different, and it might be to possess a theory that would permit exactly what the premise says it will not. First, utopian neuroscience will probably look as much like existing neuroscience as modern physics looks like Aristotelian physics. So it will not be just more of the same. Second, all one need imagine is that Mary internalizes the theory in the way an engineer has internalized Newtonian physics, and she routinely makes introspective judgments about her own states using its concepts and principles. Like the engineer who does not have to make an effort but "sees" the world in a Newtonian manner, we may consider that Mary "sees" her internal world via the utopian neuroscience. Such a neuroscience might even tell her how to be very efficient at internalizing theories. It is, after all, the premise tells us, a *complete* neuroscience.

Intuitions and imaginability are, notoriously, a function of what we believe, and when we are very ignorant, our intuitions will be correspondingly naive. Gedanken-experiments are the stuff of theoretical science, but when their venue is so surpassing distant from established science that the pivotal intuition is not uncontroversially better than its opposite, then their utility in deciding issues is questionable.

Moreover, intuitions opposite to those funding premise (2) are not only readily available, they can even be fleshed out a bit. How can I be reasonably sure that Mary would not know what a red tomato looks like? Here is a test. Present her with her first red object, and see whether she can recognize it as a red object. Given that she is supposed to know absolutely *everything* there is to know about the nervous system, perhaps she could, by introspective use of her utopian neuroscience, tell that she has, say, a gamma state in her O patterns, which she knows from her utopian neuroscience is identical to having a red sensation. Thus, she might recognize redness on that basis.

The telling point is this: whether or not she can recognize redness is clearly an empirical question, and I do not see how in our ignorance we can confidently insist that she must fail. Short of begging the question, there is no a priori reason why this is impossible. For all I know, she might even be able to produce red in her imagination if she knows what brain states are relevant. One cannot be confident that such an exercise of the imagination must be empirically impossible. To insist that our make-believe Mary could not make introspective judgments using her neuroscience *because* mental qualia are not identical to brain states would, obviously, route the argument round in a circle.

How could an alchemist assess what he could and could not know if he knew everything about substances? How could a monk living in the Middle Ages assess what he could and could not know if he knew everything there was to know about biology? He might insist, for example, that even if you knew everything there was to know about biology, you still would not know the nature of the vital spirit. Well, we still do not have a complete biology, but even so we know more than this hypothetical monk thought we could. We know (a) that there is no such thing as vital spirit, and (b) that DNA is the "secret" of life—it is what all living things on the planet share.[6]

The central point of this reply to Jackson has been that he needs independent evidence for premise (2), since it is palpably not self-evident. It cannot be defended on a priori grounds, since its truth is an empirical question, and it cannot be defended on empirical grounds, since given the data so far, as good a case can be made for the negation of premise (2) as for premise (2) itself. I do not see, therefore, how it can be defended.

CHAPTER IV

# Rationalism vs. Empiricism

# RATIONALISM

**BY Rene Descartes, translated by Donald A. Cress**

## MEDITATION ONE: CONCERNING THOSE THINGS THAT CAN BE CALLED INTO DOUBT

Several years have now passed since I first realized how numerous were the false opinions that in my youth I had taken to be true, and thus how doubtful were all those that I had subsequently built upon them. And thus I realized that once in my life I had to raze everything to the ground and begin again from the original foundations, if I wanted to establish anything firm and lasting in the sciences. But the task seemed enormous, and I was waiting until I reached a point in my life that was so timely that no more suitable time for undertaking these plans of action would come to pass. For this reason, I procrastinated for so long that I would henceforth be at fault, were I to waste the time that remains for carrying out the project by brooding over it. Accordingly, I have today suitably freed my mind of all cares, secured for myself a period of leisurely tranquillity, and am withdrawing into solitude. At last I will apply myself earnestly and unreservedly to this general demolition of my opinions.

Yet to bring this about I will not need to show that all my opinions are false, which is perhaps something I could never accomplish. But reason now persuades me that I should withhold my assent no less carefully from opinions that are not completely certain and indubitable than I would from those that are patently false. For this reason, it will suffice for the rejection of all of these opinions, if I find in each of them some reason for doubt. Nor therefore need I survey each opinion individually, a task that would be endless. Rather, because undermining the foundations will cause whatever has been built upon them to crumble of its own accord, I will attack straightaway those principles which supported everything I once believed.

Surely whatever I had admitted until now as most true I received either from the senses or through the senses. However, I have noticed that the senses are sometimes deceptive; and it is a mark of prudence never to place our complete trust in those who have deceived us even once.

But perhaps, even though the senses do sometimes deceive us when it is a question of very small and distant things, still there are many other matters concerning which one simply cannot doubt, even though they are derived from the very same senses: for example, that I am sitting here next to the fire, wearing my winter dressing gown, that I am holding this sheet of paper in my hands, and the like. But on what grounds could one deny that these hands and this entire body are mine? Unless perhaps I were to liken myself to the insane, whose brains are impaired by such an unrelenting vapor of black bile that they steadfastly insist that they are kings when they are utter paupers, or that they are arrayed in purple robes when they are naked, or that they have heads made of clay, or that they are gourds, or that they are made of glass. But such people are mad, and I would appear no less mad, were I to take their behavior as an example for myself.

This would all be well and good, were I not a man who is accustomed to sleeping at night, and to experiencing in my dreams the very same things, or now and then even less plausible ones, as these insane people do when they are awake. How often does my evening slumber persuade me of such ordinary things as these: that I am here, clothed in my dressing gown, seated next to the fireplace—when in fact I am lying undressed in bed! But right now my eyes are certainly wide awake when I gaze upon this sheet of paper. This head which I am shaking is not heavy with sleep. I extend this hand consciously and deliberately, and I feel it. Such things would not be so distinct for someone who is asleep. As if I did not recall having been deceived on other occasions even by similar thoughts in my dreams! As I consider these matters more carefully, I see so plainly that there are no definitive signs by which to distinguish being awake from being asleep. As a result, I am becoming quite dizzy, and this dizziness nearly convinces me that I am asleep.

Let us assume then, for the sake of argument, that we are dreaming and that such particulars as these are not true: that we are opening our eyes, moving our head, and extending our hands. Perhaps we do not even have such hands, or any such body at all. Nevertheless, it surely must be admitted that the things seen during slumber are, as it were, like painted images, which could only have been produced in the likeness of true things, and that therefore at least these general things—eyes, head, hands, and the whole body—are not imaginary things, but are true and exist. For indeed when painters themselves wish to represent sirens and satyrs by means of especially bizarre forms, they surely cannot assign to them utterly new natures. Rather, they simply fuse together the members of various animals. Or if perhaps they concoct something so utterly novel that nothing like it has ever been seen before (and thus is something utterly fictitious and false), yet certainly at the very least the colors from which they fashion it ought to be true. And by the same token, although even these general things—eyes, head, hands and the like—could be imaginary, still one has to admit that at least certain other things that are even more simple and universal are true. It is from these components, as if from true colors, that all those images of things that are in our thought are fashioned, be they true or false.

This class of things appears to include corporeal nature in general, together with its extension; the shape of extended things; their quantity, that is, their size and number; as well as the place where they exist; the time through which they endure, and the like.

Thus it is not improper to conclude from this that physics, astronomy, medicine, and all the other disciplines that are dependent upon the consideration of composite things are doubtful, and that, on the other hand, arithmetic, geometry, and other such disciplines, which treat of nothing but the simplest and most general things and which are indifferent as to whether these things do or do not in fact exist, contain something certain and indubitable. For whether I am awake or asleep, two plus three make five, and a square does not have more than four sides. It does not seem possible that such obvious truths should be subject to the suspicion of being false.

Be that as it may, there is fixed in my mind a certain opinion of long standing, namely that there exists a God who is able to do anything and by whom I, such as I am, have been created. How do I know that he did not bring it about that there is no earth at all, no heavens, no extended thing, no shape, no size, no place, and yet bringing it about that all these things appear to me to exist precisely as they do now? Moreover, since I judge that others sometimes make mistakes in matters that they believe they know most perfectly, may I not, in like fashion, be deceived every time I add two and three or count the sides of a square, or perform an even simpler operation, if that can be imagined? But perhaps God has not willed that I be deceived in this way, for he is said to be supremely good. Nonetheless, if it were repugnant to his goodness to have created me such that I be deceived all the time, it would also seem foreign to that same goodness to permit me to be deceived even occasionally. But we cannot make this last assertion.

Perhaps there are some who would rather deny so powerful a God than believe that everything else is uncertain. Let us not oppose them; rather, let us grant that everything said here about God is fictitious. Now they suppose that I came to be what I am either by fate, or by chance, or by a connected chain of events, or by some other way. But because being deceived and being mistaken appear to be a certain imperfection, the less powerful they take the author of my origin to be, the more probable it will be that I am so imperfect that I am always deceived. I have nothing to say in response to these arguments. But eventually I am forced to admit that there is nothing among the things I once believed to be true which it is not permissible to doubt—and not out of frivolity or lack of forethought, but for valid and considered reasons. Thus I must be no less careful to withhold assent henceforth even from these beliefs than I would from those that are patently false, if I wish to find anything certain.

But it is not enough simply to have realized these things; I must take steps to keep myself mindful of them. For long-standing opinions keep returning, and, almost against my will, they take advantage of my credulity, as if it were bound over to them by long use and the claims of intimacy. Nor will I ever get out of the habit of assenting to them and believing in them, so long as I take them to be exactly what they are, namely, in some respects doubtful, as has just now been shown, but nevertheless highly probable, so that it is much more consonant with reason to believe them than to deny them. Hence, it seems to me I would do well to deceive myself by turning my will in completely the opposite direction and pretend for a time that these opinions are wholly false and imaginary, until finally, as if with prejudices weighing down each side equally, no bad habit should turn my judgment any further from the correct perception of things. For indeed I know that meanwhile there is no danger or error in following this procedure, and that it is impossible for me to indulge in too much distrust, since I am now concentrating only on knowledge, not on action.

Accordingly, I will suppose not a supremely good God, the source of truth, but rather an evil genius, supremely powerful and clever, who has directed his entire effort at deceiving me. I will regard the heavens, the air, the earth, colors, shapes, sounds, and all external things as nothing but the bedeviling hoaxes of my dreams, with which he lays snares for my credulity. I will regard myself as not having hands, or eyes, or flesh, or blood, or any senses, but as nevertheless falsely believing that I possess all these things. I will remain resolute and steadfast in this meditation, and even if it is not within my power to know anything true, it certainly is within my power to take care resolutely to withhold my assent to what is false, lest this deceiver, however powerful, however clever he may be, have any effect on me. But this undertaking is arduous, and a certain laziness brings me back to my customary way of living. I am not unlike a prisoner who enjoyed an imaginary freedom during his sleep, but, when he later begins to suspect that he is dreaming, fears being awakened and nonchalantly conspires with these pleasant illusions. In just the same way, I fall back of my own accord into my old opinions, and dread being awakened, lest the toilsome wakefulness which follows upon a peaceful rest must be spent thenceforward not in the light but among the inextricable shadows of the difficulties now brought forward.

## MEDITATION TWO: CONCERNING THE NATURE OF THE HUMAN MIND: THAT IT IS BETTER KNOWN THAN THE BODY

Yesterday's meditation has thrown me into such doubts that I can no longer ignore them, yet I fail to see how they are to be resolved. It is as if I had suddenly fallen into a deep whirlpool; I am so tossed about that I can neither touch bottom with my foot, nor swim up to the top. Nevertheless I will work my way up and will once again attempt the same path I entered upon yesterday. I will accomplish this by putting aside everything that admits of the least doubt, as if I had discovered it to be completely false. I will stay on this course until I know something certain, or, if nothing else, until I at least know for certain that nothing is certain. Archimedes sought but one firm and immovable point in order to move the entire earth from one place to another. Just so, great things are also to be hoped for if I succeed in finding just one thing, however slight, that is certain and unshaken.

Therefore I suppose that everything I see is false. I believe that none of what my deceitful memory represents ever existed. I have no senses whatever. Body, shape, extension, movement, and place are all chimeras. What then will be true? Perhaps just the single fact that nothing is certain.

But how do I know there is not something else, over and above all those things that I have just reviewed, concerning which there is not even the slightest occasion for doubt? Is there not some God, or by whatever name I might call him, who instills these very thoughts in me? But why would I think that, since I myself could perhaps be the author of these thoughts? Am I not then at least something? But I have already denied that I have any senses and any body. Still I hesitate; for what follows from this? Am I so tied to a body and to the senses that I cannot exist without them? But I have persuaded myself that there is absolutely nothing in the world: no sky, no earth, no minds, no bodies. Is it then the case that I too do not exist? But doubtless I did exist, if I persuaded myself of something. But there is some deceiver or other who is supremely powerful and supremely sly and who is always deliberately deceiving me. Then too there is no doubt that I exist, if he is deceiving me. And let him do his best at deception, he will never bring it about that I am nothing so long as I shall think that I am something. Thus, after everything has been most carefully weighed, it must finally be established that this pronouncement "I am, I exist" is necessarily true every time I utter it or conceive it in my mind.

But I do not yet understand sufficiently what I am—I, who now necessarily exist. And so from this point on, I must be careful lest I unwittingly mistake something else for myself, and thus err in that very item of knowledge that I claim to be the most certain and evident of all. Thus, I will meditate once more on what I once believed myself to be, prior to embarking upon these thoughts. For this reason, then, I will set aside whatever can be weakened even to the slightest degree by the arguments brought forward, so that eventually all that remains is precisely nothing but what is certain and unshaken.

What then did I use to think I was? A man, of course. But what is a man? Might I not say a "rational animal"? No, because then I would have to inquire what "animal" and "rational" mean. And thus from one question I would slide into many more difficult ones. Nor do I now have enough free time that I want to waste it on subtleties of this sort.

Instead, permit me to focus here on what came spontaneously and naturally into my thinking whenever I pondered what I was. Now it occurred to me first that I had a face, hands, arms, and this entire mechanism of bodily members: the very same as are discerned in a corpse, and which I referred to by the name "body." It next occurred to me that I took in food, that I walked about, and that I sensed and thought various things; these actions I used to attribute to the soul. But as to what this soul might be, I either did not think about it or else I imagined it a rarified I-know-not-what, like a wind, or a fire, or ether, which had been infused into my coarser parts. But as to the body I was not in any doubt. On the contrary, I was under the impression that I knew its nature distinctly. Were I perhaps tempted to describe this nature such as I conceived it in my mind, I would have described it thus: by "body," I understand all that is capable of being bounded by some shape, of being enclosed in a place, and of filling up a space in such a way as to exclude any other body from it; of being perceived by touch, sight, hearing, taste, or smell; of being moved in several ways, not, of course, by itself, but by whatever else impinges upon it. For it was my view that the power of self-motion, and likewise of sensing or of thinking, in no way belonged to the nature of the body. Indeed I used rather to marvel that such faculties were to be found in certain bodies.

But now what am I, when I suppose that there is some supremely powerful and, if I may be permitted to say so, malicious deceiver who deliberately tries to fool me in any way he can? Can I not affirm that I possess at least a small measure of all those things which I have already said belong to the nature of the body? I focus my attention on them, I think about them, I review them again, but nothing comes to mind. I am tired of repeating this to no purpose. But what about those things I ascribed to the soul? What about being nourished or moving about? Since I now do not have a body, these are surely nothing but fictions. What about sensing? Surely this too does not take place without a body; and I seemed to have sensed in my dreams many things that I later realized I did not sense. What about thinking? Here I make my discovery: thought exists; it alone cannot be separated from me. I am; I exist—this is certain. But for how long? For as long as I am thinking; for perhaps it could also come to pass that if I were to cease all thinking I would then utterly cease to exist. At this time I admit nothing that is not necessarily true. I am therefore precisely nothing but a thinking thing; that is, a mind, or intellect, or understanding, or reason—words of whose meanings I was previously ignorant. Yet I am a true thing and am truly existing; but what kind of thing? I have said it already: a thinking thing.

What else am I? I will set my imagination in motion. I am not that concatenation of members we call the human body. Neither am I even some subtle air infused into these members, nor a wind, nor a fire, nor a vapor, nor a breath, nor anything I devise for myself. For I have supposed these things to be nothing. The assumption still stands; yet nevertheless I am something. But is it perhaps the case that these very things which I take to be nothing, because they are unknown to me, nevertheless are in fact no different from that "me" that I know? This I do not know, and I will not quarrel about it now. I can make a judgment only about things that are known to me. I know that I exist; I ask now who is this "I" whom I know? Most certainly, in the strict sense the knowledge of this "I" does not depend upon things of whose existence I do not yet have knowledge. Therefore it is not dependent upon any of those things that I simulate in my imagination. But this word "simulate" warns me of my error. For I would indeed be simulating were I to "imagine" that I was something, because imagining is merely the contemplating of the shape or image of a corporeal thing. But I now know with certainty that I am and also that all these images—and, generally, everything belonging to the nature of the body—could turn out to be nothing but dreams. Once I have realized this, I would seem to be speaking no less foolishly were I to say: "I will use my imagination in order to recognize more distinctly who I am," than were I to say: "Now I surely am awake, and I see something true; but since I do not yet see it clearly enough, I will deliberately fall asleep so that my dreams might represent it to me more truly and more clearly." Thus I realize that none of what I can grasp by means of the imagination pertains to this knowledge that I have of myself. Moreover, I realize that I must be most diligent about withdrawing my mind from these things so that it can perceive its nature as distinctly as possible.

But what then am I? A thing that thinks. What is that? A thing that doubts, understands, affirms, denies, wills, refuses, and that also imagines and senses.

Indeed it is no small matter if all of these things belong to me. But why should they not belong to me? Is it not the very same "I" who now doubts almost everything, who nevertheless understands something, who affirms that this one thing is true, who denies other things, who desires to know more, who wishes not to be deceived, who imagines many things even against my will, who also notices many things which appear to come from the senses?

What is there in all of this that is not every bit as true as the fact that I exist—even if I am always asleep or even if my creator makes every effort to mislead me? Which of these things is distinct from my thought? Which of them can be said to be separate from myself? For it is so obvious that it is I who doubt, I who understand, and I who will, that there is nothing by which it could be explained more clearly. But indeed it is also the same "I" who imagines; for although perhaps, as I supposed before, absolutely nothing that I imagined is true, still the very power of imagining really does exist, and constitutes a part of my thought. Finally, it is this same "I" who senses or who is cognizant of bodily things as if through the senses. For example, I now see a light, I hear a noise, I feel heat. These things are false, since I am asleep. Yet I certainly do seem to see, hear, and feel warmth. This cannot be false. Properly speaking, this is what in me is called "sensing." But this, precisely so taken, is nothing other than thinking.

From these considerations I am beginning to know a little better what I am. But it still seems (and I cannot resist believing) that corporeal things—whose images are formed by thought, and which the senses themselves examine—are much more distinctly known than this mysterious "I" which does not fall within the imagination. And yet it would be strange indeed were I to grasp the very things I consider to be doubtful, unknown, and foreign to me more distinctly than what is true, what is known—than, in short, myself. But I see what is happening: my mind loves to wander and does not yet permit itself to be restricted within the confines of truth. So be it then; let us just this once allow it completely free rein, so that, a little while later, when the time has come to pull in the reins, the mind may more readily permit itself to be controlled.

Let us consider those things which are commonly believed to be the most distinctly grasped of all: namely the bodies we touch and see. Not bodies in general, mind you, for these general perceptions are apt to be somewhat more confused, but one body in particular. Let us take, for instance, this piece of wax. It has been taken quite recently from the honeycomb; it has not yet lost all the honey flavor. It retains some of the scent of the flowers from which it was collected. Its color, shape, and size are manifest. It is hard and cold; it is easy to touch. If you rap on it with your knuckle it will emit a sound. In short, everything is present in it that appears needed to enable a body to be known as distinctly as possible. But notice that, as I am speaking, I am bringing it close to the fire. The remaining traces of the honey flavor are disappearing; the scent is vanishing; the color is changing; the original shape is disappearing. Its size is increasing; it is becoming liquid and hot; you can hardly touch it. And now, when you rap on it, it no longer emits any sound. Does the same wax still remain? I must confess that it does; no one denies it; no one thinks otherwise. So what was there in the wax that was so distinctly grasped? Certainly none of the aspects that I reached by means of the senses. For whatever came under the senses of taste, smell, sight, touch or hearing has now changed; and yet the wax remains.

Perhaps the wax was what I now think it is: namely that the wax itself never really was the sweetness of the honey, nor the fragrance of the flowers, nor the whiteness, nor the shape, nor the sound, but instead was a body that a short time ago manifested itself to me in these ways, and now does so in other ways. But just what precisely is this thing that I thus imagine? Let us focus our attention on this and see what remains after we have removed everything that does not belong to the wax: only that it is something extended, flexible, and mutable. But what is it to be flexible and mutable? Is it what my imagination shows it to be: namely, that this piece of wax can change from a round to a square shape, or from the latter to a triangular shape? Not at all; for I grasp that the wax is capable of innumerable changes of this sort, even though I am incapable of running through these innumerable changes by using my imagination. Therefore this insight is not achieved by the faculty of imagination. What is it to be extended? Is this thing's extension also unknown? For it becomes greater in wax that is beginning to melt, greater in boiling wax, and greater still as the heat is increased. And I would not judge correctly what the wax is if I did not believe that it takes on an even greater variety of dimensions than I could ever grasp with the imagination. It remains then for me to concede that I do not grasp what this wax is through the imagination; rather, I perceive it through the mind alone. The point I am making refers to this particular piece of wax, for the case of wax in general is clearer still. But what is this piece of wax which is perceived only by the mind? Surely it is the same piece of wax that I see, touch, and imagine; in short it is the same piece of wax I took it to be from the very beginning. But I need to realize that the perception of the wax is neither a seeing, nor a touching, nor an imagining. Nor has it ever been, even though it previously seemed so; rather it is an inspection on the part of the mind alone. This inspection can be imperfect and confused, as it was before, or clear and distinct, as it is now, depending on how closely I pay attention to the things in which the piece of wax consists.

But meanwhile I marvel at how prone my mind is to errors. For although I am considering these things within myself silently and without words, nevertheless I seize upon words themselves and I am nearly deceived by the ways in which people commonly speak. For we say that we see the wax itself, if it is present, and not that we judge it to be present from its color or shape. Whence I might conclude straightaway that I know the wax through the vision had by the eye, and not through an inspection on the part of the mind alone. But then were I perchance to look out my window and observe men crossing the square, I would ordinarily say I see the men themselves just as I say I see the wax. But what do I see aside from hats and clothes, which could conceal automata? Yet I judge them to be men. Thus what I thought I had seen with my eyes, I actually grasped solely with the faculty of judgment, which is in my mind.

But a person who seeks to know more than the common crowd ought to be ashamed of himself for looking for doubt in common ways of speaking. Let us then go forward and inquire when it was that I perceived more perfectly and evidently what the piece of wax was. Was it when I first saw it and believed I knew it by the external sense, or at least by the so-called common sense, that is, the power of imagination? Or do I have more perfect knowledge now, when I have diligently examined both what the wax is and how it is known? Surely it is absurd to be in doubt about this matter. For what was there in my initial perception that was distinct? What was there that any animal seemed incapable of possessing? But indeed when I distinguish the wax from its external forms, as if stripping it of its clothing, and look at the wax in its nakedness, then, even though there can be still an error in my judgment, nevertheless I cannot perceive it thus without a human mind.

But what am I to say about this mind, that is, about myself? For as yet I admit nothing else to be in me over and above the mind. What, I ask, am I who seem to perceive this wax so distinctly? Do I not know myself not only much more truly and with greater certainty, but also much more distinctly and evidently? For if I judge that the wax exists from the fact that I see it, certainly from this same fact that I see the wax it follows much more evidently that I myself exist. For it could happen that what I see is not truly wax. It could happen that I have no eyes with which to see anything. But it is utterly impossible that, while I see or think I see (I do not now distinguish these two), I who think am not something. Likewise, if I judge that the wax exists from the fact that I touch it, the same outcome will again obtain, namely that I exist. If I judge that the wax exists from the fact that I imagine it, or for any other reason, plainly the same thing follows. But what I note regarding the wax applies to everything else that is external to me. Furthermore, if my perception of the wax seemed more distinct after it became known to me not only on account of sight or touch, but on account of many reasons, one has to admit how much more distinctly I am now known to myself. For there is not a single consideration that can aid in my perception of the wax or of any other body that fails to make even more manifest the nature of my mind. But there are still so many other things in the mind itself on the basis of which my knowledge of it can be rendered more distinct that it hardly seems worth enumerating those things which emanate to it from the body.

But lo and behold, I have returned on my own to where I wanted to be. For since I now know that even bodies are not, properly speaking, perceived by the senses or by the faculty of imagination, but by the intellect alone, and that they are not perceived through their being touched or seen, but only through their being understood, I manifestly know that nothing can be perceived more easily and more evidently than my own mind. But since the tendency to hang on to long-held beliefs cannot be put aside so quickly, I want to stop here, so that by the length of my meditation this new knowledge may be more deeply impressed upon my memory.

# EMPIRICISM

BY **John Locke**

## INTRODUCTION

### 1. An Inquiry into the Understanding pleasant and useful.

Since it is the UNDERSTANDING that sets man above the rest of sensible beings, and gives him all the advantage and dominion which he has over them; it is certainly a subject, even for its nobleness, worth our labour to inquire into. The understanding, like the eye, whilst it makes us see and perceive all other things, takes no notice of itself; and it requires and art and pains to set it at a distance and make it its own object. But whatever be the difficulties that lie in the way of this inquiry; whatever it be that keeps us so much in the dark to ourselves; sure I am that all the light we can let in upon our minds, all the acquaintance we can make with our own understandings, will not only be very pleasant, but bring us great advantage, in directing our thoughts in the search of other things.

### 2. Design.

This, therefore, being my purpose—to inquire into the original, certainty, and extent of HUMAN KNOWLEDGE, together with the grounds and degrees of BELIEF, OPINION, and ASSENT;—I shall not at present meddle with the physical consideration of the mind; or trouble myself to examine wherein its essence consists; or by what motions of our spirits or alterations of our bodies we come to have any SENSATION by our organs, or any IDEAS in our understandings; and whether those ideas do in their formation, any or all of them, depend on matter or not. These are speculations which, however curious and entertaining, I shall decline, as lying out of my way in the design I am now upon. It shall suffice to my present purpose, to consider the discerning faculties of a man, as they are employed about the objects which they have to do with. And I shall imagine I have not wholly misemployed myself in the thoughts I shall have on this occasion, if, in this historical, plain method, I can give any account of the ways whereby our understandings come to attain those notions of things we have; and can set down any measures of the certainty of our knowledge; or the grounds of those persuasions which are to be found amongst men, so various, different, and wholly contradictory; and yet asserted somewhere or other with such assurance and confidence, that he that shall take a view of the opinions of mankind, observe their opposition, and at the same time consider the fondness and devotion wherewith they are embraced, the resolution and eagerness wherewith they are maintained, may perhaps have reason to suspect, that either there is no such thing as truth at all, or that mankind hath no sufficient means to attain a certain knowledge of it.

### 3. Method.

It is therefore worth while to search out the bounds between opinion and knowledge; and examine by what measures, in things whereof we have no certain knowledge, we ought to regulate our assent and moderate our persuasion. In order whereunto I shall pursue this following method:—First, I shall inquire into the original of those ideas, notions, or whatever else you please to call them, which a man observes, and is conscious to himself he has in his mind; and the ways whereby the understanding comes to be furnished with them.

Secondly, I shall endeavour to show what knowledge the understanding hath by those ideas; and the certainty, evidence, and extent of it.

John Locke, An Essay Concerning Human Understanding.

Thirdly, I shall make some inquiry into the nature and grounds of FAITH or OPINION: whereby I mean that assent which we give to any proposition as true, of whose truth yet we have no certain knowledge. And here we shall have occasion to examine the reasons and degrees of ASSENT.

### 4. Useful to know the Extent of our Comprehension.

If by this inquiry into the nature of the understanding, I can discover the powers thereof; how far they reach; to what things they are in any degree proportionate; and where they fail us, I suppose it may be of use to prevail with the busy mind of man to be more cautious in meddling with things exceeding its comprehension; to stop when it is at the utmost extent of its tether; and to sit down in a quiet ignorance of those things which, upon examination, are found to be beyond the reach of our capacities. We should not then perhaps be so forward, out of an affectation of an universal knowledge, to raise questions, and perplex ourselves and others with disputes about things to which our understandings are not suited; and of which we cannot frame in our minds any clear or distinct perceptions, or whereof (as it has perhaps too often happened) we have not any notions at all. If we can find out how far the understanding can extend its view; how far it has faculties to attain certainty; and in what cases it can only judge and guess, we may learn to content ourselves with what is attainable by us in this state.

### 5. Our Capacity suited to our State and Concerns.

For though the comprehension of our understandings comes exceeding short of the vast extent of things, yet we shall have cause enough to magnify the bountiful Author of our being, for that proportion and degree of knowledge he has bestowed on us, so far above all the rest of the inhabitants of this our mansion. Men have reason to be well satisfied with what God hath thought fit for them, since he hath given them (as St. Peter says) [words in Greek], whatsoever is necessary for the conveniences of life and information of virtue; and has put within the reach of their discovery, the comfortable provision for this life, and the way that leads to a better. How short soever their knowledge may come of an universal or perfect comprehension of whatsoever is, it yet secures their great concernments, that they have light enough to lead them to the knowledge of their Maker, and the sight of their own duties. Men may find matter sufficient to busy their heads, and employ their hands with variety, delight, and satisfaction, if they will not boldly quarrel with their own constitution, and throw away the blessings their hands are filled with, because they are not big enough to grasp everything. We shall not have much reason to complain of the narrowness of our minds, if we will but employ them about what may be of use to us; for of that they are very capable. And it will be an unpardonable, as well as childish peevishness, if we undervalue the advantages of our knowledge, and neglect to improve it to the ends for which it was given us, because there are some things that are set out of the reach of it. It will be no excuse to an idle and untoward servant, who would not attend his business by candle light, to plead that he had not broad sunshine. The Candle that is set up in us shines bright enough for all our purposes. The discoveries we can make with this ought to satisfy us; and we shall then use our understandings right, when we entertain all objects in that way and proportion that they are suited to our faculties, and upon those grounds they are capable of being proposed to us; and not peremptorily or intemperately require demonstration, and demand certainty, where probability only is to be had, and which is sufficient to govern all our concernments. If we will disbelieve everything, because we cannot certainly know all things, we shall do much what as wisely as he who would not use his legs, but sit still and perish, because he had no wings to fly.

### 6. Knowledge of our Capacity a Cure of Scepticism and Idleness.

When we know our own strength, we shall the better know what to undertake with hopes of success; and when we have well surveyed the POWERS of our own minds, and made some estimate what we may expect from them, we shall not be inclined either to sit still, and not set our thoughts on work at all, in despair of knowing anything; nor on the other side, question everything, and disclaim all knowledge, because some things are not to be understood. It is of great use to the sailor to know the length of his line, though he cannot with it fathom all the depths of the ocean. It is well he knows that it is long enough to reach the bottom, at such places as are necessary to direct his voyage, and caution him against running upon shoals that may ruin him. Our business here is not to know all things, but those which concern our conduct. If we can find out those measures, whereby a rational creature, put in that state in which man is in this world, may and ought to govern his opinions, and actions depending thereon, we need not to be troubled that some other things escape our knowledge.

### 8. What Idea stands for.

Thus much I thought necessary to say concerning the occasion of this inquiry into human Understanding. But, before I proceed on to what I have thought on this subject, I must here in the entrance beg pardon of my reader for the frequent use of the word IDEA, which he will find in the following treatise. It being that term which, I think, serves best to stand for whatsoever is the OBJECT of the understanding when a man thinks, I have used it to express whatever is meant by PHANTASM, NOTION, SPECIES, or WHATEVER IT IS WHICH THE MIND CAN BE EMPLOYED ABOUT IN THINKING; and I could not avoid frequently using it. I presume it will be easily granted me, that there are such IDEAS in men's minds: every one is conscious of them in himself; and men's words and actions will satisfy him that they are in others.

Our first inquiry then shall be,—how they come into the mind.

## BOOK I—NEITHER PRINCIPLES NOR IDEAS ARE INNATE

## CHAPTER I.—NO INNATE SPECULATIVE PRINCIPLES

### 1. The way shown how we come by any Knowledge, sufficient to prove it not innate.

It is an established opinion amongst some men, that there are in the understanding certain INNATE PRINCIPLES; some primary notions, KOIVAIVVOIAI, characters, as it were stamped upon the mind of man; which the soul receives in its very first being, and brings into the world with it. It would be sufficient to convince unprejudiced readers of the falseness of this supposition, if I should only show (as I hope I shall in the following parts of this Discourse) how men, barely by the use of their natural faculties may attain to all the knowledge they have, without the help of any innate impressions; and may arrive at certainty, without any such original notions or principles. For I imagine any one will easily grant that it would be impertinent to suppose the ideas of colours innate in a creature to whom God hath given sight, and a power to receive them by the eyes from external objects: and no less unreasonable would it be to attribute several truths to the impressions of nature, and innate characters, when we may observe in ourselves faculties fit to attain as easy and certain knowledge of them as if they were originally imprinted on the mind.

But because a man is not permitted without censure to follow his own thoughts in the search of truth, when they lead him ever so little out of the common road, I shall set down the reasons that made me doubt of the truth of that opinion, as an excuse for my mistake, if I be in one; which I leave to be considered by those who, with me, dispose themselves to embrace truth wherever they find it.

### 2. General Assent the great Argument.

There is nothing more commonly taken for granted than that there are certain PRINCIPLES, both SPECULATIVE and PRACTICAL, ( for they speak of both), universally agreed upon by all mankind: which therefore, they argue, must needs be the constant impressions which the souls of men receive in their first beings, and which they bring into the world with them, as necessarily and really as they do any of their inherent faculties.

### 3. Universal Consent proves nothing innate.

This argument, drawn from universal consent, has this misfortune in it, that if it were true in matter of fact, that there were certain truths wherein all mankind agreed, it would not prove them innate, if there can be any other way shown how men may come to that universal agreement, in the things they do consent in, which I presume may be done.

### 4. "What is is," and "It is possible for the same Thing to be and not to be," not universally assented to.

But, which is worse, this argument of universal consent, which is made use of to prove innate principles, seems to me a demonstration that there are none such: because there are none to which all mankind give an universal assent. I shall begin with the speculative, and instance in those magnified principles of demonstration, "Whatsoever is, is," and "It is impossible for the same thing to be and not to be"; which, of all others, I think have the most allowed title to innate. These have so settled a reputation of maxims universally received, that it will no doubt be thought strange if any one should seem to question it. But yet I take liberty to say, that these propositions are so far from having an universal assent, that there are a great part of mankind to whom they are not so much as known.

### 5. Not on Mind naturally imprinted, because not known to Children, Idiots, &c.

For, first, it is evident, that all children and idiots have not the least apprehension or thought of them. And the want of that is enough to destroy that universal assent which must needs be the necessary concomitant of all innate truths: it seeming to me near a contradiction to say, that there are truths imprinted on the soul, which it perceives or understands not: imprinting, if it signify anything, being nothing else but the making certain truths to be perceived. For to imprint anything on the mind without the mind's perceiving it, seems to me hardly intelligible. If therefore children and idiots have souls, have minds, with those impressions upon them, THEY must unavoidably perceive them, and necessarily know and assent to these truths; which since they do not, it is evident that there are no such impressions. For if they are not notions naturally imprinted, how can they be innate? and if they are notions imprinted, how can they be unknown? To say a notion is imprinted on the mind, and yet at the same time to say, that the mind is ignorant of it, and never yet took notice of it, is to make this impression nothing. No proposition can be said to be in the mind which it never yet knew, which it was never yet conscious of. For if any one may, then, by the same reason, all propositions that are true, and the mind is capable ever of assenting to, may be said to be in the mind, and to be imprinted: since, if any one can be said to be in the mind, which it never yet knew, it must be only because it is capable of knowing it; and so the mind is of all truths it ever shall know. Nay, thus truths may be imprinted on the mind which it never did, nor ever shall know; for a man may live long, and die at last in ignorance of many truths which his mind was capable of knowing, and that with certainty. So that if the capacity of knowing be the natural impression contended for, all the truths a man ever comes to know will, by this account, be every one of them innate; and this great point will amount to no more, but only to a very improper way of speaking; which, whilst it pretends to assert the contrary, says nothing different from those who deny innate principles. For nobody, I think, ever denied that the mind was capable of knowing several truths. The capacity, they say, is innate; the knowledge acquired. But then to what end such contest for certain innate maxims? If truths can be imprinted on the understanding without being perceived, I can see no difference there can be between any truths the mind is CAPABLE of knowing in respect of their original: they must all be innate or all adventitious: in vain shall a man go about to distinguish them. He therefore that talks of innate notions in the understanding, cannot (if he intend thereby any distinct sort of truths) mean such truths to be in the understanding as it never perceived, and is yet wholly ignorant of. For if these words "to be in the understanding" have any propriety, they signify to be understood. So that to be in the understanding, and not to be understood; to be in the mind and never to be perceived, is all one as to say anything is and is not in the mind or understanding. If therefore these two propositions, "Whatsoever is, is," and "It is impossible for the same thing to be and not to be," are by nature imprinted, children cannot be ignorant of them: infants, and all that have souls, must necessarily have them in their understandings, know the truth of them, and assent to it.

### 6. That men know them when they come to the Use of Reason answered.

To avoid this, it is usually answered, that all men know and assent to them, WHEN THEY COME TO THE USE OF REASON; and this is enough to prove them innate. I answer:

### 7. Doubtful expressions,

that have scarce any signification, go for clear reasons to those who, being prepossessed, take not the pains to examine even what they themselves say. For, to apply this answer with any tolerable sense to our present purpose, it must signify one of these two things: either that as soon as men come to the use of reason these supposed native inscriptions come to be known and observed by them; or else, that the use and exercise of men's reason, assists them in the discovery of these principles, and certainly makes them known to them.

**8. If Reason discovered them, that would not prove them innate.**

If they mean, that by the use of reason men may discover these principles, and that this is sufficient to prove them innate; their way of arguing will stand thus, viz. that whatever truths reason can certainly discover to us, and make us firmly assent to, those are all naturally imprinted on the mind; since that universal assent, which is made the mark of them, amounts to no more but this,—that by the use of reason we are capable to come to a certain knowledge of and assent to them; and, by this means, there will be no difference between the maxims of the mathematicians, and theorems they deduce from them: all must be equally allowed innate; they being all discoveries made by the use of reason, and truths that a rational creature may certainly come to know, if he apply his thoughts rightly that way.

**12. The coming of the Use of Reason not the Time we come to know these Maxims.**

If by knowing and assenting to them "when we come to the use of reason," be meant, that this is the time when they come to be taken notice of by the mind; and that as soon as children come to the use of reason, they come also to know and assent to these maxims; this also is false and frivolous. First, it is false; because it is evident these maxims are not in the mind so early as the use of reason; and therefore the coming to the use of reason is falsely assigned as the time of their discovery. How many instances of the use of reason may we observe in children, a long time before they have any knowledge of this maxim, "That it is impossible for the same thing to be and not to be?" And a great part of illiterate people and savages pass many years, even of their rational age, without ever thinking on this and the like general propositions. I grant, men come not to the knowledge of these general and more abstract truths, which are thought innate, till they come to the use of reason; and I add, nor then neither. Which is so, because, till after they come to the use of reason, those general abstract ideas are not framed in the mind, about which those general maxims are, which are mistaken for innate principles, but are indeed discoveries made and verities introduced and brought into the mind by the same way, and discovered by the same steps, as several other propositions, which nobody was ever so extravagant as to suppose innate. This I hope to make plain in the sequel of this Discourse. I allow therefore, a necessity that men should come to the use of reason before they get the knowledge of those general truths; but deny that men's coming to the use of reason is the time of their discovery.

**13. By this they are not distinguished from other knowable Truths.**

In the mean time it is observable, that this saying that men know and assent to these maxims "when they come to the use of reason," amounts in reality of fact to no more but this,—that they are never known nor taken notice of before the use of reason, but may possibly be assented to some time after, during a man's life; but when is uncertain. And so may all other knowable truths, as well as these which therefore have no advantage nor distinction from other by this note of being known when we come to the use of reason; nor are thereby proved to be innate, but quite the contrary.

**14. If coming to the Use of Reason were the Time of their Discovery, it would not prove them innate.**

But, secondly, were it true that the precise time of their being known and assented to were, when men come to the use of reason; neither would that prove them innate. This way of arguing is as frivolous as the supposition itself is false. For, by what kind of logic will it appear that any notion is originally by nature imprinted in the mind in its first constitution, because it comes first to be observed and assented to when a faculty of the mind, which has quite a distinct province, begins to exert itself? And therefore the coming to the use of speech, if it were supposed the time that these maxims are first assented to, (which it may be with as much truth as the time when men come to the use of reason,) would be as good a proof that they were innate, as to say they are innate because men assent to them when they come to the use of reason. I agree then with these men of innate principles, that there is no knowledge of these general and self-evident maxims in the mind, till it comes to the exercise of reason: but I deny that the coming to the use of reason is the precise time when they are first taken notice of; and if that were the precise time, I deny that it would prove them innate. All that can with any truth be meant by this proposition, that men 'assent to them when they come to the use of reason', is no more but this,—that the making of general abstract ideas, and the understanding of general names, being a concomitant of the rational faculty, and growing up with it, children commonly get not those general ideas, nor learn the names that stand for them, till, having for a good while exercised their reason about familiar and more particular ideas, they are, by their ordinary discourse and actions with others, acknowledged to be capable of rational conversation. If assenting to these maxims, when men come to the use of reason, can be true in any other sense, I desire it may be shown; or at least, how in this, or any other sense, it proves them innate.

### 15. The Steps by which the Mind attains several Truths.

The senses at first let in PARTICULAR ideas, and furnish the yet empty cabinet, and the mind by degrees growing familiar with some of them, they are lodged in the memory, and names got to them. Afterwards, the mind proceeding further, abstracts them, and by degrees learns the use of general names. In this manner the mind comes to be furnished with ideas and language, the MATERIALS about which to exercise its discursive faculty. And the use of reason becomes daily more visible, as these materials that give it employment increase. But though the having of general ideas and the use of general words and reason usually grow together, yet I see not how this any way proves them innate. The knowledge of some truths, I confess, is very early in the mind; but in a way that shows them not to be innate. For, if we will observe, we shall find it still to be about ideas, not innate, but acquired; it being about those first which are imprinted by external things, with which infants have earliest to do, which make the most frequent impressions on their senses. In ideas thus got, the mind discovers that some agree and others differ, probably as soon as it has any use of memory; as soon as it is able to retain and perceive distinct ideas. But whether it be then or no, this is certain, it does so long before it has the use of words; or comes to that which we commonly call "the use of reason." For a child knows as certainly before it can speak the difference between the ideas of sweet and bitter (i.e. that sweet is not bitter), as it knows afterwards (when it comes to speak) that wormwood and sugarplums are not the same thing.

## CHAPTER II.—NO INNATE PRACTICAL: PRINCIPLES

### 1. No moral Principles so clear and so generally received as the forementioned speculative Maxims.

If those speculative Maxims, whereof we discoursed in the foregoing chapter, have not an actual universal assent from all mankind, as we there proved, it is much more visible concerning PRACTICAL Principles, that they come short of an universal reception: and I think it will be hard to instance any one moral rule which can pretend to so general and ready an assent as, "What is, is"; or to be so manifest a truth as this, that "It is impossible for the same thing to be and not to be." Whereby it is evident that they are further removed from a title to be innate; and the doubt of their being native impressions on the mind is stronger against those moral principles than the other. Not that it brings their truth at all in question. They are equally true, though not equally evident. Those speculative maxims carry their own evidence with them: but moral principles require reasoning and discourse, and some exercise of the mind, to discover the certainty of their truth. They lie not open as natural characters engraved on the mind; which, if any such were, they must needs be visible by themselves, and by their own light be certain and known to everybody. But this is no derogation to their truth and certainty; no more than it is to the truth or certainty of the three angles of a triangle being equal to two right ones because it is not so evident as "the whole is bigger than a part," nor so apt to be assented to at first hearing. It may suffice that these moral rules are capable of demonstration: and therefore it is our own faults if we come not to a certain knowledge of them. But the ignorance wherein many men are of them, and the slowness of assent wherewith others receive them, are manifest proofs that they are not innate, and such as offer themselves to their view without searching.

### 2. Faith and Justice not owned as Principles by all Men.

Whether there be any such moral principles, wherein all men do agree, I appeal to any who have been but moderately conversant in the history of mankind, and looked abroad beyond the smoke of their own chimneys. Where is that practical truth that is universally received, without doubt or question, as it must be if innate? JUSTICE, and keeping of contracts, is that which most men seem to agree in. This is a principle which is thought to extend itself to the dens of thieves, and the confederacies of the greatest villains; and they who have gone furthest towards the putting off of humanity itself, keep faith and rules of justice one with another. I grant that outlaws themselves do this one amongst another: but it is without receiving these as the innate laws of nature. They practise them as rules of convenience within their own communities: but it is impossible to conceive that he embraces justice as a practical principle who acts fairly with his fellow-highwayman, and at the same time plunders or kills the next honest man he meets with. Justice and truth are the common ties of society, and therefore even outlaws and robbers, who break with all the world besides, must keep faith and rules of equity amongst themselves; or else they cannot hold together. But will any one say, that those that live by fraud or rapine have innate principles of truth and justice which they allow and assent to?

### 4. Moral Rules need a Proof, ERGO not innate.

Another reason that makes me doubt of any innate practical principles is, that I think THERE CANNOT ANY ONE MORAL RULE BE PROPOSED WHEREOF A MAN MAY NOT JUSTLY DEMAND A REASON: which would be perfectly ridiculous and absurd if they were innate; or so much as self-evident, which every innate principle must needs be, and not need any proof to ascertain its truth, nor want any reason to gain it approbation. He would be thought void of common sense who asked on the one side, or on the other side went to give a reason WHY "it is impossible for the same thing to be and not to be." It carries its own light and evidence with it, and needs no other proof: he that understands the terms assents to it for its own sake or else nothing will ever be able to prevail with him to do it. But should that most unshaken rule of morality and foundation of all social virtue, "That should do as he would be done unto," be proposed to one who never heard of it before, but yet is of capacity to understand its meaning; might he not without any absurdity ask a reason why? And were not he that proposed it bound to make out the truth and reasonableness of it to him? Which plainly shows it not to be innate; for if it were it could neither want nor receive any proof; but must needs (at least as soon as heard and understood) be received and assented to as an unquestionable truth, which a man can by no means doubt of. So that the truth of all these moral rules plainly depends upon some other antecedent to them, and from which they must be DEDUCED; which could not be if either they were innate or so much as self-evident.

## BOOK II—OF IDEAS
## CHAPTER I.—OF IDEAS IN GENERAL, AND THEIR ORIGINAL

### 1. Idea is the Object of Thinking.

Every man being conscious to himself that he thinks; and that which his mind is applied about whilst thinking being the IDEAS that are there, it is past doubt that men have in their minds several ideas,—such as are those expressed by the words whiteness, hardness, sweetness, thinking, motion, man, elephant, army, drunkenness, and others: it is in the first place then to be inquired, HOW HE COMES BY THEM?

I know it is a received doctrine, that men have native ideas, and original characters, stamped upon their minds in their very first being. This opinion I have at large examined already; and, I suppose what I have said in the foregoing Book will be much more easily admitted, when I have shown whence the understanding may get all the ideas it has; and by what ways and degrees they may come into the mind;—for which I shall appeal to every one's own observation and experience.

### 2. All Ideas come from Sensation or Reflection.

Let us then suppose the mind to be, as we say, white paper, void of all characters, without any ideas:—How comes it to be furnished? Whence comes it by that vast store which the busy and boundless fancy of man has painted on it with an almost endless variety? Whence has it all the MATERIALS of reason and knowledge? To this I answer, in one word, from EXPERIENCE. In that all our knowledge is founded; and from that it ultimately derives itself. Our observation employed either, about external sensible objects, or about the internal operations of our minds perceived and reflected on by ourselves, is that which supplies our understandings with all the MATERIALS of thinking. These two are the fountains of knowledge, from whence all the ideas we have, or can naturally have, do spring.

### 3. The Objects of Sensation one Source of Ideas

First, our Senses, conversant about particular sensible objects, do convey into the mind several distinct perceptions of things, according to those various ways wherein those objects do affect them. And thus we come by those IDEAS we have of yellow, white, heat, cold, soft, hard, bitter, sweet, and all those which we call sensible qualities; which when I say the senses convey into the mind, I mean, they from external objects convey into the mind what produces there those perceptions. This great source of most of the ideas we have, depending wholly upon our senses, and derived by them to the understanding, I call SENSATION.

### 4. The Operations of our Minds, the other Source of them.

Secondly, the other fountain from which experience furnisheth the understanding with ideas is,—the perception of the operations of our own mind within us, as it is employed about the ideas it has got;—which operations, when the soul comes to reflect on and consider, do furnish the understanding with another set of ideas, which could not be had from things without. And such are perception, thinking, doubting, believing, reasoning, knowing, willing, and all the different actings of our own minds;—which we being conscious of, and observing in ourselves, do from these receive into our understandings as distinct ideas as we do from bodies affecting our senses. This source of ideas every man has wholly in himself; and though it be not sense, as having nothing to do with external objects, yet it is very like it, and might properly enough be called INTERNAL SENSE. But as I call the other Sensation, so I call this REFLECTION, the ideas it affords being such only as the mind gets by reflecting on its own operations within itself. By reflection then, in the following part of this discourse, I would be understood to mean, that notice which the mind takes of its own operations, and the manner of them, by reason whereof there come to be ideas of these operations in the understanding. These two, I say, viz. external material things, as the objects of SENSATION, and the operations of our own minds within, as the objects of REFLECTION, are to me the only originals from whence all our ideas take their beginnings. The term OPERATIONS here I use in a large sense, as comprehending not barely the actions of the mind about its ideas, but some sort of passions arising sometimes from them, such as is the satisfaction or uneasiness arising from any thought.

## CHAPTER II.—OF SIMPLE IDEAS

### 1. Uncompounded Appearances.

The better to understand the nature, manner, and extent of our knowledge, one thing is carefully to be observed concerning the ideas we have; and that is, that some of them, are SIMPLE and some COMPLEX.

Though the qualities that affect our senses are, in the things themselves, so united and blended, that there is no separation, no distance between them; yet it is plain, the ideas they produce in the mind enter by the senses simple; and unmixed. For, though the sight and touch often take in from the same object, at the same time, different ideas;—as a man sees at once motion and colour; the hand feels softness and warmth in the same piece of wax: yet the simple ideas thus united in the same subject, are as perfectly distinct as those that come in by different senses. The coldness and hardness which a man feels in a piece of ice being as distinct ideas in the mind as the smell and whiteness of a lily; or as the taste of sugar, and smell of a rose. And there is nothing can be plainer to a man than the clear and distinct perception he has of those simple ideas; which, being each in itself uncompounded, contains in it nothing but ONE UNIFORM APPEARANCE, OR CONCEPTION IN THE MIND, and is not distinguishable into different ideas.

### 2. The Mind can neither make nor destroy them.

These simple ideas, the materials of all our knowledge, are suggested and furnished to the mind only by those two ways above mentioned, viz. sensation and reflection. When the understanding is once stored with these simple ideas, it has the power to repeat, compare, and unite them, even to an almost infinite variety, and so can make at pleasure new complex ideas. But it is not in the power of the most exalted wit, or enlarged understanding, by any quickness or variety of thought, to INVENT or FRAME one new simple idea in the mind, not taken in by the ways before mentioned: nor can any force of the understanding DESTROY those that are there. The dominion of man, in this little world of his own understanding being much what the same as it is in the great world of visible things; wherein his power, however managed by art and skill, reaches no farther than to compound and divide the materials that are made to his hand; but can do nothing towards the making the least particle of new matter, or destroying one atom of what is already in being. The same inability will every one find in himself, who shall go about to fashion in his understanding one simple idea, not received in by his senses from external objects, or by reflection from the operations of his own mind about them. I would have any one try to fancy any taste which had never affected his palate; or frame the idea of a scent he had never smelt: and when he can do this, I will also conclude that a blind man hath ideas of colours, and a deaf man true distinct notions of sounds.

**3. Only the qualities that affect the senses are imaginable.**

This is the reason why—though we cannot believe it impossible to God to make a creature with other organs, and more ways to convey into the understanding the notice of corporeal things than those five, as they are usually counted, which he has given to man—yet I think it is not possible for any MAN to imagine any other qualities in bodies, howsoever constituted, whereby they can be taken notice of, besides sounds, tastes, smells, visible and tangible qualities. And had mankind been made but with four senses, the qualities then which are the objects of the fifth sense had been as far from our notice, imagination, and conception, as now any belonging to a sixth, seventh, or eighth sense can possibly be;—which, whether yet some other creatures, in some other parts of this vast and stupendous universe, may not have, will be a great presumption to deny. He that will not set himself proudly at the top of all things, but will consider the immensity of this fabric, and the great variety that is to be found in this little and inconsiderable part of it which he has to do with, may be apt to think that, in other mansions of it, there may be other and different intelligent beings, of whose faculties he has as little knowledge or apprehension as a worm shut up in one drawer of a cabinet hath of the senses or understanding of a man; such variety and excellency being suitable to the wisdom and power of the Maker. I have here followed the common opinion of man's having but five senses; though, perhaps, there may be justly counted more;—but either supposition serves equally to my present purpose.

# CRITICAL IDEALISM

BY **Immanuel Kant, translated by J. M. D. Meiklejohn**

## INTRODUCTION

### I. Of the Difference Between Pure and Empirical Knowledge

That all our knowledge begins with experience there can be no doubt. For how is it possible that the faculty of cognition should be awakened into exercise otherwise than by means of objects which affect our senses, and partly of themselves produce representations, partly rouse our powers of understanding into activity, to compare to connect, or to separate these, and so to convert the raw material of our sensuous impressions into a knowledge of objects, which is called experience? In respect of time, therefore, no knowledge of ours is antecedent to experience, but begins with it.

But, though all our knowledge begins with experience, it by no means follows that all arises out of experience. For, on the contrary, it is quite possible that our empirical knowledge is a compound of that which we receive through impressions, and that which the faculty of cognition supplies from itself (sensuous impressions giving merely the occasion), an addition which we cannot distinguish from the original element given by sense, till long practice has made us attentive to, and skilful in separating it. It is, therefore, a question which requires close investigation, and not to be answered at first sight, whether there exists a knowledge altogether independent of experience, and even of all sensuous impressions? Knowledge of this kind is called a priori, in contradistinction to empirical knowledge, which has its sources a posteriori, that is, in experience.

But the expression, "a priori," is not as yet definite enough adequately to indicate the whole meaning of the question above started. For, in speaking of knowledge which has its sources in experience, we are wont to say, that this or that may be known a priori, because we do not derive this knowledge immediately from experience, but from a general rule, which, however, we have itself borrowed from experience. Thus, if a man undermined his house, we say, "he might know a priori that it would have fallen;" that is, he needed not to have waited for the experience that it did actually fall. But still, a priori, he could not know even this much. For, that bodies are heavy, and, consequently, that they fall when their supports are taken away, must have been known to him previously, by means of experience.

By the term "knowledge a priori," therefore, we shall in the sequel understand, not such as is independent of this or that kind of experience, but such as is absolutely so of all experience. Opposed to this is empirical knowledge, or that which is possible only a posteriori, that is, through experience. Knowledge a priori is either pure or impure. Pure knowledge a priori is that with which no empirical element is mixed up. For example, the proposition, "Every change has a cause," is a proposition a priori, but impure, because change is a conception which can only be derived from experience.

### II. The Human Intellect, Even in an Unphilosophical State, Is in Possession of Certain Cognitions "a priori".

The question now is as to a criterion, by which we may securely distinguish a pure from an empirical cognition. Experience no doubt teaches us that this or that object is constituted in such and such a manner, but not that it could not possibly exist otherwise. Now, in the first place, if we have a proposition which contains the idea of necessity in its very conception, it is priori. If, moreover, it is not derived from any other proposition, unless from one equally involving the idea of necessity, it is absolutely priori. Secondly, an empirical judgement never exhibits strict and absolute, but only assumed and comparative universality (by induction); therefore, the most we can say is—so far as we have hitherto observed, there is no exception to this or that rule. If, on the other hand, a judgement carries

Immanual Kant, "Introduction," The Critique of Pure Reason, trans. J. M. D. Meiklejohn.

with it strict and absolute universality, that is, admits of no possible exception, it is not derived from experience, but is valid absolutely a priori.

Empirical universality is, therefore, only an arbitrary extension of validity, from that which may be predicated of a proposition valid in most cases, to that which is asserted of a proposition which holds good in all; as, for example, in the affirmation, "All bodies are heavy." When, on the contrary, strict universality characterizes a judgement, it necessarily indicates another peculiar source of knowledge, namely, a faculty of cognition a priori. Necessity and strict universality, therefore, are infallible tests for distinguishing pure from empirical knowledge, and are inseparably connected with each other. But as in the use of these criteria the empirical limitation is sometimes more easily detected than the contingency of the judgement, or the unlimited universality which we attach to a judgement is often a more convincing proof than its necessity, it may be advisable to use the criteria separately, each being by itself infallible.

Now, that in the sphere of human cognition we have judgements which are necessary, and in the strictest sense universal, consequently pure a priori, it will be an easy matter to show. If we desire an example from the sciences, we need only take any proposition in mathematics. If we cast our eyes upon the commonest operations of the understanding, the proposition, "Every change must have a cause," will amply serve our purpose. In the latter case, indeed, the conception of a cause so plainly involves the conception of a necessity of connection with an effect, and of a strict universality of the law, that the very notion of a cause would entirely disappear, were we to derive it, like Hume, from a frequent association of what happens with that which precedes; and the habit thence originating of connecting representations—the necessity inherent in the judgement being therefore merely subjective. Besides, without seeking for such examples of principles existing a priori in cognition, we might easily show that such principles are the indispensable basis of the possibility of experience itself, and consequently prove their existence a priori. For whence could our experience itself acquire certainty, if all the rules on which it depends were themselves empirical, and consequently fortuitous? No one, therefore, can admit the validity of the use of such rules as first principles. But, for the present, we may content ourselves with having established the fact, that we do possess and exercise a faculty of pure a priori cognition; and, secondly, with having pointed out the proper tests of such cognition, namely, universality and necessity.

Not only in judgements, however, but even in conceptions, is an a priori origin manifest. For example, if we take away by degrees from our conceptions of a body all that can be referred to mere sensuous experience—colour, hardness or softness, weight, even impenetrability—the body will then vanish; but the space which it occupied still remains, and this it is utterly impossible to annihilate in thought. Again, if we take away, in like manner, from our empirical conception of any object, corporeal or incorporeal, all properties which mere experience has taught us to connect with it, still we cannot think away those through which we cogitate it as substance, or adhering to substance, although our conception of substance is more determined than that of an object. Compelled, therefore, by that necessity with which the conception of substance forces itself upon us, we must confess that it has its seat in our faculty of cognition a priori.

### III. Philosophy Stands in need of a Science Which Shall Determine the Possibility, Principles, and Extent of Human Knowledge "a priori"

Of far more importance than all that has been above said, is the consideration that certain of our cognitions rise completely above the sphere of all possible experience, and by means of conceptions, to which there exists in the whole extent of experience no corresponding object, seem to extend the range of our judgements beyond its bounds. And just in this transcendental or supersensible sphere, where experience affords us neither instruction nor guidance, lie the investigations of reason, which, on account of their importance, we consider far preferable to, and as having a far more elevated aim than, all that the understanding can achieve within the sphere of sensuous phenomena. So high a value do we set upon these investigations, that even at the risk of error, we persist in following them out, and permit neither doubt nor disregard nor indifference to restrain us from the pursuit. These unavoidable problems of mere pure reason are God, freedom (of will), and immortality. The science which, with all its preliminaries, has for its especial object the solution of these problems is named metaphysics—a science which is at the very outset dogmatical, that is, it confidently takes upon itself the execution of this task without any previous investigation of the ability or inability of reason for such an undertaking.

Now the safe ground of experience being thus abandoned, it seems nevertheless natural that we should hesitate to erect a building with the cognitions we possess, without knowing whence they come, and on the strength of principles, the origin of which is undiscovered. Instead of thus trying to build without a foundation, it is rather to be expected that we should long ago have put the question, how the understanding can arrive at these a priori cognitions, and what is the extent, validity, and worth which they may possess? We say, "This is natural enough," meaning by the word natural, that which is consistent with a just and reasonable way of thinking; but if we understand by the term, that which usually happens, nothing indeed could be more natural and more comprehensible than that this investigation should be left long unattempted. For one part of our pure knowledge, the science of mathematics, has been long firmly established, and thus leads us to form flattering expectations with regard to others, though these may be of quite a different nature. Besides, when we get beyond the bounds of experience, we are of course safe from opposition in that quarter; and the charm of widening the range of our knowledge is so great that, unless we are brought to a standstill by some evident contradiction, we hurry on undoubtingly in our course. This, however, may be avoided, if we are sufficiently cautious in the construction of our fictions, which are not the less fictions on that account.

Mathematical science affords us a brilliant example, how far, independently of all experience, we may carry our a priori knowledge. It is true that the mathematician occupies himself with objects and cognitions only in so far as they can be represented by means of intuition. But this circumstance is easily overlooked, because the said intuition can itself be given a priori, and therefore is hardly to be distinguished from a mere pure conception. Deceived by such a proof of the power of reason, we can perceive no limits to the extension of our knowledge. The light dove cleaving in free flight the thin air, whose resistance it feels, might imagine that her movements would be far more free and rapid in airless space. Just in the same way did Plato, abandoning the world of sense because of the narrow limits it sets to the understanding, venture upon the wings of ideas beyond it, into the void space of pure intellect. He did not reflect that he made no real progress by all his efforts; for he met with no resistance which might serve him for a support, as it were, whereon to rest, and on which he might apply his powers, in order to let the intellect acquire momentum for its progress. It is, indeed, the common fate of human reason in speculation, to finish the imposing edifice of thought as rapidly as possible, and then for the first time to begin to examine whether the foundation is a solid one or no. Arrived at this point, all sorts of excuses are sought after, in order to console us for its want of stability, or rather, indeed, to enable Us to dispense altogether with so late and dangerous an investigation. But what frees us during the process of building from all apprehension or suspicion, and flatters us into the belief of its solidity, is this. A great part, perhaps the greatest part, of the business of our reason consists in the analysation of the conceptions which we already possess of objects. By this means we gain a multitude of cognitions, which although really nothing more than elucidations or explanations of that which (though in a confused manner) was already thought in our conceptions, are, at least in respect of their form, prized as new introspections; whilst, so far as regards their matter or content, we have really made no addition to our conceptions, but only disinvolved them. But as this process does furnish a real priori knowledge, which has a sure progress and useful results, reason, deceived by this, slips in, without being itself aware of it, assertions of a quite different kind; in which, to given conceptions it adds others, a priori indeed, but entirely foreign to them, without our knowing how it arrives at these, and, indeed, without such a question ever suggesting itself. I shall therefore at once proceed to examine the difference between these two modes of knowledge.

## IV. Of the Difference between Analytical and Synthetical Judgements.

In all judgements wherein the relation of a subject to the predicate is cogitated (I mention affirmative judgements only here; the application to negative will be very easy), this relation is possible in two different ways. Either the predicate B belongs to the subject A, as somewhat which is contained (though covertly) in the conception A; or the predicate B lies completely out of the conception A, although it stands in connection with it. In the first instance, I term the judgement analytical, in the second, synthetical. Analytical judgements (affirmative) are therefore those in which the connection of the predicate with the subject is cogitated through identity; those in which this connection is cogitated without identity, are called synthetical judgements. The former may be called explicative, the latter augmentative judgements; because the former add in the predicate nothing to the conception of the subject, but only analyse it into its constituent conceptions, which were thought already in the subject, although in a confused manner; the latter add to our conceptions of the subject a predicate which was not contained in it, and which no analysis could ever have discovered therein. For example, when I say, "All bodies are extended," this is an analytical judgement. For I need not go beyond the conception of body in order to find extension connected with it, but merely analyse the conception, that is, become conscious of the manifold properties which I think in that conception, in order to discover this predicate in it: it is therefore an analytical judgement. On the other hand, when I say, "All bodies are heavy," the predicate is something totally different from that which I think in the mere conception of a body. By the addition of such a predicate, therefore, it becomes a synthetical judgement.

Judgements of experience, as such, are always synthetical. For it would be absurd to think of grounding an analytical judgement on experience, because in forming such a judgement I need not go out of the sphere of my conceptions, and therefore recourse to the testimony of experience is quite unnecessary. That "bodies are extended" is not an empirical judgement, but a proposition which stands firm a priori. For before addressing myself to experience, I already have in my conception all the requisite conditions for the judgement, and I have only to extract the predicate from the conception, according to the principle of contradiction, and thereby at the same time become conscious of the necessity of the judgement, a necessity which I could never learn from experience. On the other hand, though at first I do not at all include the predicate of weight in my conception of body in general, that conception still indicates an object of experience, a part of the totality of experience, to which I can still add other parts; and this I do when I recognize by observation that bodies are heavy. I can cognize beforehand by analysis the conception of body through the characteristics of extension, impenetrability, shape, etc., all which are cogitated in this conception. But now I extend my knowledge, and looking back on experience from which I had derived this conception of body, I find weight at all times connected with the above characteristics, and therefore I synthetically add to my conceptions this as a predicate, and say, "All bodies are heavy." Thus it is experience upon which rests the possibility of the synthesis of the predicate of weight with the conception of body, because both conceptions, although the one is not contained in the other, still belong to one another (only contingently, however), as parts of a whole, namely, of experience, which is itself a synthesis of intuitions.

But to synthetical judgements a priori, such aid is entirely wanting. If I go out of and beyond the conception A, in order to recognize another B as connected with it, what foundation have I to rest on, whereby to render the synthesis possible? I have here no longer the advantage of looking out in the sphere of experience for what I want. Let us take, for example, the proposition, "Everything that happens has a cause." In the conception of "something that happens," I indeed think an existence which a certain time antecedes, and from this I can derive analytical judgements. But the conception of a cause lies quite out of the above conception, and indicates something entirely different from "that which happens," and is consequently not contained in that conception. How then am I able to assert concerning the general conception—"that which happens"—something entirely different from that conception, and to recognize the conception of cause although not contained in it, yet as belonging to it, and even necessarily? what is here the unknown = X, upon which the understanding rests when it believes it has found, out of the conception A a foreign predicate B, which it nevertheless considers to be connected with it? It cannot be experience, because the principle adduced annexes the two representations, cause and effect, to the representation existence, not only with universality, which experience cannot give, but also with the expression of necessity, therefore completely a priori and from pure conceptions. Upon such synthetical, that is augmentative propositions, depends the whole aim of our speculative knowledge a priori; for although analytical judgements are indeed highly important and necessary, they are so, only to arrive at that clearness of conceptions which is requisite for a sure and extended synthesis, and this alone is a real acquisition.

## V. In All Theoretical Sciences of Reason, Synthetical Judgements "a priori" Are Contained as Principles

1. Mathematical judgements are always synthetical. Hitherto this fact, though incontestably true and very important in its consequences, seems to have escaped the analysts of the human mind, nay, to be in complete opposition to all their conjectures. For as it was found that mathematical conclusions all proceed according to the principle of contradiction (which the nature of every apodeictic certainty requires), people became persuaded that the fundamental principles of the science also were recognized and admitted in the same way. But the notion is fallacious; for although a synthetical proposition can certainly be discerned by means of the principle of contradiction, this is possible only when another synthetical proposition precedes, from which the latter is deduced, but never of itself.

Before all, be it observed, that proper mathematical propositions are always judgements a priori, and not empirical, because they carry along with them the conception of necessity, which cannot be given by experience. If this be demurred to, it matters not; I will then limit my assertion to pure mathematics, the very conception of which implies that it consists of knowledge altogether non-empirical and a priori.

We might, indeed at first suppose that the proposition 7 + 5 = 12 is a merely analytical proposition, following (according to the principle of contradiction) from the conception of a sum of seven and five. But if we regard it more narrowly, we find that our conception of the sum of seven and five contains nothing more than the uniting of both sums into one, whereby it cannot at all be cogitated what this single number is which embraces both. The conception of twelve is by no means obtained by merely cogitating the union of seven and five; and we may analyse our conception of such a possible sum as long as we will, still we shall never discover in it the notion of twelve. We must go beyond these conceptions, and have recourse to an intuition which corresponds to one of the two—our five fingers, for example, or like Segner in his Arithmetic five points, and so by degrees, add the units contained in the five given in the intuition, to the conception of seven. For I first take the number 7, and, for the conception of 5 calling in the aid of the fingers of my hand as objects of intuition, I add the units, which I before took together to make up the number 5, gradually now by means of the material image my hand, to the number 7, and by this process, I at length see the number 12 arise. That 7 should be added to 5, I have certainly cogitated in my conception of a sum = 7 + 5, but not that this sum was equal to 12. Arithmetical propositions are therefore always synthetical, of which we may become more clearly convinced by trying large numbers. For it will thus become quite evident that, turn and twist our conceptions as we may, it is impossible, without having recourse to intuition, to arrive at the sum total or product by means of the mere analysis of our conceptions. Just as little is any principle of pure geometry analytical. "A straight line between two points is the shortest," is a synthetical proposition. For my conception of straight contains no notion of quantity, but is merely qualitative. The conception of the shortest is therefore fore wholly an addition, and by no analysis can it be extracted from our conception of a straight line. Intuition must therefore here lend its aid, by means of which, and thus only, our synthesis is possible.

Some few principles preposited by geometricians are, indeed, really analytical, and depend on the principle of contradiction. They serve, however, like identical propositions, as links in the chain of method, not as principles—for example, a = a, the whole is equal to itself, or (a + b) —> a, the whole is greater than its part. And yet even these principles themselves, though they derive their validity from pure conceptions, are only admitted in mathematics because they can be presented in intuition. What causes us here commonly to believe that the predicate of such apodeictic judgements is already contained in our conception, and that the judgement is therefore analytical, is merely the equivocal nature of the expression. We must join in thought a certain predicate to a given conception, and this necessity cleaves already to the conception. But the question is, not what we must join in thought to the given conception, but what we really think therein, though only obscurely, and then it becomes manifest that the predicate pertains to these conceptions, necessarily indeed, yet not as thought in the conception itself, but by virtue of an intuition, which must be added to the conception.

2. The science of natural philosophy (physics) contains in itself synthetical judgements a priori, as principles. I shall adduce two propositions. For instance, the proposition, "In all changes of the material world, the quantity of matter remains unchanged"; or, that, "In all communication of motion, action and reaction must always be equal." In both of these, not only is the necessity, and therefore their origin a priori clear, but also that they are synthetical propositions. For in the conception of matter, I do not cogitate its permanency, but merely its presence in space, which it fills. I therefore really go out of and beyond the conception of matter, in order to think on to it something a priori, which I did not think in it. The proposition is therefore not analytical, but synthetical, and nevertheless conceived a priori; and so it is with regard to the other propositions of the pure part of natural philosophy.

3. As to metaphysics, even if we look upon it merely as an attempted science, yet, from the nature of human reason, an indispensable one, we find that it must contain synthetical propositions a priori. It is not merely the duty of metaphysics to dissect, and thereby analytically to illustrate the conceptions which we form a priori of things; but we seek to widen the range of our a priori knowledge. For this purpose, we must avail ourselves of such principles as add something to the original conception—something not identical with, nor contained in it, and by means of synthetical judgements a priori, leave far behind us the limits of experience; for example, in the proposition, "the

world must have a beginning," and such like. Thus metaphysics, according to the proper aim of the science, consists merely of synthetical propositions a priori.

## VI. The Universal Problem of Pure Reason

It is extremely advantageous to be able to bring a number of investigations under the formula of a single problem. For in this manner, we not only facilitate our own labour, inasmuch as we define it clearly to ourselves, but also render it more easy for others to decide whether we have done justice to our undertaking. The proper problem of pure reason, then, is contained in the question: "How are synthetical judgements a priori possible?"

That metaphysical science has hitherto remained in so vacillating a state of uncertainty and contradiction, is only to be attributed to the fact that this great problem, and perhaps even the difference between analytical and synthetical judgements, did not sooner suggest itself to philosophers. Upon the solution of this problem, or upon sufficient proof of the impossibility of synthetical knowledge a priori, depends the existence or downfall of the science of metaphysics. Among philosophers, David Hume came the nearest of all to this problem; yet it never acquired in his mind sufficient precision, nor did he regard the question in its universality. On the contrary, he stopped short at the synthetical proposition of the connection of an effect with its cause (principium causalitatis), insisting that such proposition a priori was impossible. According to his conclusions, then, all that we term metaphysical science is a mere delusion, arising from the fancied insight of reason into that which is in truth borrowed from experience, and to which habit has given the appearance of necessity. Against this assertion, destructive to all pure philosophy, he would have been guarded, had he had our problem before his eyes in its universality. For he would then have perceived that, according to his own argument, there likewise could not be any pure mathematical science, which assuredly cannot exist without synthetical propositions a priori—an absurdity from which his good understanding must have saved him.

In the solution of the above problem is at the same time comprehended the possibility of the use of pure reason in the foundation and construction of all sciences which contain theoretical knowledge a priori of objects, that is to say, the answer to the following questions:

How is pure mathematical science possible?

How is pure natural science possible?

Respecting these sciences, as they do certainly exist, it may with propriety be asked, how they are possible?—for that they must be possible is shown by the fact of their really existing.[1] But as to metaphysics, the miserable progress it has hitherto made, and the fact that of no one system yet brought forward, far as regards its true aim, can it be said that this science really exists, leaves any one at liberty to doubt with reason the very possibility of its existence.

Yet, in a certain sense, this kind of knowledge must unquestionably be looked upon as given; in other words, metaphysics must be considered as really existing, if not as a science, nevertheless as a natural disposition of the human mind (metaphysica naturalis). For human reason, without any instigations imputable to the mere vanity of great knowledge, unceasingly progresses, urged on by its own feeling of need, towards such questions as cannot be answered by any empirical application of reason, or principles derived therefrom; and so there has ever really existed in every man some system of metaphysics. It will always exist, so soon as reason awakes to the exercise of its power of speculation. And now the question arises: "How is metaphysics, as a natural disposition, possible?" In other words, how, from the nature of universal human reason, do those questions arise which pure reason proposes to itself, and which it is impelled by its own feeling of need to answer as well as it can?

But as in all the attempts hitherto made to answer the questions which reason is prompted by its very nature to propose to itself, for example, whether the world had a beginning, or has existed from eternity, it has always met with unavoidable contradictions, we must not rest satisfied with the mere natural disposition of the mind to metaphysics, that is, with the existence of the faculty of pure reason, whence, indeed, some sort of metaphysical system always arises; but it must be possible to arrive at certainty in regard to the question whether we know or do not know

1 As to the existence of pure natural science, or physics, perhaps many may still express doubts. But we have only to look at the different propositions which are commonly treated of at the commencement of proper (empirical) physical science—those, for example, relating to the permanence of the same quantity of matter, the vis inertiae, the equality of action and reaction, etc.—to be soon convinced that they form a science of pure physics (physica pura, or rationalis), which well deserves to be separately exposed as a special science, in its whole extent, whether that be great or confined.

the things of which metaphysics treats. We must be able to arrive at a decision on the subjects of its questions, or on the ability or inability of reason to form any judgement respecting them; and therefore either to extend with confidence the bounds of our pure reason, or to set strictly defined and safe limits to its action. This last question, which arises out of the above universal problem, would properly run thus: "How is metaphysics possible as a science?"

Thus, the critique of reason leads at last, naturally and necessarily, to science; and, on the other hand, the dogmatical use of reason without criticism leads to groundless assertions, against which others equally specious can always be set, thus ending unavoidably in scepticism.

Besides, this science cannot be of great and formidable prolixity, because it has not to do with objects of reason, the variety of which is inexhaustible, but merely with Reason herself and her problems; problems which arise out of her own bosom, and are not proposed to her by the nature of outward things, but by her own nature. And when once Reason has previously become able completely to understand her own power in regard to objects which she meets with in experience, it will be easy to determine securely the extent and limits of her attempted application to objects beyond the confines of experience.

We may and must, therefore, regard the attempts hitherto made to establish metaphysical science dogmatically as non-existent. For what of analysis, that is, mere dissection of conceptions, is contained in one or other, is not the aim of, but only a preparation for metaphysics proper, which has for its object the extension, by means of synthesis, of our a priori knowledge. And for this purpose, mere analysis is of course useless, because it only shows what is contained in these conceptions, but not how we arrive, a priori, at them; and this it is her duty to show, in order to be able afterwards to determine their valid use in regard to all objects of experience, to all knowledge in general. But little self-denial, indeed, is needed to give up these pretensions, seeing the undeniable, and in the dogmatic mode of procedure, inevitable contradictions of Reason with herself, have long since ruined the reputation of every system of metaphysics that has appeared up to this time. It will require more firmness to remain undeterred by difficulty from within, and opposition from without, from endeavouring, by a method quite opposed to all those hitherto followed, to further the growth and fruitfulness of a science indispensable to human reason—a science from which every branch it has borne may be cut away, but whose roots remain indestructible.

### VII. Idea and Division of a Particular Science, under the Name of a Critique of Pure Reason

From all that has been said, there results the idea of a particular science, which may be called the Critique of Pure Reason. For reason is the faculty which furnishes us with the principles of knowledge a priori. Hence, pure reason is the faculty which contains the principles of cognizing anything absolutely a priori. An organon of pure reason would be a compendium of those principles according to which alone all pure cognitions a priori can be obtained. The completely extended application of such an organon would afford us a system of pure reason. As this, however, is demanding a great deal, and it is yet doubtful whether any extension of our knowledge be here possible, or, if so, in what cases; we can regard a science of the mere criticism of pure reason, its sources and limits, as the propaedeutic to a system of pure reason. Such a science must not be called a doctrine, but only a critique of pure reason; and its use, in regard to speculation, would be only negative, not to enlarge the bounds of, but to purify, our reason, and to shield it against error—which alone is no little gain. I apply the term transcendental to all knowledge which is not so much occupied with objects as with the mode of our cognition of these objects, so far as this mode of cognition is possible a priori. A system of such conceptions would be called transcendental philosophy. But this, again, is still beyond the bounds of our present essay. For as such a science must contain a complete exposition not only of our synthetical a priori, but of our analytical a priori knowledge, it is of too wide a range for our present purpose, because we do not require to carry our analysis any farther than is necessary to understand, in their full extent, the principles of synthesis a priori, with which alone we have to do. This investigation, which we cannot properly call a doctrine, but only a transcendental critique, because it aims not at the enlargement, but at the correction and guidance, of our knowledge, and is to serve as a touchstone of the worth or worthlessness of all knowledge a priori, is the sole object of our present essay. Such a critique is consequently, as far as possible, a preparation for an organon; and if this new organon should be found to fail, at least for a canon of pure reason, according to which the complete system of the philosophy of pure reason, whether it extend or limit the bounds of that reason, might one day be set forth both analytically and synthetically. For that this is possible, nay, that such a system is not of so great extent as to preclude the hope of its ever being completed, is evident. For we have not here to do with the nature of outward objects, which is infinite, but solely with the mind, which judges of the nature of objects, and, again, with the mind only in respect of its cognition a priori. And the object of our investigations, as it is not to be sought without, but, altogether within, ourselves, cannot remain concealed, and in all probability is limited enough to be completely surveyed and fairly estimated, according to its worth or worthlessness. Still less let the reader here expect a critique of books and systems of pure reason; our present object is exclusively a critique of the faculty of pure reason itself. Only when we make this critique our foundation, do we possess a pure touchstone for estimating the philosophical value of ancient and modern writings on this subject; and without this criterion, the incompetent historian or judge decides upon and corrects the groundless assertions of others with his own, which have themselves just as little foundation.

Transcendental philosophy is the idea of a science, for which the Critique of Pure Reason must sketch the whole plan architectonically, that is, from principles, with a full guarantee for the validity and stability of all the parts which enter into the building. It is the system of all the principles of pure reason. If this Critique itself does not assume the title of transcendental philosophy, it is only because, to be a complete system, it ought to contain a full analysis of all human knowledge a priori. Our critique must, indeed, lay before us a complete enumeration of all the radical conceptions which constitute the said pure knowledge. But from the complete analysis of these conceptions themselves, as also from a complete investigation of those derived from them, it abstains with reason; partly because it would be deviating from the end in view to occupy itself with this analysis, since this process is not attended with the difficulty and insecurity to be found in the synthesis, to which our critique is entirely devoted, and partly because it would be inconsistent with the unity of our plan to burden this essay with the vindication of the completeness of such an analysis and deduction, with which, after all, we have at present nothing to do. This completeness of the analysis of these radical conceptions, as well as of the deduction from the conceptions a priori which may be given by the analysis, we can, however, easily attain, provided only that we are in possession of all these radical conceptions, which are to serve as principles of the synthesis, and that in respect of this main purpose nothing is wanting.

To the Critique of Pure Reason, therefore, belongs all that constitutes transcendental philosophy; and it is the complete idea of transcendental philosophy, but still not the science itself; because it only proceeds so far with the analysis as is necessary to the power of judging completely of our synthetical knowledge a priori.

The principal thing we must attend to, in the division of the parts of a science like this, is that no conceptions must enter it which contain aught empirical; in other words, that the knowledge a priori must be completely pure. Hence, although the highest principles and fundamental conceptions of morality are certainly cognitions a priori, yet they do not belong to transcendental philosophy; because, though they certainly do not lay the conceptions of pain, pleasure, desires, inclinations, etc. (which are all of empirical origin), at the foundation of its precepts, yet still into the conception of duty—as an obstacle to be overcome, or as an incitement which should not be made into a motive—these empirical conceptions must necessarily enter, in the construction of a system of pure morality. Transcendental philosophy is consequently a philosophy of the pure and merely speculative reason. For all that is practical, so far as it contains motives, relates to feelings, and these belong to empirical sources of cognition.

If we wish to divide this science from the universal point of view of a science in general, it ought to comprehend, first, a Doctrine of the Elements, and, secondly, a Doctrine of the Method of pure reason. Each of these main divisions will have its subdivisions, the separate reasons for which we cannot here particularize. Only so much seems necessary, by way of introduction of premonition, that there are two sources of human knowledge (which probably spring from a common, but to us unknown root), namely, sense and understanding. By the former, objects are given to us; by the latter, thought. So far as the faculty of sense may contain representations a priori, which form the conditions under which objects are given, in so far it belongs to transcendental philosophy. The transcendental doctrine of sense must form the first part of our science of elements, because the conditions under which alone the objects of human knowledge are given must precede those under which they are thought.

CHAPTER V

# Morality

# NATURAL LAW THEORY

BY **Thomas Aquinas, translated by the Fathers of the English Dominican Province**

## SECOND ARTICLE [I-II, Q. 91, ART. 2]

### Whether There Is in Us a Natural Law?

OBJECTION 1: It would seem that there is no natural law in us. Because man is governed sufficiently by the eternal law: for Augustine says (De Lib. Arb. i) that "the eternal law is that by which it is right that all things should be most orderly." But nature does not abound in superfluities as neither does she fail in necessaries. Therefore no law is natural to man.

OBJ. 2: Further, by the law man is directed, in his acts, to the end, as stated above (Q. 90, A. 2). But the directing of human acts to their end is not a function of nature, as is the case in irrational creatures, which act for an end solely by their natural appetite; whereas man acts for an end by his reason and will. Therefore no law is natural to man.

OBJ. 3: Further, the more a man is free, the less is he under the law. But man is freer than all the animals, on account of his free-will, with which he is endowed above all other animals. Since therefore other animals are not subject to a natural law, neither is man subject to a natural law.

*On the contrary,* A gloss on Rom. 2:14: "When the Gentiles, who have not the law, do by nature those things that are of the law," comments as follows: "Although they have no written law, yet they have the natural law, whereby each one knows, and is conscious of, what is good and what is evil."

*I answer that,* As stated above (Q. 90, A. 1, ad 1), law, being a rule and measure, can be in a person in two ways: in one way, as in him that rules and measures; in another way, as in that which is ruled and measured, since a thing is ruled and measured, in so far as it partakes of the rule or measure. Wherefore, since all things subject to Divine providence are ruled and measured by the eternal law, as was stated above (A. 1); it is evident that all things partake somewhat of the eternal law, in so far as, namely, from its being imprinted on them, they derive their respective inclinations to their proper acts and ends. Now among all others, the rational creature is subject to Divine providence in the most excellent way, in so far as it partakes of a share of providence, by being provident both for itself and for others. Wherefore it has a share of the Eternal Reason, whereby it has a natural inclination to its proper act and end: and this participation of the eternal law in the rational creature is called the natural law. Hence the Psalmist after saying (Ps. 4:6): "Offer up the sacrifice of justice," as though someone asked what the works of justice are, adds: "Many say, Who showeth us good things?" in answer to which question he says: "The light of Thy countenance, O Lord, is signed upon us": thus implying that the light of natural reason, whereby we discern what is good and what is evil, which is the function of the natural law, is nothing else than an imprint on us of the Divine light. It is therefore evident that the natural law is nothing else than the rational creature's participation of the eternal law.

REPLY OBJ. 1: This argument would hold, if the natural law were something different from the eternal law: whereas it is nothing but a participation thereof, as stated above.

REPLY OBJ. 2: Every act of reason and will in us is based on that which is according to nature, as stated above (Q. 10, A. 1): for every act of reasoning is based on principles that are known naturally, and every act of appetite in respect

St. Thomas Aquinas, Summa Theologica, trans. Fathers of the English Dominican Province.

of the means is derived from the natural appetite in respect of the last end. Accordingly the first direction of our acts to their end must needs be in virtue of the natural law.

REPLY OBJ. 3: Even irrational animals partake in their own way of the Eternal Reason, just as the rational creature does. But because the rational creature partakes thereof in an intellectual and rational manner, therefore the participation of the eternal law in the rational creature is properly called a law, since a law is something pertaining to reason, as stated above (Q. 90, A. 1). Irrational creatures, however, do not partake thereof in a rational manner, wherefore there is no participation of the eternal law in them, except by way of similitude.

## THIRD ARTICLE [1-11, Q. 91, ART. 3]

### Whether There Is a Human Law?

OBJECTION 1: It would seem that there is not a human law. For the natural law is a participation of the eternal law, as stated above (A. 2). Now through the eternal law "all things are most orderly," as Augustine states (De Lib. Arb. i, 6). Therefore the natural law suffices for the ordering of all human affairs. Consequently there is no need for a human law.

OBJ. 2: Further, a law bears the character of a measure, as stated above (Q. 90, A. 1). But human reason is not a measure of things, but vice versa, as stated in *Metaph.* x, text. 5. Therefore no law can emanate from human reason.

OBJ. 3: Further, a measure should be most certain, as stated in *Metaph.* x, text. 3. But the dictates of human reason in matters of conduct are uncertain, according to Wis. 9:14: "The thoughts of mortal men are fearful, and our counsels uncertain." Therefore no law can emanate from human reason.

*On the contrary,* Augustine (De Lib. Arb. i, 6) distinguishes two kinds of law, the one eternal, the other temporal, which he calls human.

*I answer that,* As stated above (Q. 90, A. 1, ad 2), a law is a dictate of the practical reason. Now it is to be observed that the same procedure takes place in the practical and in the speculative reason: for each proceeds from principles to conclusions, as stated above (ibid.). Accordingly we conclude that just as, in the speculative reason, from naturally known indemonstrable principles, we draw the conclusions of the various sciences, the knowledge of which is not imparted to us by nature, but acquired by the efforts of reason, so too it is from the precepts of the natural law, as from general and indemonstrable principles, that the human reason needs to proceed to the more particular determination of certain matters. These particular determinations, devised by human reason, are called human laws, provided the other essential conditions of law be observed, as stated above (Q. 90, AA. 2, 3, 4). Wherefore Tully says in his *Rhetoric* (De Invent. Rhet. ii) that "justice has its source in nature; thence certain things came into custom by reason of their utility; afterwards these things which emanated from nature and were approved by custom, were sanctioned by fear and reverence for the law."

REPLY OBJ. 1: The human reason cannot have a full participation of the dictate of the Divine Reason, but according to its own mode, and imperfectly. Consequently, as on the part of the speculative reason, by a natural participation of Divine Wisdom, there is in us the knowledge of certain general principles, but not proper knowledge of each single truth, such as that contained in the Divine Wisdom; so too, on the part of the practical reason, man has a natural participation of the eternal law, according to certain general principles, but not as regards the particular determinations of individual cases, which are, however, contained in the eternal law.

Hence the need for human reason to proceed further to sanction them by law.

REPLY OBJ. 2: Human reason is not, of itself, the rule of things: but the principles impressed on it by nature, are general rules and measures of all things relating to human conduct, whereof the natural reason is the rule and measure, although it is not the measure of things that are from nature.

REPLY OBJ. 3: The practical reason is concerned with practical matters, which are singular and contingent: but not with necessary things, with which the speculative reason is concerned. Wherefore human laws cannot have that inerrancy that belongs to the demonstrated conclusions of sciences. Nor is it necessary for every measure to be altogether unerring and certain, but according as it is possible in its own particular genus.

## FOURTH ARTICLE [I-II, Q. 91, ART. 4]

### Whether There Was Any Need for a Divine Law?

OBJECTION 1: It would seem that there was no need for a Divine law. Because, as stated above (A. 2), the natural law is a participation in us of the eternal law. But the eternal law is a Divine law, as stated above (A. 1). Therefore there was no need for a Divine law in addition to the natural law, and human laws derived therefrom.

OBJ. 2: Further, it is written (Ecclus. 15:14) that "God left man in the hand of his own counsel." Now counsel is an act of reason, as stated above (Q. 14, A. 1). Therefore man was left to the direction of his reason. But a dictate of human reason is a human law as stated above (A. 3). Therefore there is no need for man to be governed also by a Divine law.

OBJ. 3: Further, human nature is more self-sufficing than irrational creatures. But irrational creatures have no Divine law besides the natural inclination impressed on them. Much less, therefore, should the rational creature have a Divine law in addition to the natural law.

*On the contrary,* David prayed God to set His law before him, saying (Ps. 118:33): "Set before me for a law the way of Thy justifications, O Lord."

*I answer that,* Besides the natural and the human law it was necessary for the directing of human conduct to have a Divine law. And this for four reasons. First, because it is by law that man is directed how to perform his proper acts in view of his last end. And indeed if man were ordained to no other end than that which is proportionate to his natural faculty, there would be no need for man to have any further direction of the part of his reason, besides the natural law and human law which is derived from it. But since man is ordained to an end of eternal happiness which is improportionate to man's natural faculty, as stated above (Q. 5, A. 5), therefore it was necessary that, besides the natural and the human law, man should be directed to his end by a law given by God.

Secondly, because, on account of the uncertainty of human judgment, especially on contingent and particular matters, different people form different judgments on human acts; whence also different and contrary laws result. In order, therefore, that man may know without any doubt what he ought to do and what he ought to avoid, it was necessary for man to be directed in his proper acts by a law given by God, for it is certain that such a law cannot err.

Thirdly, because man can make laws in those matters of which he is competent to judge. But man is not competent to judge of interior movements, that are hidden, but only of exterior acts which appear: and yet for the perfection of virtue it is necessary for man to conduct himself aright in both kinds of acts. Consequently human law could not sufficiently curb and direct interior acts; and it was necessary for this purpose that a Divine law should supervene.

Fourthly, because, as Augustine says (De Lib. Arb. i, 5, 6), human law cannot punish or forbid all evil deeds: since while aiming at doing away with all evils, it would do away with many good things, and would hinder the advance of the common good, which is necessary for human intercourse. In order, therefore, that no evil might remain unforbidden and unpunished, it was necessary for the Divine law to supervene, whereby all sins are forbidden.

And these four causes are touched upon in Ps. 118:8, where it is said: "The law of the Lord is unspotted," i.e. allowing no foulness of sin; "converting souls," because it directs not only exterior, but also interior acts; "the testimony of the Lord is faithful," because of the certainty of what is true and right; "giving wisdom to little ones," by directing man to an end supernatural and Divine.

REPLY OBJ. 1: By the natural law the eternal law is participated proportionately to the capacity of human nature. But to his supernatural end man needs to be directed in a yet higher way. Hence the additional law given by God, whereby man shares more perfectly in the eternal law.

REPLY OBJ. 2: Counsel is a kind of inquiry: hence it must proceed from some principles. Nor is it enough for it to proceed from principles imparted by nature, which are the precepts of the natural law, for the reasons given above: but there is need for certain additional principles, namely, the precepts of the Divine law.

REPLY OBJ. 3: Irrational creatures are not ordained to an end higher than that which is proportionate to their natural powers: consequently the comparison fails.

## THIRD ARTICLE [I-II, Q. 94, ART. 3]

### Whether All Acts of Virtue Are Prescribed by the Natural Law?

OBJECTION 1: It would seem that not all acts of virtue are prescribed by the natural law. Because, as stated above (Q. 90, A. 2) it is essential to a law that it be ordained to the common good. But some acts of virtue are ordained to the private good of the individual, as is evident especially in regards to acts of temperance. Therefore not all acts of virtue are the subject of natural law.

OBJ. 2: Further, every sin is opposed to some virtuous act. If therefore all acts of virtue are prescribed by the natural law, it seems to follow that all sins are against nature: whereas this applies to certain special sins.

OBJ. 3: Further, those things which are according to nature are common to all. But acts of virtue are not common to all: since a thing is virtuous in one, and vicious in another. Therefore not all acts of virtue are prescribed by the natural law.

*On the contrary,* Damascene says (De Fide Orth, iii, 4) that "virtues are natural." Therefore virtuous acts also are a subject of the natural law.

*I answer that,* We may speak of virtuous acts in two ways: first, under the aspect of virtuous; secondly, as such and such acts considered in their proper species. If then we speak of acts of virtue, considered as virtuous, thus all virtuous acts belong to the natural law. For it has been stated (A. 2) that to the natural law belongs everything to which a man is inclined according to his nature. Now each thing is inclined naturally to an operation that is suitable to it according to its form: thus fire is inclined to give heat. Wherefore, since the rational soul is the proper form of man, there is in every man a natural inclination to act according to reason: and this is to act according to virtue. Consequently, considered thus, all acts of virtue are prescribed by the natural law: since each one's reason naturally dictates to him to act virtuously. But if we speak of virtuous acts, considered in themselves, i.e. in their proper species, thus not all virtuous acts are prescribed by the natural law: for many things are done virtuously, to which nature does not incline at first; but which, through the inquiry of reason, have been found by men to be conducive to well-living.

REPLY OBJ. 1: Temperance is about the natural concupiscences of food, drink and sexual matters, which are indeed ordained to the natural common good, just as other matters of law are ordained to the moral common good.

REPLY OBJ. 2: By human nature we may mean either that which is proper to man—and in this sense all sins, as being against reason, are also against nature, as Damascene states (De Fide Orth, ii, 30): or we may mean that nature which is common to man and other animals; and in this sense, certain special sins are said to be against nature; thus contrary to sexual intercourse, which is natural to all animals, is unisexual lust, which has received the special name of the unnatural crime.

REPLY OBJ. 3: This argument considers acts in themselves. For it is owing to the various conditions of men, that certain acts are virtuous for some, as being proportionate and becoming to them, while they are vicious for others, as being out of proportion to them.

## FOURTH ARTICLE [I-II, Q. 94, ART. 4]

### Whether the Natural Law Is the Same in All Men?

OBJECTION 1: It would seem that the natural law is not the same in all. For it is stated in the Decretals (Dist. i) that "the natural law is that which is contained in the Law and the Gospel." But this is not common to all men; because, as it is written (Rom. 10:16), "all do not obey the gospel." Therefore the natural law is not the same in all men.

OBJ. 2: Further, "Things which are according to the law are said to be just," as stated *in Ethic.* v. But it is stated in the same book that nothing is so universally just as not to be subject to change in regard to some men. Therefore even the natural law is not the same in all men.

OBJ. 3: Further, as stated above (AA. 2, 3), to the natural law belongs everything to which a man is inclined according to his nature. Now different men are naturally inclined to different things; some to the desire of pleasures, others to the desire of honors, and other men to other things. Therefore there is not one natural law for all.

*On the contrary,* Isidore says (Etym. v, 4): "The natural law is common to all nations."

*I answer that,* As stated above (AA. 2,3), to the natural law belong those things to which a man is inclined naturally: and among these it is proper to man to be inclined to act according to reason. Now the process of reason is from the common to the proper, as stated in *Phys.* i. The speculative reason, however, is differently situated in this matter, from the practical reason. For, since the speculative reason is busied chiefly with necessary things, which cannot be otherwise than they are, its proper conclusions, like the universal principles, contain the truth without fail. The practical reason, on the other hand, is busied with contingent matters, about which human actions are concerned: and consequently, although there is necessity in the general principles, the more we descend to matters of detail, the more frequently we encounter defects. Accordingly then in speculative matters truth is the same in all men, both as to principles and as to conclusions: although the truth is not known to all as regards the conclusions, but only as regards the principles which are called common notions. But in matters of action, truth or practical rectitude is not the same for all, as to matters of detail, but only as to the general principles: and where there is the same rectitude in matters of detail, it is not equally known to all.

It is therefore evident that, as regards the general principles whether of speculative or of practical reason, truth or rectitude is the same for all, and is equally known by all. As to the proper conclusions of the speculative reason, the truth is the same for all, but is not equally known to all: thus it is true for all that the three angles of a triangle are together equal to two right angles, although it is not known to all. But as to the proper conclusions of the practical reason, neither is the truth or rectitude the same for all, nor, where it is the same, is it equally known by all. Thus it is right and true for all to act according to reason: and from this principle it follows as a proper conclusion, that goods entrusted to another should be restored to their owner. Now this is true for the majority of cases: but it may happen in a particular case that it would be injurious, and therefore unreasonable, to restore goods held in trust; for instance, if they are claimed for the purpose of fighting against one's country. And this principle will be found to fail the more, according as we descend further into detail, e.g. if one were to say that goods held in trust should be restored with such and such a guarantee, or in such and such a way; because the greater the number of conditions added, the greater the number of ways in which the principle may fail, so that it be not right to restore or not to restore.

Consequently we must say that the natural law, as to general principles, is the same for all, both as to rectitude and as to knowledge. But as to certain matters of detail, which are conclusions, as it were, of those general principles, it is the same for all in the majority of cases, both as to rectitude and as to knowledge; and yet in some few cases it may fail, both as to rectitude, by reason of certain obstacles (just as natures subject to generation and corruption fail in some few cases on account of some obstacle), and as to knowledge, since in some the reason is perverted by passion, or evil habit, or an evil disposition of nature; thus formerly, theft, although it is expressly contrary to the natural law, was not considered wrong among the Germans, as Julius Caesar relates (De Bello Gall. vi).

REPLY OBJ. 1: The meaning of the sentence quoted is not that whatever is contained in the Law and the Gospel belongs to the natural law, since they contain many things that are above nature; but that whatever belongs to the natural law is fully contained in them. Wherefore Gratian, after saying that "the natural law is what is contained in the Law and the Gospel," adds at once, by way of example, "by which everyone is commanded to do to others as he would be done by."

REPLY OBJ. 2: The saying of the Philosopher is to be understood of things that are naturally just, not as general principles, but as conclusions drawn from them, having rectitude in the majority of cases, but failing in a few.

REPLY OBJ. 3: As, in man, reason rules and commands the other powers, so all the natural inclinations belonging to the other powers must needs be directed according to reason. Wherefore it is universally right for all men, that all their inclinations should be directed according to reason.

# SOCIAL CONTRACT THEORY

BY **Thomas Hobbes**

## CHAP. XIII

### Of the Naturall Condition of Mankind, as Concerning their Felicity, and Misery

Nature hath made men so equall, in the faculties of body, and mind; as that though there bee found one man sometimes manifestly stronger in body, or of quicker mind then another; yet when all is reckoned together, the difference between man, and man, is not so considerable, as that one man can thereupon claim to himselfe any benefit, to which another may not pretend, as well as he. For as to the strength of body, the weakest has strength enough to kill the strongest, either by secret machination, or by confederacy with others, that are in the same danger with himselfe.

*Men by nature Equall.*

And as to the faculties of the mind, (setting aside the arts grounded upon words, and especially that skill of proceeding upon generall, and infallible rules, called Science; which very few have, and but in few things; as being not a native faculty, born with us; nor attained, (as Prudence,) while we look after somewhat els,) I find yet a greater equality amongst men, than that of strength. For Prudence, is but Experience; which equall time, equally bestowes on all men, in [61] those things they equally apply themselves unto. That which may perhaps make such equality incredible, is but a vain conceipt of ones owne wisdome, which almost all men think they have in a greater degree, than the Vulgar; that is, than all men but themselves, and a few others, whom by Fame, or for concurring with themselves: they approve. For such is the nature of men, that howsoever they may acknowledge many others to be more witty, or more eloquent, or more learned; Yet they will hardly believe there be many so wise as themselves; For they see their own wit at hand, and other mens at a distance. But this proveth rather that men are in that point equall, than unequall. For there is not ordinarily a greater signe of the equall distribution of any thing, than that every man is contented with his share.

*From Equality proceeds Diffidence.*

From this equality of ability, ariseth equality of hope in the attaining of our Ends. And therefore if any two men desire the same thing, which neverthelesse they cannot both enjoy, they become enemies; and in the way to their End, (which is principally their owne conservation, and sometimes their delectation only,) endeavour to destroy, or subdue one an other. And from hence it comes to passe, that where an Invader hath no more to feare, than an other mans single power; if one plant, sow, build, or possesse a convenient Seat, others may probably be expected to come prepared with forces united, to dispossesse, and deprive him, not only of the fruit of his labour, but also of his life, or liberty. And the Invader again is in the like danger of another.

*From Diffidence Warre.*

And from this diffidence of one another, there is no way for any man to secure himselfe, so reasonable, as Anticipation; that is, by force, or wiles, to master the persons of all men he can, so long, till he see no other power great enough to endanger him: And this is no more than his own conservation requireth, and is generally allowed. Also because there be some, that taking pleasure in contemplating their own power in the acts of conquest, which they pursue farther than their security requires; if others, that otherwise would be glad to be at ease within modest bounds, should not by invasion increase their power, they

Thomas Hobbes, "Of the Naturall Condition of Mankind, as Concerning their Felicity, and Misery" and "Of the First and Second Naturall Lawes, and of Contracts," Leviathan, or The Matter, Forme, and Power of a Common-Wealth Ecclesiasticall and Civil, pp. 81-96.

would not be able, long time, by standing only on their defence, to subsist. And by consequence, such augmentation of dominion over men, being necessary to a mans conservation, it ought to be allowed him.

Againe, men have no pleasure, (but on the contrary a great deale of griefe) in keeping company, where there is no power able to over-awe them all. For every man looketh that his companion should value him, at the same rate he sets upon himselfe: And upon all signes of contempt, or undervaluing, naturally endeavours, as far as he dares (which amongst them that have no common power to keep them in quiet, is far enough to make them destroy each other,) to extort a greater value from his contemners, by dommage; and from others, by the example.

So that in the nature of man, we find three principall causes of quarrell. First, Competition; Secondly, Diffidence; Thirdly, Glory. [62]

The first, maketh men invade for Gain; the second, for Safety; and the third, for Reputation. The first use Violence, to make themselves Masters of other mens persons, wives, children, and cattell; the second, to defend them; the third, for trifles, as a word, a smile, a different opinion, and any other signe of undervalue, either direct in their Persons, or by reflexion in their Kindred, their Friends, their Nation, their Profession, or their Name.

*Out of Civil States, there is alwayes Warre of every one against every one.*

Hereby it is manifest, that during the time men live without a common Power to keep them all in awe, they are in that condition which is called Warre; and such a warre, as is of every man, against every man. For Warre, consisteth not in Battell onely, or the act of fighting; but in a tract of time, wherein the Will to contend by Battell is sufficiently known: and therefore the notion of *Time,* is to be considered in the nature of Warre; as it is in the nature of Weather. For as the nature of Foule weather, lyeth not in a showre or two of rain; but in an inclination thereto of many dayes together: So the nature of War, consisteth not in actual fighting; but in the known disposition thereto, during all the time there is no assurance to the contrary. All other time is Peace.

*The Incommodities of such a War.*

Whatsoever therefore is consequent to a time of Warre, where every man is Enemy to every man; the same is consequent to the time, wherein men live without other security, than what their own strength, and their own invention shall furnish them withall. In such condition, there is no place for Industry; because the fruit thereof is uncertain: and consequently no Culture of the Earth; no Navigation, nor use of the commodities that may be imported by Sea; no commodious Building; no Instruments of moving, and removing such things as require much force; no Knowledge of the face of the Earth; no account of Time; no Arts; no Letters; no Society; and which is worst of all, continuall feare, and danger of violent death; And the life of man, solitary, poore, nasty, brutish, and short.

It may seem strange to some man, that has not well weighed these things; that Nature should thus dissociate, and render men apt to invade, and destroy one another: and he may therefore, not trusting to this Inference, made from the Passions, desire perhaps to have the same confirmed by Experience. Let him therefore consider with himselfe, when taking a journey, he armes himselfe, and seeks to go well accompanied; when going to sleep, he locks his dores; when even in his house he locks his chests; and this when he knowes there bee Lawes, and publike Officers, armed, to revenge all injuries shall bee done him; what opinion he has of his fellow subjects, when he rides armed; of his fellow Citizens, when he locks his dores; and of his children, and servants, when he locks his chests. Does he not there as much accuse mankind by his actions, as I do by my words? But neither of us accuse mans nature in it. The Desires, and other Passions of man, are in themselves no Sin. No more are the Actions, that proceed from those Passions, till they know a Law that forbids them: which till Lawes be made they cannot know: nor can any Law be made, till they have agreed upon the Person that shall make it. [63]

It may peradventure be thought, there was never such a time, nor condition of warre as this; and I believe it was never generally so, over all the world: but there are many places, where they live so now. For the savage people in many places of *America,* except the government of small Families, the concord whereof dependeth on naturall lust, have no government at all; and live at this day in that brutish manner, as I said before. Howsoever, it may be perceived what manner of life there would be, where there were no common Power to feare; by the manner of life, which men that have formerly lived under a peacefull government, use to degenerate into, in a civill Warre.

But though there had never been any time, wherein particular men were in a condition of warre one against another; yet in all times, Kings, and Persons of Soveraigne authority, because of their Independency, are in continuall jealousies, and in the state and posture of Gladiators; having their weapons pointing, and their eyes fixed on one another; that is, their Forts, Garrisons, and Guns upon the Frontiers of their Kingdomes; and continuall Spyes upon their neighbours; which is a posture of War. But because they uphold thereby, the Industry of their Subjects; there does not follow from it, that misery, which accompanies the Liberty of particular men.

To this warre of every man against every man, this also is consequent; that nothing can be Unjust. The notions of Right and Wrong, Justice and Injustice have there no place. Where there is no common Power, there is no Law; where no Law, no Injustice. Force, and Fraud, are in warre, the two Cardinall vertues. Justice, and Injustice are none of the Faculties neither of the Body, nor Mind. If they were, they might be in a man that were alone in the world, as well as his Senses, and Passions. They are Qualities, that relate to men in Society, not in Solitude, It is consequent also to the same condition, that there be no Propriety, no Dominion, no *Mine* and *Thine* distinct; but onely that to be every mans, that he can get; and for so long, as he can keep it. And thus much for the ill condition, which man by meer Nature is actually placed in; though with a possibility to come out of it, consisting partly in the Passions, partly in his Reason.

*In such a Warre, nothing is Unjust.*

The Passions that encline men to Peace, are Feare of Death; Desire of such things as are necessary to commodious living; and a Hope by their Industry to obtain them. And Reason suggesteth convenient Articles of Peace, upon which men may be drawn to agreement. These Articles, are they, which otherwise are called the Lawes of Nature: whereof I shall speak more particularly, in the two following Chapters. [64]

*The Passions that incline men to Peace.*

## CHAP. XIV

### Of the First and Second Naturall Lawes, and of Contracts

The right of nature, which Writers commonly call *Jus Naturale,* is the Liberty each man hath, to use his own power, as he will himselfe, for the preservation of his own Nature; that is to say, of his own Life; and consequently, of doing any thing, which in his own Judgement, and Reason, hee shall conceive to be the aptest means thereunto.

*Right of Nature what.*

By Liberty, is understood, according to the proper signification of the word, the absence of externall Impediments: which Impediments, may oft take away part of a mans power to do what hee would; but cannot hinder him from using the power left him, according as his judgement, and reason shall dictate to him.

*Liberty what.*

A Law of Nature, *(Lex Naturalis,)* is a Precept, or generall Rule, found out by Reason, by which a man is forbidden to do, that, which is destructive of his life, or taketh away the means of preserving the same; and to omit, that, by which he thinketh it may be best preserved. For though they that speak of this subject, use to confound *Jus,* and *Lex, Right* and *Law*; yet they ought to distinguished; because Right, consisteth in liberty to do, or to forbeare; Whereas Law, determineth, and bindeth to one of them: so that Law, and Right, differ as much, as Obligation, and Liberty; which in one and the same matter are inconsistent.

*A Law of Nature what.*

*Difference of Right and Law.*

And because the condition of Man, (as hath been declared in the precedent Chapter) is a condition of Warre of every one against every one; in which case every one is governed by his own Reason; and there is nothing he can make use of, that may not be a help unto him, in preserving his life against his enemyes; It followeth, that in such a condition, every man has a Right to every thing; even to one anothers body. And therefore, as long as this naturall Right of every man to every thing endureth, there can be no security to any man, (how strong or wise soever he be,) of living out the time, which Nature ordinarily alloweth men to live. And consequently it is a precept, or generall rule of Reason, *That every man, ought to endeavour Peace, as farre as he has hope of obtaining it; and when he cannot obtain it, that he may seek, and use, all helps, and advantages of Warre.* The first branch of which Rule, containeth the first, and Fundamentall Law of Nature; which is, *to seek Peace, and follow it.* The Second, the summe of the Right of Nature; which is, *By all means we can, to defend our selves.*

*Naturally every man has Right to every thing.*

*The Fundamentall Law of Nature.*

From this Fundamentall Law of Nature, by which men are commanded to endeavour Peace, is derived this second Law; *That a man be willing, when others are so too, as farre-forth, as for Peace, and* [65] *defence of himselfe he shall think it necessary, to lay down this right to all things; and be contented with so much liberty against other men, as he would allow other men against himselfe.* For as long as every man holdeth this Right, of doing any thing he liketh; so long are all men in the condition of Warre. But if other men will

*The se[c]ond Law of Nature.*

not lay down their Right, as well as he; then there is no Reason for any one, to devest himselfe of his: For that were to expose himselfe to Prey, (which no man is bound to) rather than to dispose himselfe to Peace. This is that Law of the Gospell; *Whatsoever you require that others should do to you, that do ye to them.* And that Law of all men, *Quod tibi fieri non vis, alteri ne feceris.*

*What it is to lay down a Right.*

To *lay downe* a mans *Right* to any thing, is to *devest* himselfe of the *Liberty*, of hindring another of the benefit of his own Right to the same. For he that renounceth, or passeth away his Right, giveth not to any other man a Right which he had not before; because there is nothing to which every man had not Right by Nature: but onely standeth out of his way, that he may enjoy his own originall Right, without hindrance from him; not without hindrance from another. So that the effect which redoundeth to one man, by another mans defect of Right, is but so much diminution of impediments to the use of his own Right originall.

*Renouncing a Right what it is.*

*Transferring Right what.*

*Obligation.*

*Duty.*

*Injustice.*

Right is layd aside, either by simply Renouncing it; or by Transferring it to another. By *Simply* Renouncing; when he cares not to whom the benefit thereof redoundeth. By Transferring; when he intendeth the benefit thereof to some certain person, or persons. And when a man hath in either manner abandoned, or granted away his Right; then is he said to be Obliged, or Bound, not to hinder those, to whom such Right is granted, or abandoned, from the benefit of it: and that he *Ought*, and it is his Duty, not to make voyd that voluntary act of his own: and that such hindrance is Injustice, and Injury, as being *Sine Jure;* the Right being before renounced, or transferred. So that *Injury*, or *Injustice*, in the controversies of the world, is somewhat like to that, which in the disputations of Scholers is called *Absurdity.* For as it is there called an Absurdity, to contradict what one maintained in the Beginning: so in the world, it is called Injustice, and Injury, voluntarily to undo that, which from the beginning he had voluntarily done. The way by which a man either simply Renounceth, or Transferreth his Right, is a Declaration, or Signification, by some voluntary and sufficient signe, or signes, that he doth so Renounce, or Transferre; or hath so Renounced, or Transferred the same, to him that accepteth it. And these Signes are either Words onely, or Actions onely; or (as it happeneth most often) both Words, and Actions. And the same are the Bonds, by which men are bound, and obliged: Bonds, that have their strength, not from their own Nature, ( for nothing is more easily broken then a mans word,) but from Feare of some evill consequence upon the rupture.

*Not all Rights are alienable.*

Whensoever a man Transferreth his Right, or Renounceth it; it is either in consideration of some Right reciprocally transferred to [66] himselfe; or for some other good he hopeth for thereby. For it is a voluntary act: and of the voluntary acts of every man, the object is some *Good to himselfe.* And therefore there be some Rights, which no man can be understood by any words, or other signes, to have abandoned, or transferred. As first a man cannot lay down the right of resisting them, that assault him by force, to take away his life; because he cannot be understood to ayme thereby, at any Good to himselfe. The same may be sayd of Wounds, and Chayns, and Imprisonment; both because there is no benefit consequent to such patience; as there is to the patience of suffering another to be wounded, or imprisoned: as also because a man cannot tell, when he seeth men proceed against him by violence, whether they intend his death or not. And lastly the motive, and end for which this renouncing, and transferring of Right is introduced, is nothing else but the security of a mans person, in his life, and in the means of so preserving life, as not to be weary of it. And therefore if a man by words, or other signes, seem to despoyle himselfe of the End, for which those signes were intended; he is not to be understood as if he meant it, or that it was his will; but that he was ignorant of how such words and actions were to be interpreted.

*Contract what.*

The mutuall transferring of Right, is that which men call Contract.

There is difference, between transferring of Right to the Thing; and transferring, or tradition, that is, delivery of the Thing it selfe. For the Thing may be delivered together with the Translation of the Right; as in buying and selling with ready mony; or exchange of goods, or lands: and it may be delivered some time after.

*Covenant what.*

Again, one of the Contractors, may deliver the Thing contracted for on his part, and leave the other to perform his part at some determinate time after, and in the mean time be trusted; and then the Contract on his part, is called Pact, or Covenant: Or both parts may contract now, to performe hereafter: in which cases, he that is to performe in time to come, being trusted, his performance is called *Keeping of Promise*, or Faith; and the fayling of performance (if it be voluntary) *Violation of Faith.*

When the transferring of Right, is not mutuall; but one of the parties transferreth, in hope to gain thereby friendship, or service from another, or from his friends; or in hope to gain the reputation of Charity, or Magnanimity; or to deliver his mind from the pain of compassion; or in hope of reward in heaven; This is not Contract, but Gift, Free-gift, Grace: which words signifie one and the same thing.

*Free-gift.*

Signes of Contract, are either *Expresse,* or *by Inference.* Expresse, are words spoken with understanding of what they signifie: And such words are either of the time *Present,* or *Past;* as, *I Give, I Grant, I have Given, I have Granted, I will that this be yours:* Or of the future; as, *I will Give, I will Grant:* which words of the future, are called Promise.

*Signes of Contract Expresse.*

Signes by Inference, are sometimes the consequence of Words; [67] sometimes the consequence of Silence; somtimes the consequence of Actions; somtimes the consequence of Forbearing an Action: and generally a signe by Inference, of any Contract, is whatsoever sufficiently argues the will of the Contractor.

*Signes of Contract by Inference.*

Words alone, if they be of the time to come, and contain a bare promise, are an insufficient signe of a Free-gift and therefore not obligatory. For if they be of the time to Come, as, *To morrow I will Give,* they are a signe I have not given yet, and consequently that my right is not transferred, but remaineth till I transferre it by some other Act. But if the words be of the time Present, or Past, as, *I have given, or do give to be delivered to morrow,* then is my to morrows Right given away to day; and that by the vertue of the words, though there were no other argument of my will. And there is a great difference in the signification of these words, *Volo hoc tuum esse cras,* and *Cras dabo;* that is, between *I will that this be thine to morrow,* and, *I will give it thee to morrow:* For the word *I will,* in the former manner of speech, signifies an act of the will Present; but in the later, it signifies a promise of an act of the will to Come: and therefore the former words, being of the Present, transferre a future right; the later, that be of the Future, transferre nothing. But if there be other signes of the Will to transferre a Right, besides Words; then, though the gift be Free, yet may the Right be understood to passe by words of the future: as if a man propound a Prize to him that comes first to the end of a race, The gift is Free; and though the words be of the Future, yet the Right passeth: for if he would not have his words so be understood, he should not have let them runne.

*Free gift passeth by words of the Present or Past.*

In Contracts, the right passeth, not onely where the words are of the time Present, or Past; but also where they are of the Future: because all Contract is mutuall translation, or change of Right; and therefore he that promiseth onely, because he hath already received the benefit for which he promiseth, is to be understood as if he intended the Right should passe: for unlesse he had been content to have his words so understood, the other would not have performed his part first. And for that cause, in buying, and selling, and other acts of Contract, a Promise is equivalent to a Covenant; and therefore obligatory.

*Signes of Contract are words both of the Past, Present, and Future.*

He that performeth first in the case of a Contract, is said to Merit that which he is to receive by the performance of the other; and he hath it as *Due.* Also when a Prize is propounded to many, which is to be given to him onely that winneth; or mony is thrown amongst many, to be enjoyed by them that catch it; though this be a Free gift; yet so to Win, or so to Catch, is to *Merit,* and to have it as Due. For the Right is transferred in the Propounding of the Prize, and in throwing down the mony; though it be not determined to whom, but by the Event of the contention. But there is between these two sorts of Merit, this difference, that In Contract, I Merit by vertue of my own power, and the Contractors need; but in this case of Free gift, I am enabled to Merit onely by the benignity of the Giver: In Contract, I merit at the Contractors hand that hee [68] should depart with his right; In this case of Gift, I Merit not that the giver should part with his right; but that when he has parted with it, it should be mine, rather than anothers. And this I think to be the meaning of that distinction of the Schooles, between *Meritum congrui,* and *Meritum condigni.* For God Almighty, having promised Paradise to those men (hoodwinkt with carnall desires,) that can walk through this world according to the Precepts, and Limits prescribed by him; they say, he that shall so walk, shall Merit Paradise *Ex congruo.* But because no man can demand a right to it, by his own Righteousnesse, or any other power in himselfe, but by the Free Grace of God onely; they say, no man can Merit Paradise *ex condigno.* This I say, I think is the meaning of that distinction; but because Disputers do not agree upon the signification of their own termes of Art, longer than it serves their turn; I will not affirme any thing of their meaning: onely this I say; when a gift is given indefinitely, as a prize to be contended for, he that winneth Meriteth, and may claime the Prize as Due.

*Merit what.*

If a Covenant be made, wherein neither of the parties performe presently, but trust one another; in the condition of meer Nature, (which is a condition of Warre of every man against every man,) upon any reasonable suspition, it is Voyd: But if there be a common Power set over them both, with

*Covenants of Mutuall trust, when Invalid.*

right and force sufficient to compell performance; it is not Voyd. For he that performeth first, has no assurance of other will performe after; because the bonds of words are too weak to bridle mens ambition, avarice, anger, and other Passions, without the feare of some coerceive Power; which in the condition of meer Nature, where all men are equall, and judges of the justnesse of their own fears, cannot possibly be supposed. And therefore he which performeth first, does but betray himselfe to his enemy; contrary to the Right (he can never abandon) of defending his life, and means of living.

But in a civill estate, where there is a Power set up to constrain those that would otherwise violate their faith, that feare is no more reasonable; and for that cause, he which by the Covenant is to perform first, is obliged so to do.

The cause of feare, which maketh such a Covenant invalid, must be alwayes something arising after the Covenant made; as some new fact, or other signe of the Will not to performe: else it cannot make the Covenant voyd. For that which could not hinder a man from promising, ought not to be admitted as a hindrance of performing.

*Right to the End, Containeth Right to the Means.*

He that transferreth any Right, transferreth the Means of enjoying it, as farre as lyeth in his power. As he that selleth Land, is understood to transferre the Herbage, and whatsoever growes upon it; Nor can he that sells a Mill turn away the Stream that drives it. And they that give to a man the Right of government in Sovereignty, are understood to give him the right of levying mony to maintain Souldiers; and of appointing Magistrates for the administration of Justice.

*No Covenant with Beasts.*

To make Covenants with bruit Beasts, is impossible; because not understanding our speech, they understand not, nor accept of any [69] translation of Right; nor can translate any Right to another: and without mutuall acceptation, there is no Covenant.

*Nor with God without speciall Revelation.*

To make Covenant with God, is impossible, but by Mediation of such as God speaketh to, either by Revelation supernaturall, or by his Lieutenants that govern under him, and in his Name: For otherwise we know not whether our Covenants be accepted, or not. And therefore they that Vow any thing contrary to an ylaw of Nature, Vow in vain; as being a thing unjust to pay such Vow. And if it be a thing commanded by the Law of Nature, it is not the Vow, but the Law that binds them.

*No Covenant, but of Possible and Future.*

The matter, or subject of a Covenant, is alwayes something that falleth under deliberation; (For to Covenant, is an act of the Will; that is to say an act, and the last act, of deliberation;) and is therefore alwayes understood to be something to come; and which is judged Possible for him that Covenanteth, to performe.

And therefore, to promise that which is known to be Impossible, is no Covenant. But if that prove impossible afterwards; which before was thought possible, the Covenant is valid, and bindeth, (though not to the thing it selfe,) yet to the value; or, if that also be impossible, to the unfeigned endeavour of performing as much as is possible: for to more no man can be obliged.

*Covenants how made voyd.*

Men are freed of their Covenants two wayes; by Performing; or by being Forgiven. For Performance, is the naturall end of obligation; and Forgivenesse, the restitution of liberty; as being a re-transferring of that Right, in which the obligation consisted.

*Covenants extorted by feare are valide.*

Covenants entred into by fear, in the condition of meer Nature, are obligatory. For example, if I Covenant to pay a ransome, or service for my life, to an enemy; I am bound by it. For it is a Contract, wherein one receiveth the benefit of life; the other is to receive mony, or service for it; and consequently, where no other Law (as in the condition, of meer Nature) forbiddeth the performance, the Covenant is valid. Therefore Prisoners of warre, if trusted with the payment of their Ransome, are obliged to pay it: And if a weaker Prince, make a disadvantageous peace with a stronger, for feare; he is bound to keep it; unlesse (as hath been sayd before) there ariseth some new, and just cause of feare, to renew the war. And even in Common-wealths, if I be forced to redeem my selfe from a Theefe by promising him mony, I am bound to pay it, till the Civill Law discharge me. For whatsoever I may lawfully do without Obligation, the same I may lawfully Covenant to do through feare: and what I lawfully Covenant, I cannot lawfully break.

*The former Covenant to one, makes voyd the later to another.*

A former Covenant, makes voyd a later. For a man that hath passed away his Right to one man to day, hath it not to passe to morrow to another: and therefore the later promise passeth no Right, but is null.

A Covenant not to defend my selfe from force, by force, is alwayes voyd. For (as I have shewed before) no man can transferre, or lay down his Right to save himselfe from Death, Wounds, and

Imprisonment, (the avoyding whereof is the onely End of laying [70] down any Right, and therefore the promise of not resisting force, in no Covenant transferreth any right; nor is obliging. For though a man may Covenant thus, *Unlesse I do so, or so, kill me;* he cannot Covenant thus, *Unlesse I do so, or so, I will not resist you, when you come to kill me.* For man by nature chooseth the lesser evill, which is danger of death in resisting; rather than the greater, which is certain and present death in not resisting. And this is granted to be true by all men, in that they lead Criminals to Execution, and Prison, with armed men, notwithstanding that such Criminals have consented to the Law, by which they are condemned.

*A mans Covenant not to defend himselfe, is voyd.*

A Covenant to accuse ones selfe, without assurance of pardon, is likewise invalide. For in the condition of Nature, where every man is Judge, there is no place for Accusation: and in the Civill State, the Accusation is followed with Punishment; which being Force, a man is not obliged not to resist. The same is also true, of the Accusation of those, by whose Condemnation a man falls into misery; as of a Father, Wife, or Benefactor. For the Testimony of such an Accuser, if it be not willingly given, is presumed to be corrupted by Nature; and therefore not to be received: and where a mans Testimony is not to be credited, he is not bound to give it. Also Accusations upon Torture, are not to be reputed as Testimonies. For Torture is to be used but as means of conjecture, and light, in the further examination, and search of truth: and what is in that case confessed, tendeth to the ease of him that is Tortured; not to the informing of the Torturers: and therefore ought not to have the credit of a sufficient Testimony: for whether he deliver himselfe by true, or false Accusation, he does it by the Right of preserving his own life.

*No man obliged to accuse himself.*

The force of Words, being (as I have formerly noted) too weak to hold men to the performance of their Covenants; there are in mans nature, but two imaginable helps to strengthen it. And those are either a Feare of the consequence of breaking their word; or a Glory, or Pride in appearing not to need to breake it. This later is a Generosity too rarely found to be presumed on, especially in the pursuers of Wealth, Command, or sensuall Pleasure; which are the greatest part of Mankind. The Passion to be reckoned upon, is Fear; whereof there be two very generall Objects: one, The Power of Spirits Invisible; the other, The Power of those men they shall therein Offend. Of these two, though the former be the greater Power, yet the feare of the later is commonly the greater Feare. The Feare of the former is in every man, his own Religion: which hath place in the nature of man before Civill Society. The later hath not so; at least not place enough, to keep men to their promises; because in the condition of meer Nature, the inequality of Power is not discerned, but by the event of Battell. So that before the time of Civill Society, or in the interruption thereof by Warre, there is nothing can strengthen a Covenant of Peace agreed on, against the temptations of Avarice, Ambition, Lust, or other strong desire, but the feare of that Invisible Power, which they every one Worship as God; and Feare as a Revenger of their perfydy. All therefore that can be done [71] between two men not subject to Civill Power, is to put one another to swear by the God he feareth: Which *Swearing*, or Oath, is a *Forme of Speech, added to a Promise; by which be that promiseth, signifieth, that unlesse be performe, be renounceth the mercy of his God, or calleth to him far vengeance on himselfe.* Such was the Heathen Forme, *Let* Jupiter *kill me else, as I kill this Beast.* So is our Forme, *I shall do thus, and thus, so help me God.* And this, with the Rites and Ceremonies, which every one useth in his own Religion, that the feare of breaking faith might be the greater.

*The End of an Oath.*

*The forme of an Oath.*

By this it appears, that an Oath taken according to any other Forme, or Rite, then his, that sweareth, is in vain; and no Oath: And that there is no Swearing by any thing which the Swearer thinks not God. For though men have sometimes used to swear by their Kings, for feare, or flattery; yet they would have it thereby understood, they attributed to them Divine honour. And that Swearing unnecessarily by God, is but prophaning of his name: and Swearing by other things, as men do in common discourse, is not Swearing, but an impious Custome, gotten by too much vehemence of talking.

*No Oath, but by God.*

It appears also, that the Oath addes nothing to the Obligation. For a Covenant, if lawfull, binds in the sight of God, without the Oath, as much as with it: if unlawfull, bindeth not at all; though it be confirmed with an Oath.

*An Oath addes nothing to the Obligation.*

# EMOTIVISM (PART 1)

BY **David Hume**

## BOOK III OF MORALS:
## PART I OF VIRTUE AND VICE IN GENERAL

### Sect. I Moral Distinctions Not Derived from Reason

There is an inconvenience which attends all abstruse reasoning that it may silence, without convincing an antagonist, and requires the same intense study to make us sensible of its force, that was at first requisite for its invention. When we leave our closet, and engage in the common affairs of life, its conclusions seem to vanish, like the phantoms of the night on the appearance of the morning; and it is difficult for us to retain even that conviction, which we had attained with difficulty. This is still more conspicuous in a long chain of reasoning, where we must preserve to the end the evidence of the first propositions, and where we often lose sight of all the most received maxims, either of philosophy or common life. I am not, however, without hopes, that the present system of philosophy will acquire new force as it advances; and that our reasonings concerning morals will corroborate whatever has been said concerning the UNDERSTANDING and the PASSIONS. Morality is a subject that interests us above all others: We fancy the peace of society to be at stake in every decision concerning it; and it is evident, that this concern must make our speculations appear more real and solid, than where the subject is, in a great measure, indifferent to us. What affects us, we conclude can never be a chimera; and as our passion is engaged on the one side or the other, we naturally think that the question lies within human comprehension; which, in other cases of this nature, we are apt to entertain some doubt of. Without this advantage I never should have ventured upon a third volume of such abstruse philosophy, in an age, wherein the greatest part of men seem agreed to convert reading into an amusement, and to reject every thing that requires any considerable degree of attention to be comprehended.

It has been observed, that nothing is ever present to the mind but its perceptions; and that all the actions of seeing, hearing, judging, loving, hating, and thinking, fall under this denomination. The mind can never exert itself in any action, which we may not comprehend under the term of perception; and consequently that term is no less applicable to those judgments, by which we distinguish moral good and evil, than to every other operation of the mind. To approve of one character, to condemn another, are only so many different perceptions.

Now as perceptions resolve themselves into two kinds, viz. impressions and ideas, this distinction gives rise to a question, with which we shall open up our present enquiry concerning morals. WHETHER IT IS BY MEANS OF OUR IDEAS OR IMPRESSIONS WE DISTINGUISH BETWIXT VICE AND VIRTUE, AND PRONOUNCE AN ACTION BLAMEABLE OR PRAISEWORTHY? This will immediately cut off all loose discourses and declamations, and reduce us to something precise and exact on the present subject.

Those who affirm that virtue is nothing but a conformity to reason; that there are eternal fitnesses and unfitnesses of things, which are the same to every rational being that considers them; that the immutable measures of right and wrong impose an obligation, not only on human creatures, but also on the Deity himself: All these systems concur in the opinion, that morality, like truth, is discerned merely by ideas, and by their juxtaposition and comparison. In order, therefore, to judge of these systems, we need only consider, whether it be possible, from reason alone, to distinguish betwixt moral good and evil, or whether there must concur some other principles to enable us to make that distinction.

If morality had naturally no influence on human passions and actions, it were in vain to take such pains to inculcate it; and nothing would be more fruitless than that multitude of rules and precepts, with which all moralists

David Hume, "Moral Distinctions Not Derived from Reason," A Treatise of Human Nature.

abound. Philosophy is commonly divided into speculative and practical; and as morality is always comprehended under the latter division, it is supposed to influence our passions and actions, and to go beyond the calm and indolent judgments of the understanding. And this is confirmed by common experience, which informs us, that men are often governed by their duties, and are detered from some actions by the opinion of injustice, and impelled to others by that of obligation.

Since morals, therefore, have an influence on the actions and affections, it follows, that they cannot be derived from reason; and that because reason alone, as we have already proved, can never have any such influence. Morals excite passions, and produce or prevent actions. Reason of itself is utterly impotent in this particular. The rules of morality therefore, are not conclusions of our reason.

No one, I believe, will deny the justness of this inference; nor is there any other means of evading it, than by denying that principle, on which it is founded. As long as it is allowed, that reason has no influence on our passions and action, it is in vain to pretend, that morality is discovered only by a deduction of reason. An active principle can never be founded on an inactive; and if reason be inactive in itself, it must remain so in all its shapes and appearances, whether it exerts itself in natural or moral subjects, whether it considers the powers of external bodies, or the actions of rational beings.

It would be tedious to repeat all the arguments, by which I have proved [Book II. Part III. Sect 3.], that reason is perfectly inert, and can never either prevent or produce any action or affection, it will be easy to recollect what has been said upon that subject. I shall only recall on this occasion one of these arguments, which I shall endeavour to render still more conclusive, and more applicable to the present subject.

Reason is the discovery of truth or falshood. Truth or falshood consists in an agreement or disagreement either to the real relations of ideas, or to real existence and matter of fact. Whatever, therefore, is not susceptible of this agreement or disagreement, is incapable of being true or false, and can never be an object of our reason. Now it is evident our passions, volitions, and actions, are not susceptible of any such agreement or disagreement; being original facts and realities, compleat in themselves, and implying no reference to other passions, volitions, and actions. It is impossible, therefore, they can be pronounced either true or false, and be either contrary or conformable to reason.

This argument is of double advantage to our present purpose. For it proves DIRECTLY, that actions do not derive their merit from a conformity to reason, nor their blame from a contrariety to it; and it proves the same truth more INDIRECTLY, by shewing us, that as reason can never immediately prevent or produce any action by contradicting or approving of it, it cannot be the source of moral good and evil, which are found to have that influence. Actions may be laudable or blameable; but they cannot be reasonable: Laudable or blameable, therefore, are not the same with reasonable or unreasonable. The merit and demerit of actions frequently contradict, and sometimes controul our natural propensities. But reason has no such influence. Moral distinctions, therefore, are not the offspring of reason. Reason is wholly inactive, and can never be the source of so active a principle as conscience, or a sense of morals.

But perhaps it may be said, that though no will or action can be immediately contradictory to reason, yet we may find such a contradiction in some of the attendants of the action, that is, in its causes or effects. The action may cause a judgment, or may be obliquely caused by one, when the judgment concurs with a passion; and by an abusive way of speaking, which philosophy will scarce allow of, the same contrariety may, upon that account, be ascribed to the action. How far this truth or faishood may be the source of morals, it will now be proper to consider.

It has been observed, that reason, in a strict and philosophical sense, can have influence on our conduct only after two ways: Either when it excites a passion by informing us of the existence of something which is a proper object of it; or when it discovers the connexion of causes and effects, so as to afford us means of exerting any passion. These are the only kinds of judgment, which can accompany our actions, or can be said to produce them in any manner; and it must be allowed, that these judgments may often be false and erroneous. A person may be affected with passion, by supposing a pain or pleasure to lie in an object, which has no tendency to produce either of these sensations, or which produces the contrary to what is imagined. A person may also take false measures for the attaining his end, and may retard, by his foolish conduct, instead of forwarding the execution of any project. These false judgments may be thought to affect the passions and actions, which are connected with them, and may be said to render them unreasonable, in a figurative and improper way of speaking. But though this be acknowledged, it is easy to observe, that these errors are so far from being the source of all immorality, that they are commonly very innocent, and draw no manner of guilt upon the person who is so unfortunate as to fail into them. They extend not beyond a mistake of fact, which moralists have not generally supposed criminal, as being perfectly involuntary. I am more to be lamented than blamed, if I am mistaken with regard to the influence of objects in producing pain or pleasure, or if I know not the proper means of satisfying my desires. No one can ever regard such errors as a defect in my moral character. A fruit, for instance, that is really disagreeable, appears to me at a distance, and through mistake I fancy it to be pleasant and delicious. Here is one error. I choose certain means of reaching this fruit, which are not proper for my end. Here is a second error; nor is there any third one, which can ever possibly enter into our reasonings concerning actions. I ask, therefore, if a man, in this situation, and guilty of these two errors, is to be regarded as vicious and criminal, however unavoidable they might have been? Or if it be possible to imagine, that such errors are the sources of all immorality?

And here it may be proper to observe, that if moral distinctions be derived from the truth or falshood of those judgments, they must take place wherever we form the judgments; nor will there be any difference, whether the question be concerning an apple or a kingdom, or whether the error be avoidable or unavoidable. For as the very essence of morality is supposed to consist in an agreement or disagreement to reason, the other circumstances are entirely arbitrary, and can never either bestow on any action the character of virtuous or vicious, or deprive it of that character. To which we may add, that this agreement or disagreement, not admitting of degrees, all virtues and vices would of course be equal.

Should it be pretended, that though a mistake of fact be not criminal, yet a mistake of right often is; and that this may be the source of immorality: I would answer, that it is impossible such a mistake can ever be the original source of immorality, since it supposes a real right and wrong; that is, a real distinction in morals, independent of these judgments. A mistake, therefore, of right may become a species of immorality; but it is only a secondary one, and is founded on some other, antecedent to it.

As to those judgments which are the effects of our actions, and which, when false, give occasion to pronounce the actions contrary to truth and reason; we may observe, that our actions never cause any judgment, either true or false, in ourselves, and that it is only on others they have such an influence. It is certain, that an action, on many occasions, may give rise to false conclusions in others; and that a person, who through a window sees any lewd behaviour of mine with my neighbour's wife, may be so simple as to imagine she is certainly my own. In this respect my action resembles somewhat a lye or falshood; only with this difference, which is material, that I perform not the action with any intention of giving rise to a false judgment in another, but merely to satisfy my lust and passion. It causes, however, a mistake and false judgment by accident; and the falshood of its effects may be ascribed, by some odd figurative way of speaking, to the action itself. But still I can see no pretext of reason for asserting, that the tendency to cause such an error is the first spring or original source of all immorality.

Thus upon the whole, it is impossible, that the distinction betwixt moral good and evil, can be made to reason; since that distinction has an influence upon our actions, of which reason alone is incapable. Reason and judgment may, indeed, be the mediate cause of an action, by prompting, or by directing a passion: But it is not pretended, that a judgment of this kind, either in its truth or falshood, is attended with virtue or vice. And as to the judgments, which are caused by our judgments, they can still less bestow those moral qualities on the actions, which are their causes.

But to be more particular, and to shew, that those eternal immutable fitnesses and unfitnesses of things cannot be defended by sound philosophy, we may weigh the following considerations.

If the thought and understanding were alone capable of fixing the boundaries of right and wrong, the character of virtuous and vicious either must lie in some relations of objects, or must be a matter of fact, which is discovered by our reasoning. This consequence is evident. As the operations of human understanding divide themselves into two kinds, the comparing of ideas, and the inferring of matter of fact; were virtue discovered by the understanding; it must be an object of one of these operations, nor is there any third operation of the understanding. which can discover it. There has been an opinion very industriously propagated by certain philosophers, that morality is susceptible of demonstration; and though no one has ever been able to advance a single step in those demonstrations; yet it is taken for granted, that this science may be brought to an equal certainty with geometry or algebra. Upon this supposition vice and virtue must consist in some relations; since it is allowed on all hands, that no matter of fact is capable of being demonstrated. Let us, therefore, begin with examining this hypothesis, and endeavour, if possible, to fix those moral qualities, which have been so long the objects of our fruitless researches. Point out distinctly the relations, which constitute morality or obligation, that we may know wherein they consist, and after what manner we must judge of them.

If you assert, that vice and virtue consist in relations susceptible of certainty and demonstration, you must confine yourself to those four relations, which alone admit of that degree of evidence; and in that case you run into absurdities, from which you will never be able to extricate yourself. For as you make the very essence of morality to lie in the relations, and as there is no one of these relations but what is applicable, not only to an irrational, but also to an inanimate object; it follows, that even such objects must be susceptible of merit or demerit. RESEMBLANCE, CONTRARIETY, DEGREES IN QUALITY, and PROPORTIONS IN QUANTITY AND NUMBER; all these relations belong as properly to matter, as to our actions, passions, and volitions. It is unquestionable, therefore, that morality lies not in any of these relations, nor the sense of it in their discovery.

Should it be asserted, that the sense of morality consists in the discovery of some relation, distinct from these, and that our enumeration was not compleat, when we comprehended all demonstrable relations under four general heads: To this I know not what to reply, till some one be so good as to point out to me this new relation. It is impossible to refute a system, which has never yet been explained. In such a manner of fighting in the dark, a man loses his blows in the air, and often places them where the enemy is not present.

I must, therefore, on this occasion, rest contented with requiring the two following conditions of any one that would undertake to clear up this system. First, As moral good and evil belong only to the actions of the mind, and are derived from our situation with regard to external objects, the relations, from which these moral distinctions arise, must lie only betwixt internal actions, and external objects, and must not be applicable either to internal actions, compared among themselves, or to external objects, when placed in opposition to other external objects. For as morality is supposed to attend certain relations, if these relations coued belong to internal actions considered singly, it would follow, that we might be guilty of crimes in ourselves, and independent of our situation, with respect to the universe: And in like manner, if these moral relations coued be applied to external objects, it would follow, that even inanimate beings would be susceptible of moral beauty and deformity. Now it seems difficult to imagine, that any relation can be discovered betwixt our passions, volitions and actions, compared to external objects, which relation might not belong either to these passions and volitions, or to these external objects, compared among themselves. But it will be still more difficult to fulfil the second condition, requisite to justify this system. According to the principles of those who maintain an abstract rational difference betwixt moral good and evil, and a natural fitness and unfitness of things, it is not only supposed, that these relations, being eternal and immutable, are the same, when considered by every rational creature, but their effects are also supposed to be necessarily the same; and it is concluded they have no less, or rather a greater, influence in directing the will of the deity, than in governing the rational and virtuous of our own species. These two particulars are evidently distinct. It is one thing to know virtue, and another to conform the will to it. In order, therefore, to prove, that the measures of right and wrong are eternal laws, obligatory on every rational mind, it is not sufficient to shew the relations upon which they are founded: We must also point out the connexion betwixt the relation and the will; and must prove that this connexion is so necessary, that in every well-disposed mind, it must take place and have its influence; though the difference betwixt these minds be in other respects immense and infinite. Now besides what I have already proved, that even in human nature no relation can ever alone produce any action: besides this, I say, it has been shewn, in treating of the understanding, that there is no connexion of cause and effect, such as this is supposed to be, which is discoverable otherwise than by experience, and of which we can pretend to have any security by the simple consideration of the objects. All beings in the universe, considered in themselves, appear entirely loose and independent of each other. It is only by experience we learn their influence and connexion; and this influence we ought never to extend beyond experience.

Thus it will be impossible to fulfil the first condition required to the system of eternal measures of right and wrong; because it is impossible to shew those relations, upon which such a distinction may be founded: And it is as impossible to fulfil the second condition; because we cannot prove A PRIORI, that these relations, if they really existed and were perceived, would be universally forcible and obligatory.

But to make these general reflections more dear and convincing, we may illustrate them by some particular instances, wherein this character of moral good or evil is the most universally acknowledged. Of all crimes that human creatures are capable of committing, the most horrid and unnatural is ingratitude, especially when it is committed against parents, and appears in the more flagrant instances of wounds and death. This is acknowledged by all mankind, philosophers as well as the people; the question only arises among philosophers, whether the guilt or moral deformity of this action be discovered by demonstrative reasoning, or be felt by an internal sense, and by means of some sentiment, which the reflecting on such an action naturally occasions. This question will soon be decided against the former opinion, if we can shew the same relations in other objects, without the notion of any guilt or iniquity attending them. Reason or science is nothing but the comparing of ideas, and the discovery of their relations; and if the same relations have different characters, it must evidently follow, that those characters are not discovered merely by reason. To put the affair, therefore, to this trial, let us chuse any inanimate object, such as an oak or elm; and let us suppose, that by the dropping of its seed, it produces a sapling below it, which springing up by degrees, at last overtops and destroys the parent tree: I ask, if in this instance there be wanting any relation, which is discoverable in parricide or ingratitude? Is not the one tree the cause of the other's existence; and the latter the cause of the destruction of the former, in the same manner as when a child murders his parent? It is not sufficient to reply, that a choice or will is wanting. For in the case of parricide, a will does not give rise to any DIFFERENT relations, but is only the cause from which the action is derived; and consequently produces the same relations, that in the oak or elm arise from some other principles. It is a will or choice, that determines a man to kill his parent; and they are the laws of matter and motion, that determine a sapling to destroy the oak, from which it sprung. Here then the same relations have different causes; but still the relations are the same: And as their discovery is not in both cases attended with a notion of immorality, it follows, that that notion does not arise from such a discovery.

But to chuse an instance, still more resembling; I would fain ask any one, why incest in the human species is criminal, and why the very same action, and the same relations in animals have not the smallest moral turpitude and deformity? If it be answered, that this action is innocent in animals, because they have not reason sufficient to discover its turpitude; but that man, being endowed with that faculty which ought to restrain him to his duty, the same action instantly becomes criminal to him; should this be said, I would reply, that this is evidently arguing in a circle. For before reason can perceive this turpitude, the turpitude must exist; and consequently is independent of the decisions of our reason, and is their object more properly than their effect. According to this system, then, every animal, that has sense, and appetite, and will; that is, every animal must be susceptible of all the same virtues and vices, for which we ascribe praise and blame to human creatures. All the difference is, that our superior reason may serve to discover the vice or virtue, and by that means may augment the blame or praise: But still this discovery supposes a separate being in these moral distinctions, and a being, which depends only on the will and appetite, and which, both in thought and reality, may be distinguished from the reason. Animals are susceptible of the same relations, with respect to each other, as the human species, and therefore would also be susceptible of the same morality, if the essence of morality consisted in these relations. Their want of a sufficient degree of reason may hinder them from perceiving the duties and obligations of morality, but can never hinder these duties from existing; since they must antecedently exist, in order to their being perceived. Reason must find them, and can never produce them. This argument deserves to be weighed, as being, in my opinion, entirely decisive.

Nor does this reasoning only prove, that morality consists not in any relations, that are the objects of science; but if examined, will prove with equal certainty, that it consists not in any matter of fact, which can be discovered by the understanding. This is the second part of our argument; and if it can be made evident, we may conclude, that morality is not an object of reason. But can there be any difficulty in proving, that vice and virtue are not matters of fact, whose existence we can infer by reason? Take any action allowed to be vicious: Wilful murder, for instance. Examine it in all lights, and see if you can find that matter of fact, or real existence, which you call vice. In which-ever way you take it, you find only certain passions, motives, volitions and thoughts. There is no other matter of fact in the case. The vice entirely escapes you, as long as you consider the object. You never can find it, till you turn your reflection into your own breast, and find a sentiment of disapprobation, which arises in you, towards this action. Here is a matter of fact; but it is the object of feeling, not of reason. It lies in yourself, not in the object. So that when you pronounce any action or character to be vicious, you mean nothing, but that from the constitution of your nature you have a feeling or sentiment of blame from the contemplation of it. Vice and virtue, therefore, may be compared to sounds, colours, heat and cold, which, according to modern philosophy, are not qualities in objects, but perceptions in the mind: And this discovery in morals, like that other in physics, is to be regarded as a considerable advancement of the speculative sciences; though, like that too, it has little or no influence on practice. Nothing can be more real, or concern us more, than our own sentiments of pleasure and uneasiness; and if these be favourable to virtue, and unfavourable to vice, no more can be requisite to the regulation of our conduct and behaviour.

I cannot forbear adding to these reasonings an observation, which may, perhaps, be found of some importance. In every system of morality, which I have hitherto met with, I have always remarked, that the author proceeds for some time in the ordinary way of reasoning, and establishes the being of a God, or makes observations concerning human affairs; when of a sudden I am surprized to find, that instead of the usual copulations of propositions, is, and is not, I meet with no proposition that is not connected with an ought, or an ought not. This change is imperceptible; but is, however, of the last consequence. For as this ought, or ought not, expresses some new relation or affirmation, it is necessary that it should be observed and explained; and at the same time that a reason should be given, for what seems altogether inconceivable, how this new relation can be a deduction from others, which are entirely different from it. But as authors do not commonly use this precaution, I shall presume to recommend it to the readers; and am persuaded, that this small attention would subvert all the vulgar systems of morality, and let us see, that the distinction of vice and virtue is not founded merely on the relations of objects, nor is perceived by reason.

# EMOTIVISM (PART 2)

BY **David Hume**

## APPENDIX I. CONCERNING MORAL SENTIMENT

If the foregoing hypothesis be received, it will now be easy for us to determine the question first started,[1] concerning the general principles of morals; and though we postponed the decision of that question, lest it should then involve us in intricate speculations, which are unfit for moral discourses, we may resume it at present, and examine how far either REASON or SENTIMENT enters into all decisions of praise or censure.

One principal foundation of moral praise being supposed to lie in the usefulness of any quality or action, it is evident that REASON must enter for a considerable share in all decisions of this kind; since nothing but that faculty can instruct us in the tendency of qualities and actions, and point out their beneficial consequences to society and to their possessor. In many cases this is an affair liable to great controversy: doubts may arise; opposite interests may occur; and a preference must be given to one side, from very nice views, and a small overbalance of utility. This is particularly remarkable in questions with regard to justice; as is, indeed, natural to suppose, from that species of utility which attends this virtue.[2] Were every single instance of justice, like that of benevolence, useful to society; this would be a more simple state of the case, and seldom liable to great controversy. But as single instances of justice are often pernicious in their first and immediate tendency, and as the advantage to society results only from the observance of the general rule, and from the concurrence and combination of several persons in the same equitable conduct; the case here becomes more intricate and involved. The various circumstances of society; the various consequences of any practice; the various interests which may be proposed; these, on many occasions, are doubtful, and subject to great discussion and inquiry. The object of municipal laws is to fix all the questions with regard to justice: the debates of civilians; the reflections of politicians; the precedents of history and public records, are all directed to the same purpose. And a very accurate REASON or JUDGEMENT is often requisite, to give the true determination, amidst such intricate doubts arising from obscure or opposite utilities.

But though reason, when fully assisted and improved, be sufficient to instruct us in the pernicious or useful tendency of qualities and actions; it is not alone sufficient to produce any moral blame or approbation. Utility is only a tendency to a certain end; and were the end totally indifferent to us, we should feel the same indifference towards the means. It is requisite a SENTIMENT should here display itself, in order to give a preference to the useful above the pernicious tendencies. This SENTIMENT can be no other than a feeling for the happiness of mankind, and a resentment of their misery; since these are the different ends which virtue and vice have a tendency to promote. Here therefore REASON instructs us in the several tendencies of actions, and HUMANITY makes a distinction in favour of those which are useful and beneficial.

This partition between the faculties of understanding and sentiment, in all moral decisions, seems clear from the preceding hypothesis. But I shall suppose that hypothesis false: it will then be requisite to look out for some other theory that may be satisfactory; and I dare venture to affirm that none such will ever be found, so long as we suppose reason to be the sole source of morals. To prove this, it will be proper to weigh the five following considerations.

I. It is easy for a false hypothesis to maintain some appearance of truth, while it keeps wholly in generals, makes use of undefined terms, and employs comparisons, instead of instances. This is particularly remarkable in that philosophy, which ascribes the discernment of all moral distinctions to reason alone, without the concurrence of

1 Sect. 1

2 See App. II

David Hume, "Moral Distinctions Not Derived from Reason," A Treatise of Human Nature.

sentiment. It is impossible that, in any particular instance, this hypothesis can so much as be rendered intelligible, whatever specious figure it may make in general declamations and discourses. Examine the crime of INGRATITUDE, for instance; which has place, wherever we observe good-will, expressed and known, together with good-offices performed, on the one side, and a return of ill-will or indifference, with ill-offices or neglect on the other: anatomize all these circumstances, and examine, by your reason alone, in what consists the demerit or blame. You never will come to any issue or conclusion.

Reason judges either of MATTER OF FACT or of RELATIONS. Enquire then, first, where is that matter of fact which we here call crime; point it out; determine the time of its existence; describe its essence or nature; explain the sense or faculty to which it discovers itself. It resides in the mind of the person who is ungrateful. He must, therefore, feel it, and be conscious of it. But nothing is there, except the passion of ill-will or absolute indifference. You cannot say that these, of themselves, always, and in all circumstances, are crimes. No, they are only crimes when directed towards persons who have before expressed and displayed good-will towards us. Consequently, we may infer, that the crime of ingratitude is not any particular individual FACT; but arises from a complication of circumstances, which, being presented to the spectator, excites the SENTIMENT of blame, by the particular structure and fabric of his mind.

This representation, you say, is false. Crime, indeed, consists not in a particular FACT, of whose reality we are assured by reason; but it consists in certain MORAL RELATIONS, discovered by reason, in the same manner as we discover by reason the truths of geometry or algebra. But what are the relations, I ask, of which you here talk? In the case stated above, I see first good-will and good-offices in one person; then ill-will and ill-offices in the other. Between these, there is a relation of CONTARIETY. Does the crime consist in that relation? But suppose a person bore me ill-will or did me ill-offices; and I, in return, were indifferent towards him, or did him good offices. Here is the same relation of CONTRARIETY; and yet my conduct is often highly laudable. Twist and turn this matter as much as you will, you can never rest the morality on relation; but must have recourse to the decisions of sentiment.

When it is affirmed that two and three are equal to the half of ten, this relation of equality I understand perfectly. I conceive, that if ten be divided into two parts, of which one has as many units as the other; and if any of these parts be compared to two added to three, it will contain as many units as that compound number. But when you draw thence a comparison to moral relations, I own that I am altogether at a loss to understand you. A moral action, a crime, such as ingratitude, is a complicated object. Does the morality consist in the relation of its parts to each other? How? After what manner? Specify the relation: be more particular and explicit in your propositions, and you will easily see their falsehood.

No, say you, the morality consists in the relation of actions to the rule of right; and they are denominated good or ill, according as they agree or disagree with it. What then is this rule of right? In what does it consist? How is it determined? By reason, you say, which examines the moral relations of actions. So that moral relations are determined by the comparison of action to a rule. And that rule is determined by considering the moral relations of objects. Is not this fine reasoning?

All this is metaphysics, you cry. That is enough; there needs nothing more to give a strong presumption of falsehood. Yes, reply I, here are metaphysics surely; but they are all on your side, who advance an abstruse hypothesis, which can never be made intelligible, nor quadrate with any particular instance or illustration. The hypothesis which we embrace is plain. It maintains that morality is determined by sentiment. It defines virtue to be WHATEVER MENTAL ACTION OR QUALITY GIVES TO A SPECTATOR THE PLEASING SENTIMENT OF APPROBATION; and vice the contrary. We then proceed to examine a plain matter of fact, to wit, what actions have this influence. We consider all the circumstances in which these actions agree, and thence endeavour to extract some general observations with regard to these sentiments. If you call this metaphysics, and find anything abstruse here, you need only conclude that your turn of mind is not suited to the moral sciences.

II. When a man, at any time, deliberates concerning his own conduct (as, whether he had better, in a particular emergence, assist a brother or a benefactor), he must consider these separate relations, with all the circumstances and situations of the persons, in order to determine the superior duty and obligation; and in order to determine the proportion of lines in any triangle, it is necessary to examine the nature of that figure, and the relation which its several parts bear to each other. But notwithstanding this appearing similarity in the two cases, there is, at bottom, an extreme difference between them. A speculative reasoner concerning triangles or circles considers the several known and given relations of the parts of these figures; and thence infers some unknown relation, which is dependent on the former. But in moral deliberations we must be acquainted beforehand with all the objects, and all their relations to each other; and from a comparison of the whole, fix our choice or approbation. No new fact to be ascertained; no new relation to be discovered. All the circumstances of the case are supposed to be laid before us, ere we can fix any sentence of blame or approbation. If any material circumstance be yet unknown or doubtful, we must first employ our inquiry or intellectual faculties to assure us of it; and must suspend for a time all moral decision or sentiment. While we are ignorant whether a man were aggressor or not, how can we determine whether the person who killed him be criminal or innocent? But after every circumstance, every relation is known, the understanding has no further room to operate, nor any object on which it could employ itself. The approbation or blame which then ensues, cannot be the work of the judgement, but of the heart; and is not a speculative proposition or affirmation, but an active feeling or sentiment. In the disquisitions of the understanding, from known circumstances and relations, we infer some new and unknown. In moral decisions, all the circumstances and relations must be previously known; and the mind, from the contemplation of the whole, feels some new impression of affection or disgust, esteem or contempt, approbation or blame.

Hence the great difference between a mistake of FACT and one of RIGHT; and hence the reason why the one is commonly criminal and not the other. When Oedipus killed Laius, he was ignorant of the relation, and from circumstances, innocent and involuntary, formed erroneous opinions concerning the action which he committed. But when Nero killed Agrippina, all the relations between himself and the person, and all the circumstances of the fact, were previously known to him; but the motive of revenge, or fear, or interest, prevailed in his savage heart over the sentiments of duty and humanity. And when we express that detestation against him to which he himself, in a little time, became insensible, it is not that we see any relations, of which he was ignorant; but that, for the rectitude of our disposition, we feel sentiments against which he was hardened from flattery and a long perseverance in the most enormous crimes.

In these sentiments then, not in a discovery of relations of any kind, do all moral determinations consist. Before we can pretend to form any decision of this kind, everything must be known and ascertained on the side of the object or action. Nothing remains but to feel, on our part, some sentiment of blame or approbation; whence we pronounce the action criminal or virtuous.

III. This doctrine will become still more evident, if we compare moral beauty with natural, to which in many particulars it bears so near a resemblance. It is on the proportion, relation, and position of parts, that all natural beauty depends; but it would be absurd thence to infer, that the perception of beauty, like that of truth in geometrical problems, consists wholly in the perception of relations, and was performed entirely by the understanding or intellectual faculties. In all the sciences, our mind from the known relations investigates the unknown. But in all decisions of taste or external beauty, all the relations are beforehand obvious to the eye; and we thence proceed to feel a sentiment of complacency or disgust, according to the nature of the object, and disposition of our organs.

Euclid has fully explained all the qualities of the circle; but has not in any proposition said a word of its beauty. The reason is evident. The beauty is not a quality of the circle. It lies not in any part of the line, whose parts are equally distant from a common centre. It is only the effect which that figure produces upon the mind, whose peculiar fabric of structure renders it susceptible of such sentiments. In vain would you look for it in the circle, or seek it, either by your senses or by mathematical reasoning, in all the properties of that figure.

Attend to Palladio and Perrault, while they explain all the parts and proportions of a pillar. They talk of the cornice, and frieze, and base, and entablature, and shaft, and architrave; and give the description and position of each of these members. But should you ask the description and position of its beauty, they would readily reply, that the beauty is not in any of the parts or members of a pillar, but results from the whole, when that complicated figure is presented to an intelligent mind, susceptible to those finer sensations. Till such a spectator appear, there is nothing but a figure of such particular dimensions and proportions: from his sentiments alone arise its elegance and beauty.

Again; attend to Cicero, while he paints the crimes of a Verres or a Catiline. You must acknowledge that the moral turpitude results, in the same manner, from the contemplation of the whole, when presented to a being whose organs have such a particular structure and formation. The orator may paint rage, insolence, barbarity on the one side; meekness, suffering, sorrow, innocence on the other. But if you feel no indignation or compassion arise in you from this complication of circumstances, you would in vain ask him, in what consists the crime or villainy, which he so vehemently exclaims against? At what time, or on what subject it first began to exist? And what has a few months afterwards become of it, when every disposition and thought of all the actors is totally altered or annihilated? No satisfactory answer can be given to any of these questions, upon the abstract hypothesis of morals; and we must at last acknowledge, that the crime or immorality is no particular fact or relation, which can be the object of the understanding, but arises entirely from the sentiment of disapprobation, which, by the structure of human nature, we unavoidably feel on the apprehension of barbarity or treachery.

IV. Inanimate objects may bear to each other all the same relations which we observe in moral agents; though the former can never be the object of love or hatred, nor are consequently susceptible of merit or iniquity. A young tree, which over-tops and destroys its parent, stands in all the same relations with Nero, when he murdered Agrippina; and if morality consisted merely in relations, would no doubt be equally criminal.

V. It appears evident that—the ultimate ends of human actions can never, in any case, be accounted for by reason, but recommend themselves entirely to the sentiments and affections of mankind, without any dependance on the intellectual faculties. Ask a man WHY HE USES EXERCISE; he will answer, BECAUSE HE DESIRES TO KEEP HIS HEALTH. If you then enquire, WHY HE DESIRES HEALTH, he will readily reply, BECAUSE SICKNESS IS PAINFUL. If you push your enquiries farther, and desire a reason WHY HE HATES PAIN, it is impossible he can ever give any. This is an ultimate end, and is never referred to any other object.

Perhaps to your second question, WHY HE DESIRES HEALTH, he may also reply, that IT IS NECESSARY FOR THE EXERCISE OF HIS CALLING. If you ask, WHY HE IS ANXIOUS ON THAT HEAD, he will answer, BECAUSE HE DESIRES TO GET MONEY. If you demand WHY? IT IS THE INSTRUMENT OF PLEASURE, says he. And beyond this it is an absurdity to ask for a reason. It is impossible there can be a progress IN INFINITUM; and that one thing can always be a reason why another is desired. Something must be desirable on its own account, and because of its immediate accord or agreement with human sentiment and affection.

Now as virtue is an end, and is desirable on its own account, without fee and reward, merely for the immediate satisfaction which it conveys; it is requisite that there should be some sentiment which it touches, some internal taste or feeling, or whatever you may please to call it, which distinguishes moral good and evil, and which embraces the one and rejects the other.

Thus the distinct boundaries and offices of REASON and of TASTE are easily ascertained. The former conveys the knowledge of truth and falsehood: the latter gives the sentiment of beauty and deformity, vice and virtue. The one discovers objects as they really stand in nature, without addition and diminution: the other has a productive faculty, and gilding or staining all natural objects with the colours, borrowed from internal sentiment, raises in a manner a new creation. Reason being cool and disengaged, is no motive to action, and directs only the impulse received from appetite or inclination, by showing us the means of attaining happiness or avoiding misery: Taste, as it gives pleasure or pain, and thereby constitutes happiness or misery, becomes a motive to action, and is the first spring or impulse to desire and volition. From circumstances and relations, known or supposed, the former leads us to the discovery of the concealed and unknown: after all circumstances and relations are laid before us, the latter makes us feel from the whole a new sentiment of blame or approbation. The standard of the one, being founded on the nature of things, is eternal and inflexible, even by the will of the Supreme Being: the standard of the other arising from the eternal frame and constitution of animals, is ultimately derived from that Supreme Will, which bestowed on each being its peculiar nature, and arranged the several classes and orders of existence.

# MORAL RELATIVISM

BY **Ruth Benedict**

Ruth F. Benedict (1887–1948) was a leading anthropologist of the 20th century. She began her studies in 1919 at Columbia University under John Dewey, then continued at the New School for Social Research with Elsie Clews Parsons. Back at Columbia, she wrote her doctoral dissertation under Franz Boas, receiving her doctorate in 1923, and staying on as a professor. Apart from more scholarly work, her book *Patterns of Culture* (1934) was a bestseller. What follows is an abridgment of an essay that first appeared in the *Journal of General Psychology*, 10:59–80 (1934). This essay is widely reprinted as making a strong case for ethical relativism.

Modern social anthropology has become more and more a study of the varieties and common elements of cultural environment and the consequences of these in human behavior. For such a study of diverse social orders, primitive peoples fortunately provide a laboratory not yet entirely vitiated by the spread of standardized worldwide civilizations. Dyaks and Hopis, Fijians and Yakuts are significant for psychological and sociological study because only among these simpler peoples has there been sufficient isolation to give opportunity for the development of localized social forms. In the higher cultures, the standardization of custom and belief over a couple of continents has given a false sense of the inevitability of the particular forms that have gained currency, and we need to turn to a wider survey in order to check the conclusions we hastily base upon this near-universality of familiar customs. Most of the simpler cultures did not gain the wide currency of the one which, out of our experience, we identify with human nature, but this was for various historical reasons, and certainly not for any that gives us as its carriers a monopoly of social good or of social sanity. Modern civilization, from this point of view, becomes not a necessary pinnacle of human achievement but one entry in a long series of possible adjustments.

These adjustments, whether they are in mannerisms like the ways of showing anger, or joy, or grief in any society, or in major human drives like those of sex, prove to be far more variable than experience in any one culture would suggest. In certain fields, such as that of religion or of formal marriage arrangements, these wide limits of variability are well known and can be fairly described. In others it is not yet possible to give a generalized account, but that does not absolve us of the task of indicating the significance of the work that has been done and of the problems that have arisen.

One of these problems relates to the customary modern normal-abnormal categories and our conclusions regarding them. In how far are such categories culturally determined, or in how far can we with assurance regard them as absolute? In how far can we regard inability to function socially as diagnostic of abnormality, or in how far is it necessary to regard this as a function of the culture? [...]

The most spectacular illustrations of the extent to which normality may be culturally defined are those cultures where an abnormality of our culture is the cornerstone of their social structure. It is not possible to do justice to these possibilities in a short discussion. A recent study of an island of northwest Melanesia by *Fortune* describes a society built upon traits which we regard as beyond the border of paranoia. In this tribe the exogamic groups look upon each other as prime manipulators of black magic, so that one marries always into an enemy group which remains for life one's deadly and unappeasable foes. They look upon a good garden crop as a confession of theft, for everyone is engaged in making magic to induce into his garden the productiveness of his neighbor's; therefore no secrecy in the island is so rigidly insisted upon as the secrecy of a man's harvesting of his yams. Their polite phrase at the acceptance of a gift is, "And if you now poison me, how shall I repay you this present?" Their preoccupation with poisoning is constant; no woman ever leaves her cooking pot for a moment unattended. Even the great affinal economic exchanges that are characteristic of this Melanesian culture area are quite altered in Dobu since they are incompatible with this fear and distrust that pervades the culture. [...] They go farther and people the whole world outside their own quarters with such malignant spirits that all-night feasts and ceremonials simply do not occur here. They have even religiously enforced customs that forbid the sharing of seed even in one family group. Anyone else's food is deadly poison to you, so that communality of stores is out of the question. For some months before harvest the whole society is on the verge of starvation, but if one falls to the temptation and eats up one's seed yams, one is an outcast and beachcomber for life. There is no coming back. It involves, as a matter of course, divorce and the breaking of all social ties.

Now in this society where no one may work with another and no one may share with another, *Fortune* describes the individual who was regarded by all his fellows as crazy. He was not one of those who periodically ran amok and, beside himself and frothing at the mouth, fell with a knife upon anyone he could reach. Such behavior they did not regard as putting anyone outside the pale. They did not even put the individuals who were known to be liable to these attacks under any kind of control. They merely fled when they saw the attack coming on and kept out of the way. "He would be all right tomorrow." But there was one man of sunny, kindly disposition who liked work and liked to be helpful. The compulsion was too strong for him to repress it in favor of the opposite tendencies of his culture. Men and women never spoke of him without laughing; he was silly and simple and definitely crazy. Nevertheless, to the ethnologist used to a culture that has, in Christianity, made his type the model of all virtue, he seemed a pleasant fellow.

An even more extreme example, because it is of a culture that has built itself upon a more complex abnormality, is that of the North Pacific Coast of North America. The civilization of the Kwakiutl, at the time when it was first recorded in the last decades of the nineteenth century, was one of the most vigorous in North America. It was built upon an ample economic supply of goods, the fish which furnished their food staple being practically inexhaustible and obtainable with comparatively small labor, and the wood which furnished the material for their houses, their furnishings, and their arts being, with however much labor, always procurable. They lived in coastal villages that compared favorably in size with those of any other American Indians and they kept up constant communication by means of sea-going dugout canoes.

It was one of the most vigorous and zestful of the aboriginal cultures of North America, with complex crafts and ceremonials, and elaborate and striking arts. It certainly had none of the earmarks of a sick civilization. The tribes of the Northwest Coast had wealth, and exactly in our terms. That is, they had not only a surplus of economic goods, but they made a game of the manipulation of wealth. It was by no means a mere direct transcription of economic needs and the filling of those needs. It involved the idea of capital, of interest, and of conspicuous waste. It was a game with all the binding rules of a game, and a person entered it as a child. His father distributed wealth for him, according to his ability, at a small feast or potlatch, and each gift the receiver was obliged to accept and to return after a short interval with interest that ran to about 100 per cent a year. By the time the child was grown, therefore, he was well launched, a larger potlatch had been given for him on various occasions of exploit or initiation, and he had wealth either out at usury or in his own possession. Nothing in the civilization could be enjoyed without validating it by the distribution of this wealth. Everything that was valued, names and songs as well as material objects, were passed down in family lines, but they were always publicly assumed with accompanying sufficient distributions of property. It was a game of validating and exercising all the privileges one could accumulate from one's various forebears, or by gift, or by marriage, that made the chief interest of the culture. Everyone in his degree took part in it, but many, of course, mainly as spectators. In its highest form it was played out between rival chiefs representing not only themselves and their family lines but their communities, and the object of the contest was to glorify oneself and to humiliate one's opponent. On this level of greatness the property involved was no longer represented by blankets, so many thousand of them to a pot-latch, but by higher units of value. These higher units were like our bank notes. They were incised copper tablets, each of them named, and having a value that depended upon their illustrious history. This was as high as ten thousand blankets, and to possess one of them, still more to enhance its value at a great potlatch, was one of the greatest glories within the compass of the chiefs of the Northwest Coast. [...]

Every contingency of life was dealt with in ... two traditional ways. To them the two were equivalent. Whether one fought with weapons or "fought with property," as they say, the same idea was at the bottom of both. In the olden times, they say, they fought with spears, but now they fight with property. One overcomes one's opponents in equivalent fashion in both, matching forces and seeing that one comes out ahead, and one can thumb one's nose at the vanquished rather more satisfactorily at a potlatch than on a battlefield. Every occasion in life was noticed not in its own terms, as a stage in the sex life of the individual or as a climax of joy or of grief, but as furthering this drama of consolidating one's own prestige and bringing shame to one's guests. Whether it was the occasion of the birth of a child, or a daughter's adolescence, or of the marriage of one's son, they were all equivalent raw material for the culture to use for this one traditionally selected end. They were all to raise one's own personal status and to entrench oneself by the humiliation of one's fellows. A girl's adolescence among the Nootka was an event for which her father gathered property from the time she was first able to run about. When she was adolescent he would demonstrate his greatness by an unheard of distribution of these goods, and cut down all his rivals. It was not as a fact of the girl's sex life that it figured in their culture, but as the occasion for a major move in the great game of vindicating one's own greatness and humiliating one's associates.

In their behavior at great bereavements this set of the culture comes out most strongly. Among the Kwakiutl it did not matter whether a relative had died in bed of disease, or by the hand of an enemy; in either case death was an affront to be wiped out by the death of another person. The fact that one had been caused to mourn was proof that one had been put upon. A chief's sister and her daughter had gone up to Victoria, and either because they drank bad whiskey or because their boat capsized they never came back. The chief called together his warriors. "Now, I ask you, tribes, who shall wail? Shall I do it or shall another?" The spokesman answered, of course, "Not you, Chief. Let some other of the tribes." Immediately they set up the war pole to announce their intention of wiping out the injury, and gathered a war party. They set out, and found seven men and two children asleep and killed them. "Then they felt good when they arrived at Sebaa in the evening."

The point which is of interest to us is that in our society those who on that occasion would feel good when they arrived at Sebaa that evening would be the definitely abnormal. There would be some, even in our society, but it is not a recognized and approved mood under the circumstances. On the Northwest Coast those are favored and fortunate to whom that mood under those circumstances is congenial, and those to whom it is repugnant are unlucky. This latter minority can register in their own culture only by doing violence to their congenial responses and acquiring others that are difficult for them. The person, for instance, who, like a Plains Indian whose wife has been taken from him, is too proud to fight, can deal with the Northwest Coast civilization only by ignoring its strongest bents. If he cannot achieve it, he is the deviant in that culture, their instance of abnormality.

This head-hunting that takes place on the Northwest Coast after a death is no matter of blood revenge or of organized vengeance. There is no effort to tie up the subsequent killing with any responsibility on the part of the victim for the death of the person who is being mourned. A chief whose son has died goes visiting wherever his fancy dictates, and he says to his host, "My prince has died today, and you go with him." Then he kills him. In this, according to their interpretation, he acts nobly because he has not been downed. He has thrust back in return. The whole procedure is meaningless without the fundamental paranoid reading of bereavement. Death, like all the other untoward accidents of existence, confounds man's pride and can only be handled in the category of insults. [...]

These illustrations, which it has been possible to indicate only in the briefest manner, force upon us the fact that normality is culturally defined. An adult shaped to the drives and standards of either of these cultures, if he were transported into our civilization, would fall into our categories of abnormality. He would be faced with the psychic dilemmas of the socially unavailable. In his own culture, however, he is the pillar of society, the end result of socially inculcated mores, and the problem of personal instability in his case simply does not arise.

No one civilization can possibly utilize in its mores the whole potential range of human behavior. Just as there are great numbers of possible phonetic articulations, and the possibility of language depends on a selection and standardization of a few of these in order that speech communication may be possible at all, so the possibility of organized behavior of every sort, from the fashions of local dress and houses to the dicta of a people's ethics and religion, depends upon a similar selection among the possible behavior traits. In the field of recognized economic obligations or sex taboos, this selection is as nonrational and subconscious a process as it is in the field of phonetics. It is a process which goes on in the group for long periods of time and is historically conditioned by innumerable accidents of isolation or of contact of peoples. In any comprehensive study of psychology, the selection that different cultures have made in the course of history within the great circumference of potential behavior is of great significance.

Every society, beginning with some slight inclination in one direction or another, carries its preference farther and farther, integrating itself more and more completely upon its chosen basis, and discarding those types of behavior that are uncongenial. Most of those organizations of personality that seem to us most incontrovertibly abnormal have been used by different civilizations in the very foundations of their institutional life. Conversely, the most valued traits of our normal individuals have been looked on in differently organized cultures as aberrant. Normality, in short, within a very wide range, is culturally defined. It is primarily a term for the socially elaborated segment of human behavior in any culture; and abnormality, a term for the segment that that particular civilization does not use. The very eyes with which we see the problem are conditioned by the long traditional habits of our own society.

It is a point that has been made more often in relation to ethics than in relation to psychiatry. We do not any longer make the mistake of deriving the morality of our own locality and decade directly from the inevitable constitution of human nature. We do not elevate it to the dignity of a first principle. We recognize that morality differs in every society, and is a convenient term for socially approved habits. Mankind has always preferred to say, "It is morally good," rather than "It is habitual," and the fact of this preference is matter enough for a critical science of ethics. But historically the two phases are synonymous.

The concept of the normal is properly a variant of the concept of the good. It is that which society has approved. A normal action is one which falls well within the limits of expected behavior for a particular society. Its variability among different peoples is essentially a function of the variability of the behavior patterns that different societies have created for themselves, and can never be wholly divorced from a consideration of culturally institutionalized types of behavior.

Each culture is a more or less elaborate working-out of the potentialities of the segment it has chosen. In so far as a civilization is well integrated and consistent within itself, it will tend to carry farther and farther, according to its nature, its initial impulse toward a particular type of action, and from the point of view of any other culture those elaborations will include more and more extreme and aberrant traits.

Each of these traits, in proportion as it reinforces the chosen behavior patterns of that culture, is for that culture normal. Those individuals to whom it is congenial either congenitally, or as the result of childhood sets, are accorded prestige in that culture, and are not visited with the social contempt or disapproval which their traits would call down upon them in a society that was differently organized. On the other hand, those individuals whose characteristics are not congenial to the selected type of human behavior in that community are the deviants, no matter how valued their personality traits may be in a contrasted civilization. [...]

The problem of understanding abnormal human behavior in any absolute sense independent of cultural factors is still far in the future. The categories of borderline behavior which we derive from the study of the neuroses and psychoses of our civilization are categories of prevailing local types of instability. They give much information about the stresses and strains of Western civilization, but no final picture of inevitable human behavior. Any conclusions about such behavior must await the collection by trained observers of psychiatric data from other cultures. Since no adequate work of the kind has been done at the present time, it is impossible to say what core of definition of abnormality may be found valid from the comparative material. It is as it is in ethics; all our local conventions of moral behavior and of immoral are without absolute validity, and yet it is quite possible that a modicum of what is considered right and what wrong could be disentangled that is shared by the whole human race. When data are available in psychiatry, this minimum definition of abnormal human tendencies will be probably quite unlike our culturally conditioned, highly elaborated psychoses such as those that are described, for instance, under the terms of schizophrenia and manic-depressive.

# VIRTUE ETHICS

BY **Aristotle, translated by Joe Sachs**

## BOOK II

**Chapter 1.** Now since virtue is of two sorts, one pertaining to thinking and the other to character, excellence of thinking is for the most part, both in its coming to be and in its growth, a result of teaching, for which reason it has need of experience and time, while excellence of character comes into being as a consequence of habit, on account of which it even gets its name by a small inflection from habit.[1] It is also clear from this that none of the virtues of character comes to be present in us by nature, since none of the things that are by nature can be habituated to be otherwise; for example, a stone, which by nature falls downward, could not be habituated to fall upward, not even if one were to train it by throwing it upward ten thousand times, nor could fire be habituated to move downward, nor could any of the things that happen by nature in one way be habituated to happen in another way. Therefore the virtues come to be present neither by nature nor contrary to nature, but in us who are of such a nature as to take them on, and to be brought to completion in them by means of habit.

Also, with those things that come to belong to us by nature, we are provided with the potencies for these beforehand, and we produce the being-at-work of them in return. (This very thing is obvious in the case of the senses, for it was not from repeatedly seeing or repeatedly hearing that we took on the senses, but on the contrary, having them, we used them—we did not get them by using them.) But we do take on the virtues by first being at work in them, just as also in other things, namely the arts; the things that one who has learned them needs to do, we learn by doing, and people become, say, housebuilders by building houses or harpists by playing the harp. So too, we become just by doing things that are just, temperate by doing things that are temperate, and courageous by doing things that are courageous. What happens in cities gives evidence of this, for lawmakers make the citizens good by habituating them, and since this is the intention of every lawmaker, those that do not do it well are failures, and one regime differs from another in this respect as a good one from a worthless one.

Also, it is from and by means of the same things that every virtue both comes into being and is destroyed, and similarly every art, for people become both good harpists and bad harpists from harp playing, and it is analogous with housebuilders and all the rest; from building houses well people will be good housebuilders and from building them badly they will be bad ones. If it were not that way, there would have been no need of a teacher, but everyone would have been born good or bad at the arts. And it is the same way in the case of the virtues, for by acting in our dealings with people some of us become just, others unjust, and by acting in frightening situations and getting habituated to be afraid or to be confident, some of us become courageous and others become cowards. And it is similar with the things that are involved with desires and with angry impulses, for some people become temperate and gentle, while others become spoiled and irritable, the ones from turning themselves this way in these situations, the others from turning themselves that way. In a word, active states come into being from being at work in similar ways. Hence it is necessary to make our ways of being at work be of certain sorts, for our active states follow in accordance with the

1 The word character (*êthos*) derives from habit (*ethos*) by a mere lengthening of the initial vowel from epsilon to eta. How the condition meant by character derives from habit is more complex. Ethical virtue is by no means simply a set of socially approved habits. It requires a pre-existent natural capacity meant to be completed properly in a certain way, as the following discussion explains; an appropriate habit, which might be imposed by parents or by other social training, is a second necessary condition for its development. But there is a third and crucial necessary factor that brings a virtue into being, that is the deliberate contribution of the person who comes to have it, the *hexis* or active condition that enters the discussion in Chap. 5 below, as a result of which Aristotle considers us to be responsible for our own characters (1114b 22–24).

distinctions among these. It makes no small difference, then, to be habituated in this way or in that straight from childhood, but an enormous difference, or rather all the difference.

**Chapter 2.** Now since our present occupation is not for the sake of contemplation, as the other kinds of study are (for we are investigating not in order that we might know what virtue is, but in order that we might become good, since otherwise there would be no benefit from it), it is necessary to investigate, with respect to the things involved in actions, how one ought to perform them, since these actions also determine the sorts of active states that come into being, as we have said. Now the phrase "acting in accordance with right reason" is commonly accepted, and let it be set down—there will be a discussion of it later, both what right reason is and how it is related to the other virtues.[2] But let this be acknowledged in advance—that every discourse that concerns actions is obliged to speak in outline and not precisely—just as we said also at the beginning that one ought to demand that discourses be in accord with their material, while matters that are involved in actions and are advantageous have nothing rigidly fixed about them, any more than do matters of health. And since the general discourse is of this sort, still more does the discourse that concerns particulars lack precision, for it falls under no art nor under any skill that has been handed down, but it is always necessary for those who are acting to look at the circumstances surrounding the occasion themselves, just as is the case also with the medical art or the art of steering a ship. But even though the present discourse is of this sort, one ought to try to help it along.

First, then, one must recognize this, that things such as virtues are of such a nature as to be destroyed by deficiency and by excess, as we see (since one must use visible examples as evidence for invisible things) in the case of strength and health; for excessive gymnastic exercises, as well as deficient ones, destroy one's strength, and similarly drink and food, when they come to be too much or too little, destroy one's health, while proportionate amounts produce, increase, and preserve these. And it is the same way also with temperance and courage and the other virtues. Someone who runs away from and fears everything and endures nothing becomes a coward, while someone who fears nothing at all but goes out to confront everything becomes rash; similarly, someone who indulges in every pleasure and refrains from none becomes spoiled, while someone who shuns them all, like a boorish bumpkin, becomes in a certain way insensible. So temperance and courage are destroyed by excess and by deficiency, but are preserved by an intermediate condition.

But it is not only the case that the same things from which and by the action of which their coming into being and increase comes about, produce their destruction as well, but it is also in these same things that the being-at-work of the virtues will consist. For it is that way also in the more visible cases, such as that of strength, since strength comes about from taking in a lot of food and enduring a lot of labor, while it is especially the strong person who would be capable of doing these very things. And so it is in the case of the virtues as well, for by refraining from pleasures we become temperate, and once having become temperate we are most capable of refraining from them; and it is similar in the case of courage, for by habituating ourselves to disdain frightening things, and by enduring them, we become courageous, and having become courageous we shall be most capable of enduring frightening things.

**Chapter 3.** As a sign of the active states of one's soul, one must consider the pleasure or pain that accompanies one's deeds, for someone who refrains from bodily pleasures and delights in this very thing is temperate, but someone who does so while feeling burdened by it is spoiled, and someone who endures terrifying things and delights in them, or is at any rate not pained by them, is courageous, but someone who does so while being pained is a coward. For the sort of virtue that belongs to character is concerned with pleasures and pains, since it is on account of pleasure that we perform base actions, and on account of pain that we refrain from beautiful actions. Hence it is necessary to be brought up in some way straight from childhood, as Plato says, so as to take delight and feel pain in those things in which one ought, for this is the right education.[3]

Also, if the virtues are concerned with actions and feelings, while pleasure or pain follows upon every feeling and every action, for this reason too virtue would be concerned with pleasures and pains. Punishments indicate this too, since they come about by means of these, for they are a certain kind of medicines, and medicines by their nature

2 See Book VI, Chapters 5–13, where the final formulation at 1144b 26–28 identifies right reason in matters of action with practical judgment.

3 This is what is called an education in music in Plato's *Republic*, and is discussed from 376E to 403C. Aristotle's reference is to 402A, where Socrates gives the reason for what contemporary readers call "censorship" of the stories and music children are allowed to hear. The point is not whether depictions of sex and violence, or music without grace, will make children act in certain ways, but that it will coarsen their sensibilities before they are able to make choices on their own.

work through opposites. Also, as we said just now, every active condition of the soul is in its nature related to and concerned with the sorts of things by the action of which it naturally becomes worse or better, and it is by means of pleasures and pains that people become base, through pursuing and avoiding them, either the ones one ought not, or when one ought not, or in a way one ought not, or in as many other ways as such distinctions are articulated. This is also why people define the virtues as certain states of freedom from passion, and of calmness, but they do not define them well, because they say this simply but do not add "as one ought" and "as one ought not" and "when" and the rest.

Therefore, it is established that virtue of this sort is an aptitude productive of the best actions that concern pleasures and pains, and that vice is the opposite. And this might become evident to us from the following considerations that concern the same things. For since there are three things that lead to choices and three that lead to avoidance, the former being what is beautiful, what is advantageous, and what is pleasant, and the contraries being what is ugly, what is harmful, and what is painful, the good person is apt to go right and the bad person is apt to go astray concerning all of these, but especially concerning pleasure, for this is shared with the animals, and follows along with everything that comes by choice, since even the beautiful and the advantageous seem pleasant.[4] Also, this has grown up with us all from infancy, and for this reason it is difficult to scrub away this feeling, since it is ingrained in our life. And we measure our actions, some of us more, others less, against the yardstick of pleasure and pain. On account of this, then, it is necessary that our whole concern be about these things, for to be delighted or pained well or badly plays no small role in our actions. And it is even harder to fight against pleasure than Heracleitus says it is to fight against anger,[5] but artfulness and virtue always come to be concerned with what is more difficult, for it is better to do well at this. And so for this reason the whole concern both of virtue and of politics is about pleasures and pains, since one who deals with these well will be a good person, and one who deals with them badly will be bad.

Let it stand as stated, then, that virtue is concerned with pleasures and pains, that it grows by the action of those things out of which it comes into being, or is destroyed by them when they do not happen in the same way, and that it is at work in connection with those things out of which it has come into being.

**Chapter 4.** One might raise as an impasse, though, how we mean that it is necessary to become just by performing just actions and temperate by performing temperate actions, for if people do things that are just or temperate they already are just or temperate people, just as, if they do the things that have to do with writing or with music, they are literate or musical people. Or is it not even this way in the case of the arts? For it is possible to produce something literate by chance or by being advised by someone else. One will be literate, then, only when one produces something literate and does so in a literate way, that is, in accordance with the art of writing within oneself. Anyway, it is not the same in the case of the arts as with the virtues, for the things that come into being by means of the arts have their being-well-made in themselves; it is sufficient for these to come into being in a certain condition. But with the things that come about as a result of the virtues, just because they themselves are a certain way it is not the case that one does them justly or temperately, but only if the one doing them also does them being a certain way: if one does them first of all knowingly, and next, having chosen them and chosen them for their own sake, and third, being in a stable condition and not able to be moved all the way out of it.[6]

For having the other kinds of artfulness, these things do not count, except the mere knowing, but for having the virtues, the knowing is of little or no strength, while the other conditions have not a little but all the power, and they

---

4 The word used here for choice has a reduced meaning that can apply to an animal-like act guided exclusively by imagination and aimed solely at pleasure. Note too, by the way, that Aristotle includes some of his most important observations in subordinate clauses within throw-away arguments; a spectacular example has occurred here, with the meaning of *good* being distinguished into its three primary senses. This picks up the question that was dismissed at 1096b 30, not with the precision that would carry it outside the inquiry about ethics, but with a definite dialectical step forward, and later observations will continue the upward motion from the evidence of human action toward a single governing meaning of the good.

5 "It is hard to fight against anger, for what it wants to happen, it purchases in exchange for life" (Fragment 85 in the Diels numbering). Exactly what Heracleitus meant by *thumos*, translated here as "anger," is uncertain. In Plato's *Republic* (439E–441C), Socrates distinguishes it as the middle, spirited part of the soul, that can ally itself with either reason or desire to control the third part. The "musical" education Socrates prescribes, which Aristotle has called the right education at 1104b 13 above, is aimed at taming and winning over this irrationally spirited element straight from childhood.

6 The last eleven words of the sentence translate Aristotle's marvelous adverb *ametakinêtôs; akinêtôs* would mean in the manner of someone immovable or rigid, but the added prefix makes it convey the condition of those toys that can be knocked over but always come back upright on their own, a flexible stability or equilibrium.

are the very ones which arise from repeatedly performing just or temperate actions. Thus, while the actions are called just or temperate whenever they are the sorts of things that a just or temperate person would do, the one who does them is not just or temperate unless he also does them in the way that just and temperate people do them. It is well said, then, that by performing just actions one becomes a just person and by performing temperate actions one becomes a temperate person, and no one is going to become good by not performing these actions. But most people do not perform them, but believe that by taking refuge in talk[7] they are philosophizing and in that way will be people of serious stature, doing something similar to those sick people who listen to the doctors carefully but do none of the things they order. So just as they will be in no good condition in body if they treat themselves in this way, neither will those who philosophize in this way be in any good condition in soul.

**Chapter 5.** After these things, one must examine what virtue is. Now since there are three kinds of things that come to be present in the soul—feelings, predispositions, and active conditions—virtue would be one of these. And by feelings I mean desire, anger, fear, confidence, envy, joy, affection, hatred, yearning, jealousy, pity, and generally those things which are accompanied by pleasure or pain. It is the predispositions in accordance with which we are said to be apt to feel these, such as those by which we are predisposed to be angry or to be annoyed or to feel pity. And it is the active conditions in accordance with which we bear ourselves well or badly toward the feelings; for example, in relation to being angry, if we are that way violently or slackly, we bear ourselves badly, but if in a measured way, we bear ourselves well, and similarly in relation to other feelings.

Now neither virtues nor vices are feelings, because we are not said to be of serious or trifling moral stature as a result of our feelings, but we are said to be so as a result of our virtues and vices, and because we are neither praised nor blamed as a result of our feelings (for one is not praised for being afraid or for being angry, nor is one blamed simply for being angry, but for being so in a certain way), but we are praised or blamed as a result of our virtues and vices. Also, we are angry and frightened without choice, but the virtues are certain kinds of choices, or not present without choice. And on top of these things, as a result of the feelings we are said to be moved, but as a result of the virtues and vices we are said not to be moved but to be disposed in a certain way.

And for these reasons, the virtues and vices are not predispositions either, since we are not called good or bad, nor are we praised or blamed, simply for being predisposed to feel something. Also, we are predisposed by nature, but we do not become good or bad by nature; but we spoke about this before.[8] So if the virtues are neither feelings nor predispositions, what remains is that they are active conditions. Therefore what virtue is, in the sense of the general class to which it belongs, has been said.

**Chapter 6.** But it is necessary to say not only this, that it is an active condition, but also what sort of active condition it is. And something one ought to state is that every virtue, as well as bringing that of which it is the virtue to completion in a good condition, also makes it yield work of a good kind, as the excellence of the eye makes both the eye and its work first-rate, since by means of the excellence of the eye we see well. Similarly, the excellence of a horse both makes it a first-rate horse, and makes it good at running, at carrying its rider, and at holding still in the face of enemies. So if this is the way things are in all cases, then also the virtue of a human being would be the active condition from which one becomes a good human being and from which one will yield up one's own work well.

How this will be, we have already spoken of, but it will be clear in the following manner as well, if we examine what sort of nature virtue has. Now in everything continuous and divisible it is possible to take a greater amount, a lesser amount, or an equal measure, and these either on account of the thing itself or in relation to us, and the equal measure is a certain kind of mean between excess and deficiency. By a mean that belongs to the thing, I am speaking of what holds a position equally apart from either of the extremes, which is one and the same thing for everyone, but the mean in relation to us is what neither goes too far nor falls short, and this is not one thing nor the same thing for everyone. For example, if ten are a lot and two are few, then six are a mean amount for those who take it according to the thing, since it both exceeds and is exceeded by an equal amount, and this is a mean according to the arithmetic proportion. But the mean in relation to us is not something one needs to take in this way, for it is not the case, if ten pounds is a lot for someone to eat and two pounds a little, that the gymnastic trainer will prescribe six pounds,

7 Aristotle's words here allude to something Socrates says in Plato's *Phaedo* at 99E, but are in no way intended to apply to him; Socrates ends that dialogue by accepting death in accordance with his philosophic talk, knowingly, by deliberate choice, and from a firm conviction.

8 See 1103a18–32.

for perhaps even this is a lot for the one who is going to take it, or a little. For it is a little to Milo,[9] but to someone beginning gymnastic training it is a lot. And it is similar with running and wrestling.

Now in this way everyone who has knowledge avoids excess and deficiency, but seeks the mean and chooses this, but not the mean that belongs to the thing but the mean in relation to us. So if every kind of knowledge accomplishes its work well in this way, by looking to the mean and guiding its works toward this (which is why people are accustomed to remark about works that are in a good condition that it is not possible either to take anything away from or to add anything to them, on the grounds that excess and deficiency destroy what is well made, but the mean condition preserves it; and good craftsmen, as we are saying, do their work looking toward this), while virtue is something more precise and better than any art, just as nature is, then virtue would be something apt to hit the mean.

I am speaking of virtue of character, for this is concerned with feelings and actions, and among these there is excess and deficiency, and the mean. For instance, it is possible to be afraid or be confident or to desire or be angry or feel pity, or in general to feel pleasure or feel pain both more and less, and on both sides not in the right way; but to feel them when one ought, and in the cases in which, and toward the people whom, and for the reasons for the sake of which, and in the manner one ought is both a mean and the best thing, which is what belongs to virtue. And similarly, concerning actions also, there is excess and deficiency, and the mean. And virtue is concerned with feelings and actions, in which excess and deficiency go astray, while the mean is praised and gets them right, and both of these belong to virtue. Therefore, virtue is a certain kind of mean condition, since it is, at any rate, something that makes one apt to hit the mean. Also, it is possible to go wrong in many ways (for what is bad belongs to what is unlimited, as the Pythagoreans conjectured, and what is good belongs among what is limited), but there is only one way to get something right (which is why the one is easy and the other is difficult, it being easy to miss the target and difficult to hit it); so for these reasons excess and deficiency belong to vice and the mean condition belongs to virtue,

> For the good are good simply, but the bad are bad in every sort of way.

Therefore, virtue is an active condition that makes one apt at choosing, consisting in a mean condition in relation to us, which is determined by a proportion and by the means by which a person with practical judgment would determine it. And it is a mean condition between two vices, one resulting from excess and the other from deficiency, and is also a mean in the sense that the vices of the one sort fall short and those of the other sort go beyond what is appropriate both in feelings and in actions, while virtue both discovers and chooses the mean. Hence, in terms of its thinghood and the articulation that spells out what it is for it to be, virtue is a mean condition, but in terms of what is best and what is done well, it is an extreme. But not every action admits of a mean condition, nor does every feeling, for some of them as soon as they are named are understood as having baseness involved with them, such as joy at others' misfortunes, shamelessness, and envy, and in the case of actions, adultery, stealing, and murder; for with all these things and things like them what is meant is that the things themselves are base, and not the excesses or deficiencies of them. There is, then, never any possibility of getting anything right about them, but one always goes astray, nor is there any doing well or not well about such things by committing adultery with the right woman and when and in the way one ought, but simply doing any of these things is to go wrong. It would be like believing that there was also a mean condition and an excess and deficiency concerned with being unjust or a coward or dissipated, for at that rate there would be a mean condition in excess and in deficiency, and an excess in excess and a deficiency in deficiency. But just as there is no excess or deficiency of temperance or courage, because the mean is in a certain way an extreme, so there is no mean condition or excess and deficiency of those other things, but however one does them one is in the wrong; in general there is no mean in excess and in deficiency, nor any excess or deficiency of the mean condition.[10]

---

9 Milo of Croton was the Olympic champion wrestler six times. Reports credited him with being able both to carry and to eat a whole ox.

10 Failure to pay attention to this argument causes serious misunderstandings of what Aristotle intends by a mean. Since there cannot be too much courage, the mean is not a synonym for playing it safe; since there cannot be too little courage, it is a condition that, when present at all, is all-sufficient. A virtue such as courage is not a limited thing but the thing that confers limit on something else. It is in fear and confidence, and in the actions they lead to, that there can be excess and deficiency, but courage is not a position on the scale of fear and confidence. It is a condition of the soul in which one holds oneself, in which actions can be clearly envisioned and freely chosen without being determined by fear

**Chapter 7.** But it is necessary not just to speak of this universally, but also to apply it to the particulars, for in discourses about actions, those that are universal are common to more instances, but those that are about parts of the topic are more truthful, since actions are concerned with particulars, and discourse needs to harmonize with them. So one should take these from the list.[11] Now concerning fear and confidence, the mean condition is courage; of people who go to excess, the one who exceeds in fearlessness is without a name (and many of these things are nameless), the one who exceeds in confidence is rash, and the one who exceeds in fearing but falls short in being confident is a coward.[12] Concerning pleasures and pains—though not all of them and less so concerning pains—the mean condition is temperance and the excess is dissipation. Those who fall short concerning pleasure don't turn up very often, for which reason they and their sort have not happened on a name, but let them be termed "insensible." Concerning giving and taking money, the mean condition is generosity, the excess and deficiency being wastefulness and stinginess. In the latter, people exceed and fall short in contrary ways, for the wasteful person exceeds in letting go of things but falls short in getting them, while the stingy person exceeds in getting and falls short in letting go. Though we are speaking now in outline and under headings, content with just this, more precise distinctions will be made later about these topics.

There are also other dispositions concerned with money, the mean condition being magnificence (for a magnificent person is different from a generous one, since the former is concerned with great things and the latter with small ones), the excess being gaudiness or vulgarity, and the deficiency being chintziness; and these differ from those that concern generosity, but in what way they differ will be said later. And concerning honor and dishonor, the mean condition is greatness of soul, the excess is spoken of as a certain sort of vanity, and the deficiency is smallness of soul, and as we were saying generosity was related to magnificence, differing by being concerned with small things, so too, related in that way to greatness of soul, which is concerned with great honor, there is a certain disposition which is concerned with small honor, for it is possible to have an appetite for honor in the way one ought and also more or less than one ought; the person who exceeds in such appetites is called passionate for honor, the one who falls short is said to be lacking the passion for honor, and the person at the mean is without a name. The dispositions too are without names, except that of the person passionate for honor, which is called the passion for honor, which shows that the people at the extremes claim the right to the mean territory, and we do the same; there are times when we call the person at the mean passionate for honor and times when we speak of such a person as lacking the passion for honor, and times when we praise the person who is passionate for honor, but times when we praise the person who lacks the passion for honor. The reason why we do this will be stated in what follows, but for now let us mention the rest of the virtues in the way we have been led along.[13]

Concerning anger, there are also excess, deficiency, and a mean condition, and while they are pretty much without names, since we speak of the person at the mean as gentle, let us call the mean condition gentleness; of the extremes, let the person who exceeds be irritable and the vice irritability, and let the one who falls short be slow to anger and the deficiency slowness to anger. And there are three other mean conditions, that have some likeness to

---

or confidence. These things gradually become more evident as the inquiry proceeds, but it should be clear at this point that a virtue, while it occupies a mean between vices and hits a mean in making choices, is not itself any kind of quantity.

11 In 1220b–1221a of the *Eudemian Ethics*, there is a list of fourteen virtues of character alongside their corresponding vices of excess and deficiency. In the present chapter thirteen virtues (or quasi-virtues) of character, with their corresponding vices, are mentioned, but not displayed in a diagram. There are two minor virtues in each work that do not appear in the other (proper passion for honor and charm here, dignity and patience there), and one virtue taken in the *Eudemian Ethics* list as belonging to character (practical judgment) is treated in this work as an intellectual virtue. The avoidance of a diagram here seems deliberate, as Aristotle's stated purpose of attending to the particular virtues would be undermined by forcing them into too rigid an application of a general scheme.

12 We might call the nameless type incautious. The threefold distinction suggests that we recognize someone as a coward whether he gets that way from too much fear or too little confidence, while we see rashness as overconfidence rather than under-cautiousness. See 1115b 24–1116a 9.

13 This phrase implies following the "beaten path" of popular or conventional opinion, though commentators often twist it to mean Aristotle's own "usual method." In the *Politics* (1256a 2, b 15–22), the beaten path of opinion is Aristotle's warrant for accepting a kind of teleology at variance from his own opinions, as these are developed in all his theoretical works. Political inquiry does not impose philosophic conclusions on human communities, but studies people who have certain ineradicable opinions. In the *Parts of Animals* (643b 11), the beaten path is Aristotle's guide to the natural, though not neatly logical, classification of animals. Here in the study of ethics, the recognition that excellence of character is always a mean between opposite vices is like the popular classification of animals as birds, fish, and so on; Aristotle takes it as deeply revealing, not the whole story, and not to be taken as having logical precision or pushed to extremes.

each other but differ from one another, for while they are all concerned with communal life in words and actions, they differ because one is concerned with what is true in them and the others with what is pleasant; of the latter, one sort occurs in playfulness and the other in all things in the course of life. So one ought to speak about these also, in order that we might see more clearly that the mean condition is praised in everything, while the extremes are neither praised nor are they right, but they are blamed. Now most of these are also without names, but we ought to try, as in the other cases, to make up names ourselves for the sake of clarity and to make it easy to follow.

Concerning truth, then, one who is at the mean is a truthful person, and let the mean condition be called truthfulness; pretence in the direction of exaggeration is bragging and the one who has it is a braggart, while pretence in the direction of understatement is irony and the one who has it is ironic. Concerning what is pleasant in playfulness, the person at the mean is charming and the disposition is charm, the excess is buffoonery and one who has it is a buffoon, and the one who falls short is a certain sort of boor and the active condition is boorishness. Concerning the remaining sort of pleasantness in life, the one who is pleasant in the way one ought to be is friendly and the mean condition is friendliness,[14] the one who goes to excess, if it is for no purpose, is obsequious, but if it is for his own advantage, he is a flatterer, and the one who falls short and is unpleasant in everything is a certain sort of contrary person and hard to get along with.

And there are also mean conditions among and involving the feelings, for while a sense of shame is not a virtue, the person with a sense of shame is also praised, since even in these matters one sort of person is spoken of as a mean, and another sort as going to excess, as the shy person is ashamed about everything; the one who falls short, or is ashamed about nothing at all, is shameless, while the one at the mean is the person with a sense of shame. Righteous indignation is a mean condition between joy at the misfortunes of others and envy, which are concerned with pain and pleasure at what occurs among those who happen to be one's neighbors, for the person inclined toward righteous indignation is pained at those who fare well without deserving it, while the envious person, exceeding that, is pained at all those who fare well, and the one who takes joy in others' misfortune falls so far short of being pained as to be delighted. But there will be a fitting occasion concerning these things in another place; and concerning justice, since it is not meant in a single sense, after distinguishing these we will speak about the way in which both its kinds are mean conditions.[15]

**Chapter 8.** Since there are three dispositions, two of them vices, one resulting from excess and the other from deficiency, and one of them a virtue, the mean condition, they are all in some way opposite to all; for the extremes are opposite both to the mean and to one another, while the mean is opposite to the extremes. Just as the equal amount is greater in relation to the lesser and less in relation to the greater, so too the mean active conditions exceed in relation to the deficiencies and fall short in relation to the excesses in both feelings and actions. For the courageous person appears rash in relation to the coward and cowardly in relation to the rash person, and similarly the temperate person appears dissipated in relation to the insensible person and insensible in relation to the dissolute person, and the generous person appears wasteful in relation to the stingy person and stingy in relation to the wasteful person. Hence the people at each of the extremes push the person at the mean away toward the other extreme, and the coward calls the courageous person rash while the rash person calls him a coward, and analogously in the other cases.[16] But while these are opposed to one another in this way, the greatest contrariety belongs to the extremes in relation to one another rather than to the mean, for these stand farther apart from one another than from the mean, just as the great is farther from the small and the small from the great than the two of them are from the equal. Also, a certain likeness to the mean shows up in some of the extremes, as in rashness in relation to courage or in wastefulness in relation to generosity, while in the extremes in relation to one another there is the greatest

---

14 In Bk. IV, Chap. 6, this is said to be a nameless virtue that resembles friendship. The full treatment of friendship and its relation to action, character, and feeling occupies Bks. VIII and IX.

15 The two sorts of mean mentioned in this paragraph are only quasi-virtues, mere habits or predispositions of feeling. Righteous indignation (*nemesis*) is the natural basis of justice, evident in the child's heartfelt protest "that's not fair," but it is not a developed state of character that disposes one toward right choices. It is not mentioned again, but is superseded by the discussion of justice in Bk. V. A sense of shame is discussed again in Bk. IV, Chap. 9, but as a temporary stage of development that people need to grow out of. All the other active states identified in this chapter as virtues are discussed at greater length in Bks. III and IV.

16 A powerful historical example of this may be found in Thucydides's account of a civil war in Corcyra, in Bk. III, Chap. 82 of *The Peloponnesian War*.

unlikeness; but things standing at the greatest remove from one another are defined as contraries, so that the things standing at the greater remove would be the more contrary.

In comparison with the mean it is in some cases the deficiency that is more opposite, but in other cases the excess; for example, in relation to courage it is not rashness, which is the excess, that is more opposite, but cowardice, which is the deficiency, but in relation to temperance it is not insensibility, which is the lack, that is more opposite, but dissipation, which is the excess. This turns out to be the case for two reasons, one of which comes from the thing itself, for on account of one extreme's being nearer to and more like the mean, we do not place this but its contrary as more opposite to the mean; for example, since rashness seems to be more like courage and nearer to it, while cowardice seems more unlike it, we set the latter down as more opposite, since the things that stand at a greater remove from the mean seem to be more contrary to it. This, then, is one reason, coming from the thing itself, but the other reason comes from us ourselves, for those things toward which we ourselves tend more by nature in any way appear more contrary to the mean. For example, we ourselves tend more by nature toward pleasures, on account of which we are more easily carried away toward dissipation than toward orderliness. So we more so call those things contrary toward which the extra tendency occurs more, and for this reason dissipation, which is the excess, is more contrary to temperance.

**Chapter 9.** It has been said sufficiently, then, that virtue of character is a mean condition, and in what way, namely because it is a mean between two kinds of vice, the one resulting from excess and the other from deficiency, and that it is such a mean condition on account of being apt to hit the mean in feelings and actions. And this is why it is work to be of serious moral stature, since in each kind of thing it is work to get hold of the mean; for instance, to take the center of a circle belongs not to everyone but to one who knows something, and so too, while getting angry, or giving and spending money, belong to everyone and are easy, to whom and how much and when and for what purpose and in what way to do these things are no longer in everyone's power, nor are they easy; for this reason what is done well is rare and praiseworthy and beautiful.

Hence the one who aims at the mean ought first to pull back from what is more contrary to it, just as Calypso advises,[17]

> Keep the ship out beyond that thick spray and swell,

for of the extremes the one is a greater error, the other a lesser. Since then, to hit the mean with extreme precision is a difficult thing, as the second best way to sail,[18] as people say, one ought to take the least of the evils, and this will be most the case in the way which we are speaking of. Also, one ought to consider what we ourselves are carried away toward, since different people are of a nature to incline toward different things, and this will be recognizable from the pleasure or pain that comes about in our own case. We ought then to drag ourselves over toward the opposite side, for by pulling far away from going wrong we will come to the mean, the very thing that people do who straighten warped pieces of lumber. And in everything one must guard most against the pleasant thing and against pleasure, for we do not judge it without bribes. So exactly the way the town elders felt toward Helen, we ought to feel toward pleasure, and to think over in every instance what they said, for by sending it off in that way we shall go astray less.[19]

17 The line is spoken by Odysseus to his men at XII, 219 of the *Odyssey*, as a result of Circe's advice to him in lines 106–110 that he would lose six men near Scylla but lose everyone near Charybdis. (Calypso's advice to him to keep the North star always on his left when he sailed from Ogygia is at V, 276–7. The order and location of events in the first half of the *Odyssey* are notoriously difficult to keep straight.)

18 This is generally taken to mean that, when the wind fails, one sails in the second best way by rowing. A famous occurrence of this metaphor is in Plato's *Phaedo*, at 99D.

19 At III, 156–160 of the *Iliad*, the old men of Troy say, in effect, let her beauty exert its power somewhere else. At 398A of the *Republic*, Plato elaborates the same message toward Homer himself, that a poet so holy, wondrous, and pleasant must be sent off, crowned and anointed, to some other city.

The three pieces of general advice in this paragraph are extensively referred to in the secondary literature as "rules." This goes back at least to the footnotes in John Burnet's 1900 text of this work, creeps even into the translation in the Loeb edition, and then turns up in later commentary as though it had been Aristotle's own word. But Aristotle uses the word rule (*kanôn*) only in two places in this work, and only in order to say that there can be no such thing in ethics; the only rule is the judgment of a good human being (1113a 33), because a rule applied to particulars would need to be flexible (1137b 29–32), that is, not a straightedge at all. In the course of this inquiry, as the understanding of pleasure is progressively deepened, major exceptions to the second and third of the generalizations given here will emerge.

By doing these things, then, to say it in summary, we shall be most able to hit the mean. But this no doubt is difficult, and especially in particular cases, for it is not easy to determine how and with whom and on what sort of grounds and for how much time one ought to be angry, and we sometimes praise those who underdo it and call them gentle, while at other times we praise those who are severe by proclaiming them manly. But the person who deviates a little from what is done well is not blamed, whether the deviation is toward the more or toward the less, but someone who deviates more is blamed for it, since this person does not escape notice. But at what point and for how much of a deviation one is to be blamed is not easy to determine by a formulation, for no other perceptible thing is either; such things are in the particulars, and the judgment is in the perceiving. Therefore this much is clear: that while the mean active condition is praised in all things, one ought to incline away from it sometimes toward the excess and sometimes toward the deficiency, for in that way we shall most easily hit the mark of the mean and of what is done well.

# PLEASURE AND UTILITARIAN ETHICS

BY **Jeremy Bentham**

## CHAPTER I: OF THE PRINCIPLE OF UTILITY

I. Nature has placed mankind under the governance of two sovereign masters, *pain* and *pleasure*. It is for them alone to point out what we ought to do, as well as to determine what we shall do. On the one hand the standard of right and wrong, on the other the chain of causes and effects, are fastened to their throne. They govern us in all we do, in all we say, in all we think: every effort we can make to throw off our subjection, will serve but to demonstrate and confirm it. In words a man may pretend to abjure their empire: but in reality he will remain subject to it all the while. The *principle of utility*[1] recognises this subjection, and assumes it for the foundation of that system, the object of which is to rear the fabric of felicity by the hands of reason and of law. Systems which attempt to question it, deal in sounds instead of sense, in caprice instead of reason, in darkness instead of light.

*Mankind governed by pain and pleasure.*

But enough of metaphor and declamation: it is not by such means that moral science is to be improved.

II. The principle of utility is the foundation of the presen work: it will be proper therefore at the outset to give an explicit and determinate account of what is meant by it. By the principle[2] of utility is meant that principle which approves or disapproves of every action whatsoever, according to the tendency which it appears to have to augment or diminish the happiness of the party whose interest is in question: or, what is the same thing in other words, to promote or to oppose that happiness. I say of every action whatsoever; and therefore not only of every action of a private individual, but of every measure of government.

*Principle of utility, what.*

III. By utility is meant that property in any object, whereby it tends to produce benefit, advantage, pleasure, good, or happiness, (all this in the present case comes to the same thing) or (what comes again to the same thing) to prevent the happening of mischief, pain, evil, or unhappiness to the party

*Utility what.*

1 Note by the Author, July 1822.

To this denomination has of late been added, or substituted, the *greatest happiness* or *greatest felicity* principle: this for shortness, instead of saying at length *that principle* which states the greatest happiness of all those whose interest is in question, as being the right and proper, and only right and proper and universally desirable, end of human action: of human action in every situation, and in particular in that of a functionary or set of functionaries exercising the powers of Government. The word *utility* does not so clearly point to the ideas of *pleasure* and *pain* as the words *happiness* and *felicity* do: nor does it lead us to the consideration of the *number*, of the interests affected; to the *number*, as being the circumstance, which contributes, in the largest proportion, to the formation of the standard here in question; the *standard of right and wrong*, by which alone the propriety of human conduct, in every situation, can with propriety be tried. This want of a sufficiently manifest connexion between the ideas of *happiness* and *pleasure* on the one hand, and the idea of *utility* on the other, I have every now and then found operating, and with but too much efficiency, as a bar to the acceptance, that might otherwise have been given, to this principle.

2 The word principle is derived from the Latin principium: which seems to be compounded of the two words *primus*, first, or chief, and *cipium*, a termination which seems to be derived from *capio*, to take, as in *moncipium*, *municipium*; to which are analogous, *auceps*, *forceps*, and others. It is a term of very vague and very extensive signification: it is applied to any thing which is conceived to serve as a foundation or beginning to any series of operations: in some cases, of physical operations; but of mental operations in the present case.

*A principle, what.*

The principle here in question may be taken for an act of the mind; a sentiment; a sentiment of approbation; a sentiment which, when applied to an action, approves of its utility, as that quality of it by which the measure of approbation or disapprobation bestowed upon it ought to be governed.

Jeremy Bentham, *An Introduction to the Principles of Morals and Legislation*, pp. 1-22, 29-32, 97-129.

whose interest is considered: if that party be the community in general, then the happiness of the community: if a particular individual, then the happiness of that individual.

*Interest of the community, what.*

IV. The interest of the community is one of the most general expressions that can occur in the phraseology of morals: no wonder that the meaning of it is often lost. When it has a meaning, it is this. The community is a fictitious *body*, composed of the individual persons who are considered as constituting as it were its *members*. The interest of the community then is, what?—the sum of the interests of the several members who compose it.

V. It is in vain to talk of the interest of the community, without understanding what is the interest of the individual.[3] A thing is said to promote the interest, or to be *for* the interest, of an individual, when it tends to add to the sum total of his pleasures: or, what comes to the same thing, to diminish the sum total of his pains.

*An action conformable to the principle of utility, what.*

VI. An action then may be said to be conformable to the principle of utility, or, for shortness sake, to utility, (meaning with respect to the community at large) when the tendency it has to augment the happiness of the community is greater than any it has to diminish it.

*A measure of government conformable to the principle of utility, what.*

VII. A measure of government (which is but a particular kind of action, performed by a particular person or persons) may be said to be conformable to or dictated by the principle of utility, when in like manner the tendency which it has to augment the happiness of the community is greater than any which it has to diminish it.

*Laws or dictates of utility, what.*

VIII. When an action, or in particular a measure of government, is supposed by a man to be conformable to the principle of utility, it may be convenient, for the purposes of discourse, to imagine a kind of law or dictate, called a law or dictate of utility: and to speak of the action in question, as being conformable to such law or dictate.

*A partizan of the principle of utility, who.*

IX. A man may be said to be a partizan of the principle of utility, when the approbation or disapprobation he annexes to any action, or to any measure, is determined by and proportioned to the tendency which he conceives it to have to augment or to diminish the happiness of the community: or in other words, to its conformity or unconformity to the laws or dictates of utility.

*Ought, ought not, right and wrong, &c. how to be understood.*

X. Of an action that is conformable to the principle of utility one may always say either that it is one that ought to be done, or at least that it is not one that ought not to be done. One may say also, that it is right it should be done; at least that it is not wrong it should be done: that it is a right action; at least that it is not a wrong action. When thus interpreted, the words *ought*, and *right* and *wrong*, and others of that stamp, have a meaning: when otherwise, they have none.

*To prove the rectitude of this principle is at once unnecessary and impossible.*

XI. Has the rectitude of this principle been ever formally contested? It should seem that it had, by those who have not known what they have been meaning. Is it susceptible of any direct proof? it should seem not: for that which is used to prove every thing else, cannot itself be proved: a chain of proofs must have their commencement somewhere. To give such proof is as impossible as it is needless.

*It has seldom, however, as yet been consistently pursued.*

XII. Not that there is or ever has been that human creature breathing, however stupid or perverse, who has not on many, perhaps on most occasions of his life, deferred to it. By the natural constitution of the human frame, on most occasions of their lives men in general embrace this principle, without thinking of it: if not for the ordering of their own actions, yet for the trying of their own actions, as well as of those of other men. There have been, at the same time, not many, perhaps, even of the most intelligent, who have been disposed to embrace it purely and without reserve. There are even few who have not taken some occasion or other to quarrel with it, either on account of their not understanding always how to apply it, or on account of some prejudice or other which they were afraid to examine into, or could not bear to part with. For such is the stuff that man is made of: in principle and in practice, in a right track and in a wrong one, the rarest of all human qualities is consistency.

3 Interest is one of those words, which not having any superior *genus*, cannot in the ordinary way be defined.

XIII. When a man attempts to combat the principle of utility, it is with reasons drawn, without his being aware of it, from that very principle itself.[4] His arguments, if they prove any thing, prove not that the principle is *wrong*, but that, according to the applications he supposes to be made of it, it is *misapplied.* Is it possible for a man to move the earth? Yes; but he must first find out another earth to stand upon.

*It can never be consistently combated.*

XIV. To disprove the propriety of it by arguments is impossible; but, from the causes that have been mentioned, or from some confused or partial view of it, a man may happen to be disposed not to relish it. Where this is the case, if he thinks the settling of his opinions on such a subject worth the trouble, let him take the following steps, and at length, perhaps, he may come to reconcile himself to it.

*Course to be taken for surmounting prejudices that may have been entertained against it.*

1. Let him settle with himself, whether he would wish to discard this principle altogether; if so, let him consider what it is that all his reasonings (in matters of politics especially) can amount to?
2. If he would, let him settle with himself, whether he would judge and act without any principle, or whether there is any other he would judge and act by?
3. If there be, let him examine and satisfy himself whether the principle he thinks he has found is really any separate intelligible principle; or whether it be not a mere principle in words, a kind of phrase, which at bottom expresses neither more nor less than the mere averment of his own unfounded sentiments; that is, what in another person he might be apt to call caprice?
4. If he is inclined to think that his own approbation or disapprobation, annexed to the idea of an act, without any regard to its consequences, is a sufficient foundation for him to judge and act upon, let him ask himself whether his sentiment is to be a standard of right and wrong, with respect to every other man, or whether every man's sentiment has the same privilege of bring a standard to itself?
5. In the first case, let him ask himself whether his principle is not despotical, and hostile to all the rest of human race?
6. In the second case, whether it is not anarchial, and whether at this rate there are not as many different standards of right and wrong as there are men? and whether even to the same man, the same thing, which is right to-day, may not(without the least change in its nature) be wrong to-morrow? and whether the same thing is not right and wrong in the same place at the same time? and in either case, whether all argument is not at an end? and whether, when two men have said, 'I like this,' and 'I don't like it,' they can (upon such a principle) have any thing more to say?

---

4 'The principle of utility, (I have heard it said) is a dangerous principle: it is dangerous on certain occasions to consult it.' This is as much as to say, what? that it is not consonant to utility, to consult utility: in short, that it is *not* consulting it, to consult it.

Addition by the Author, July 1822.

Not long after the publication of the Fragment on Government, anno 1776, in which, in the character of an all-comprehensive and all-commanding principle, the principle of *utility* was brought to view, one person by whom observation to the above effect was made was *Alexander Wedderburn*, at that time Attorney or Solicitor General, afterwards successively Chief Justice of the Common Pleas, and Chancellor of England, under the successive titles of Lord Loughborough and Earl of Rosslyn. It was made—not indeed in my hearing, but in the hearing of a person by whom it was almost immediately communicated to me. So far from being self-contradictory, it was a shrewd and perfectly true one. By that distinguished functionary, the state of the Government was thoroughly understood: by the obscure individual, at that time not so much as supposed to be so: his disquisitions had not been as yet applied, with any thing like a comprehensive view, to the field of Constitutional Law, nor therefore to those features of the English Government, by which the greatest happiness of the ruling *one* with or without that of a favoured few, are now so plainly seen to be the only ends to which the course of it has at any time been directed. The *principle of utility* was an appellative, at that time employed—employed by me, as it had been by others, to designate that which, in a more perspicuous and instructive manner, may, as above, be designated by the name of the *greatest happiness principle*. 'This principle (said Wedderburn) is a dangerous one.' Saying so, he said that which, to a certain extent, is strictly true: a principle, which lays down, as the only *right* and justifiable end of Government, the greatest happiness of the greatest number—how can it be denied to be a dangerous one? dangerous it unquestionably is, to every government which has for its *actual* end or object, the greatest happiness of a certain *one*, with or without the addition of some comparatively small number of others, whom it is matter of pleasure or accommodation to him to admit, each of them, to a share in the concern, on the footing of so many junior partners. *Dangerous* it therefore really was, to the interest—the sinister interest—of all those functionaries, himself included, whose interest it was, to maximize delay, vexation, and expense, in judicial and other modes of procedure, for the sake of the profit, extractible out of the expense. In a Government which had for its end in view the greatest happiness of the greatest number, Alexander Wedderburn might have been Attorney General and then Chancellor: but he would not have been Attorney General with £15,000 a year, nor Chancellor, with a peerage with a veto upon all justice, with £25,000 a year, and with 500 sinecures at his disposal, under the name of Ecclesiastical Benefices, besides *el casteras*.

7. If he should have said to himself, No: for that the sentiment which he proposes as a standard must be grounded on reflection, let him say on what particulars the reflection is to turn? if on particulars having relation to the utility of the act, then let him say whether this is not deserting his own principle, and borrowing assistance from that very one in opposition to which he sets it up: or if not on those particulars, on what other particulars?
8. If he should be for compounding the matter, and adopting his own principle in part, and the principle of utility in part, let him say how far he will adopt it?
9. When he has settled with himself where he will stop, then let him ask himself how he justifies to himself the adopting it so far? and why he will not adopt it any farther?
10. Admitting any other principle than the principle of utility to be a right principle, a principle that it is right for a man to pursue; admitting (what is not true) that the word *right* can have a meaning without reference to utility, let him say whether there is any such thing as a *motive* that a man can have to pursue the dictates of it: if there is, let him say what that motive is, and how it is to be distinguished from those which enforce the dictates of utility: if not, then lastly let him say what it is this other principle can be good for?

## CHAPTER II: OF PRINCIPLES ADVERSE TO THAT OF UTILITY

*All other principles than that of utility must be wrong.*

I. If the principle of utility be a right principle to be governed by, and that in all cases, it follows from what has been just observed, that whatever principle differs from it in any case must necessarily be a wrong one. To prove any other principle, therefore, to be a wrong one, there needs no more than just to show it to be what it is, a principle of which the dictates are in some point or other different from those of the principle of utility: to state it is to confute it.

*Ways in which a principle may be wrong.*

II. A principle may be different from that of utility in two ways: 1. By being constantly opposed to it: this is the case with a principle which may be termed the principle of *asceticism*.[5] 2. By being sometimes opposed to it, and sometimes not, as it may happen: this is the case with another, which may be termed the principle of *sympathy* and *antipathy*.

*Principle of asceticism, what.*

III. By the principle of asceticism I mean that principle, which, like the principle of utility, approves or disapproves of any action, according to the tendency which it appears to have to augment or diminish the happiness of the party whose interest is in question; but in an inverse manner: approving of actions in as far as they tend to diminish his happiness; disapproving of them in as far as they tend to augment it.

*A partizan of the principle of asceticism, who.*

IV. It is evident that any one who reprobates any the least particle of pleasure, as such, from whatever source derived, is *pro tanto* a partizan of the principle of asceticism. It is only upon that principle, and not from the principle of utility, that the most abominable pleasure which the vilest of malefactors ever reaped from his crime would be to be reprobated, if it stood alone. The case is, that it never does stand alone; but is necessarily followed by such a quantity of pain (or, what comes to the same thing, such a chance for a certain quantity of pain) that the pleasure in comparison of it, is as nothing: and this is the true and sole, but perfectly sufficient, reason for making it a ground for punishment.

---

5 Ascetic is a term that has been sometimes applied to Monks. It comes from a Greek word which signifies *exercise*. The practices by which Monks sought to distinguish themselves from other men were called their Exercises. These exercises consisted in so many contrivances they had for tormenting themselves. By this they thought to ingratiate themselves with the Deity. For the Deity, said they, is a Being of infinite

*Asceticism, origin of the word.*

benevolence: now a Being of the most ordinary benevolence is pleased to see others make themselves as happy as they can: therefore to make ourselves as unhappy as we can is the way to please the Deity. If any body asked them, what motive they could find for doing all this? Oh! said they, you are not to imagine that we are punishing ourselves for nothing: we know very well what we are about. You are to know, that for every grain of pain it costs us now, we are to have a hundred grains of pleasure by and by. The case is, that God loves to see us torment ourselves at present: indeed he has as good as told us so. But this is

*Principles or the Monks.*

done only to try us, in order just to see how we should behave: which it is plain he could not know, without making the experiment. Now then, from the satisfaction it gives him to see us make ourselves as unhappy as we can make ourselves in this present life, we have a sure proof of the satisfaction it will give him to see us as happy as he can make us in a life to come.

V. There are two classes of men of very different complexions, by whom the principle of asceticism appears to have been embraced; the one a set of moralists, the other a sot of religionists. Different accordingly have been the motives which appear to have recommended it to the notice of these different parties. Hope, that is the prospect of pleasure, seems to have animated the former: hope, the aliment of philosophic pride: the hope of honour and reputation at the hands of men. Fear, that is the prospect of pain, the latter: fear, the offspring of superstitious fancy: the fear of future punishment at the hands of a splenetic and revengeful Deity. I say in this case fear: for of the invisible future, fear is more powerful than hope. These circumstances characterize the two different parties among the partizans of the principle of asceticism; the parties and their motives different, the principle the same.

*This principle has had in some a philosophical, in others a religious origin.*

VI. The religious party, however, appear to have carried it farther than the philosophical: they have acted more consistently and less wisely. The philosophical party have scarcely gone farther than to reprobate pleasure: the religious party have frequently gone so far as to make it a matter of merit and of duty to court pain. The philosophical party have hardly gone farther than the making pain a matter of indifference. It is no evil, they have said: they have not said, it is a good. They have not so much as reprobated all pleasure in the lump. They have discarded only what they have called the gross; that is, such as are organical, or of which the origin is easily traced up to such as are organical: they have even cherished and magnified the refined. Yet this, however, not under the name of pleasure: to cleanse itself from the sordea of its impure original, it was necessary it should change its name: the honourable, the glorious, the reputable, the becoming, the *honestum,* the *decorum,* it was to be called: in short, any thing but pleasure.

*It has been carried farther by the religious party than by the philosophical.*

VII. From these two sources have flowed the doctrines from which the sentiments of the bulk of mankind have all along received a tincture of this principle; some from the philosophical, some from the religious, some from both. Men of education more frequently from the philosophical, as more suited to the elevation of their sentiments: the vulgar more frequently from the superstitious, as more suited to the narrowness of their intellect, undilated by knowledge: and to the abjectness of their condition, continually open to the attacks of fear. The tinctures, however, derived from the two sources, would naturally inter-mingle, insomuch that a man would not always know by which of them he was most influenced: and they would often serve to corroborate and enliven one another. It was this conformity that made a kind of alliance between parties of a complexion otherwise so dissimilar: and disposed them to unite upon various occasions against the common enemy, the partizan of the principle of utility, whom they joined in branding with the odious name of Epicurean.

*The philosophical branch of it has had most influence among persons of education, the religious among the vulgar.*

VIII. The principle of asceticism, however, with whatever warmth it may have been embraced by its partizans as a rule of private conduct, seems not to have been carried to any considerable length, when applied to the business of government. In a few instances it has been carried a little way by the philosophical party: witness the Spartan regimen. Though then, perhaps, it may be considered as having been a measure of security: and an application, though a precipitate and perverse application, of the principle of utility. Scarcely in any instances, to any considerable length, by the religious: for the various monastic orders, and the societies of the Quakers, Dumplers, Moravians, and other religionists, have been free societies, whose regimen no man has been astricted to without the intervention of his own consent. Whatever merit a man may have thought there would be in making himself miserable, no such notion seems ever to have occurred to any of them, that it may be a merit, much less a duty, to make others miserable: although it should seem, that if a certain quantity of misery were a thing so desirable, it would not matter much whether it were brought by each man upon himself, or by one man upon another. It is true, that from the same source from whence, among the religionists, the attachment to the principle of asceticism took its rise, flowed other doctrines and practices, from which misery in abundance was produced in one man by the instrumentality of another: witness the holy wars, and the persecutions for religion. But the passion for producing misery in these cases proceeded upon some special ground: the exercise of it was confined to persons of particular descriptions: they were tormented, not as men, but as heretics and infidels. To have inflicted the same miseries on their fellow-believers and fellow-sectaries, would have been as blameable in the eyes even of these religionists, as in those of a partizan of the principle of utility. For a man to give himself a certain number of stripes was indeed meritorious: but to give the same number of stripes to another man, not consenting, would have been a sin. We read

*The principle of asceticism has never been steadily applied by either party to the Business of Government.*

of saints, who for the good of their souls, and the mortification of their bodies, have voluntarily yielded themselves a prey to vermin: but though many persons of this class have wielded the reins of empire, we read of none who have set themselves to work, and made laws on purpose, with a view of stocking the body politic with the breed of highwaymen, housebreakers, or incendiaries. If at any time they have suffered the nation to be preyed upon by swarms of idle pensioners, or useless placemen, it has rather been from negligence and imbecility, than from any settled plan for oppressing and plundering of the people. If at any time they have sapped the sources of national wealth, by cramping commerce, and driving the inhabitants into emigration, it has been with other views, and in pursuit of other ends. If they have declaimed against the pursuit of pleasure, and the use of wealth, they have commonly stopped at declamation: they have not, like Lycurgus, made express ordinances for the purpose of banishing the precious metals. If they have established idleness by a law, it has been not because idleness, the mother of vice and misery, is itself a virtue, but because idleness (say they) is the road to holiness. If under the notion of fasting, they have joined in the plan of confining their subjects to a diet, thought by some to be of the most nourishing and prolific nature, it has been not for the sake of making them tributaries to the nations by whom that diet was to be supplied, but for the sake of manifesting their own power, and exercising the obedience of the people. If they have established, or suffered to be established, punishments for the breach of celibacy, they have done no more than comply with the petitions of those deluded rigorists, who, dupes to the ambitious and deep-laid policy of their rulers, first laid themselves under that idle obligation by a vow.

*The principle of asceticism, in its origin, was but that of utility misapplied.*

IX. The principle of asceticism seems originally to have been the reverie of certain hasty speculators, who having perceived, or fancied, that certain pleasures, when reaped in certain circumstances, have, at the long run, been attended with pains more than equivalent to them, took occasion to quarrel with every thing that offered itself under the name of pleasure. Having then got thus far, and having forgot the point which they set out from, they pushed on, and went so much further as to think it meritorious to fall in love with pain. Even this, we see, is at bottom but the principle of utility misapplied.

*It can never be consistently pursued.*

X. The principle of utility is capable of being consistently pursued; and it is but tautology to say, that the more consistently it is pursued, the better it must ever be for humankind. The principle of asceticism never was, nor ever can be, consistently pursued by any living creature. Let but one tenth part of the inhabitants of this earth pursue it consistently, and in a day's time they will have turned it into a hell.

*The principle of sympathy and antipathy, what.*

XI. Among principles adverse[6] to that of utility, that which at this day seems to have most influence in matters of government, is what may be called the principle of sympathy and antipathy. By the

6 The following Note was first printed in January 1789.

It ought rather to have been styled, more extensively, the principle of *caprice*. Where it applies to the choice of actions to be marked out for injunction or prohibition, for reward or punishment, (to stand, in a word, as subjects for *obligations* to be imposed,) it may indeed with propriety be termed, as in the text, the principle of *sympathy* and *antipathy*. But this appellative does not so well apply to it, when occupied in the choice of the *events* which are to serve as sources of *title* with respect to *rights*: where the actions prohibited and allowed the obligations and rights, being already fixed, the only question is, under what circumstances a man is to be invested with the one or subjected to the other? from what incidents occasion is to be taken to invest a man, or to refuse to invest him, with the one, or to subject him to the other? In this latter case it may more appositely be characterized by the name of the *phantastic principle*. Sympathy and antipathy are affections of the *sensible* faculty. But the choice of *titles* with respect to *rights*, especially with respect to proprietary rights, upon grounds unconnected with utility, has been in many instances the work, not of the affections but of the imagination.

When, in justification of an article of English Common Law, calling uncles to succeed in certain cases in preference to fathers, Lord Coke produced a sort of ponderosity he had discovered in rights, disqualifying them from ascending in a straight line, it was not that he loved uncles particularly, or *hated* fathers, but because the analogy, such as it was, was what his imagination presented him with, instead of a reason, and because, to a judgment unobservant of the standard of utility, or unacquainted with the art of consulting it, where affection is out of the way, imagination is the only guide.

When I know not what ingenious grammarian invented the proposition *Delegatus non potest delegare*, to serve as a rule of law, it was not surely that he had any antipathy to delegates of the second order, or that it was any pleasure to him to think of the ruin which, for want of a manager at home, may befal the affaire of a traveller, whom an unforeseen accident has deprived of the object of his choice: it was, that the incongruity, of giving the same law to objects so contrasted as *active* and *passive* are, was not to be surmounted, and that *-atus* chimes, as well as it contrasts, with *-are*.

When that inexorable maxim, (of which the dominion is no more to be defined, than the date of its birth, or the name of its father, is to be found,) was imported from England for the government of Bengal, and the whole fabric of judicature was crushed by the thunders of *ex post facto* justice, it was hot surely that the prospect of a blameless magistraoy perishing in prison afforded any enjoyment to the unoffended authors

principle of sympathy and antipathy, I mean that principle which approves or disapproves of certain actions, not on account of their tending to augment the happiness, nor yet on account of their tending to diminish the happiness of the party whose interest is in question, but merely because a man finds himself disposed to approve or disapprove of them: holding up that approbation or disapprobation as a sufficient reason for itself, and disclaiming the necessity of looking out for any extrinsic ground. Thus far in the general department of morals: and in the particular department of politics, measuring out the quantum (as well as determining the ground) of punishment, by the degree of the disapprobation.

*This is rather the negation of all principle, than any thing positive.*

XII. It is manifest, that this is rather a principle in name than in reality: it is not a positive principle of itself, so much as a term employed to signify the negation of all principle. What one expects to find in a principle is something that points out some external consideration, as a means of warranting and guiding the internal sentiments of approbation and disapprobation: this expectation is but ill fulfilled by a proposition, which does neither more nor less than hold up each of those sentiments as a ground and standard for itself.

*Sentiments of a partizan of the principle of antipathy.*

XIII. In looking over the catalogue of human actions (says a partizan of this principle) in order to determine which of them are to be marked with the seal of disapprobation, you need but to take counsel of your own feelings: whatever you find in yourself a propensity to condemn, is wrong for

---

of their misery; but that the music of the maxim, absorbing the whole imagination, had drowned the cries of humanity along with the dictates of common sense.[1] *Fiat Justitia, ruat caelum,* says another maxim, as full of extravagance as it is of harmony: Go heaven to wreck—so justice be but done:—and what is the ruin of kingdoms, in comparison of the wreck of heaven?

So again, when the Prussian chancellor, inspired with the wisdom of I know not what Roman sage, proclaimed in good Latin, for the edification of German ears, *Servitus servitulis non datur,* [Cod. Fred. tom. ii. par. 2. liv. 2. tit. x. § 6. p. 308.] it was not that he had conceived any aversion to the life-holder who, during the continuance of his term, should wish to gratify a neighbour with a right of way or water, or to the neighbour who should wish to accept of the indulgence; but that, to a jurisprudential ear, *-tus -tutis* sound little less melodious than *-atus -are.* Whether the melody of the maxim was the real reason of the rule, is not left open to dispute: for it is ushered in by the conjunction *quia,* reason's appointed harbinger: *quia servitus servitutis non datur.*

Neither would equal melody have been produced, nor indeed could similar melody have been called for, in either of these instances, by the opposite provision: it is only when they are opposed to general rules, and not when by their conformity they are absorbed in them, that more specific ones can obtain a separate existence. *Delegatus potest delegare,* and *Servitus servitutis datur,* provisions already included under the general adoption of contracts, would have been as unnecessary to the apprehension and the memory, as, in comparison of their energetic negatives, they are insipid to the ear.

Were the inquiry diligently made, it would be found that the goddess of harmony has exercised more influence, however latent, over the dispensations of Themis, than her most diligent historiographers, or even her most passionate panegyrists, seem to have been aware of. Every one knows, how, by the ministry of Orpheus, it was she who first collected the sons of men beneath the shadow of the sceptre: yet, in the midst of continual experience, men seem yet to learn, with what successful diligence she has laboured to guide it in its course. Every one knows, that measured numbers were the language of the infancy of law: none seem to have observed, with what imperious sway they have governed her maturer age. In English jurisprudence in particular, the connexion betwixt law and music, however less perceived than in Spartan legislation, is not perhaps less real nor less close. The music of the Office, though not of the same kind, is not less musical in its kind, than the music of the Theatre; that which hardens the heart, than that which softens it:—sostenutos as long, cadences as sonorous; and those governed by rules, though not yet promulgated, not less determinate. Search indictments, pleadings, proceedings in chancery, conveyances: whatever trespasses you may find against truth or common sense, you will find none against the laws of harmony. The English Liturgy, justly as this quality has been extolled in that sacred office, possesses not a greater measure of it, than is commonly to be found in an English Act of Parliament. Dignity,

1 Additional Note by the Author, July 1822.

Add, and that the bad system, of Mahometan and other native law was to be put down at all events, to make way for the inapplicable and still more mischievous system of English Judge-made law, and, by the hand of his accomplice Hastings, was to be put into the pocket of Impey—Importer of this instrument of subversion, £8,000 a-year contrary to law, in addition to the £8,000 a-year lavished upon him, with the customary profusion, by the hand of law.—See the Account of this transaction in *Mars British India.*

To this Governor a statue is erecting by a vote of East India Directors and Proprietors: on it should be inscribed—*Let it but put money into our pockets, no tyranny too flagtious to be worshipped by us.*

To this statue of the Arch-malefactor should be added, for a companion, that of the long-robed accomplice: the one lodging the bribe in the hand of the other. The hundred millions of plundered and oppressed Hindoos and Mahometans pay for the one; a Westminster Hall subscription might pay for the other.

What they have done for Ireland with her seven millions of souls, the authorised deniers and perverters of justice have done for Hindustan with her hundred millions. In this there is nothing wonderful. The wonder is—that, under such institutions, men, though in ever such small number, should be found, whom the view of the injustices which, by *English Judge-made law,* they are compelled to commit, and the miseries they are thus compelled to produce, deprive of health and rest, Witnees the Letter of an English Hindostan Judge, Sept. 1, 1819, which lies before me. I will not make so cruel a requital for his honesty, as to put his name in print: indeed the House of Commons' Documents already published leave little need of it.

that very reason. For the same reason it is also meet for punishment: in what proportion it is adverse to utility, or whether it be adverse to utility at all, is a matter that makes no difference. In that same *proportion* also is it meet for punishment: if you hate much, punish much: if you hate little, punish little: punish as you hate. If you hate not at all, punish not at all: the fine feelings of the soul are not to be overborne and tyrannized by the harsh and rugged dictates of political utility.

*The systems that have been formed concerning the standard of right and wrong, are all reducible to this principle.*

XIV. The various systems that have been formed concerning the standard of right and wrong, may all be reduced to the principle of sympathy and antipathy. One account may serve for all of them. They consist all of them in so many contrivances for avoiding the obligation of appealing to any external standard, and for prevailing upon the reader to accept of the author's sentiment or opinion as a reason for itself. The phrases different, but the principle the same[7].

---

simplicity, brevity, precision, intelligibility, possibility of being retained or so much as apprehended, every thing yields to Harmony. Volumes might be filled, shelves loaded, with the sacrifices that are made to this insatiate power. Expletives, her ministers in Grecian poetry are not less busy, though in different shape and bulk, in English legislation: in the former, they are monosyllables:[2] in the latter, they are whole lines.[3]

To return to the *principle of sympathy and antipathy:* a term preferred at first, on account of its impartiality, to the *principle of caprice*. The choice of an appellative, in the above respects too narrow, was owing to my not having, at that time, extended my views over the civil branch of law, any otherwise than as I had found it inseparably involved in the penal. But when we come to the former branch, we shall see the *phantastic* principle making at least as great a figure there, as the principle of *sympathy and antipathy* in the latter.

In the days of Lord Coke, the light of utility can scarcely be said to have as yet shone upon the face of Common Law. If a faint ray of it, under the name of the *argumentum ab inconvenienti*, is to be found in a list of about twenty topics exhibited by that great lawyer as the co-ordinate leaders of that all-perfect system, the admission, so circumstanced, is as sure a proof of neglect, as, to the statues of Brutus and Cassius, exclusion was a cause of notice. It stands, neither in the front, nor in the rear, nor in any post of honour; but huddled in towards the middle, without the smallest mark of preference. [Coke, Littleton, 11. a.] Nor is this Latin *inconvenience* by any means the same thing with the English one. It stands distinguished from *mischief*: and because by the vulgar it is taken for something less bad, it is given by the learned as something worse. *The law prefers a mischief to an inconvenience*, says an admired maxim, and the more admired, because as nothing is expressed by it, the more is supposed to be understood.

Not that there is any avowed, much less a constant opposition, between the prescriptions of utility and the operations of the common law: such constancy we have seen to be too much even for ascetic fervor. [Supra, par. x] From time to time instinct would unavoidably betray them into the paths of reason: instinct which, however it may be cramped, can never be killed by education. The cobwebs spun out of the materials brought together by 'the competition of opposite analogies,' can never have ceased being warped by the silent attraction of the rational principle: though it should have been, as the needle is by the magnet, without the privity of conscience.

2 Μεν, τοι, γε, νυν, &c.

3 And be it further enacted by the authority aforesaid, that—Provided always, and it is hereby further enacted and declared that—&c. &c.

7 It is curious enough to observe the variety of inventions men have hit upon, and the variety of phrases they have brought forward, in order to conceal from the world, and, if possible, from themselves, this very general and therefore very pardonable self-sufficiency.

*1 Moral Sense.*

1. One man says, he has a thing made on purpose to tell him what is right and what is wrong; and that it is called a *moral sense:* and then he goes to work at his ease, and says, such a thing is right, and such a thing is wrong—why? 'because my moral sense tells me it is.'

*2. Common Sense.*

2. Another man comes and alters the phrase: leaving out *moral*, and putting in *common*, in the room of it. He then tells you, that his common sense teaches him what is right and wrong, as surely as the other's moral sense did: meaning by common sense, a sense of some kind or other, which, he says, is possessed by all mankind: the sense of those, whose sense is not the same as the author's, being struck out of the account as not worth taking. This contrivance does better than the other; for a moral sense, being a new thing, a man may feel about him a good while without being able to find it out: but common sense is as old as the creation; and there is no man but would be ashamed to be thought not to have as much of it as his neighbours. It has another great advantage: by appearing to share power, it lessens envy: for when a man gets up upon this ground, in order to anathematize those who differ from him, it is not by a *sic volo sic jubeo*, but by a *velitis jubeatis*.

*3. Understanding.*

3. Another man comes, and says, that as to a moral sense indeed, he cannot find that he has any such thing: that however he has an *understanding*, which will do quite as well. This understanding, he says, is the standard of right and wrong: it tells him so and so. All good and wise men understand as he does: if other men's understandings differ in any point from his, so much the worse for them: it is a sure sign they are either defective or corrupt.

*4. Rule of Right.*

4. Another man says, that there is an eternal and immutable Rule of Right: that that rule of right dictates so and so: and then he begins giving you his sentiments upon any thing that comes uppermost: and these sentiments (you are to take for granted) are so many branches of the eternal rule of right.

*5. Fitness of Things.*

5. Another man, or perhaps the same man (it's no matter) says, that there are certain practices conformable, and others repugnant, to the Fitness of Things; and then he tells you, at his leisure, what practices are conformable and what repugnant: just as he happens to like a practice or dislike it.

XV. It is manifest, that the dictates of this principle will frequently coincide with those of utility, though perhaps without intending any such thing. Probably more frequently than not: and hence it is that the business of penal justice is carried on upon that tolerable sort of footing upon which we see it carried on in common at this day. For what more natural or more general ground of hatred to a practice can there be, than the mischievousness of such practice? What all men are exposed to suffer by, all men

*This principle will frequently coincide with that of utility.*

6. A great multitude of people are continually talking of the Law of Nature; and then they go on giving you their sentiments about what is right and what is wrong: and these sentiments, you are to understand, are so many chapters and sections of the Law of Nature.

*6. Law of Nature.*

7. Instead of the phrase, Law of Nature, you have sometimes, Law of Reason, Right Reason, Natural Justice, Natural Equity, Good Order. Any of them will do equally well. This latter is most used in politics. The three last are much more tolerable than the others, because they do not very explicitly claim to be any thing more than phrases: they insist but feebly upon the being looked upon as so many positive standards of themselves, and seem content to be taken, upon occasion, for phrases expressive of the conformity of the thing in question to the proper standard, whatever that may be. On most occasions, however, it will be better to say *utility: utility* is clearer, as referring more explicitly to pain and pleasure.

*7. Law of Reason, Right Reason, Natural Justice, Natural Equity, Good Order.*

*Various phrases that have served as the characteristic marks of so many pretended systems.*

8. We have one philosopher, who says, there is no harm in any thing in the world but in telling a lie; and that if, for example, you were to murder your own father, this would only be a particular way of saying, he was not your father. Of course, when this philosopher sees any thing that he does not like, he says, it is a particular way of telling a lie. It is saying, that the act ought to be done, or may be done, when, *in truth,* it ought not to be done.

*8. Truth.*

9. The fairest and openest of them all is that sort of man who speaks out, and says, I am of the number of the Elect: now God himself takes care to inform the Elect what is right: and that with so good effect, and let them strive ever so, they cannot help not only knowing it but practising it. If therefore a man wants to know what is right and what is wrong, he has nothing to do but to come to me.

*9. Doctrine of Election.*

It is upon the principle of antipathy that such and such acts are often reprobated on the score of their being *unnatural:* the practice of exposing children, established among the Greeks and Romans, was an unnatural practice. Unnatural, when it means any thing, means unfrequent: and there it means something; although nothing to the present purpose. But here it means no such thing: for the frequency of such acts is perhaps the great complaint. It therefore means nothing; nothing, I mean, which there is in the act itself. All it can serve to express is, the disposition of the person who is talking of it: the disposition he is in to be angry at the thoughts of it. Does it merit his anger? Very likely it may: but whether it does or no is a question, which, to be answered rightly, can only be answered upon the principle of utility.

*Repugnancy to Nature.*

Unnatural, is as good a word as moral sense, or common sense; and would be as good a foundation for a system. Such an act is unnatural; that is, repugnant to nature: for I do not like to practise it: and, consequently, do not practise it. It is therefore repugnant to what ought to be the nature of every body else.

The mischief common to all these ways of thinking and arguing (which, in truth, as we have seen, are but one and the same method, couched in different forms of words) is their serving as a cloke, and pretence, and aliment, to despotism: if not a despotism in practice, a despotism however in disposition: which is but too apt, when pretence and power offer, to show itself in practice. The consequence is, that with intentions very commonly of the purest kind, a man becomes a torment either to himself or his fellow-creatures. If he be of the melancholy cast, he sits in silent grief, bewailing their blindness and depravity: if of the irascible, he declaims with fury and virulence against all who differ from him; blowing up the coals of fanaticism, and branding with the charge of corruption and insincerity, every man who does not think, or profess to think, as he does.

*Mischief they produce.*

If such a man happens to possess the advantages of style, his book may do a considerable deal of mischief before the nothingness of it is understood.

These principles, if such they can be called, it is more frequent to see applied to morals than to politics: but their influence extends itself to both. In politics, as well as morals, a man will be at least equally glad of a pretence for deciding any question in the manner that best pleases him, without the trouble of inquiry. If a man is an infallible judge of what is right and wrong in the actions of private individuals, why not in the measures to be observed by public men in the direction of those actions? accordingly (not to mention other chimeras) I have more than once known the pretended law of nature set up in legislative debates, in opposition to arguments derived from the principle of utility.

'But is it never, then, from any other considerations than those of utility, that we derive our notions of right and wrong?' I do not know: I do not care. Whether a moral sentiment can be originally conceived from any other source than a view of utility, is one question: whether upon examination and reflection it can, in point of fact, be actually persisted in and justified on any other ground, by a person reflecting within himself, is another: whether in point of right it can properly be justified on any other ground, by a person addressing himself to the community, is a third. The two first are questions of speculation: it matters not, comparatively speaking, how they are decided. The last is a question of practice: the decision of it is of as much importance as that of any can be.

*Whether utility is actually the sole ground of all the approbation we ever bestow, is a different consideration.*

'I feel in myself,' (say you) 'a disposition to approve of such or such an action in a moral view: but this is not owing to any notions I have of its being a useful one to the community. I do not pretend to know whether it be an useful one or not: it may be, for aught I know, a mischievous one.' 'But is it then,' (say I) 'a mischievous one? examine; and if you can make yourself sensible that it is so, then, if duty means any thing, that is, moral *duty*, it is your duly at least to abstain from it: and more than that, if it is what lies in your power, and can be done without too great a sacrifice, to endeavour to prevent it. It is not your cherishing the notion of it in your bosom, and giving it the name of virtue, that will excuse you.'

will be disposed to hate. It is far yet, however, from being a constant ground: for when a man suffers, it is not always that he knows what it is he suffers by. A man may suffer grievously, for instance, by a new tax, without being able to trace up the cause of his sufferings to the injustice of some neighbour, who has eluded the payment of an old one.

*This principle is most apt to err on the side of severity.*

XVI. The principle of sympathy and antipathy is most apt to err on the side of severity. It is for applying punishment in many cases which deserve none: in many cases which deserve some, it is for applying more than they deserve. There is no incident imaginable, be it ever so trivial, and so remote from mischief, from which this principle may not extract a ground of punishment. Any difference in taste: any difference in opinion: upon one subject as well as upon another. No disagreement so trifling which perseverance and altercation will not render serious. Each becomes in the other's eyes an enemy, and, if laws permit, a criminal[8]. This is one of the circumstances by which the human race is distinguished (not much indeed to its advantage) from the brute creation.

*But errs, in some instances, on the side of lenity.*

XVII. It is not, however, by any means unexampled for this principle to err on the side of lenity. A near and perceptible mischief moves antipathy. A remote and imperceptible mischief, though not less real, has no effect. Instances in proof of this will occur in numbers in the course of the work.[9] It would be breaking in upon the order of it to give them here.

*The theological principle, what—not a separate principle.*

XVIII. It may be wondered, perhaps, that in all this while no mention has been made of the *theological* principle; meaning that principle which professes to recur for the standard of right and wrong to the will of God. But the case is, this is not in fact a distinct principle. It is never any thing more or less than one or other of the three before-mentioned principles presenting itself under another shape. The *will* of God here meant cannot be his revealed will, as contained in the sacred writings: for that is a system which nobody ever thinks of recurring to at this time of day, for the details of political administration: and even before it can be applied to the details of private conduct, it is universally allowed, by the most eminent divines of all persuasions, to stand in need of pretty ample interpretations; else to what use are the works of those divines? And for the guidance of these interpretations, it is also allowed, that some other standard must be assumed. The will then which is meant on this occasion, is that which may be called the *presumptive* will: that is to say, that which is presumed to be his will on account of the conformity of its dictates to those of some other principle. What then may be this other principle? it must be one

---

'I feel in myself,' (say you again) 'a disposition to detest such or such an action in a moral view; but this is not owing to any notions I have of its being a mischievous one to the community. I do not pretend to know whether it be a mischievous one or not: it may be not a mischievous one: it may be, for aught I know, an useful one.'—'May it indeed,' (say I) 'an useful one? but let me tell you then, that unless duty, and right and wrong, be just what you please to make them, if it really be not a mischievous one, and any body has a mind to do it, it is no duty of yours, but, on the contrary, it would be very wrong in you, to take upon you to prevent him: detest it within yourself as much as you please; that may be a very good reason (unless it be also a useful one) for your not doing it yourself: but if you go about, by word or deed, to do any thing to hinder him, or make him suffer for it, it is you, and not he, that have done wrong: it is not your setting yourself to blame his conduct, or branding it with the name of vice, that will make him culpable, or you blameless. Therefore, if you can make yourself content that he shall be of one mind, and you of another, about that matter, and so continue, it is well: but if nothing will serve you, but that you and be must needs be of the same mind, I'll tell you what you have to do: it is for you to get the better of your antipathy, not for him to truckle to it'

8 King James the First of England had conceived a violent antipathy against Arians: two of whom he burnt[1]. This gratification he procured himself without much difficulty; the notions of the times were favourable to it. He wrote a furious book against Vorstius, for being what was called an Arminian: for Vorstius was at a distance. He also wrote a furious book, called 'A Counterblast to Tobacco,' against the use of that drug, which Sir Walter Raleigh had then lately introduced. Had the notions of the times co-operated with him, he would have burnt the Anabaptist and the smoker of tobacco in the same fire. However he had the satisfaction of putting Raleigh to death afterwards, though for another crime.

Disputes concerning the comparative excellence of French and Italian music have occasioned very serious bickerings at Paris. One of the parties would not have been sorry (says Mr. D'Alembert[1]) to have brought government into the quarrel. Pretences were sought after and urged. Long before that, a dispute of like nature, and of at least equal warmth, had been kindled at London upon the comparative merits of two composers at London; where riots between the approvers and disapprovers of a new play are, at this day, not unfrequent. The ground of quarrel between the Big-endians and the Little-endians in the fable, was not more frivolous than many an one which has laid empires desolate. In Russia, it is said, there was a time when some thousands of persons lost their lives in a quarrel, in which the government had taken part, about the number of fingers to be used in making the sign of the cross. This was in days of yore: the ministers of Catherine II. are better *instructed*,[2] than to take any other part in such disputes, than that of preventing the parties concerned from doing one another a mischief.

1 Melanges Essai sur la Liberté de la Musique.

2 Instruct. art. 474, 475, 476.

9 See ch. xvi. [Division], par. 42, 44.

or other of the three mentioned above: for there cannot, as we have seen, be any more. It is plain, therefore, that, setting revelation out of the question, no light can ever be thrown upon the standard of right and wrong, by any thing that can be said upon the question, what is God's will. We may be perfectly sure, indeed, that whatever is right is conformable to the will of God but so far is that from answering the purpose of showing us what is right, that it is necessary to know first whether a thing is right, in order to know from thence whether it be conformable to the will of God.[10]

*Antipathy, let the actions it dictates be ever so right, is never of itself a right ground of action.*

XIX. There are two things which are very apt to be confounded, but which it imports us carefully to distinguish:—the motive or cause, which, by operating on the mind of an individual, is productive of any act: and the ground or reason which warrants a legislator, or other by-stander, in regarding that act with an eye of approbation. When the act happens, in the particular instance in question, to be productive of effects which we approve of, much more if we happen to observe that the same motive may frequently be productive, in other instances, of the like effects, we are apt to transfer our approbation to the motive itself, and to assume, as the just ground for the approbation we bestow on the act, the circumstance of its originating from that motive. It is in this way that the sentiment of antipathy has often been considered as a just ground of action. Antipathy, for instance, in such or such a case, is the cause of an action which is attended with good effects: but this does not make it a right ground of action in that case, any more than in any other. Still farther. Not only the effects are good, but the agent sees beforehand that they will be so. This may make the action indeed a perfectly right action: but it does not make antipathy a right ground of action. For the same sentiment of antipathy, if implicitly deferred to, may be, and very frequently is, productive of the very worst effects. Antipathy, therefore, can never be a right ground of action. No more, therefore, can resentment, which, as will be seen more particularly hereafter, is but a modification of antipathy. The only right ground of action, that can possibly subsist, is, after all, the consideration of utility, which, if it is a right principle of action, and of approbation, in any one case, is so in every other. Other principles in abundance, that is, other motives, may be the reasons why such and such an act *has* been done: that is, the reasons or causes of its being done: but it is this alone that can be the reason why it might or ought to have been done. Antipathy or resentment requires always to be regulated, to prevent its doing mischief: to be regulated by what? always by the principle of utility. The principle of utility neither requires nor admits of any other regulator than itself.

## CHAPTER IV: VALUE OF A LOT OF PLEASURE OR PAIN, HOW TO BE MEASURED

*Use of this chapter.*

I. Pleasures then, and the avoidance of pains, are the *ends* which the legislator has in view: it behoves him therefore to understand their *value*. Pleasures and pains are the *instruments* he has to work with: it behoves him therefore to understand their force, which is again, in other words, their value.

II. To a person considered *by himself*, the value of a pleasure or pain considered *by itself*, will be greater or less, according to the four following circumstances:[11]

---

*The principle of theology how reducible to one or an other of the other three principles.*

10 The principle of theology refers every thing to God's pleasure. But what is God's pleasure? God does not, he confessedly does not now, either speak or write to us. How then are we to know what is his pleasure? By observing what is our own pleasure, and pronouncing it to be his. Accordingly, what is called the pleasure of God, is and must necessarily be (revelation apart) neither more nor less than the good pleasure of the person, whoever he be, who is pronouncing what he believes, or pretends, to be God's pleasure. How know you it to be God's pleasure that such or such an act should be abstained from? whence come you even to suppose as much? 'Because the engaging in it would, I imagine, be prejudicial upon the whole to the happiness of mankind;' says the partizan of the principle of utility: 'Because the commission of it is attended with a gross and sensual, or at least with a trifling and transient satisfaction;' says the partizan of the principle of asceticism: 'Because I detest the thoughts of it; and I cannot, neither ought I to be called upon to tell why;' says he who proceeds upon the principle of antipathy. In the words of one or other of these must that person necessarily answer (revelation apart) who professes to take for his standard the will of God.

11 These circumstances have since been denominated *elements* or *dimensions* of *value*, in a pleasure or a pain.

Not long after the publication of the first edition, the following memoriter verses were framed, in the view of lodging more effectually, in the memory, these points, on which the whole fabric of morals and legislation may be seen to rest.

*Intense, long, certain, speedy, fruitful, pure—*
Such marks in *pleasures* and in *pains* endure.
Such pleasures seek if *private* be thy end:
If it be *public*, wide let them *extend*.
Such *pains* avoid, whichever be thy view:
If pains *must* come, let them *extend* to few.

*Circumstances to be taken into the account in estimating the value of a pleasure or pain considered with reference to a single person, and by itself.*

1. Its *intensity.*
2. Its *duration.*
3. Its *certainty* or *uncertainty.*
4. Its *propinquity* or *remoteness.*

III. These are the circumstances which are to be considered in estimating a pleasure or a pain considered each of them by itself. But when the value of any pleasure or pain is considered for the purpose of estimating the tendency of any *act* by which it is produced, there are two other circumstances to be taken into the account; these are,

*—considered as connected with other pleasures or pains.*

5. Its *fecundity,* or the chance it has of being followed by sensations of the *same* kind: that is, pleasures, if it be a pleasure: pains, if it be a pain.
6. Its *purity,* or the chance it has of *not* being followed by sensations of the *opposite* kind: that is, pains, if it be a pleasure: pleasures, if it be a pain.

These two last, however, are in strictness scarcely to be deemed properties of the pleasure or the pain itself; they are not, therefore, in strictness to be taken into the account of the value of that pleasure or that pain. They are in strictness to be deemed properties only of the act, or other event, by which such pleasure or pain has been produced; and accordingly are only to be taken into the account of the tendency of such act or such event.

*—considered with reference to a number of persons.*

IV. To a *number* of persons, with reference to each of whom the value of a pleasure or a pain is considered, it will be greater or less, according to seven circumstances: to wit, the six preceding ones; *viz.*

1. Its *intensity.*
2. Its *duration.*
3. Its *certainty* or *uncertainty.*
4. Its *propinquity* or *remoteness.*
5. Its *fecundity.*
6. Its *purity.*

And one other; to wit:

7. Its *extent;* that is, the number of persons to whom it *extends;* or (in other words) who are affected by it.

*Process for estimating the tendency of any act or event.*

V. To take an exact account then of the general tendency of any act, by which the interests of a community are affected, proceed as follows. Begin with any one person of those whose interests seem most immediately to be affected by it: and take an account,

1. Of the value of each distinguishable *pleasure* which appears to be produced by it in the *first* instance.
2. Of the value of each *pain* which appears to be produced by it in the *first* instance.
3. Of the value of each pleasure which appears to be produced by it *after* the first. This constitutes the *fecundity* of the first *pleasure* and the *impurity* of the first *pain.*
4. Of the value of each *pain* which appears to be produced by it after the first. This constitutes the *fecundity* of the first *pain,* and the *impurity* of the first pleasure.
5. Sum up all the values of all the *pleasures* on the one side, and those of all the pains on the other. The balance, if it be on the side of pleasure, will give the *good* tendency of the act upon the whole, with respect to the interests of that *individual* person; if on the side of pain, the *bad* tendency of it upon the whole.

6. Take an account of the *number* of persons whose interests appear to be concerned; and repeat the above process with respect to each. *Sum up* the numbers expressive of the degrees of *good* tendency, which the act has, with respect to each individual, in regard to whom the tendency of it is *good* upon the whole: do this again with respect to each individual, in regard to whom the tendency of it is *good* upon the whole: do this again with respect to each individual, in regard to whom the tendency of it is *bad* upon the whole. Take the *balance;* which, if on the side of *pleasure,* will give the general *good tendency* of the act, with respect to the total number or community of individuals concerned; if on the side of pain, the general *evil tendency,* with respect to the same community.

*Use of the foregoing process.*

VI. It is not to be expected that this process should be strictly pursued previously to every moral judgment, or to every legislative or judicial operation. It may, however, be always kept in view: and as near as the process actually pursued on these occasions approaches to it, so near will such process approach to the character of an exact one.

*The same process applicable to good and evil, profit and mischief, and all other modifications of pleasure and pain.*

VII. The same process is alike applicable to pleasure and pain, in whatever shape they appear: and by whatever denomination they are distinguished: to pleasure, whether it be called *good* (which is properly the cause or instrument of pleasure) or *profit* (which is distant pleasure, or the cause or instrument of distant pleasure,) or *convenience,* or *advantage, benefit, emolument, happiness,* and so forth: to pain, whether it be called *evil,* (which corresponds to *good)* or *mischief,* or *inconvenience,* or *disadvantage,* or *loss,* or *unhappiness,* and so forth.

*Conformity of men's practice to this theory.*

VIII. Nor is this a novel and unwarranted, any more than it is a useless theory. In all this there is nothing but what the practice of mankind, wheresoever they have a clear view of their own interest, is perfectly conformable to. An article of property, an estate in land, for instance, is valuable, on what account? On account of the pleasures of all kinds which it enables a man to produce, and what comes to the same thing the pains of all kinds which it enables him to avert. But the value of such an article of property is universally understood to rise or fall according to the length or shortness of the time which a man has in it: the certainty or uncertainty of its coming into possession: and the nearness or remoteness of the time at which, if at all, it is to come into possession. As to the *intensity* of the pleasures which a man may derive from it, this is never thought of, because it depends upon the use which each particular person may come to make of it; which cannot be estimated till the particular pleasures he may come to derive from it, or the particular pains he may come to exclude by means of it, are brought to view. For the same reason, neither does he think of the *fecundity* or *purity* of those pleasures.

Thus much for pleasure and pain, happiness and unhappiness, in *general.* We come now to consider the several particular kinds of pain and pleasure.

## CHAPTER X: OF MOTIVES

### § 1. Different Senses of the Word Motive[12]

*Motives, why considered.*

I. It is an acknowledged truth, that every kind of act whatever, and consequently every kind of offence, is apt to assume a different character, and beattended with different effects, according to the nature of the *motive* which gives birth to it. This makes it requisite to take a view of the several motives by which human conduct is liable to be influenced.

*Purely speculative motives have nothing to do here.*

II. By a motive, in the most extensive sense in which the word is ever used with reference to a thinking being, is meant any thing that can contribute to give birth to, or even to prevent, any kind of action. Now the action of a thinking being is the act either of the body, or only of the mind: and an act of the mind

12 Note by the author, July, 1822.

For a tabular simultaneous view of the whole list of MOTIVES, in conjunction with the correspondent *pleasures* and *pains, interests* and *desires,* see, by the same author, *Table of the Springs of Action,* &c., with Explanatory Notes and Observations. London: 1817, Hunter, St. Paul's Church Yard, 8vo. pp. 32.

The word *inducement* has of late presented itself, as being in its signification more comprehensive than the word *motive,* and on some occasions more apposite.

is an act either of the intellectual faculty, or of the will. Acts of the intellectual faculty will sometimes rest in the understanding merely, without exerting any influence in the production of any acts of the will. Motives, which are not of a nature to influence any other acts than those, may be styled purely *speculative* motives, or motives resting in speculation. But as to these acts, neither do they exercise any influence over external acts, or over their consequences, nor consequently over any pain or any pleasure that may be in the number of such consequences. Now it is only on account of their tendency to produce either pain or pleasure, that any acts can be material. With acts, therefore, that rest purely in the understanding, we have not here any concern: nor therefore with any object, if any such there be, which, in the character of a motive, can have no influence on any other acts than those.

*Motives to the will.*

III. The motives with which alone we have any concern, are such as are of a nature to act upon the will. By a motive then, in this sense of the word, is to be understood any thing whatsoever, which, by influencing the will of a sensitive being, is supposed to serve as a means of determining him to act, or voluntarily to forbear to act,[13] upon any occasion. Motives of this sort, in contradistinction to the former, may be styled *practical* motives, or motives applying to practice.

*Figurative and unfigurative senses of the word.*

IV. Owing to the poverty and unsettled state of language, the word *motive* is employed indiscriminately to denote two kinds of objects, which, for the better understanding of the subject, it is necessary should be distinguished. On some occasions it is employed to denote any of those really existing incidents from whence the act in question is supposed to take its rise. The sense it bears on these occasions may be styled its literal or *unfigurative* sense. On other occasions it is employed to denote a certain fictitious entity, a passion, an affection of the mind, an ideal being which upon the happening of any such incident is considered as operating upon the mind, and prompting it to take that course, towards which it is impelled by the influence of such incident. Motives of this class are Avarice, Indolence, Benevolence, and so forth; as we shall see more particularly farther on. This latter may be styled the *figurative* sense of the term *motive.*

*Motives interior and exterior.*

V. As to the real incidents to which the name of motive is also given, these too are of two very different kinds. They may be either, 1. The *internal* perception of any individual lot of pleasure or pain, the expectation of which is looked upon as calculated to determine you to act in such or such a manner; as the pleasure of acquiring such a sum of money, the pain of exerting yourself on such an occasion, and so forth: or, 2. Any *external* event, the happening whereof is regarded as having a tendency to bring about the perception of such pleasure or such pain; for instance, the coming up of a lottery ticket, by which the possession of the money devolves to you; or the breaking out of a fire in the house you are in, which makes it necessary for you to quit it. The former kind of motives may be termed interior, or internal: the latter exterior, or external.

*Motive in prospect motive in esse.*

VI. Two other senses of the term *motive* need also to be distinguished. Motive refers necessarily to action. It is a pleasure, pain, or other event, that prompts to action. Motive then, in one sense of the word, must be previous to such event. But, for a man to be governed by any motive, he must in every case look beyond that event which is called his action; he must look to the consequences of it: and it is only in this way that the idea of pleasure, of pain, or of any other event, can give birth to it. He must look, therefore, in every case, to some event posterior to the act in contemplation: an event which as yet exists not, but stands only in prospect. Now, as it is in all cases difficult, and in most cases unnecessary, to distinguish between objects so intimately connected, as the posterior possible object which is thus looked forward to, and the present existing object or event which takes place upon a man's looking forward to the other, they are both of them spoken of under the same appellation, *motive.* To distinguish them, the one first mentioned may be termed a motive in *prospect,* the other a motive in *esse:* and under each of these denominations will come as well exterior as internal motives. A fire breaks out in your neighbour's house: you are under apprehension of its extending to your own: you are apprehensive, that if you stay in it, you will be burnt: you accordingly run out of it. This then is the act: the others are all motives to it. The event of the fire's breaking out in your neighbour's house is an external motive, and that in *esse:* the idea or belief of the probability of the fire's extending to your own house, that of your being burnt if you continue,

13 When the effect or tendency of a motive is to determine a man to forbear to act, it may seem improper to make use of the term *motive*: since motive, properly speaking, means that which disposes an object to *move*. We must however use that improper term, or a term which, though proper enough, is scarce in use, the word *determinative*. By way of justification, or at least apology, for the popular usage in this behalf, it may be observed, that even forbearance to act, or the negation of motion (that is, of bodily motion) supposes an act done, when such forbearance is voluntary. It supposes, to wit, an act of the will, which is as much a positive act, as much a motion, as any other act of the thinking substance.

and the pain you feel at the thought of such a catastrophe, are all so many internal events, but still in *esse:* the event of the fire's actually extending to your own house, and that of your being actually burnt by it, external motives in prospect: the pain you would feel at seeing your house a burning, and the pain you would feel while you yourself were burning, internal motives in prospect: which events, according as the matter turns out, may come to be in *esse:* but then of course they will cease to act as motives.

*Motives immediate and remote.*

VII. Of all these motives, which stand nearest to the act, to the production of which they all contribute, is that internal motive in *esse* which consists in the expectation of the internal motive in prospect: the pain or uneasiness you feel at the thoughts of being burnt.[14] All other motives are more or less remote: the motives in prospect, in proportion as the period at which they are expected to happen is more distant from the period at which the act takes place, and consequently later in point of time: the motives in *esse,* in proportion as they also are more distant from that period, and consequently earlier in point of time.[15]

*Motives to the understanding, how they may influence the will.*

VIII. It has already been observed, that with motives of which the influence terminates altogether in the understanding, we have nothing here to do. If then, amongst objects that are spoken of as motives with reference to the understanding, there be any which concern us here, it is only in as far as such objects may, through the medium of the understanding, exercise an influence over the will. It is in this way, and in this way only, that any objects, in virtue of any tendency they may have to influence the sentiment of belief, may in a practical sense act in the character of motives. Any objects, by tending to induce a belief concerning the existence, actual, or probable, of a practical motive; that is, concerning the probability of a motive in prospect, or the existence of a motive in *esse;* may exercise an influence on the will, and rank with those other motives that have been placed under the name of practical. The pointing out of motives such as these, is what we frequently mean when we talk of giving *reasons.* Your neighbour's house is on fire as before. I observe to you, that at the lower part of your neighbour's house is some wood-work, which joins on to yours; that the flames have caught this wood-work, and so forth; which I do in order to dispose you to believe as I believe, that if you stay in your house much longer you will be burnt. In doing this, then, I suggest motives to your understanding; which motives, by the tendency they have to give birth to or strengthen a pain, which operates upon you in the character of an internal motive in *esse,* join their force, and act as motives upon the will.

## § 2. No Motives Either Constantly Good or Constantly Bad

*Nothing can set of itself as a motive but the ideas of pleasure or pain.*

IX. In all this chain of motives, the principal or original link seems to be the last internal motive in prospect: it is to this that all the other motives in prospectowe their materiality: and the immediately acting motive its existence. This motive in prospect, we see, is always some pleasure, or some pain; some pleasure, which the act in question is expected to be a means of continuing or producing: some pain which it is expected to be a means of discontinuing or preventing. A motive is substantially nothing more than pleasure or pain, operating in a certain manner.

*No sort of motive is in itself a bad one.*

X. Now, pleasure is in *itself a* good: nay, even setting aside immunity from pain, the only good: pain is in itself an evil; and, indeed, without exception, the only evil; or else the words good and evil have no meaning. And this is alike true of every sort of pain, and of every sort of pleasure. It follows, therefore, immediately and incontestibly, that *there is no such thing as any sort of motive that is in itself a bad one.*[16]

14 Whether it be the expectation of being burnt, or the pain that accompanies that expectation, that is the immediate internal motive spoken of, may be difficult to determine. It may even be questioned, perhaps, whether they are distinct entities. Both questions, however, seem to be mere questions of words, and the solution of them altogether immaterial. Even the other kinds of motives, though for some purposes they demand a separate consideration, are, however, so intimately allied, that it will often be scarce practicable, and not always material, to avoid confounding them, as they have always hitherto been confounded.

15 Under the term *esse* must be included as well *past* existence, with reference to a given period, as *present.* They are equally real, in comparison with what is as yet but future. Language is materially deficient, in not enabling us to distinguish with precision between *existence* as opposed to *unreality* and *present existence* as opposed to past. The word existence in English, and *esse,* adopted by lawyers from the Latin, have the inconvenience of appearing to confine the existence in question to some single period considered as being present.

16 Let a man's motive be ill-will; call it even malice, envy, cruelty; it is still a kind of pleasure that is his motive: the pleasure he takes at the thought of the pain which he sees, or expects to see, his adversary undergo. Now even this wretched pleasure, taken by itself, is good: it may be faint; it may be short: it must at any rate be impure: yet while it lasts, and before any bad consequences arrive, it is as good as any other that is not more intense. See ch. iv. [Value].

*Inaccuracy of expressions in which good or bad are applied to motives.*

XI. It is common, however, to speak of actions as proceeding from *good* or *bad* motives: in which case the motives meant are such as are internal. The expression is far from being an accurate one; and as it is apt to occur in the consideration of almost every kind of offence, it will be requisite to settle the precise meaning of it, and observe how far it quadrates with the truth of things.

*Any sort of motive may give birth to any sort of act.*

XII. With respect to goodness and badness, as it is with everything else that is not itself either pain or pleasure, so is it with motives. If they are good or bad, it is only on account of their effects: good, on account of their tendency to produce pleasure, or avert pain: bad, on account of their tendency to produce pain, or avert pleasure. Now the case is, that from one and the same motive, and from every kind of motive, may proceed actions that are good, others that are bad, and others that are indifferent. This we shall proceed to shew with respect to all the different kinds of motives, as determined by the various kinds of pleasures and pains.

*Difficulties which stand in the way of an analysis of this sort.*

XIII. Such an analysis, useful as it is, will be found to be a matter of no small difficulty; owing, in great measure, to a certain perversity of structure which prevails more or less throughout all languages. To speak of motives, as of anything else, one must call them by their names. But the misfortune is, that it is rare to meet with a motive of which the name expresses that and nothing more. Commonly along with the very name of the motive, is tacitly involved a proposition imputing to it a certain quality; a quality which, in many cases, will appear to include that very goodness or badness, concerning which we are here inquiring whether, properly speaking, it be or be not imputable to motives. To use the common phrase, in most cases, the name of the motive is a word which is employed either only in a *good sense*, or else only in a *bad sense*. Now, when a word is spoken of as being used in a good sense, all that is necessarily meant is this: that in conjunction with the idea of the object it is put to signify, it conveys an idea of *approbation:* that is, of a pleasure or satisfaction, entertained by the person who employs the term at the thoughts of such object. In like manner, when a word is spoken of as being used in a bad sense, all that is necessarily meant is this: that, in conjunction with the idea of the object it is put to signify, it conveys an idea of *disapprobation:* that is, of a displeasure entertained by the person who employs the term at the thoughts of such object. Now, the circumstance on which such approbation is grounded will, as naturally as any other, be the opinion of the *goodness* of the object in question, as above explained: such, at least, it must be, upon the principle of utility: so, on the other hand, the circumstance on which any such disapprobation is grounded, will, as naturally as any other, be the opinion of the *badness* of the object: such, at least, it must be, in as far as the principle of utility is taken for the standard.

Now there are certain motives which, unless in a few particular cases, have scarcely any other name to be expressed by but such a word as is used only in a good sense. This is the case, for example, with the motives of piety and honour. The consequence of this is, that if, in speaking of such a motive, a man should have occasion to apply the epithet bad to any actions which he mentions as apt to result from it, he must appear to be guilty of a contradiction in terms. But the names of motives which have scarcely any other name to be expressed by, but such a word as is used only in a bad sense, are many more.[17] This is the case, for example, with the motives of lust and avarice. And accordingly, if in speaking of any such motive, a man should have occasion to apply the epithets good or indifferent to any actions which he mentions as apt to result from it, he must here also appear to be guilty of a similar contradiction.[18]

This perverse association of ideas cannot, it is evident, but throw great difficulties in the way of the inquiry now before us. Confining himself to the language most in use, a man can scarce avoid running, in appearance, into perpetual contradictions. His propositions will appear, on the one hand, repugnant to truth; and on the other hand, adverse to utility. As paradoxes, they will excite contempt: as mischievous paradoxes, indignation. For the truths he labours to convey, however important, and however salutary, his reader is never the better: and he himself is much the worse. To obviate this inconvenience, completely, he has but this one unpleasant remedy; to lay aside the old phraseology and invent a new one. Happy the man whose language is ductile enough to permit him this resource. To

17 For the reason, see chap. xi. [Dispositions], par. xvii. note.

18 To this imperfection of language, and nothing more, are to be attributed, in great measure, the violent clamours that have from time to time been raised against those ingenious moralists, who, travelling out of the beaten tract of speculation, have found more or less difficulty in disentangling themselves from the shackles of ordinary language: such as Rochefoucault, Mandeville and Helvetius. To the unsoundness of their opinions, and, with still greater injustice, to the corruption of their hearts, was often imputed, what was most commonly owing either to a want of skill, in matters of language on the part of the author, or a want of discernment, possibly now and then in some instances a want of probity, on the part of the commentator.

palliate the inconvenience, where that method of obviating it is impracticable, he has nothing left for it but to enter into a long discussion, to state the whole matter at large, to confess, that for the sake of promoting the purposes, he has violated the established laws of language, and to throw himself upon the mercy of his readers.[19]

## § 3. Catalogue of Motives Corresponding to that of Pleasures and Pains

*Physical desire corresponding to pleasures of sense in general.*

XIV. From the pleasures of the senses, considered in the gross, results the motive which, in a neutral sense, may be termed physical desire: in a bad sense, it is termed sensuality. Name used in a good sense it has none. Of this, nothing can be determined, till it be considered separately, with reference to the several species of pleasures to which it corresponds.

*The motive corresponding to the pleasures of the palate.*

XV. In particular, then, to the pleasures of the taste or palate corresponds a motive, which in a neutral sense having received no name that can serve to express it in all cases, can only be termed, by circumlocution, the love of the pleasures of the palate. In particular cases it is styled hunger: in others, thirst.[20] The love of good cheer expresses this motive, but seems to go beyond: intimating, that the pleasure is to be partaken of in company, and involving a kind of sympathy. In a bad sense, it is styled in some cases greediness, voraciousness, gluttony: in others, principally when applied to children, lickerishness. It may in some cases also be represented by the word daintiness. Name used in a good sense it has none, 1. A boy, who does not want for victuals, steals a cake out of a pastry-cook's shop, and eats it. In this case his motive will be universally deemed a bad one: and if it be asked what it is, it may be answered, perhaps, lickerishness. 2. A boy buys a cake out of a pastry-cook's shop, and eats it. In this case his motive can scarcely be looked upon as either good or bad, unless his master should be out of humour with him; and then perhaps he may call it lickerishness, as before. In both cases, however, his motive is the same. It is neither more nor less than the motive corresponding to the pleasures of the palate.[21]

*Sexual desires corresponding to the pleasure of the sexual sense.*

XVI. To the pleasures of the sexual sense corresponds the motive which, in a neutral sense, may be termed sexual desire. In a bad sense, it is spoken of under the name of lasciviousness, and a variety of other names of reprobation. Name used in a good sense it has none.[22]

1. A man ravishes a virgin. In this case the motive is, without scruple, termed by the name of lust, lasciviousness, and so forth; and is universally looked upon as a bad one. 2. The same man, at another time, exercises the rights of marriage with his wife. In this case the motive is accounted, perhaps, a good one, or at least indifferent: and here people would scruple to call it by any of those names. In both cases, however, the motive may be precisely the same. In both cases it may be neither more nor less than sexual desire.

*Curiosity, &c. corresponding to the pleasures of curiosity.*

XVII. To the pleasures of curiosity corresponds the motive known by the same name: and which may be otherwise called the love of novelty, or the love of experiment; and, on particular occasions, sport, and sometimes play.

---

19 Happily, language is not always so intractable, but that by making use of two words instead of one, a man may avoid the inconvenience of fabricating words that are absolutely new. Thus instead of the word lust, by putting together two words in common use, he may frame the neutral expression, sexual desire: instead of the word avarice, by putting together two other words also in common use, he may frame the neutral expression, pecuniary interest. This, accordingly, is the course which I have taken. In these instances, indeed, even the combination is not novel: the only novelty there is consists in the steady adherence to the one neutral expression, rejecting altogether the terms, of which the import is infected by adventitious and unsuitable ideas.

In the catalogue of motives, corresponding to the several sorts of pains and pleasures, I have inserted such as have occurred to me. I cannot pretend to warrant it complete. To make sure of rendering it so, the only way would be, to turn over the dictionary from beginning to end: an operation which, in a view to perfection, would be necessary for more purposes than this. See B. I. tit. [Defamation], and Append, tit. [Composition].

20 Hunger and thirst, considered in the light of motives, import not so much the desire of a particular kind of pleasure, as the desire of removing a positive kind of pain. They do not extend to the desire of that kind of pleasure which depends on the choice of foods and liquors.

21 It will not be worth while, in every case, to give an instance in which the action may be indifferent: if good as well as bad actions may result from the same motive, it is easy to conceive, that also may be indifferent.

22 Love indeed includes sometimes this idea: but then it can never answer the purpose of exhibiting it separately: since there are three motives, at least, that may all of them be included in it, besides this: the love of beauty corresponding to the pleasures of the eye, and the motives corresponding to those of amity and benevolence. We speak of the love of children, of the love of parents, of the love of God. These pious uses protect the appellation, and preserve it from the ignominy poured forth upon its profane associates. Even sensual love would not answer the purpose; since that would include the love of beauty.

1. A boy, in order to divert himself, reads an improving book: the motive is accounted, perhaps, a good one: at any rate not a bad one. 2. He sets his top a spinning: the motive is deemed, at any rate, not a bad one. 3. He sets loose a mad ox among a crowd; his motive is now, perhaps, termed an abominable one. Yet in all three cases the motive may be the very same; it may be neither more nor less than curiosity.

*None to pleasures of sense.*

XVIII. As to the other pleasures of sense they are of too little consequence to have given any separate denominations to the corresponding motives.

*Pecuniary interest to the pleasures of wealth.*

XIX. To the pleasures of wealth corresponds the sort of motive which, in a neutral sense, may be termed pecuniary interest: in a bad sense, it is termed, in some cases, avarice, covetousness, rapacity, or lucre: in other cases, niggardliness: in a good sense, but only in particular cases, economy and frugality; and in some cases the word industry may be applied to it: in a sense nearly indifferent, but rather bad than otherwise, it is styled, though only in particular cases, parsimony.

1. For money you gratify a man's hatred, by putting his adversary to death. 2. For money you plough his field for him.—In the first case your motive is termed lucre, and is accounted corrupt and abominable: and in the second, for want of a proper appellation, it is styled industry; and is looked upon as innocent at least, if not meritorious. Yet the motive is in both cases precisely the same: it is neither more nor less than pecuniary interest.

*None to the pleasures of skill.*

XX. The pleasures of skill are neither distinct enough, nor of consequence enough, to have given any name to the corresponding motive.

XXI. To the pleasures of amity corresponds a motive which, in a neutral sense, may be termed the desire of ingratiating one's self. In a bad sense it is in certain cases styled servility: in a good sense it has no name that is peculiar to it: in the cases in which it has been looked on with a favourable eye, it has seldom been distinguished from the motive of sympathy or benevolence, with which, in such cases, it is commonly associated.

*To the pleasures of amity the desire of ingratiating one's self.*

XXI. To the pleasures of amity the desire of ingratiating one's self. In a bad sence it is in certain cases styled servility: in a good sense it has no name that is peculiar to it: in the cases in which it has been looked on with a favourable eye, it has seldom been distinguished from the motive of sympathy or benevolence, with which, in such cases, it is commonly associated.

1. To acquire the affections of a woman before marriage, to preserve them afterwards, you do every thing, that is consistent with other duties, to make her happy: in this case your motive is looked upon as laudable, though there is no name for it. 2. For the same purpose, you poison a woman with whom she is at enmity: in this case your motive is looked upon as abominable, though still there is no name for it. 3. To acquire or preserve the favour of a man who is richer or more powerful than yourself, you make yourself subservient to his pleasures. Let them even be lawful pleasures, if people choose to attribute your behaviour to this motive, you will not get them to find any other name for it than servility. Yet in all three cases the motive is the same: it is neither more nor less than the desire of ingratiating yourself.

*To the pleasures of a good name, the love of reputation.*

XXII. To the pleasures of the moral sanction, or, as they may otherwise be called, the pleasures of a good name, corresponds a motive which, in a neutral sense, has scarcely yet obtained any adequate appellative. It may be styled, the love of reputation. It is nearly related to the motive last preceding: being neither more nor less than the desire of ingratiating one's self with, or, as in this case we should rather say, of recommending one's self to, the world at large. In a good sense, it is termed honour, or the sense of honour: or rather, the word honour is introduced somehow or other upon the occasion of its being brought to view: for in strictness the word honour is put rather to signify that imaginary object, which a man is spoken of as possessing upon the occasion of his obtaining a conspicuous share of the pleasures that are in question. In particular cases, it is styled the love of glory. In a bad sense, it is styled, in some cases, false honour; in others, pride; in others, vanity. In a sense not decidedly bad, but rather bad than otherwise, ambition. In an indiffercnt sense, in some cases, the love of fame: in others, the sense of shame. And, as the pleasures belonging to the moral sanction run undistinguishably into the pains derived from the same source,[23] it may also be styled, in some cases, the fear of dishonour, the fear of disgrace, the fear of infamy, the fear of ignominy, or the fear of shame.

23 Sec Chap. vi. [Pleasures and Pains], par. xxiv. note.

1. You have received an affront from a man: according to the custom of the country, in order, on the one hand, to save yourself from the shame of being thought to bear it patiently;[24] on the other hand, to obtain the reputation of courage; you challenge him to fight with mortal weapons. In this case your motive will by some people be accounted laudable, and styled honour: by others it will be accounted blameable, and these, if they call it honour, will prefix an epithet of improbation to it, and call it false honour. 2. In order to obtain a post of rank and dignity, and thereby to increase the respects paid you by the public, you bribe the electors who are to confer it, or the judge before whom the title to it is in dispute. In this case your motive is commonly accounted corrupt and abominable, and is styled, perhaps, by some such name as dishonest or corrupt ambition, as there is no single name for it. 3. In order to obtain the good-will of the public, you bestow a large sum in works of private charity or public utility. In this case people will be apt not to agree about your motive. Your enemies will put a bad colour upon it, and call it ostentation: your friends, to save you from this reproach, will choose to impute your conduct not to this motive but to some other: such as that of charity (the denomination in this case given to private sympathy) or that of public spirit. 4. A king, for the sake of gaining the admiration annexed to the name of conqueror (we will suppose power and resentment out of the question) engages his kingdom in a bloody war. His motive, by the multitude (whose sympathy for millions is easily overborne by the pleasure which their imagination finds in gaping at any novelty they observe in the conduct of a single person) is deemed an admirable one. Men of feeling and reflection, who disapprove of the dominion exercised by this motive on this occasion, without always perceiving that it is the same motive which in other instances meets with their approbation, deem it an abominable one; and because the multitude, who are the manufacturers of language, have not given them a simple name to call it by, they will call it by some such compound name as the love of false glory or false ambition. Yet in all four cases the motive is the same: it is neither more nor less than the love of reputation.

*To the pleasures of power, the love of power.*

XXIII. To the pleasures of power corresponds the motive which, in a neutral sense, may be termed the love of power. People, who are out of humour with it sometimes, call it the lust of power. In a good sense, it is scarcely provided with a name. In certain cases this motive, as well as the love of reputation, are confounded under the same name, ambition. This is not to be wondered at, considering the intimate connexion there is between the two motives in many cases: since it commonly happens, that the same object which affords the one sort of pleasure, affords the other sort at the same time: for instance, offices, which are at once posts of honour and places of trust: and since at any rate reputation is the road to power.

1. If, in order to gain a place in administration, you poison the man who occupies it. 2. If, in the same view, you propose a salutary plan for the advancement of the public welfare; your motive is in both cases the same. Yet in the first case it is accounted criminal and abominable: in the second case allowable, and even laudable.

*The motive belonging to the religious sanction.*

XXIV. To the pleasures as well as to the pains of the religious sanction corresponds a motive which has, strictly speaking, no perfectly neutral name applicable to all cases, unless the word religion be admitted in this character: though the word religion, strictly speaking, seems to mean not so much the motive

24 A man's bearing an affront patiently, that is, without taking this method of doing what is called wiping it off, is thought to import one or other of two things: either that he does not possess that sensibility to the pleasures and pains of the moral sanction, which, in order to render himself a respectable member of society, a man ought to possess: or, that he does not possess courage enough to stake his life for the chance of gratifying that resentment which a proper sense of the value of those pleasures and those pains it is thought would not fail to inspire. True it is, that there are divers other motives, by any of which the same conduct might equally be produced: the motives corresponding to the religious sanction, and the motives that come under the head of benevolence. Piety towards God, the practice in question being generally looked upon as repugnant to the dictates of the religious sanction: sympathy for your antagonist himself, whose life would be put to hazard at the same time with your own; sympathy for his connexions; the persons who are dependent on him in the way of support, or connected with him in the way of sympathy: sympathy for your own connexions: and even sympathy for the public, in cases where the man is such that the public appears to have a material interest in his life. But in comparison with the love of life, the influence of the religious sanction is known to be in general but weak: especially among people of those classes who are here in question: a sure proof of which is the prevalence of this very custom. Where it is so strong as to preponderate, it is so rare, that, perhaps, it gives a man a place in the calendar: and, at any rate, exalts him to the rank of martyr. Moreover, the instances in which either private benevolence or public spirit predominate over the love of life, will also naturally be but rare: and, owing to the general propensity to detraction, it will also be much rarer for them to be thought to do so. Now, when three or more motives, any one of them capable of producing a given mode of conduct, apply at once, that which appears to be the most powerful, is that which will of course be deemed to have actually done the *most:* and, as the bulk of mankind, on this as on other occasions, are disposed to decide peremptorily upon superficial estimates, it will generally be looked upon as having done the whole.

The consequence is, that when a man of a certain rank forbears to take this chance of revenging an affront, his conduct will, by most people, be imputed to the love of life: which, when it predominates over the love of reputation, is, by a not unsalutary association of ideas, stigmatized with the reproachful name of cowardice.

itself, as a kind of fictitious personage, by whom the motive is supposed to be created, or an assemblage of acts, supposed to be dictated by that personage: nor does it seem to be completely settled into a neutral sense. In the same sense it is also, in some cases, styled religious zeal: in other cases, the fear of God. The love of God, though commonly contrasted with the fear of God, does not come strictly under this head. It coincides properly with a motive of a different denomination; viz. a kind of sympathy or good-will, which has the Deity for its object. In a good sense, it is styled devotion, piety, and pious zeal. In a bad sense, it is styled, in some cases, superstition, or superstitious zeal: in other cases, fanaticism, or fanatic zeal: in a sense not decidedly bad, because not appropriated to this motive, enthusiasm, or enthusiastic zeal.

1. In order to obtain the favour of the Supreme Being, a man assassinates his lawful sovereign. In this case the motive is now almost universally looked upon as abominable, and is termed fanaticism: formerly it was by great numbers accounted laudable, and was by them called pious zeal. 2. In the same view, a man lashes himself with thongs. In this case, in yonder house, the motive is accounted laudable, and is called pious zeal: in the next house it is deemed contemptible, and called superstition. 3. In the same view, a man eats a piece of bread (or at least what to external appearance is a piece of bread) with certain ceremonies. In this case, in yonder house, his motive is looked upon as laudable, and is styled piety and devotion: in the next house it is deemed abominable, and styled superstition, as before: perhaps even it is absurdly styled impiety. 4. In the same view, a man holds a cow by the tail while he is dying. On the Thames the motive would in this case be deemed contemptible, and called superstition. On the Ganges it is deemed meritorious, and called piety. 5. In the same view, a man bestows a large sum in works of charity, or public utility. In this case the motive is styled laudable, by those at least to whom the works in question appear to come under this description: and by these at least it would be styled piety. Yet in all these cases the motive is precisely the same: it is neither more nor less than the motive belonging to the religious sanction.[25]

*Good-will, &c. to the pleasures of sympathy.*

XXV. To the pleasures of sympathy corresponds the motive which, in a neutral sense, is termed good-will. The word sympathy may also be used on this occasion: though the sense of it seems to be rather more extensive. In a good sense, it is styled benevolence: and in certain cases, philanthropy; and, in a figurative way,brotherly love; in others, humanity; in others, charity; in others, pity and compassion; in others, mercy; in others, gratitude; in others, tenderness; in others, patriotism; in others, public spirit. Love is also employed in this as in so many other senses. In a bad sense, it has no name applicable to it in all cases: in particular cases it is styled partiality. The word zeal, with certain epithets prefixed to it, might also be employed sometimes on this occasion, though the sense of it be more extensive; applying sometimes to ill as well as to good will. It is thus we speak of party zeal, national zeal, and public zeal. The word attachment is also used with the like epithets: we also say family-attachment. The French expression, *esprit de corps,* for which as yet there seems to be scarcely any name in English, might be rendered, in some cases, though rather inadequately, by the terms corporation spirit, corporation attachment, or corporation zeal.

1. A man who has set a town on fire is apprehended and committed: out of regard or compassion for him, you help him to break prison. In this case the generality of people will probably scarcely know whether to condemn your motive or to applaud it; those who condemn your conduct, will be disposed rather to impute it to some other motive: if they style it benevolence or compassion, they will be for prefixing an epithet, and calling it false benevolence or false compassion.[26] 2. The man is taken again, and is put upon his trial: to save him you swear falsely in his favour. People, who would not call your motive a bad one before, will perhaps call it so now. 3. A man is at law with you about an estate: he has no right to it: the judge knows this, yet, having an esteem or affection for your adversary, adjudges it to him. In this case the motive is by every body deemed abominable, and is termed injustice and partiality. 4. You detect a statesman

25 I am aware, or at least I hope, that people in general, when they see the matter thus stated, will be ready to acknowledge, that the motive in these cases, whatever be the tendency of the acts which it produces, is not a bad one: but this will not render it the less true, that hitherto, in popular discourse it has been common for men to speak of acts, which they could not but acknowledge to have originated from this source, as proceeding from a bad motive. The same observation will apply to many of the other cases.

26 Among the Greeks, perhaps the motive, and the conduct it gave birth to, would, in such a case, have been rather approved than disapproved of. It seems to have been deemed an act of heroism on the part of Hercules, to have delivered his friend Theseus from hell: though divine justice, which held him there, should naturally have been regarded as being at least upon a footing with human justice. But to divine justice, even when acknowledged under that character, the respect paid at that time of day does not seem to have been very profound, or well-settled: at present, the respect paid to it is profound and settled enough, though the name of it is but too often applied to dictates which could have had no other origin than the worst sort of human caprice.

in receiving bribes: out of regard to the public interest, you give information of it, and prosecute him. In this case, by all who acknowledge your conduct to have originated from this motive, your motive will be deemed a laudable one, and styled public spirit. But his friends and adherents will not choose to account for your conduct in any such manner: they will rather attribute it to party enmity. 5. You find a man on the point of starving: you relieve him; and save his life. In this case your motive will by every body be accounted laudable, and it will be termed compassion, pity, charity, benevolence. Yet in all these cases the motive is the same: it is neither more nor less than the motive of good-will.

*Ill-will, &c. to the pleasures of antipathy.*

XXVI. To the pleasures of malevolence, or antipathy, corresponds the motive which, in a neutral sense, is termed antipathy or displeasure: and, in particular cases, dislike, aversion, abhorrence, and indignation: in a neutral sense, or perhaps a sense leaning a little to the bad side, ill-will: and, in particular cases, anger, wrath, and enmity. In a bad sense it is styled, in different cases, wrath, spleen, ill-humour, hatred, malice, rancour, rage, fury, cruelty, tyranny, envy, jealousy, revenge, misanthropy, and by other names, which it is hardly worth while to endeavour to collect.[27] Like good-will, it is used with epithets expressive of the persons who are the objects of the affection. Hence we hear of party enmity, party rage, and so forth. In a good sense there seems to be no single name for it. In compound expressions it may be spoken of in such a sense, by epithets, such as *just* and *laudable*, prefixed to words that are used in a neutral or nearly neutral sense.

1. You rob a man: he prosecutes you, and gets you punished: out of resentment you set upon him, and hang him with your own hands. In this case your motive will universally be deemed detestable, and will be called malice, cruelty, revenge, and so forth. 2. A man has stolen a little money from you: out of resentment you prosecute him, and get him hanged by course of law. In this case people will probably be a little divided in their opinions about your motive: your friends will deem it a laudable one, and call it a just or laudable resentment: your enemies will perhaps be disposed to deem it blamcable, and call it cruelty, malice, revenge, and so forth: to obviate which, your friends will try perhaps to change the motive, and call it public spirit. 3. A man has murdered your father: out of resentment you prosecute him, and get him put to death in course of law. In this case your motive will be universally deemed a laudable one, and styled, as before, a just or laudable resentment: and your friends, in order to bring forward the more amiable principle from which the malevolent one, which was your immediate motive, took its rise, will be for keeping the latter out of sight, speaking of the former only, under some such name as filial piety. Yet in all these cases the motive is the same: it is neither more nor less than the motive of ill-will.

*Self-preservation, to the several kinds of pains.*

XXVII. To the several sorts of pains, or at least to all such of them as are conceived to subsist in an intense degree, and to the death, which, as far as we can perceive, is the termination of all the pleasures, as well as all the pains we are acquainted with, corresponds the motive, which in a neutral sense is styled, in general, self-preservation: the desire of preserving one's self from the pain or evil in question. Now in many instances the desire of pleasure, and the sense of pain, run into one another undistinguishably. Self-preservation, therefore, where the degree of the pain which it corresponds to is but slight will scarcely be distinguishable, by any precise line, from the motives corresponding to the several sorts of pleasures. Thus in the case of the pains of hunger and thirst: physical want will in many cases be scarcely distinguishable from physical desire. In some cases it is styled, still in a neutral sense, self-defence. Between the pleasures and the pains of the moral and religious sanctions, and consequently of the motives that correspond to them, as likewise between the pleasures of amity, and the pains of enmity, this want of boundaries has already been taken notice of.[28] The case is the same between the pleasures of wealth, and the pains of privation corresponding to those pleasures. There are many cases, therefore, in which it will be difficult to distinguish the motive of self-preservation from pecuniary interest, from the desire of ingratiating one's self, from the love of reputation, and from religious hope: in which cases, those more specific and explicit names will naturally be preferred to this general and inexplicit one. There are also a multitude of compound names, which either are already in use, or might be devised, to distinguish the specific branches of the motive of self-preservation from those several motives of a pleasurable origin: such as the fear of poverty, the fear of losing such or such a man's regard, the fear of shame, and the fear of God. Moreover, to

27 Here, as elsewhere, it may be observed, that the same words which are mentioned as names of motives, are also many of them names of passions, appetites, and affections: fictitious entities, which are framed only by considering pleasures or pains in some particular point of view. Some of them are also names of moral qualities. This branch of nomenclature is remarkably entangled: to unravel it completely would take up a whole volume; not a syllable of which would belong properly to the present design.

28 See ch v. [Pleasures and Pains], par. xxiv, xxv.

the evil of death corresponds, in a neutral sense, the love of life; in a bad sense, cowardice: which 'corresponds also to the pains of the senses, at least when considered as subsisting in an acute degree. There seems to be no name for the love of life that has a good sense; unless it be the vague and general name of prudence.

1. To save yourself from being hanged, pilloried, imprisoned, or fined, you poison the only person who can give evidence against you. In this case your motive will universally be styled abominable: but as the term self-preservation has no bad sense, people will not care to make this use of it: they will be apt rather to change the motive, and call it malice. 2. A woman, having been just delivered of an illegitimate child, in order to save herself from shame, destroys the child, or abandons it. In this case, also, people will call the motive a bad one, and, not caring to speak of it under a neutral name, they will be apt to change the motive, and call it by some such name as cruelty. 3. To save the expense of a halfpenny, you suffer a man, whom you could preserve at that expense, to perish with want, before your eyes. In this case your motive will be universally deemed an abominable one; and, to avoid calling it by so indulgent a name as self-preservation, people will be apt to call it avarice and niggardliness, with which indeed in this case it indistinguishably coincides: for the sake of finding a more reproachful appellation, they will be apt likewise to change the motive, and term it cruelty. 4. To put an end to the pain of hunger, you steal a loaf of bread. In this case your motive will scarcely, perhaps, be deemed a very bad one; and, in order to express more indulgence for it, people will be apt to find a stronger name for it than self-preservation, terming it *necessity.* 5. To save yourself from drowning, you beat off an innocent man who has got hold of the same plank. In this case your motive will in general be deemed neither good nor bad, and it will be termed self-preservation, or necessity, or the love of life. 6. To save your life from a gang of robbers, you kill them in the conflict. In this case the motive may, perhaps, be deemed rather laudable than otherwise, and, besides self-preservation, is styled also self-defence. 7. A soldier is sent out upon a party against a weaker party of the enemy: before he gets up with them, to save his life, he runs away. In this case the motive will universally be deemed a contemptible one, and will be called cowardice. Yet in all these various cases, the motive is still the same. It is neither more nor less than self-preservation.

*To the pains of exertion, the love of ease.*

XXVIII. In particular, to the pains of exertion corresponds the motive, which, in a neutral sense, may be termed the love of case, or by a longer circumlocution, the desire of avoiding trouble. In a bad sense, it is termed indolence.[29] It seems to have no name that carries with it a good sense.

1. To save the trouble of taking care of it, a parent leaves his child to perish. In this case the motive will be deemed an abominable one, and, because indolence will seem too mild a name for it, the motive will, perhaps, be changed, and spoken of under some such term as cruelty. 2. To save yourself from an illegal slavery, you make your escape. In this case the motive will be deemed certainly not a bad one: and, because indolence, or even the love of ease, will be thought too unfavourable a name for it, it will, perhaps, be styled the love of liberty. 3. A mechanic, in order to save his labour, makes an improvement in his machinery. In this ease, people will look upon his motive as a good one; and finding no name for it that carries a good sense, they will be disposed to keep the motive out of sight: they will speak rather of his ingenuity, than of the motive which was the means of his manifesting that quality. Yet in all these cases the motive is the same: it is neither more nor less than the love of ease.

*Motives can only be bad with reference to the most frequent complexion of their effects.*

XXIX. It appears then that there is no such thing as any sort of motive which is a bad one in itself: nor, consequently, any such thing as a sort of motive, which in itself is exclusively a good one. And as to their effects, it appears too that these are sometimes bad, at other times either indifferent or good: and this appears to be the case with every sort of motive. *If any sort of motive then is either good or bad on the score of its effects, this is the case only on individual occasions, and with individual motives;* and this is the case with one sort of motive as well as with another. *If any sort of motive then can, in consideration of its effects, be termed with any propriety a bad one,* it can only be with reference to the balance of all the effects it may have had of both kinds within a given period, that is, of its most usual tendency.

*How it is that motives, such as lust, avarice, &c. are constantly bad.*

XXX. What then? (it will be said) are not lust, cruelty, avarice, bad motives? Is there so much as any one individual occasion, in which motives like these can be otherwise than bad? No, certainly: and yet the proposition, that there is no one *sort* of motive but what will on many occasions be a good one, is nevertheless true. The fact is, that these are names which, if properly applied, are never applied but in the cases where the motives they signify happen to he bad. The names of these motives, considered apart

29 It may seem odd at first sight to speak of the love of ease as giving birth to action: but exertion is as natural an effect of the love of ease as inaction is, when a smaller degree of exertion promises to exempt a man from a greater.

from their effects, are sexual desire, displeasure, and pecuniary interest. To sexual desire, when the effects of it are looked upon as bad, is given the name of lust. Now lust is always a bad motive. Why? Because if the case be such, that the effects of the motive are not bad, it does not go, or at least ought not to go, by the name of lust. The case is, then, that when I say, 'Lust is a bad motive,' it is a proposition that merely concerns the import of the word lust; and which would be false if transferred to the other word used for the same motive, sexual desire. Hence we see the emptiness of all those rhapsodies of common-place morality, which consist in the taking of such names as lust, cruelty, and avarice, and branding them with marks of reprobation: applied to the *thing,* they are false; applied to the *name,* they are true indeed, but nugatory. Would you do a real service to mankind, show them the cases in which sexual desire *merits* the name of lust; displeasure, that of cruelty; and pecuniary interest, that of avarice.

*Under the above restrictions, motives may be distinguished into good, bad, and indifferent or neutral.*

XXXI. If it were necessary to apply such denominations as good, bad, and indifferent to motives, they might be classed in the following manner, in consideration of the most frequent complexion of their effects.

In the class of good motives might placed the articles of, 1. Good-will. 2. Love of reputation. 3. Desire of amity. And, 4. Religion. In the class of bad motives, 5. Displeasure. In the class of neutral or indifferent motives, 6. Physical desire. 7. Pecuniary interest. 8. Love of power. 9. Self-preservation; as including the fear of the pains of the senses, the love of ease, and the love of life.

*Inconveniences of this distribution.*

XXXII. This method of arrangement, however, cannot but be imperfect; and the nomenclature belonging to it is in danger of being fallacious. For by what method of investigation can a man be assured, that with regard to the motives ranked under the name of good, the good effects they have had, from the beginning of the world, have, in each of the four species comprised under this name, been superior to the bad? still more difficulty would a man find in assuring himself, that with regard to those which are ranked under the name of neutral or indifferent, the effects they have had have exactly balanced each other, the value of the good being neither greater nor leas than that of the bad. It is to be considered, that the interests of the person himself can no more be left out of the estimate, than those of the rest of the community. For what would become of the species, if it were not for the motives of hunger and thirst, sexual desire, the fear of pain, and the love of life? Nor in the actual constitution of human nature is the motive of displeasure less necessary, perhaps, than any of the others: although a system, in which the business of life might be carried on without it, might possibly be conceived. It seems, therefore, that they could scarcely, without great danger of mistakes, be distinguished in this manner even with reference to each other.

*It is only in individual instances that motives can be good or bad.*

XXXIII. The only way, it should seem, in which a motive can with safety and propriety be styled good or bad, is with reference to its effects in each individual instance; and principally from the intention it gives birth to: from which arise, as will be shown hereafter, the most material part of its effects. A motive is good, when the intention it gives birth to is a good one; bad, when the intention is a bad one: and an intention is good or bad, according to the material consequences that are the objects of it. So far is it from the goodness of the intention's being to be known only from the species of the motive. But from one and the same motive, as we have seen, may result intentions of every sort of complexion whatsoever. This circumstance, therefore, can afford no clue for the arrangement of the several sorts of motives.

*Motives distinguished into social, dissocial, and self-regarding.*

XXXIV. A more commodious method, therefore, it should seem, would be to distribute them according to the influence which they appear to have on the interests of the other members of the community, laying those of the party himself out of the question: to wit, according to the tendency which they appear to have to unite, or disunite, his interests and theirs. On this plan they may be distinguished into *social, dissocial,* and *self-regarding.* In the social class may be reckoned, 1. Good-will. 2. Love of reputation. 3. Desire of amity. 4. Religion. In the dissocial may be placed, 5. Displeasure. In the self-regarding class, 6. Physical desire. 7. Pecuniary interest. 8. Love of power. 9. Self-preservation; as including the fear of the pains of the senses, the love of ease, and the love of life.

*—social into purely-social, and semi-social.*

XXXV. With respect to the motives that have been termed social, if any farther distinction should be of use, to that of social good-will alone may be applied the epithet of *purely-social;* while the love of reputation, the desire of amity, and the motive of religion, may together be comprised under the division of *semi-social:* the social tendency being much more constant and unequivocal in the former than in any of the three latter.

Indeed these last, social as they may be termed, are self-regarding at the same time.[30]

---

30 'Religion,' says the pious Addison, somewhere in the Spectator, 'is the highest species of self-love.'

*The dictates of good-will are the surest of coinciding with those of utility.*

### § 4. Order of Pre-eminence among Motives

XXXVI. Of all these sorts of motives, good-will is that of which the dictates,[31] taken in a general view, are surest of coinciding with those of the principle of utility. For the dictates of utility are neither more nor less than the dictates of the most extensive[32] and enlightened (that is *well-advised*[33]) benevolence.

The dictates of the other motives may be conformable to those of utility, or repugnant, as it may happen.

*Yet do not in all cases.*

XXXVII. In this, however, it is taken for granted, that in the case in question the dictates of benevolence are not contradicted by those of a more extensive, that is enlarged, benevolence. Now when the dictates of benevolence, as respecting the interests of a certain set of persons, are repugnant to the dictates of the same motive, as respecting the more important[34] interests of another set of persons, the former dictates, it is evident, are repealed, as it were, by the latter: and a man, were he to be governed by the former, could scarcely, with propriety, be said to be governed by the dictates of benevolence. On this account, were the motives on both sides sure to be alike present to a man's mind, the case of such a repugnancy would hardly be worth distinguishing, since the partial benevolence might be considered as swallowed up in the more extensive: if the former prevailed, and governed the action, it must be considered as not owing its birth to benevolence, but to some other motive: if the latter prevailed, the former might be considered as having no effect. But the case is, that a partial benevolence may govern the action, without entering into any direct competition with the more extensive benevolence, which would forbid it; because the interests of the less numerous assemblage of persons may be present to a man's mind, at a time when those of the more numerous are either not present, or, if present, make no impression. It is in this way that the dictates of this motive may be repugnant to utility, yet still be the dictates of benevolence. What makes those of private benevolence conformable upon the whole to the principle of utility, is, that in general they stand unopposed by those of public: if they are repugnant to them, it is only by accident. What makes them the more conformable, is, that in a civilized society, in most of the cases in which they would of themselves be apt to run counter to those of public benevolence, they find themselves opposed by stronger motives of the self-regarding class, which are played off against them by the laws; and that it is only in cases where they stand unopposed by the other more salutary dictates, that they are left free. An act of injustice or cruelty, committed by a man for the sake of his father or his son, is punished, and with reason, as much as if it were committed for his own.

*Next to them come those of the love of reputation.*

XXXVIII. After good-will, the motive of which the dictates seem to have the next best chance for coinciding with those of utility, is that of the love of reputation. There is but one circumstance which prevents the dictates of this motive from coinciding in all cases with those of the former. This is, that men in their likings and dislikings, in the dispositions they manifest to annex to any mode of conduct their approbation or their disapprobation, and in consequence to the person who appears to practise it, their good or their ill will, do not govern themselves exclusively by the principle of utility. Sometimes it is the principle of asceticism they are guided by: sometimes the principle of sympathy and antipathy. There is another circumstance, which diminishes, not their conformity to the principle of utility, but only their efficacy in comparison with the dictates of the motive of benevolence. The dictates of this motive will operate as strongly in secret as in public: whether it appears likely that the conduct which they recommend will he known or not: those of the love of reputation will coincide with those of benevolence only in proportion as a man's conduct seems likely to be known. This circumstance, however, does not make so much difference as at first sight might appear. Acts, in proportion as they are material, are apt to become known:[35] and in point of reputation, the slightest suspicion often serves for proof. Besides, if an act be a disreputable one, it is not any assurance a man can have of the secrecy of the particular act in question, that will of course surmount the objections he may have against engaging in it. Though the act in question should remain secret, it will go towards

---

*Laws and dictates conceived as issuing from motives.*

31 When a man is supposed to be prompted by any motive to engage, or not to engage, in such or such an action, it may be of use, for the convenience of discourse, to speak of such motive as giving birth to an imaginary kind of *law* or *dictate*, injoining him to engage, or not to engage, in it[1].

1 See ch. I,

32 See ch iv. [Value], and ch. vi. [Sensibility], par. xxi.

33 See ch. ix. [Consciousness].

34 Or valuable. See ch. iv. [Value].

35 See B. II. tit. [Evidence].

forming a habit, which may give birth to other acts, that may not meet with the same good fortune. There is no human being, perhaps, who is at years of discretion, on whom considerations of this sort have not some weight: and they have the more weight upon a man, in proportion to the strength of his intellectual powers, and the firmness of his mind.[36] Add to this, the influence which habit itself, when once formed, has in restraining a man from acts towards which, from the view of the disrepute annexed to them, as well as from any other cause, he has contracted an aversion. The influence of habit, in such cases, is a matter of fact, which, though not readily accounted for, is acknowledged and indubitable.[37]

*Next those of the desire of amity.*

XXXIX. After the dictates of the love of reputation come, as it should seem, those of the desire of amity. The former are disposed to coincide with those of utility, inasmuch as they are disposed to coincide with those of benevolence. Now those of the desire of amity are apt also to coincide, in a certain sort, with those of benevolence. But the sort of benevolence with the dictates of which the love of reputation coincides, is the more extensive; that with which those of the desire of amity coincide, the less extensive. Those of the love of amity have still, however, the advantage of those of the self-regarding motives. The former, at one period or other of his life, dispose a man to contribute to the happiness of a considerable number of persons: the latter, from the beginning of life to the end of it, confine themselves to the care of that single individual. The dictates of the desire of amity, it is plain, will approach nearer to a coincidence with those of the love of reputation, and thence with those of utility, in proportion, *ceteris paribus,* to the number of the persons whose amity a man has occasion to desire: and hence it is, for example, that an English member of parliament, with all his own weaknesses, and all the follies of the people whose amity he has to cultivate, is probably, in general, a better character than the secretary of a visier at Constantinople, or of a naib in Indostan.

*Difficulty of placing those of religion.*

XL. The dictates of religion are, under the infinite diversity of religions, so extremely variable, that it is difficult to know what general account to give of them, or in what rank to place the motive they belong to. Upon the mention of religion, people's first thoughts turn naturally to the religion they themselves profess. This is a great source of miscalculation, and has a tendency to place this sort of motive in a higher rank than it deserves. The dictates of religion would coincide, in all cases, with those of utility, were the Being, who is the object of religion, universally supposed to be as benevolent as he is supposed to be wise and powerful; and were the notions entertained of his benevolence, at the same time, as correct as those which are entertained of his wisdom and his power. Unhappily, however, neither of these is the case. He is universally supposed to be all-powerful: for by the Deity, what else does any man mean than the Being, whatever he be, by whom every thing is done? And as to knowledge, by the same rule that he should know one thing he should know another. These notions seem to be as correct, for all material purposes, as they are universal. But among the votaries of religion (of which number the multifarious fraternity of Christians is but a small part) there seem to be but few (I will not say how few) who are real believers in his benevolence. They call him benevolent in words, but they do not mean that he is so in reality. They do not mean, that he is benevolent as man is conceived to be benevolent: they do not mean that he is benevolent in the only sense in which benevolence has a meaning. For if they did, they would recognise that the dictates of religion could be neither more nor less than the dictates of utility: not a tittle different: not a tittle less or more. But the case is, that on a thousand occasions they turn their backs on the principle of utility. They go astray after the strange principles its antagonists: sometimes it is the principle of asceticism: sometimes the principle of sympathy and antipathy.[38] Accordingly, the idea they bear in their minds, on such occasions, is but too often the idea of malevolence; to which idea, stripping it of its own proper name, they bestow the specious appellation of the social motive.[39] The dictates of religion, in short, are no other than the dictates of that principle which has

---

36 See ch. vi [Sensibility], par. xii, viii.

37 Strictly speaking, habit, being but a fictitious entity, and not really any thing distinct from the acts or perceptions by which it is said to be formed, cannot be the cause of any thing. The enigma, however, may be satisfactorily solved upon the principle of association, of the nature and force of which a very satisfactory account may be seen in Dr. Priestley's edition of Hartley on Man.

38 Ch. ii. [Principles Adverse], par. xviii.

39 Sometimes, in order the better to conceal the cheat (from their own eyes doubtless as well as from others) they set up a phantom of their own, which they call Justice: whose dictates are to modify (which being explained, means to oppose) the dictates of benevolence. But justice, in the only sense in which it has a meaning, is an imaginary personage, feigned for the convenience of discourse, whose dictates are the dictates of utility, applied to certain particular cases. Justice, then, is nothing more than an imaginary instrument, employed to forward on certain occasions, and by certain means, the purposes of benevolence. The dictates of justice are nothing more than a part of the dictates of benevolence, which, on certain occasions, are applied to certain subjects; to wit, to certain actions.

been already mentioned under the name of the theological principle.[40] These, as has been observed, are just as it may happen, according to the biases of the person in question, copies of the dictates of one or other of the three original principles: sometimes, indeed, of the dictates of utility: but frequently of those of asceticism, or those of sympathy and antipathy. In this respect they are only on a par with the dictates of the love of reputation: in another they are below it. The dictates of religion are in all places intermixed more or less with dictates unconformable to those of utility, deduced from texts, well or ill interpreted, of the writings held for sacred by each sect: unconformable, by imposing practices sometimes inconvenient to a man's self, sometimes pernicious to the rest of the community. The sufferings of uncalled martyrs, the calamities of holy wars and religious persecutions, the mischiefs of intolerant laws, (objects which can here only be glanced at, not detailed) are so many additional mischiefs over and above the number of those which were ever brought into the world by the love of reputation. On the other hand, it is manifest, that with respect to the power of operating in secret, the dictates of religion have the same advantage over those of the love of reputation, and the desire of amity, as is possessed by the dictates of benevolence.

*Tendency they have to improve.*

XLI. Happily, the dictates of religion seem to approach nearer and nearer to a coincidence with those of utility every day. But why? Because the dictates of the moral sanction do so: and those coincide with or are influenced by these. Men of the worst religions, influenced by the voice and practice of the surrounding world, borrow continually a new and a new leaf out of the book of utility: and with these, in order not to break with their religion, they endeavour, sometimes with violence enough, to patch together and adorn the repositories of their faith.

*Afterwards come the self-regarding motives and, lastly, that of displeasure.*

XLII. As to the self-regarding and dissocial motives, the order that takes place among these, and the preceding one, in point of extra-regarding influence, is too evident to need insisting on. As to the order that takes place among the motives of the self-regarding class, considered in comparison with one another, there seems to be no difference which on this occasion would be worth mentioning. With respect to the dissocial motive, it makes a difference (with regard to its extra-regarding effects) from which of two sources it originates; whether from self-regarding or from social considerations. The displeasure you conceive against a man may be founded either on some act which offends you in the first instance, oron an act which offends you no otherwise than because you look upon it as being prejudicial to some other party on whose behalf you interest yourself: which other party may be of course either a determinate individual, or any assemblage of individuals, determinate or indeterminate.[41] It is obvious enough, that a motive, though in itself dissocial, may, by issuing from a social origin, possess a social tendency; and that its tendency, in this case, is likely to be the more social, the more enlarged the description is of the persons whose interests you espouse. Displeasure, venting itself against a man, on account of a mischief supposed to be done by him to the public, may be more social in its effects than any good-will, the exertions of which are confined to an individual.[42]

### § 5. Conflict Among Motives

*Motives impelling and restraining, what.*

XLIII. When a man has it in contemplation to engage in any action, he is frequently acted upon at the same time by the force of divers motives: one motive, or set of motives, acting in one direction; another motive, or set of motives, acting as it were in an opposite direction. The motives on one side disposing him to engage in the action: those on the other, disposing him not to engage in it. Now, any motive, the influence of which tends to dispose him to engage in the action in question, may be termed an *impelling* motive: any motive, the influence of which tends to dispose him not to engage in it, a *restraining* motive. But these appellations may of course be interchanged, according as the act is of the positive kind, or the negative.[43]

*What are the motives most frequently at variance.*

XLIV. It has been shown, that there is no sort of motive but may give birth to any sort of action. It follows, therefore, that there are no two motives but may come to be opposed to one another. Where the tendency of the act is bad, the most common case is for it to have been dictated by a motive either of the

40 See ch. ii. [Frinciplea Adverse, &c.]

41 See ch. vi. [Sensibility], par. xxi.

42 See *supra*, par. xxxvii.

43 See ch. vii. [Actions], par. viii.

self-regarding, or of the dissocial class. In such case the motive of benevolence has commonly been acting, though ineffectually, in the character of a restraining motive.

*Example to illustrate a struggle among contending motives.*

XLV. An example may be of use, to show the variety of contending motives, by which a man may be acted upon at the same time. Crillon, a Catholic (at a time when it was generally thought meritorious among Catholics to extirpate Protestants), was ordered by his king, Charles IX. of France, to fall privately upon Coligny, a Protestant, and assassinate him: his answer was, 'Excuse me, Sire; but I'll fight him with all my heart.'[44] Here, then, were all the three forces above mentioned, including that of the political sanction, acting upon him at once. By the political sanction, or at least so much of the force of it as such a mandate, from such a sovereign, issued on such an occasion, might be supposed to carry with it, he was enjoined to put Coligny to death in the way of assassination: by the religious sanction, that is, by the dictates of religious zeal, he was enjoined to put him to death in any way: by the moral sanction, or in other words, by the dictates of honour, that is, of the love of reputation, he was permitted (which permission, when coupled with the mandates of his sovereign, operated, he conceived, as an injunction) to fight the adversary upon equal terms: by the dictates of enlarged benevolence (supposing the mandate to be unjustifiable) he was enjoined not to attempt his life in any way, but to remain at peace with him: supposing the mandate to be unjustifiable, by the dictates of private benevolence he was enjoined not to meddle with him at any rate. Among this confusion of repugnant dictates, Crillon, it seems, gave the preference, in the first place, to those of honour: in the next place, to those of benevolence. He would have fought, had his offer been accepted; as it was not, he remained at peace.

Here a multitude of questions might arise. Supposing the dictates of the political sanction to follow the mandate of the sovereign, of what kind were the motives which they afforded him for compliance? The answer is, of the self-regarding kind at any rate: inasmuch as, by the supposition, it was in the power of the sovereign to punish him for non-compliance, or reward him for compliance. Did they afford him the motive of religion? (I mean independently of the circumstance of heresy above mentioned) the answer is, Yes, if his notion was, that it was God's pleasure he should comply with them; No, if it was not. Did they afford him the motive of the love of reputation? Yes, if it was his notion that the world would expect and require that he should comply with them: No, if it was not. Did they afford him that of benevolence? Yes, if it was his notion that the community would upon the whole be the better for his complying with them; No, if it was not. But did the dictates of the political sanction, in the case in question, actually follow the mandates of the sovereign: in other words, was such a mandate legal? This we see is a mere question of local jurisprudence, altogether foreign to the present purpose.

*Practical use of the above disquisitions relative to motives.*

XLVI. What is here said about the goodness and badness of motives, is far from being a mere matter of words. There will be occasion to make use of it hereafter for various important purposes. I shall have need of it for the sake of dissipating various prejudices, which are of disservice to the community, sometimes by cherishing the flame of civil dissensions,[45] at other times, by obstructing the course of justice. It will be shown, that in the case of many offences,[46] the consideration of the motive is a most material one: for that in the first place it makes a very material difference in the magnitude of the mischief:[47] in the next place, that it is easy to be ascertained; and thence may be made a ground for a difference in the demand for punishment: but that in other cases it is altogether incapable of being ascertained; and that, were it capable of being ever so well ascertained, good or bad, it could make no difference in the demand for punishment: that in all cases, the motive that may happen to govern a prosecutor, is a consideration totally immaterial: whence maybe seen the mischievousness of the prejudice that is so apt to be entertained against informers; and the consequence it is of that the judge, in particular, should be proof against the influence of such delusions.

Lastly, The subject of motives is one with which it is necessary to be acquainted, in order to pass a judgment on any means that may be proposed for combating offences in their source.[48]

But before the theoretical foundation for these practical observations can be completely laid, it is necessary we should say something on the subject of *disposition:* which, accordingly, will furnish matter for the ensuing chapter.

---

44 The idea of the case here supposed is taken from an anecdote in real history, but varies from it in several particulars.

45 See B. I. tit. [Rebellion].

46 See B. I. tit. [Simp. corp. injuries]. Ib. tit. [Homicide].

47 See ch. xi. [Dispositions].

48 See Append. tit. [Preventive Institutions].

# HAPPINESS AND UTILITARIAN ETHICS

BY **John Stuart Mill**

## CHAPTER II: WHAT UTILITARIANISM IS

A passing remark is all that needs be given to the ignorant blunder of supposing that those who stand up for utility as the test of right and wrong, use the term in that restricted and merely colloquial sense in which utility is opposed to pleasure. An apology is due to the philosophical opponents of utilitarianism, for even the momentary appearance of confounding them with any one capable of so absurd a misconception; which is the more extraordinary, inasmuch as the contrary accusation, of referring everything to pleasure, and that too in its grossest form, is another of the common charges against utilitarianism: and, as has been pointedly remarked by an able writer, the same sort of persons, and often the very same persons, denounce the theory "as impracticably dry when the word utility precedes the word pleasure, and as too practicably voluptuous when the word pleasure precedes the word utility." Those who know anything about the matter are aware that every writer, from Epicurus to Bentham, who maintained the theory of utility, meant by it, not something to be contradistinguished from pleasure, but pleasure itself, together with exemption from pain; and instead of opposing the useful to the agreeable or the ornamental, have always declared that the useful means these, among other things. Yet the common herd, including the herd of writers, not only in newspapers and periodicals, but in books of weight and pretension, are perpetually falling into this shallow mistake. Having caught up the word utilitarian, while knowing nothing whatever about it but its sound, they habitually express by it the rejection, or the neglect, of pleasure in some of its forms; of beauty, of ornament, or of amusement. Nor is the term thus ignorantly misapplied solely in disparagement, but occasionally in compliment; as though it implied superiority to frivolity and the mere pleasures of the moment. And this perverted use is the only one in which the word is popularly known, and the one from which the new generation are acquiring their sole notion of its meaning. Those who introduced the word, but who had for many years discontinued it as a distinctive appellation, may well feel themselves called upon to resume it, if by doing so they can hope to contribute anything towards rescuing it from this utter degradation.[1]

The creed which accepts as the foundation of morals, Utility, or the Greatest Happiness Principle, holds that actions are right in proportion as they tend to promote happiness, wrong as they tend to produce the reverse of happiness. By happiness is intended pleasure, and the absence of pain; by unhappiness, pain, and the privation of pleasure. To give a clear view of the moral standard set up by the theory, much more requires to be said; in particular, what things it includes in the ideas of pain and pleasure; and to what extent this is left an open question. But these supplementary explanations do not affect the theory of life on which this theory of morality is grounded—namely, that pleasure, and freedom from pain, are the only things desirable as ends; and that all desirable things (which are as numerous in the utilitarian as in any other scheme) are desirable either for the pleasure inherent in themselves, or as means to the promotion of pleasure and the prevention of pain.

1 The author of this essay has reason for believing himself to be the first person who brought the word utilitarian into use. He did not invent it, but adopted it from a passing expression in Mr. Galt's *Annals of the Parish*. After using it as a designation for several years, he and others abandoned it from a growing dislike to anything resembling a badge or watchword of sectarian distinction. But as a name for one single opinion, not a set of opinions—to denote the recognition of utility as a standard, not any particular way of applying it—the term supplies a want in the language, and offers, in many cases, a convenient mode of avoiding tiresome circumlocution.

John Stuart Mill, "General Remarks and Of the Ultimate Sanction of the Principle of Utility," *Utilitarianism*.

Now, such a theory of life excites in many minds, and among them in some of the most estimable in feeling and purpose, inveterate dislike. To suppose that life has (as they express it) no higher end than pleasure—no better and nobler object of desire and pursuit—they designate as utterly mean and grovelling; as a doctrine worthy only of swine, to whom the followers of Epicurus were, at a very early period, contemptuously likened; and modern holders of the doctrine are occasionally made the subject of equally polite comparisons by its German, French, and English assailants.

When thus attacked, the Epicureans have always answered, that it is not they, but their accusers, who represent human nature in a degrading light; since the accusation supposes human beings to be capable of no pleasures except those of which swine are capable. If this supposition were true, the charge could not be gainsaid, but would then be no longer an imputation; for if the sources of pleasure were precisely the same to human beings and to swine, the rule of life which is good enough for the one would be good enough for the other. The comparison of the Epicurean life to that of beasts is felt as degrading, precisely because a beast's pleasures do not satisfy a human being's conceptions of happiness. Human beings have faculties more elevated than the animal appetites, and when once made conscious of them, do not regard anything as happiness which does not include their gratification. I do not, indeed, consider the Epicureans to have been by any means faultless in drawing out their scheme of consequences from the utilitarian principle. To do this in any sufficient manner, many Stoic, as well as Christian elements require to be included. But there is no known Epicurean theory of life which does not assign to the pleasures of the intellect; of the feelings and imagination, and of the moral sentiments, a much higher value as pleasures than to those of mere sensation. It must be admitted, however, that utilitarian writers in general have placed the superiority of mental over bodily pleasures chiefly in the greater permanency, safety, uncostliness, &c., of the former—that is, in their circumstantial advantages rather than in their intrinsic nature. And on all these points utilitarians have fully proved their case; but they might have taken the other, and, as it may be called, higher ground, with entire consistency. It is quite compatible with the principle of utility to recognise the fact, that some *kinds* of pleasure are more desirable and more valuable than others. It would be absurd that while, in estimating all other things, quality is considered as well as quantity, the estimation of pleasures should be supposed to depend on quantity alone.

If I am asked, what I mean by difference of quality in pleasures, or what makes one pleasure more valuable than another, merely as a pleasure, except its being greater in amount, there is but one possible answer. Of two pleasures, if there be one to which all or almost all who have experience of both give a decided preference, irrespective of any feeling of moral obligation to prefer it, that is the more desirable pleasure. If one of the two is, by those who are competently acquainted with both, placed so far above the other that they prefer it, even though knowing it to be attended with a greater amount of discontent, and would not resign it for any quantity of the other pleasure which their nature is capable of, we are justified in ascribing to the preferred enjoyment a superiority in quality, so far outweighing quantity as to render it, in comparison, of small account.

Now it is an unquestionable fact that those who are equally acquainted with, and equally capable of appreciating and enjoying, both, do give a most marked preference to the manner of existence which employs their higher faculties. Few human creatures would consent to be changed into any of the lower animals, for a promise of the fullest allowance of a beast's pleasures; no intelligent human being would consent to be a fool, no instructed person would be an ignoramus, no person of feeling and conscience would be selfish and base, even though they should be persuaded that the fool, the dunce, or the rascal is better satisfied with his lot than they are with theirs. They would not resign what they possess more than he, for the most complete satisfaction of all the desires which they have in common with him. If they ever fancy they would, it is only in cases of unhappiness so extreme, that to escape from it they would exchange their lot for almost any other, however undesirable in their own eyes. A being of higher faculties requires more to make him happy, is capable probably of more acute suffering, and is certainly accessible to it at more points, than one of an inferior type; but in spite of these liabilities, he can never really wish to sink into what he feels to be a lower grade of existence. We may give what explanation we please of this unwillingness; we may attribute it to pride, a name which is given indiscriminately to some of the most and to some of the least estimable feelings of which mankind are capable; we may refer it to the love of liberty and personal independence, an appeal to which was with the Stoics one of the most effective means for the inculcation of it; to the love of power, or to the love of excitement, both of which do really enter into and contribute to it: but its most appropriate appellation is a sense of dignity, which all human beings possess in one form or other, and in some, though by no means in exact, proportion to their higher faculties, and which is so essential a part of the happiness of those in whom it is strong, that nothing which conflicts with it could be, otherwise than momentarily, an object of desire to them. Whoever supposes that this preference takes place at a sacrifice of happiness—that the superior being, in anything like equal circumstances, is not happier than the inferior—confounds the two very different ideas, of happiness, and content. It is indisputable that the being whose capacities of enjoyment are low, has the greatest chance of having them fully satisfied; and a highly-endowed being will always feel that any happiness which he can look for, as the world is constituted, is imperfect. But he can learn to bear its imperfections, if they are at all bearable; and they will not make him envy the being who is indeed unconscious of the imperfections, but only because he feels not at all the good which those imperfections qualify. It is better to be a human being dissatisfied than a pig satisfied; better to be Socrates dissatisfied than a fool satisfied. And if the fool, or the pig, is of a different opinion, it is because they only know their own side of the question. The other party to the comparison knows both sides.

It may be objected, that many who are capable of the higher pleasures, occasionally, under the influence of temptation, postpone them to the lower. But this is quite compatible with a full appreciation of the intrinsic superiority of the higher. Men often, from infirmity of character, make their election for the nearer good, though they know it to be the less valuable; and this no less when the choice is between two bodily pleasures, than when it is between bodily and mental. They pursue sensual indulgences to the injury of health, though perfectly aware that health is the greater good. It may be further objected, that many who begin with youthful enthusiasm for everything noble, as they advance in years sink into indolence and selfishness. But I do not believe that those who undergo this very common change, voluntarily choose the lower description of pleasures in preference to the higher. I believe that before they devote themselves exclusively to the one, they have already become incapable of the other. Capacity for the nobler feelings is in most natures a very tender plant, easily killed, not only by hostile influences, but by mere want of sustenance; and in the majority of young persons it speedily dies away if the occupations to which their position in life has devoted them, and the society into which it has thrown them, are not favourable to keeping that higher capacity in exercise. Men lose their high aspirations as they lose their intellectual tastes, because they have not time or opportunity for indulging them; and they addict themselves to inferior pleasures, not because they deliberately prefer them, but because they are either the only ones to which they have access, or the only ones which they are any longer capable of enjoying. It may be questioned whether any one who has remained equally susceptible to both classes of pleasures, ever knowingly and calmly preferred the lower; though many, in all ages, have broken down in an ineffectual attempt to combine both.

From this verdict of the only competent judges, I apprehend there can be no appeal. On a question which is the best worth having of two pleasures, or which of two modes of existence is the most grateful to the feelings, apart from its moral attributes and from its consequences, the judgment of those who are qualified by knowledge of both, or, if they differ, that of the majority among them, must be admitted as final. And there needs be the less hesitation to accept this judgment respecting the quality of pleasures, since there is no other tribunal to be referred to even on the question of quantity. What means are there of determining which is the acutest of two pains, or the intensest of two pleasurable sensations, except the general suffrage of those who are familiar with both? Neither pains nor pleasures are homogeneous, and pain is always heterogeneous with pleasure. What is there to decide whether a particular pleasure is worth purchasing at the cost of a particular pain, except the feelings and judgment of the experienced? When, therefore, those feelings and judgment declare the pleasures derived from the higher faculties to be preferable *in kind*, apart from the question of intensity, to those of which the animal nature, disjoined from the higher faculties, is susceptible, they are entitled on this subject to the same regard.

I have dwelt on this point, as being a necessary part of a perfectly just conception of Utility or Happiness, considered as the directive rule of human conduct. But it is by no means an indispensable condition to the acceptance of the utilitarian standard; for that standard is not the agent's own greatest happiness, but the greatest amount of happiness altogether; and if it may possibly be doubted whether a noble character is always the happier for its nobleness, there can be no doubt that it makes other people happier, and that the world in general is immensely a gainer by it. Utilitarianism, therefore, could only attain its end by the general cultivation of nobleness of character, even if each individual were only benefited by the nobleness of others, and his own, so far as happiness is concerned, were a sheer deduction from the benefit. But the bare enunciation of such an absurdity as this last, renders refutation superfluous.

According to the Greatest Happiness Principle, as above explained, the ultimate end, with reference to and for the sake of which all other things are desirable (whether we are considering our own good or that of other people), is an existence exempt as far as possible from pain, and as rich as possible in enjoyments, both in point of quantity and quality; the test of quality, and the rule for measuring it against quantity, being the preference felt by those who, in their opportunities of experience, to which must be added their habits of self-consciousness and self-observation, are best furnished with the means of comparison. This, being, according to the utilitarian opinion, the end of human action, is necessarily also the standard of morality; which may accordingly be defined, the rules and precepts for human conduct, by the observance of which an existence such as has been described might be, to the greatest extent possible, secured to all mankind; and not to them only, but, so far as the nature of things admits, to the whole sentient creation.

Against this doctrine, however, arises another class of objectors, who say that happiness, in any form, cannot be the rational purpose of human life and action; because, in the first place, it is unattainable: and they contemptuously ask, What right hast thou to be happy? a question which Mr. Carlyle clenches by the addition, What right, a short time ago, hadst thou even *to be*? Next, they say, that men can do *without* happiness; that all noble human beings have felt this, and could not have become noble but by learning the lesson of Entsagen, or renunciation; which lesson, thoroughly learnt and submitted to, they affirm to be the beginning and necessary condition of all virtue.

The first of these objections would go to the root of the matter were it well founded; for if no happiness is to be had at all by human beings, the attainment of it cannot be the end of morality, or of any rational conduct. Though, even in that case, something might still be said for the utilitarian theory; since utility includes not solely the pursuit of happiness, but the prevention or mitigation of unhappiness; and if the former aim be chimerical, there will be all the greater scope and more imperative need for the latter, so long at least as mankind think fit to live, and do not take refuge in the simultaneous act of suicide recommended under certain conditions by Novalis. When, however, it is thus positively asserted to be impossible that human life should be happy, the assertion, if not something like a verbal quibble, is at least an exaggeration. If by happiness be meant a continuity of highly pleasurable excitement, it is evident enough that this is impossible. A state of exalted pleasure lasts only moments, or in some cases, and with some intermissions, hours or days, and is the occasional brilliant flash of enjoyment, not its permanent and steady flame. Of this the philosophers who have taught that happiness is the end of life were as fully aware as those who taunt them. The happiness which they meant was not a life of rapture, but moments of such, in an existence made up of few and transitory pains, many and various pleasures, with a decided predominance of the active over the passive, and having as the foundation of the whole, not to expect more from life than it is capable of bestowing. A life thus composed, to those who have been fortunate enough to obtain it, has always appeared worthy of the name of happiness. And such an existence is even now the lot of many, during some considerable portion of their lives. The present wretched education, and wretched social arrangements, are the only real hindrance to its being attainable by almost all.

The objectors perhaps may doubt whether human beings, if taught to consider happiness as the end of life, would be satisfied with such a moderate share of it. But great numbers of mankind have been satisfied with much less. The main constituents of a satisfied life appear to be two, either of which by itself is often found sufficient for the purpose: tranquillity, and excitement. With much tranquillity, many find that they can be content with very little pleasure: with much excitement, many can reconcile themselves to a considerable quantity of pain. There is assuredly no inherent impossibility in enabling even the mass of mankind to unite both; since the two are so far from being incompatible that they are in natural alliance, the prolongation of either being a preparation for, and exciting a wish for, the other. It is only those in whom indolence amounts to a vice, that do not desire excitement after an interval of repose; it is only those in whom the need of excitement is a disease, that feel the tranquillity which follows excitement dull and insipid, instead of pleasurable in direct proportion to the excitement which preceded it. When people who are tolerably fortunate in their outward lot do not find in life sufficient enjoyment to make it valuable to them, the cause generally is, caring for nobody but themselves. To those who have neither public nor private affections, the excitements of life are much curtailed, and in any case dwindle in value as the time approaches when all selfish interests must be terminated by death: while those who leave after them objects of personal affection, and especially those who have also cultivated a fellow-feeling with the collective interests of mankind, retain as lively an interest in life on the eve of death as in the vigour of youth and health. Next to selfishness, the principal cause which makes life unsatisfactory, is want of mental cultivation. A cultivated mind—I do not mean that of a philosopher, but any mind to which the fountains of knowledge have been opened, and which has been taught, in any tolerable degree, to exercise its faculties—finds sources of inexhaustible interest in all that surrounds it; in the objects of nature, the achievements of art, the imaginations of poetry, the incidents of history, the ways of mankind past and present, and their prospects in the future. It is possible, indeed, to become indifferent to all this, and that too without having exhausted a thousandth part of it; but only when one has had from the beginning no moral or human interest in these things, and has sought in them only the gratification of curiosity.

Now there is absolutely no reason in the nature of things why an amount of mental culture sufficient to give an intelligent interest in these objects of contemplation, should not be the inheritance of every one born in a civilized country. As little is there an inherent necessity that any human being should be a selfish egotist, devoid of every feeling or care but those which centre in his own miserable individuality. Something far superior to this is sufficiently common even now, to give ample earnest of what the human species may be made. Genuine private affections, and a sincere interest in the public good, are possible, though in unequal degrees, to every rightly brought-up human being. In a world in which there is so much to interest, so much to enjoy, and so much also to correct and improve, every one who has this moderate amount of moral and intellectual requisites is capable of an existence which may be called enviable; and unless such a person, through bad laws, or subjection to the will of others, is denied the liberty to use the sources of happiness within his reach, he will not fail to find this enviable existence, if he escape the positive evils of life, the great sources of physical and mental suffering—such as indigence, disease, and the unkindness, worthlessness, or premature loss of objects of affection. The main stress of the problem lies, therefore, in the contest with these calamities, from which it is a rare good fortune entirely to escape; which, as things now are, cannot be obviated, and often cannot be in any material degree mitigated. Yet no one whose opinion deserves a moment's consideration can doubt that most of the great positive evils of the world are in themselves removable, and will, if human affairs continue to improve, be in the end reduced within narrow limits. Poverty, in any sense implying suffering, may be completely extinguished by the wisdom of society, combined with the good sense and providence of individuals. Even that most intractable of enemies, disease, may be indefinitely reduced in dimensions by good physical and moral education, and proper control of noxious influences; while the progress of science holds out a promise for the future of still more direct conquests over this detestable foe. And every advance in that direction relieves us from some, not only of the chances which cut short our own lives, but, what concerns us still more, which deprive us of those in whom our happiness is wrapt up. As for vicissitudes of fortune, and other disappointments connected with worldly circumstances, these are principally the effect either of gross imprudence, of ill-regulated desires, or of bad or imperfect social institutions. All the grand sources, in short, of human suffering are in a great degree, many of them almost entirely, conquerable by human care and effort; and though their removal is grievously slow—though a long succession of generations will perish in the breach before the conquest is completed, and this world becomes all that, if will and knowledge were not wanting, it might easily be made—yet every mind sufficiently intelligent and generous to bear a part, however small and unconspicuous, in the endeavour, will draw a noble enjoyment from the contest itself, which he would not for any bribe in the form of selfish indulgence consent to be without.

And this leads to the true estimation of what is said by the objectors concerning the possibility, and the obligation, of learning to do without happiness. Unquestionably it is possible to do without happiness; it is done involuntarily by nineteen-twentieths of mankind, even in those parts of our present world which are least deep in barbarism; and it often has to be done voluntarily by the hero or the martyr, for the sake of something which he prizes more than his individual happiness. But this something, what is it, unless the happiness of others, or some of the requisites of happiness? It is noble to be capable of resigning entirely one's own portion of happiness, or chances of it: but, after all, this self-sacrifice must be for some end; it is not its own end; and if we are told that its end is not happiness, but virtue, which is better than happiness, I ask, would the sacrifice be made if the hero or martyr did not believe that it would earn for others immunity from similar sacrifices? Would it be made, if he thought that his renunciation of happiness for himself would produce no fruit for any of his fellow creatures, but to make their lot like his, and place them also in the condition of persons who have renounced happiness? All honour to those who can abnegate for themselves the personal enjoyment of life, when by such renunciation they contribute worthily to increase the amount of happiness in the world; but he who does it, or professes to do it, for any other purpose, is no more deserving of admiration than the ascetic mounted on his pillar. He may be an inspiriting proof of what men *can* do, but assuredly not an example of what they *should*.

Though it is only in a very imperfect state of the world's arrangements that any one can best serve the happiness of others by the absolute sacrifice of his own, yet so long as the world is in that imperfect state, I fully acknowledge that the readiness to make such a sacrifice is the highest virtue which can be found in man. I will add, that in this condition of the world, paradoxical as the assertion may be, the conscious ability to do without happiness gives the best prospect of realizing such happiness as is attainable. For nothing except that consciousness can raise a person above the chances of life, by making him feel that, let fate and fortune do their worst, they have not power to subdue him: which, once felt, frees him from excess of anxiety concerning the evils of life, and enables him, like many a Stoic in the worst times of the Roman Empire, to cultivate in tranquillity the sources of satisfaction accessible to him, without concerning himself about the uncertainty of their duration, any more than about their inevitable end.

Meanwhile, let utilitarians never cease to claim the morality of self-devotion as a possession which belongs by as good a right to them, as either to the Stoic or to the Transcendentalist. The utilitarian morality does recognise in human beings the power of sacrificing their own greatest good for the good of others. It only refuses to admit that the sacrifice is itself a good. A sacrifice which does not increase, or tend to increase, the sum total of happiness, it considers as wasted. The only self-renunciation which it applauds, is devotion to the happiness, or to some of the means of happiness, of others; either of mankind collectively, or of individuals within the limits imposed by the collective interests of mankind.

I must again repeat, what the assailants of utilitarianism seldom have the justice to acknowledge, that the happiness which forms the utilitarian standard of what is right in conduct, is not the agent's own happiness, but that of all concerned. As between his own happiness and that of others, utilitarianism requires him to be as strictly impartial as a disinterested and benevolent spectator. In the golden rule of Jesus of Nazareth, we read the complete spirit of the ethics of utility. To do as one would be done by, and to love one's neighbour as oneself, constitute the ideal perfection of utilitarian morality. As the means of making the nearest approach to this ideal, utility would enjoin, first, that laws and social arrangements should place the happiness, or (as speaking practically it may be called) the interest, of every individual, as nearly as possible in harmony with the interest of the whole; and secondly, that education and opinion, which have so vast a power over human character, should so use that power as to establish in the mind of every individual an indissoluble association between his own happiness and the good of the whole; especially between his own happiness and the practice of such modes of conduct, negative and positive, as regard for the universal happiness prescribes: so that not only he may be unable to conceive the possibility of happiness to himself, consistently with conduct opposed to the general good, but also that a direct impulse to promote the general good may be in every individual one of the habitual motives of action, and the sentiments connected therewith may fill a large and prominent place in every human being's sentient existence. If the impugners of the utilitarian morality represented it to their own minds in this its true character, I know not what recommendation possessed by any other morality they could possibly affirm to be wanting to it: what more beautiful or more exalted developments of human nature any other ethical system can be supposed to foster, or what springs of action, not accessible to the utilitarian, such systems rely on for giving effect to their mandates.

The objectors to utilitarianism cannot always be charged with representing it in a discreditable light. On the contrary, those among them who entertain anything like a just idea of its disinterested character, sometimes find fault with its standard as being too high for humanity. They say it is exacting too much to require that people shall always act from the inducement of promoting the general interests of society. But this is to mistake the very meaning of a standard of morals, and to confound the rule of action with the motive of it. It is the business of ethics to tell us what are our duties, or by what test we may know them; but no system of ethics requires that the sole motive of all we do shall be a feeling of duty; on the contrary, ninety-nine hundredths of all our actions are done from other motives, and rightly so done, if the rule of duty does not condemn them. It is the more unjust to utilitarianism that this particular misapprehension should be made a ground of objection to it, inasmuch as utilitarian moralists have gone beyond almost all others in affirming that the motive has nothing to do with the morality of the action, though much with the worth of the agent. He who saves a fellow creature from drowning does what is morally right, whether his motive be duty, or the hope of being paid for his trouble: he who betrays the friend that trusts him, is guilty of a crime, even if his object be to serve another friend to whom he is under greater obligations.[2] But to speak only of actions done from the motive of duty, and in direct obedience to principle: it is a misapprehension of the utilitarian mode of thought, to conceive it as implying that people should fix their minds upon so wide a generality as the world, or society at large. The great majority of good actions are intended, not for the benefit of the world, but for that of individuals, of which the good of the world is made up; and the thoughts of the most virtuous man need not on these occasions travel beyond the particular persons concerned, except so far as is necessary to assure himself that in benefiting them he is not violating the rights—that is, the legitimate and authorized expectations—of any one else. The multiplication of happiness is, according to the utilitarian ethics, the object of virtue: the occasions on which any person (except one in a thousand) has it in his power to do this on an extended scale, in other words, to be a public benefactor, are but exceptional; and on these occasions alone is he called on to consider public utility; in every other case, private utility, the interest or happiness of some few persons, is all he has to attend to. Those alone the influence of whose actions extends to society in general, need concern themselves habitually about so large an object. In the case of abstinences indeed—of things which people forbear to do, from moral considerations, though the consequences in the particular case might be beneficial—it would be unworthy of an intelligent agent not to be consciously aware that the action is of a class which, if practised generally, would be generally injurious, and that this is the ground of the obligation to abstain from it. The amount of regard for the public interest implied in this recognition, is no greater than is demanded by every system of morals; for they all enjoin to abstain from whatever is manifestly pernicious to society.

The same considerations dispose of another reproach against the doctrine of utility, founded on a still grosser misconception of the purpose of a standard of morality, and of the very meaning of the words right and wrong. It is often affirmed that utilitarianism renders men cold and unsympathizing; that it chills their moral feelings towards individuals; that it makes them regard only the dry and hard consideration of the consequences of actions, not taking into their moral estimate the qualities from which those actions emanate. If the assertion means that they do not allow their judgment respecting the rightness or wrongness of an action to be influenced by their opinion of the qualities of the person who does it, this is a complaint not against utilitarianism, but against having any standard of morality at all; for certainly no known ethical standard decides an action to be good or bad because it is done by a good or a bad man, still less because done by an amiable, a brave, or a benevolent man or the contrary. These considerations are relevant, not to the estimation of actions, but of persons; and there is nothing in the utilitarian theory inconsistent with the fact that there are other things which interest us in persons besides the rightness and wrongness of their actions. The Stoics, indeed, with the paradoxical misuse of language which was part of their system, and by which they strove to raise themselves above all concern about anything but virtue, were fond of saying that he who has that has everything; that he, and only he, is rich, is beautiful, is a king. But no claim of this description is made for the virtuous man by the utilitarian doctrine. Utilitarians are quite aware that there are other desirable possessions and qualities besides virtue, and are perfectly willing to allow to all of them their full worth. They are also aware that a right action does not necessarily indicate a virtuous character, and that actions which are blameable often proceed from qualities entitled to praise. When this is apparent in any particular case, it modifies their estimation, not certainly of the act, but of the agent. I grant that they are, notwithstanding, of opinion, that in

---

2 An opponent, whose intellectual and moral fairness it is a pleasure to acknowledge (the Rev. J. Llewellyn Davis), has objected to this passage, saying, "Surely the rightness or wrongness of saving a man from drowning does depend very much upon the motive with which it is done. Suppose that a tyrant, when his enemy jumped into the sea to escape from him, saved him from drowning simply in order that he might inflict upon him more exquisite tortures, would it tend to clearness to speak of that rescue as 'a morally right action?' Or suppose again, according to one of the stock illustrations of ethical inquiries, that a man betrayed a trust received from a friend, because the discharge of it would fatally injure that friend himself or some one belonging to him, would utilitarianism compel one to call the betrayal 'a crime' as much as if it had been done from the meanest motive?"

I submit, that he who saves another from drowning in order to kill him by torture afterwards, does not differ only in motive from him who does the same thing from duty or benevolence; the act itself is different. The rescue of the man is, in the case supposed, only the necessary first step of an act far more atrocious than leaving him to drown would have been. Had Mr. Davis said, "The rightness or wrongness of saving a man from drowning does depend very much"—not upon the motive, but—"upon the *intention*" no utilitarian would have differed from him. Mr. Davis, by an oversight too common not to be quite venial, has in this case confounded the very different ideas of Motive and Intention. There is no point which utilitarian thinkers (and Bentham pre-eminently) have taken more pains to illustrate than this. The morality of the action depends entirely upon the intention—that is, upon what the agent *wills to do*. But the motive, that is, the feeling which makes him will so to do, when it makes no difference in the act, makes none in the morality: though it makes a great difference in our moral estimation of the agent, especially if it indicates a good or a bad habitual *disposition*—a bent of character from which useful, or from which hurtful actions are likely to arise.

the long run the best proof of a good character is good actions; and resolutely refuse to consider any mental disposition as good, of which the predominant tendency is to produce bad conduct. This makes them unpopular with many people; but it is an unpopularity which they must share with every one who regards the distinction between right and wrong in a serious light; and the reproach is not one which a conscientious utilitarian need be anxious to repel.

If no more be meant by the objection than that many utilitarians look on the morality of actions, as measured by the utilitarian standard, with too exclusive a regard, and do not lay sufficient stress upon the other beauties of character which go towards making a human being loveable or admirable, this may be admitted. Utilitarians who have cultivated their moral feelings, but not their sympathies nor their artistic perceptions, do fall into this mistake; and so do all other moralists under the same conditions. What can be said in excuse for other moralists is equally available for them, namely, that if there is to be any error, it is better that it should be on that side. As a matter of fact, we may affirm that among utilitarians as among adherents of other systems, there is every imaginable degree of rigidity and of laxity in the application of their standard: some are even puritanically rigorous, while others are as indulgent as can possibly be desired by sinner or by sentimentalist. But on the whole, a doctrine which brings prominently forward the interest that mankind have in the repression and prevention of conduct which violates the moral law, is likely to be inferior to no other in turning the sanctions of opinion against such violations. It is true, the question, What does violate the moral law? is one on which those who recognise different standards of morality are likely now and then to differ. But difference of opinion on moral questions was not first introduced into the world by utilitarianism, while that doctrine does supply, if not always an easy, at all events a tangible and intelligible mode of deciding such differences.

It may not be superfluous to notice a few more of the common misapprehensions of utilitarian ethics, even those which are so obvious and gross that it might appear impossible for any person of candour and intelligence to fall into them: since persons, even of considerable mental endowments, often give themselves so little trouble to understand the bearings of any opinion against which they entertain a prejudice, and men are in general so little conscious of this voluntary ignorance as a defect, that the vulgarest misunderstandings of ethical doctrines are continually met with in the deliberate writings of persons of the greatest pretensions both to high principle and to philosophy. We not uncommonly hear the doctrine of utility inveighed against as a *godless* doctrine. If it be necessary to say anything at all against so mere an assumption, we may say that the question depends upon what idea we have formed of the moral character of the Deity. If it be a true belief that God desires, above all things, the happiness of his creatures, and that this was his purpose in their creation, utility is not only not a godless doctrine, but more profoundly religious than any other. If it be meant that utilitarianism does not recognise the revealed will of God as the supreme law of morals, I answer, that an utilitarian who believes in the perfect goodness and wisdom of God, necessarily believes that whatever God has thought fit to reveal on the subject of morals, must fulfil the requirements of utility in a supreme degree. But others besides utilitarians have been of opinion that the Christian revelation was intended, and is fitted, to inform the hearts and minds of mankind with a spirit which should enable them to find for themselves what is right, and incline them to do it when found, rather than to tell them, except in a very general way, what it is: and that we need a doctrine of ethics, carefully followed out, to *interpret* to us the will of God. Whether this opinion is correct or not, it is superfluous here to discuss; since whatever aid religion, either natural or revealed, can afford to ethical investigation, is as open to the utilitarian moralist as to any other. He can use it as the testimony of God to the usefulness or hurtfulness of any given course of action, by as good a right as others can use it for the indication of a transcendental law, having no connexion with usefulness or with happiness.

Again, Utility is often summarily stigmatized as an immoral doctrine by giving it the name of Expediency, and taking advantage of the popular use of that term to contrast it with Principle. But the Expedient, in the sense in which it is opposed to the Right, generally means that which is expedient for the particular interest of the agent himself: as when a minister sacrifices the interest of his country to keep himself in place. When it means anything better than this, it means that which is expedient for some immediate object, some temporary purpose, but which violates a rule whose observance is expedient in a much higher degree. The Expedient, in this sense, instead of being the same thing with the useful, is a branch of the hurtful. Thus, it would often be expedient, for the purpose of getting over some momentary embarrassment, or attaining some object immediately useful to ourselves or others, to tell a lie. But inasmuch as the cultivation in ourselves of a sensitive feeling on the subject of veracity, is one of the most useful, and the enfeeblement of that feeling one of the most hurtful, things to which our conduct can be instrumental; and inasmuch as any, even unintentional, deviation from truth, does that much towards weakening the trustworthiness of human assertion, which is not only the principal support of all present social well-being, but the insufficiency of which does more than any one thing that can be named to keep back civilisation, virtue, everything on which human happiness on the largest scale depends; we feel that the violation, for a present advantage, of a rule of such transcendent expediency, is not expedient, and that he who, for the sake of a convenience to himself or to some other individual, does what depends on him to deprive mankind of the good, and inflict upon them the evil, involved in the greater or less reliance which they can place in each other's word, acts the part of one of their worst enemies. Yet that even this rule, sacred as it is, admits of possible exceptions, is acknowledged by all moralists; the chief of which is when the withholding of some fact (as of information from a malefactor, or of bad news from a person dangerously ill) would preserve some one (especially a person other than oneself) from great and unmerited evil, and when the withholding can only be effected by denial. But in order that the exception may not extend itself beyond the need, and may have the least possible effect in weakening reliance on veracity, it ought to be recognized, and, if possible, its limits defined; and if the principle of utility is good for anything, it must be good for weighing these conflicting utilities against one another, and marking out the region within which one or the other preponderates.

Again, defenders of utility often find themselves called upon to reply to such objections as this—that there is not time, previous to action, for calculating and weighing the effects of any line of conduct on the general happiness. This is exactly as if any one were to say that it is impossible to guide our conduct by Christianity, because there is not time, on every occasion on which anything has to be done, to read through the Old and New Testaments. The answer to the objection is, that there has been ample time, namely, the whole past duration of the human species. During all that time mankind have been learning by experience the tendencies of actions; on which experience all the prudence, as well as all the morality of life, is dependent. People talk as if the commencement of this course of experience had hitherto been put off, and as if, at the moment when some man feels tempted to meddle with the property or life of another, he had to begin considering for the first time whether murder and theft are injurious to human happiness. Even then I do not think that he would find the question very puzzling; but, at all events, the matter is now done to his hand. It is truly a whimsical supposition, that if mankind were agreed in considering utility to be the test of morality, they would remain without any agreement as to what is useful, and would take no measures for having their notions on the subject taught to the young, and enforced by law and opinion. There is no difficulty in proving any ethical standard whatever to work ill, if we suppose universal idiocy to be conjoined with it, but on any hypothesis short of that, mankind must by this time have acquired positive beliefs as to the effects of some actions on their happiness; and the beliefs which have thus come down are the rules of morality for the multitude, and for the philosopher until he has succeeded in finding better. That philosophers might easily do this, even now, on many subjects; that the received code of ethics is by no means of divine right; and that mankind have still much to learn as to the effects of actions on the general happiness, I admit, or rather, earnestly maintain. The corollaries from the principle of utility, like the precepts of every practical art, admit of indefinite improvement, and, in a progressive state of the human mind, their improvement is perpetually going on. But to consider the rules of morality as improvable, is one thing; to pass over the intermediate generalizations entirely, and endeavour to test each individual action directly by the first principle, is another. It is a strange notion that the acknowledgment of a first principle is inconsistent with the admission of secondary ones. To inform a traveller respecting the place of his ultimate destination, is not to forbid the use of landmarks and direction-posts on the way. The proposition that happiness is the end and aim of morality, does not mean that no road ought to be laid down to that goal, or that persons going thither should not be advised to take one direction rather than another. Men really ought to leave off talking a kind of nonsense on this subject, which they would neither talk nor listen to on other matters of practical concernment. Nobody argues that the art of navigation is not founded on astronomy, because sailors cannot wait to calculate the Nautical Almanack. Being rational creatures, they go to sea with it ready calculated; and all rational creatures go out upon the sea of life with their minds made up on the common questions of right and wrong, as well as on many of the far more difficult questions of wise and foolish. And this, as long as foresight is a human quality, it is to be presumed they will continue to do. Whatever we adopt as the fundamental principle of morality, we require subordinate principles to apply it by: the impossibility of doing without them, being common to all systems, can afford no argument against any one in particular: but gravely to argue as if no such secondary principles could be had, and as if mankind had remained till now, and always must remain, without drawing any general conclusions from the experience of human life, is as high a pitch, I think, as absurdity has ever reached in philosophical controversy.

The remainder of the stock arguments against utilitarianism mostly consist in laying to its charge the common infirmities of human nature, and the general difficulties which embarrass conscientious persons in shaping their course through life. We are told that an utilitarian will be apt to make his own particular case an exception to moral rules, and, when under temptation, will see an utility in the breach of a rule, greater than he will see in its observance. But is utility the only creed which is able to furnish us with excuses for evil doing, and means of cheating our own conscience? They are afforded in abundance by all doctrines which recognise as a fact in morals the existence of conflicting considerations; which all doctrines do, that have been believed by sane persons. It is not the fault of any creed, but of the complicated nature of human affairs, that rules of conduct cannot be so framed as to require no exceptions, and that hardly any kind of action can safely be laid down as either always obligatory or always condemnable. There is no ethical creed which does not temper the rigidity of its laws, by giving a certain latitude, under the moral responsibility of the agent, for accommodation to peculiarities of circumstances; and under every creed, at the opening thus made, self-deception and dishonest casuistry get in. There exists no moral system under which there do not arise unequivocal cases of conflicting obligation. These are the real difficulties, the knotty points both in the theory of ethics, and in the conscientious guidance of personal conduct. They are overcome practically with greater or with less success according to the intellect and virtue of the individual; but it can hardly be pretended that any one will be the less qualified for dealing with them, from possessing an ultimate standard to which conflicting rights and duties can be referred. If utility is the ultimate source of moral obligations, utility may be invoked to decide between them when their demands are incompatible. Though the application of the standard may be difficult, it is better than none at all: while in other systems, the moral laws all claiming independent authority, there is no common umpire entitled to interfere between them; their claims to precedence one over another rest on little better than sophistry, and unless determined, as they generally are, by the unacknowledged influence of considerations of utility, afford a free scope for the action of personal desires and partialities. We must remember that only in these cases of conflict between secondary principles is it requisite that first principles should be appealed to. There is no case of moral obligation in which some secondary principle is not involved; and if only one, there can seldom be any real doubt which one it is, in the mind of any person by whom the principle itself is recognized.

# DEONTOLOGICAL ETHICS

BY **Immanuel Kant, translated by Thomas Kingsmill Abbott**

## TRANSITION FROM POPULAR MORAL PHILOSOPHY TO THE METAPHYSIC OF MORALS

If we have hitherto drawn our notion of duty from the common use of our practical reason, it is by no means to be inferred that we have treated it as an empirical notion. On the contrary, if we attend to the experience of men's conduct, we meet frequent and, as we ourselves allow, just complaints that one cannot find a single certain example of the disposition to act from pure duty. Although many things are done in conformity with what duty prescribes, it is nevertheless always doubtful whether they are done strictly from duty, so as to have a moral worth. Hence there have at all times been philosophers who have altogether denied that this disposition actually exists at all in human actions, and have ascribed everything to a more or less refined self-love. Not that they have on that account questioned the soundness of the conception of morality; on the contrary, they spoke with sincere regret of the frailty and corruption of human nature, which, though noble enough to take its rule an idea so worthy of respect, is yet weak to follow it and employs reason which ought to give it the law only for the purpose of providing for the interest of the inclinations, whether singly or at the best in the greatest possible harmony with one another.

In fact, it is absolutely impossible to make out by experience with complete certainty a single case in which the maxim of an action, however right in itself, rested simply on moral grounds and on the conception of duty. Sometimes it happens that with the sharpest self-examination we can find nothing beside the moral principle of duty which could have been powerful enough to move us to this or that action and to so great a sacrifice; yet we cannot from this infer with certainty that it was not really some secret impulse of self-love, under the false appearance of duty, that was the actual determining cause of the will. We like them to flatter ourselves by falsely taking credit for a more noble motive; whereas in fact we can never, even by the strictest examination, get completely behind the secret springs of action; since, when the question is of moral worth, it is not with the actions which we see that we are concerned, but with those inward principles of them which we do not see.

Moreover, we cannot better serve the wishes of those who ridicule all morality as a mere chimera of human imagination over stepping itself from vanity, than by conceding to them that notions of duty must be drawn only from experience (as from indolence, people are ready to think is also the case with all other notions); for or is to prepare for them a certain triumph. I am willing to admit out of love of humanity that even most of our actions are correct, but if we look closer at them we everywhere come upon the dear self which is always prominent, and it is this they have in view and not the strict command of duty which would often require self-denial. Without being an enemy of virtue, a cool observer, one that does not mistake the wish for good, however lively, for its reality, may sometimes doubt whether true virtue is actually found anywhere in the world, and this especially as years increase and the judgement is partly made wiser by experience and partly, also, more acute in observation. This being so, nothing can secure us from falling away altogether from our ideas of duty, or maintain in the soul a well-grounded respect for its law, but the clear conviction that although there should never have been actions which really sprang from such pure sources, yet whether this or that takes place is not at all the question; but that reason of itself, independent on all experience, ordains what ought to take place, that accordingly actions of which perhaps the world has hitherto never given an example, the feasibility even of which might be very much doubted by one who founds everything on experience, are nevertheless inflexibly commanded by reason; that, e.g., even though there might never yet have been a sincere friend, yet not a whit the less is pure sincerity in friendship required of every man, because, prior to all experience, this duty is involved as duty in the idea of a reason determining the will by a priori principles.

Immanuel Kant, *Groundwork of the Metaphysics of Morals,* trans. Thomas Kingsmill Abbott.

When we add further that, unless we deny that the notion of morality has any truth or reference to any possible object, we must admit that its law must be valid, not merely for men but for all rational creatures generally, not merely under certain contingent conditions or with exceptions but with absolute necessity, then it is clear that no experience could enable us to infer even the possibility of such apodeictic laws. For with what right could we bring into unbounded respect as a universal precept for every rational nature that which perhaps holds only under the contingent conditions of humanity? Or how could laws of the determination of our will be regarded as laws of the determination of the will of rational beings generally, and for us only as such, if they were merely empirical and did not take their origin wholly a priori from pure but practical reason?

Nor could anything be more fatal to morality than that we should wish to derive it from examples. For every example of it that is set before me must be first itself tested by principles of morality, whether it is worthy to serve as an original example, i.e., as a pattern; but by no means can it authoritatively furnish the conception of morality. Even the Holy One of the Gospels must first be compared with our ideal of moral perfection before we can recognise Him as such; and so He says of Himself, "Why call ye Me (whom you see) good; none is good (the model of good) but God only (whom ye do not see)?" But whence have we the conception of God as the supreme good? Simply from the idea of moral perfection, which reason frames a priori and connects inseparably with the notion of a free will. Imitation finds no place at all in morality, and examples serve only for encouragement, i.e., they put beyond doubt the feasibility of what the law commands, they make visible that which the practical rule expresses more generally, but they can never authorize us to set aside the true original which lies in reason and to guide ourselves by examples.

If then there is no genuine supreme principle of morality but what must rest simply on pure reason, independent of all experience, I think it is not necessary even to put the question whether it is good to exhibit these concepts in their generality (in abstracto) as they are established a priori along with the principles belonging to them, if our knowledge is to be distinguished from the vulgar and to be called philosophical.

In our times indeed this might perhaps be necessary; for if we collected votes whether pure rational knowledge separated from everything empirical, that is to say, metaphysic of morals, or whether popular practical philosophy is to be preferred, it is easy to guess which side would preponderate.

This descending to popular notions is certainly very commendable, if the ascent to the principles of pure reason has first taken place and been satisfactorily accomplished. This implies that we first found ethics on metaphysics, and then, when it is firmly established, procure a hearing for it by giving it a popular character. But it is quite absurd to try to be popular in the first inquiry, on which the soundness of the principles depends. It is not only that this proceeding can never lay claim to the very rare merit of a true philosophical popularity, since there is no art in being intelligible if one renounces all thoroughness of insight; but also it produces a disgusting medley of compiled observations and half-reasoned principles. Shallow pates enjoy this because it can be used for every-day chat, but the sagacious find in it only confusion, and being unsatisfied and unable to help themselves, they turn away their eyes, while philosophers, who see quite well through this delusion, are little listened to when they call men off for a time from this pretended popularity, in order that they might be rightfully popular after they have attained a definite insight.

We need only look at the attempts of moralists in that favourite fashion, and we shall find at one time the special constitution of human nature (including, however, the idea of a rational nature generally), at one time perfection, at another happiness, here moral sense, there fear of God. a little of this, and a little of that, in marvellous mixture, without its occurring to them to ask whether the principles of morality are to be sought in the knowledge of human nature at all (which we can have only from experience); or, if this is not so, if these principles are to be found altogether a priori, free from everything empirical, in pure rational concepts only and nowhere else, not even in the smallest degree; then rather to adopt the method of making this a separate inquiry, as pure practical philosophy, or (if one may use a name so decried) as metaphysic of morals,[1] to bring it by itself to completeness, and to require the public, which wishes for popular treatment, to await the issue of this undertaking.

Such a metaphysic of morals, completely isolated, not mixed with any anthropology, theology, physics, or hyperphysics, and still less with occult qualities (which we might call hypophysical), is not only an indispensable substratum

1 Just as pure mathematics are distinguished from applied, pure logic from applied, so if we choose we may also distinguish pure philosophy of morals (metaphysic) from applied (viz., applied to human nature). By this designation we are also at once reminded that moral principles are not based on properties of human nature, but must subsist a priori of themselves, while from such principles practical rules must be capable of being deduced for every rational nature, and accordingly for that of man.

of all sound theoretical knowledge of duties, but is at the same time a desideratum of the highest importance to the actual fulfilment of their precepts. For the pure conception of duty, unmixed with any foreign addition of empirical attractions, and, in a word, the conception of the moral law, exercises on the human heart, by way of reason alone (which first becomes aware with this that it can of itself be practical), an influence so much more powerful than all other springs[2] which may be derived from the field of experience, that, in the consciousness of its worth, it despises the latter, and can by degrees become their master; whereas a mixed ethics, compounded partly of motives drawn from feelings and inclinations, and partly also of conceptions of reason, must make the mind waver between motives which cannot be brought under any principle, which lead to good only by mere accident and very often also to evil.

From what has been said, it is clear that all moral conceptions have their seat and origin completely a priori in the reason, and that, moreover, in the commonest reason just as truly as in that which is in the highest degree speculative; that they cannot be obtained by abstraction from any empirical, and therefore merely contingent, knowledge; that it is just this purity of their origin that makes them worthy to serve as our supreme practical principle, and that just in proportion as we add anything empirical, we detract from their genuine influence and from the absolute value of actions; that it is not only of the greatest necessity, in a purely speculative point of view, but is also of the greatest practical importance, to derive these notions and laws from pure reason, to present them pure and unmixed, and even to determine the compass of this practical or pure rational knowledge, i.e., to determine the whole faculty of pure practical reason; and, in doing so, we must not make its principles dependent on the particular nature of human reason, though in speculative philosophy this may be permitted, or may even at times be necessary; but since moral laws ought to hold good for every rational creature, we must derive them from the general concept of a rational being. In this way, although for its application to man morality has need of anthropology, yet, in the first instance, we must treat it independently as pure philosophy, i.e., as metaphysic, complete in itself (a thing which in such distinct branches of science is easily done); knowing well that unless we are in possession of this, it would not only be vain to determine the moral element of duty in right actions for purposes of speculative criticism, but it would be impossible to base morals on their genuine principles, even for common practical purposes, especially of moral instruction, so as to produce pure moral dispositions, and to engraft them on men's minds to the promotion of the greatest possible good in the world.

But in order that in this study we may not merely advance by the natural steps from the common moral judgement (in this case very worthy of respect) to the philosophical, as has been already done, but also from a popular philosophy, which goes no further than it can reach by groping with the help of examples, to metaphysic (which does allow itself to be checked by anything empirical and, as it must measure the whole extent of this kind of rational knowledge, goes as far as ideal conceptions, where even examples fail us), we must follow and clearly describe the practical faculty of reason, from the general rules of its determination to the point where the notion of duty springs from it.

Everything in nature works according to laws. Rational beings alone have the faculty of acting according to the conception of laws, that is according to principles, i.e., have a will. Since the deduction of actions from principles requires reason, the will is nothing but practical reason. If reason infallibly determines the will, then the actions of such a being which are recognised as objectively necessary are subjectively necessary also, i.e., the will is a faculty to choose that only which reason independent of inclination recognises as practically necessary, i.e., as good. But if reason of itself does not sufficiently determine the will, if the latter is subject also to subjective conditions (particular impulses) which do not always coincide with the objective conditions; in a word, if the will does not in itself completely accord with reason (which is actually the case with men), then the actions which objectively are recognised as necessary are subjectively contingent, and the determination of such a will according to objective laws is obligation,

2 I have a letter from the late excellent Sulzer, in which he asks me what can be the reason that moral instruction, although containing much that is convincing for the reason, yet accomplishes so little? My answer was postponed in order that I might make it complete. But it is simply this: that the teachers themselves have not got their own notions clear, and when they endeavour to make up for this by raking up motives of moral goodness from every quarter, trying to make their physic right strong, they spoil it. For the commonest understanding shows that if we imagine, on the one hand, an act of honesty done with steadfast mind, apart from every view to advantage of any kind in this world or another, and even under the greatest temptations of necessity or allurement, and, on the other hand, a similar act which was affected, in however low a degree, by a foreign motive, the former leaves far behind and eclipses the second; it elevates the soul and inspires the wish to be able to act in like manner oneself. Even moderately young children feel this impression and one should never represent duties to them in any other light.

that is to say, the relation of the objective laws to a will that is not thoroughly good is conceived as the determination of the will of a rational being by principles of reason, but which the will from its nature does not of necessity follow.

The conception of an objective principle, in so far as it is obligatory for a will, is called a command (of reason), and the formula of the command is called an imperative.

All imperatives are expressed by the word ought [or shall], and thereby indicate the relation of an objective law of reason to a will, which from its subjective constitution is not necessarily determined by it (an obligation). They say that something would be good to do or to forbear, but they say it to a will which does not always do a thing because it is conceived to be good to do it. That is practically good, however, which determines the will by means of the conceptions of reason, and consequently not from subjective causes, but objectively, that is on principles which are valid for every rational being as such. It is distinguished from the pleasant, as that which influences the will only by means of sensation from merely subjective causes, valid only for the sense of this or that one, and not as a principle of reason, which holds for every one.[3]

A perfectly good will would therefore be equally subject to objective laws (viz., laws of good), but could not be conceived as obliged thereby to act lawfully, because of itself from its subjective constitution it can only be determined by the conception of good. Therefore no imperatives hold for the Divine will, or in general for a holy will; ought is here out of place, because the volition is already of itself necessarily in unison with the law. Therefore imperatives are only formulae to express the relation of objective laws of all volition to the subjective imperfection of the will of this or that rational being, e.g., the human will.

Now all imperatives command either hypothetically or categorically. The former represent the practical necessity of a possible action as means to something else that is willed (or at least which one might possibly will). The categorical imperative would be that which represented an action as necessary of itself without reference to another end, i.e., as objectively necessary.

Since every practical law represents a possible action as good and, on this account, for a subject who is practically determinable by reason, necessary, all imperatives are formulae determining an action which is necessary according to the principle of a will good in some respects. If now the action is good only as a means to something else, then the imperative is hypothetical; if it is conceived as good in itself and consequently as being necessarily the principle of a will which of itself conforms to reason, then it is categorical.

Thus the imperative declares what action possible by me would be good and presents the practical rule in relation to a will which does not forthwith perform an action simply because it is good, whether because the subject does not always know that it is good, or because, even if it know this, yet its maxims might be opposed to the objective principles of practical reason.

Accordingly the hypothetical imperative only says that the action is good for some purpose, possible or actual. In the first case it is a problematical, in the second an assertorial practical principle. The categorical imperative which declares an action to be objectively necessary in itself without reference to any purpose, i.e., without any other end, is valid as an apodeictic (practical) principle.

Whatever is possible only by the power of some rational being may also be conceived as a possible purpose of some will; and therefore the principles of action as regards the means necessary to attain some possible purpose are in fact infinitely numerous. All sciences have a practical part, consisting of problems expressing that some end is possible for us and of imperatives directing how it may be attained. These may, therefore, be called in general imperatives of skill. Here there is no question whether the end is rational and good, but only what one must do in order to attain it. The precepts for the physician to make his patient thoroughly healthy, and for a poisoner to ensure certain death, are of equal value in this respect, that each serves to effect its purpose perfectly. Since in early youth it

3 The dependence of the desires on sensations is called inclination, and this accordingly always indicates a want. The dependence of a contingently determinable will on principles of reason is called an interest. This therefore, is found only in the case of a dependent will which does not always of itself conform to reason; in the Divine will we cannot conceive any interest. But the human will can also take an interest in a thing without therefore acting from interest. The former signifies the practical interest in the action, the latter the pathological in the object of the action. The former indicates only dependence of the will on principles of reason in themselves; the second, dependence on principles of reason for the sake of inclination, reason supplying only the practical rules how the requirement of the inclination may be satisfied. In the first case the action interests me; in the second the object of the action (because it is pleasant to me). We have seen in the first section that in an action done from duty we must look not to the interest in the object, but only to that in the action itself, and in its rational principle (viz., the law).

cannot be known what ends are likely to occur to us in the course of life, parents seek to have their children taught a great many things, and provide for their skill in the use of means for all sorts of arbitrary ends, of none of which can they determine whether it may not perhaps hereafter be an object to their pupil, but which it is at all events possible that he might aim at; and this anxiety is so great that they commonly neglect to form and correct their judgement on the value of the things which may be chosen as ends.

There is one end, however, which may be assumed to be actually such to all rational beings (so far as imperatives apply to them, viz., as dependent beings), and, therefore, one purpose which they not merely may have, but which we may with certainty assume that they all actually have by a natural necessity, and this is happiness. The hypothetical imperative which expresses the practical necessity of an action as means to the advancement of happiness is assertorial. We are not to present it as necessary for an uncertain and merely possible purpose, but for a purpose which we may presuppose with certainty and a priori in every man, because it belongs to his being. Now skill in the choice of means to his own greatest well-being may be called prudence,[4] in the narrowest sense. And thus the imperative which refers to the choice of means to one's own happiness, i.e., the precept of prudence, is still always hypothetical; the action is not commanded absolutely, but only as means to another purpose.

Finally, there is an imperative which commands a certain conduct immediately, without having as its condition any other purpose to be attained by it. This imperative is categorical. It concerns not the matter of the action, or its intended result, but its form and the principle of which it is itself a result; and what is essentially good in it consists in the mental disposition, let the consequence be what it may. This imperative may be called that of morality.

There is a marked distinction also between the volitions on these three sorts of principles in the dissimilarity of the obligation of the will. In order to mark this difference more clearly, I think they would be most suitably named in their order if we said they are either rules of skill, or counsels of prudence, or commands (laws) of morality. For it is law only that involves the conception of an unconditional and objective necessity, which is consequently universally valid; and commands are laws which must be obeyed, that is, must be followed, even in opposition to inclination. Counsels, indeed, involve necessity, but one which can only hold under a contingent subjective condition, viz., they depend on whether this or that man reckons this or that as part of his happiness; the categorical imperative, on the contrary, is not limited by any condition, and as being absolutely, although practically, necessary, may be quite properly called a command. We might also call the first kind of imperatives technical (belonging to art), the second pragmatic[5] (to welfare), the third moral (belonging to free conduct generally, that is, to morals).

Now arises the question, how are all these imperatives possible? This question does not seek to know how we can conceive the accomplishment of the action which the imperative ordains, but merely how we can conceive the obligation of the will which the imperative expresses. No special explanation is needed to show how an imperative of skill is possible. Whoever wills the end, wills also (so far as reason decides his conduct) the means in his power which are indispensably necessary thereto. This proposition is, as regards the volition, analytical; for, in willing an object as my effect, there is already thought the causality of myself as an acting cause, that is to say, the use of the means; and the imperative educes from the conception of volition of an end the conception of actions necessary to this end. Synthetical propositions must no doubt be employed in defining the means to a proposed end; but they do not concern the principle, the act of the will, but the object and its realization. E.g., that in order to bisect a line on an unerring principle I must draw from its extremities two intersecting arcs; this no doubt is taught by mathematics only in synthetical propositions; but if I know that it is only by this process that the intended operation can be performed, then to say that, if I fully will the operation, I also will the action required for it, is an analytical proposition; for it is one and the same thing to conceive something as an effect which I can produce in a certain way, and to conceive myself as acting in this way.

---

4 The word prudence is taken in two senses: in the one it may bear the name of knowledge of the world, in the other that of private prudence. The former is a man's ability to influence others so as to use them for his own purposes. The latter is the sagacity to combine all these purposes for his own lasting benefit. This latter is properly that to which the value even of the former is reduced, and when a man is prudent in the former sense, but not in the latter, we might better say of him that he is clever and cunning, but, on the whole, imprudent.

5 It seems to me that the proper signification of the word pragmatic may be most accurately defined in this way. For sanctions are called pragmatic which flow properly not from the law of the states as necessary enactments, but from precaution for the general welfare. A history is composed pragmatically when it teaches prudence, i.e., instructs the world how it can provide for its interests better, or at least as well as, the men of former time.

If it were only equally easy to give a definite conception of happiness, the imperatives of prudence would correspond exactly with those of skill, and would likewise be analytical. For in this case as in that, it could be said: "Whoever wills the end, wills also (according to the dictate of reason necessarily) the indispensable means thereto which are in his power." But, unfortunately, the notion of happiness is so indefinite that although every man wishes to attain it, yet he never can say definitely and consistently what it is that he really wishes and wills. The reason of this is that all the elements which belong to the notion of happiness are altogether empirical, i.e., they must be borrowed from experience, and nevertheless the idea of happiness requires an absolute whole, a maximum of welfare in my present and all future circumstances. Now it is impossible that the most clear-sighted and at the same time most powerful being (supposed finite) should frame to himself a definite conception of what he really wills in this. Does he will riches, how much anxiety, envy, and snares might he not thereby draw upon his shoulders? Does he will knowledge and discernment, perhaps it might prove to be only an eye so much the sharper to show him so much the more fearfully the evils that are now concealed from him, and that cannot be avoided, or to impose more wants on his desires, which already give him concern enough. Would he have long life? who guarantees to him that it would not be a long misery? would he at least have health? how often has uneasiness of the body restrained from excesses into which perfect health would have allowed one to fall? and so on. In short, he is unable, on any principle, to determine with certainty what would make him truly happy; because to do so he would need to be omniscient. We cannot therefore act on any definite principles to secure happiness, but only on empirical counsels, e.g. of regimen, frugality, courtesy, reserve, etc., which experience teaches do, on the average, most promote well-being. Hence it follows that the imperatives of prudence do not, strictly speaking, command at all, that is, they cannot present actions objectively as practically necessary; that they are rather to be regarded as counsels (consilia) than precepts precepts of reason, that the problem to determine certainly and universally what action would promote the happiness of a rational being is completely insoluble, and consequently no imperative respecting it is possible which should, in the strict sense, command to do what makes happy; because happiness is not an ideal of reason but of imagination, resting solely on empirical grounds, and it is vain to expect that these should define an action by which one could attain the totality of a series of consequences which is really endless. This imperative of prudence would however be an analytical proposition if we assume that the means to happiness could be certainly assigned; for it is distinguished from the imperative of skill only by this, that in the latter the end is merely possible, in the former it is given; as however both only ordain the means to that which we suppose to be willed as an end, it follows that the imperative which ordains the willing of the means to him who wills the end is in both cases analytical. Thus there is no difficulty in regard to the possibility of an imperative of this kind either.

On the other hand, the question how the imperative of morality is possible, is undoubtedly one, the only one, demanding a solution, as this is not at all hypothetical, and the objective necessity which it presents cannot rest on any hypothesis, as is the case with the hypothetical imperatives. Only here we must never leave out of consideration that we cannot make out by any example, in other words empirically, whether there is such an imperative at all, but it is rather to be feared that all those which seem to be categorical may yet be at bottom hypothetical. For instance, when the precept is: "Thou shalt not promise deceitfully"; and it is assumed that the necessity of this is not a mere counsel to avoid some other evil, so that it should mean: "Thou shalt not make a lying promise, lest if it become known thou shouldst destroy thy credit," but that an action of this kind must be regarded as evil in itself, so that the imperative of the prohibition is categorical; then we cannot show with certainty in any example that the will was determined merely by the law, without any other spring of action, although it may appear to be so. For it is always possible that fear of disgrace, perhaps also obscure dread of other dangers, may have a secret influence on the will. Who can prove by experience the non-existence of a cause when all that experience tells us is that we do not perceive it? But in such a case the so-called moral imperative, which as such appears to be categorical and unconditional, would in reality be only a pragmatic precept, drawing our attention to our own interests and merely teaching us to take these into consideration.

We shall therefore have to investigate a priori the possibility of a categorical imperative, as we have not in this case the advantage of its reality being given in experience, so that [the elucidation of] its possibility should be requisite only for its explanation, not for its establishment. In the meantime it may be discerned beforehand that the categorical imperative alone has the purport of a practical law; all the rest may indeed be called principles of the will but not laws, since whatever is only necessary for the attainment of some arbitrary purpose may be considered as in itself contingent, and we can at any time be free from the precept if we give up the purpose; on the contrary, the unconditional command leaves the will no liberty to choose the opposite; consequently it alone carries with it that necessity which we require in a law.

Secondly, in the case of this categorical imperative or law of morality, the difficulty (of discerning its possibility) is a very profound one. It is an a priori synthetical practical proposition;[6] and as there is so much difficulty in discerning the possibility of speculative propositions of this kind, it may readily be supposed that the difficulty will be no less with the practical.

In this problem we will first inquire whether the mere conception of a categorical imperative may not perhaps supply us also with the formula of it, containing the proposition which alone can be a categorical imperative; for even if we know the tenor of such an absolute command, yet how it is possible will require further special and laborious study, which we postpone to the last section.

When I conceive a hypothetical imperative, in general I do not know beforehand what it will contain until I am given the condition. But when I conceive a categorical imperative, I know at once what it contains. For as the imperative contains besides the law only the necessity that the maxims[7] shall conform to this law, while the law contains no conditions restricting it, there remains nothing but the general statement that the maxim of the action should conform to a universal law, and it is this conformity alone that the imperative properly represents as necessary.

There is therefore but one categorical imperative, namely, this: Act only on that maxim whereby thou canst at the same time will that it should become a universal law.

Now if all imperatives of duty can be deduced from this one imperative as from their principle, then, although it should remain undecided what is called duty is not merely a vain notion, yet at least we shall be able to show what we understand by it and what this notion means.

Since the universality of the law according to which effects are produced constitutes what is properly called nature in the most general sense (as to form), that is the existence of things so far as it is determined by general laws, the imperative of duty may be expressed thus: Act as if the maxim of thy action were to become by thy will a universal law of nature.

We will now enumerate a few duties, adopting the usual division of them into duties to ourselves and ourselves and to others, and into perfect and imperfect duties.[8]

1. A man reduced to despair by a series of misfortunes feels wearied of life, but is still so far in possession of his reason that he can ask himself whether it would not be contrary to his duty to himself to take his own life. Now he inquires whether the maxim of his action could become a universal law of nature. His maxim is: "From self-love I adopt it as a principle to shorten my life when its longer duration is likely to bring more evil than satisfaction." It is asked then simply whether this principle founded on self-love can become a universal law of nature. Now we see at once that a system of nature of which it should be a law to destroy life by means of the very feeling whose special nature it is to impel to the improvement of life would contradict itself and, therefore, could not exist as a system of nature; hence that maxim cannot possibly exist as a universal law of nature and, consequently, would be wholly inconsistent with the supreme principle of all duty.
2. Another finds himself forced by necessity to borrow money. He knows that he will not be able to repay it, but sees also that nothing will be lent to him unless he promises stoutly to repay it in a definite time. He desires to make this promise, but he has still so much conscience as to ask himself: "Is it not unlawful and inconsistent with duty

6 I connect the act with the will without presupposing any condition resulting from any inclination, but a priori, and therefore necessarily (though only objectively, i.e., assuming the idea of a reason possessing full power over all subjective motives). This is accordingly a practical proposition which does not deduce the willing of an action by mere analysis from another already presupposed (for we have not such a perfect will), but connects it immediately with the conception of the will of a rational being, as something not contained in it.

7 A maxim is a subjective principle of action, and must be distinguished from the objective principle, namely, practical law. The former contains the practical rule set by reason according to the conditions of the subject (often its ignorance or its inclinations), so that it is the principle on which the subject acts; but the law is the objective principle valid for every rational being, and is the principle on which it ought to act that is an imperative.

8 It must be noted here that I reserve the division of duties for a future metaphysic of morals; so that I give it here only as an arbitrary one (in order to arrange my examples). For the rest, I understand by a perfect duty one that admits no exception in favour of inclination and then I have not merely external but also internal perfect duties. This is contrary to the use of the word adopted in the schools; but I do not intend to justify there, as it is all one for my purpose whether it is admitted or not.

to get out of a difficulty in this way?" Suppose however that he resolves to do so: then the maxim of his action would be expressed thus: "When I think myself in want of money, I will borrow money and promise to repay it, although I know that I never can do so." Now this principle of self-love or of one's own advantage may perhaps be consistent with my whole future welfare; but the question now is, "Is it right?" I change then the suggestion of self-love into a universal law, and state the question thus: "How would it be if my maxim were a universal law?" Then I see at once that it could never hold as a universal law of nature, but would necessarily contradict itself. For supposing it to be a universal law that everyone when he thinks himself in a difficulty should be able to promise whatever he pleases, with the purpose of not keeping his promise, the promise itself would become impossible, as well as the end that one might have in view in it, since no one would consider that anything was promised to him, but would ridicule all such statements as vain pretences.

3. A third finds in himself a talent which with the help of some culture might make him a useful man in many respects. But he finds himself in comfortable circumstances and prefers to indulge in pleasure rather than to take pains in enlarging and improving his happy natural capacities. He asks, however, whether his maxim of neglect of his natural gifts, besides agreeing with his inclination to indulgence, agrees also with what is called duty. He sees then that a system of nature could indeed subsist with such a universal law although men (like the South Sea islanders) should let their talents rest and resolve to devote their lives merely to idleness, amusement, and propagation of their species—in a word, to enjoyment; but he cannot possibly will that this should be a universal law of nature, or be implanted in us as such by a natural instinct. For, as a rational being, he necessarily wills that his faculties be developed, since they serve him and have been given him, for all sorts of possible purposes.
4. A fourth, who is in prosperity, while he sees that others have to contend with great wretchedness and that he could help them, thinks: "What concern is it of mine? Let everyone be as happy as Heaven pleases, or as he can make himself; I will take nothing from him nor even envy him, only I do not wish to contribute anything to his welfare or to his assistance in distress!" Now no doubt if such a mode of thinking were a universal law, the human race might very well subsist and doubtless even better than in a state in which everyone talks of sympathy and good-will, or even takes care occasionally to put it into practice, but, on the other side, also cheats when he can, betrays the rights of men, or otherwise violates them. But although it is possible that a universal law of nature might exist in accordance with that maxim, it is impossible to will that such a principle should have the universal validity of a law of nature. For a will which resolved this would contradict itself, inasmuch as many cases might occur in which one would have need of the love and sympathy of others, and in which, by such a law of nature, sprung from his own will, he would deprive himself of all hope of the aid he desires.

These are a few of the many actual duties, or at least what we regard as such, which obviously fall into two classes on the one principle that we have laid down. We must be able to will that a maxim of our action should be a universal law. This is the canon of the moral appreciation of the action generally. Some actions are of such a character that their maxim cannot without contradiction be even conceived as a universal law of nature, far from it being possible that we should will that it should be so. In others this intrinsic impossibility is not found, but still it is impossible to will that their maxim should be raised to the universality of a law of nature, since such a will would contradict itself It is easily seen that the former violate strict or rigorous (inflexible) duty; the latter only laxer (meritorious) duty. Thus it has been completely shown how all duties depend as regards the nature of the obligation (not the object of the action) on the same principle.

If now we attend to ourselves on occasion of any transgression of duty, we shall find that we in fact do not will that our maxim should be a universal law, for that is impossible for us; on the contrary, we will that the opposite should remain a universal law, only we assume the liberty of making an exception in our own favour or (just for this time only) in favour of our inclination. Consequently if we considered all cases from one and the same point of view, namely, that of reason, we should find a contradiction in our own will, namely, that a certain principle should be objectively necessary as a universal law, and yet subjectively should not be universal, but admit of exceptions. As however we at one moment regard our action from the point of view of a will wholly conformed to reason, and then again look at the same action from the point of view of a will affected by inclination, there is not really any contradiction, but an antagonism of inclination to the precept of reason, whereby the universality of the principle is changed into a mere generality, so that the practical principle of reason shall meet the maxim half way. Now, although this cannot be justified in our own impartial judgement, yet it proves that we do really recognise the validity of the categorical imperative and (with all respect for it) only allow ourselves a few exceptions, which we think unimportant and forced from us.

We have thus established at least this much, that if duty is a conception which is to have any import and real legislative authority for our actions, it can only be expressed in categorical and not at all in hypothetical imperatives. We have also, which is of great importance, exhibited clearly and definitely for every practical application the content of the categorical imperative, which must contain the principle of all duty if there is such a thing at all. We have not yet, however, advanced so far as to prove a priori that there actually is such an imperative, that there is a practical law which commands absolutely of itself and without any other impulse, and that the following of this law is duty.

With the view of attaining to this, it is of extreme importance to remember that we must not allow ourselves to think of deducing the reality of this principle from the particular attributes of human nature. For duty is to be a practical, unconditional necessity of action; it must therefore hold for all rational beings (to whom an imperative can apply at all), and for this reason only be also a law for all human wills. On the contrary, whatever is deduced from the particular natural characteristics of humanity, from certain feelings and propensions, nay, even, if possible, from any particular tendency proper to human reason, and which need not necessarily hold for the will of every rational being; this may indeed supply us with a maxim, but not with a law; with a subjective principle on which we may have a propension and inclination to act, but not with an objective principle on which we should be enjoined to act, even though all our propensions, inclinations, and natural dispositions were opposed to it. In fact, the sublimity and intrinsic dignity of the command in duty are so much the more evident, the less the subjective impulses favour it and the more they oppose it, without being able in the slightest degree to weaken the obligation of the law or to diminish its validity.

Here then we see philosophy brought to a critical position, since it has to be firmly fixed, notwithstanding that it has nothing to support it in heaven or earth. Here it must show its purity as absolute director of its own laws, not the herald of those which are whispered to it by an implanted sense or who knows what tutelary nature. Although these may be better than nothing, yet they can never afford principles dictated by reason, which must have their source wholly a priori and thence their commanding authority, expecting everything from the supremacy of the law and the due respect for it, nothing from inclination, or else condemning the man to self-contempt and inward abhorrence.

Thus every empirical element is not only quite incapable of being an aid to the principle of morality, but is even highly prejudicial to the purity of morals, for the proper and inestimable worth of an absolutely good will consists just in this, that the principle of action is free from all influence of contingent grounds, which alone experience can furnish. We cannot too much or too often repeat our warning against this lax and even mean habit of thought which seeks for its principle amongst empirical motives and laws; for human reason in its weariness is glad to rest on this pillow, and in a dream of sweet illusions (in which, instead of Juno, it embraces a cloud) it substitutes for morality a bastard patched up from limbs of various derivation, which looks like anything one chooses to see in it, only not like virtue to one who has once beheld her in her true form.[9]

The question then is this: "Is it a necessary law for all rational beings that they should always judge of their actions by maxims of which they can themselves will that they should serve as universal laws?" If it is so, then it must be connected (altogether a priori) with the very conception of the will of a rational being generally. But in order to discover this connexion we must, however reluctantly, take a step into metaphysic, although into a domain of it which is distinct from speculative philosophy, namely, the metaphysic of morals. In a practical philosophy, where it is not the reasons of what happens that we have to ascertain, but the laws of what ought to happen, even although it never does, i.e., objective practical laws, there it is not necessary to inquire into the reasons why anything pleases or displeases, how the pleasure of mere sensation differs from taste, and whether the latter is distinct from a general satisfaction of reason; on what the feeling of pleasure or pain rests, and how from it desires and inclinations arise, and from these again maxims by the co-operation of reason: for all this belongs to an empirical psychology, which would constitute the second part of physics, if we regard physics as the philosophy of nature, so far as it is based on empirical laws. But here we are concerned with objective practical laws and, consequently, with the relation of the

9 To behold virtue in her proper form is nothing else but to contemplate morality stripped of all admixture of sensible things and of every spurious ornament of reward or self-love. How much she then eclipses everything else that appears charming to the affections, every one may readily perceive with the least exertion of his reason, if it be not wholly spoiled for abstraction.

will to itself so far as it is determined by reason alone, in which case whatever has reference to anything empirical is necessarily excluded; since if reason of itself alone determines the conduct (and it is the possibility of this that we are now investigating), it must necessarily do so a priori.

The will is conceived as a faculty of determining oneself to action in accordance with the conception of certain laws. And such a faculty can be found only in rational beings. Now that which serves the will as the objective ground of its self-determination is the end, and, if this is assigned by reason alone, it must hold for all rational beings. On the other hand, that which merely contains the ground of possibility of the action of which the effect is the end, this is called the means. The subjective ground of the desire is the spring, the objective ground of the volition is the motive; hence the distinction between subjective ends which rest on springs, and objective ends which depend on motives valid for every rational being. Practical principles are formal when they abstract from all subjective ends; they are material when they assume these, and therefore particular springs of action. The ends which a rational being proposes to himself at pleasure as effects of his actions (material ends) are all only relative, for it is only their relation to the particular desires of the subject that gives them their worth, which therefore cannot furnish principles universal and necessary for all rational beings and for every volition, that is to say practical laws. Hence all these relative ends can give rise only to hypothetical imperatives.

Supposing, however, that there were something whose existence has in itself an absolute worth, something which, being an end in itself, could be a source of definite laws; then in this and this alone would lie the source of a possible categorical imperative, i.e., a practical law.

Now I say: man and generally any rational being exists as an end in himself, not merely as a means to be arbitrarily used by this or that will, but in all his actions, whether they concern himself or other rational beings, must be always regarded at the same time as an end. All objects of the inclinations have only a conditional worth, for if the inclinations and the wants founded on them did not exist, then their object would be without value. But the inclinations, themselves being sources of want, are so far from having an absolute worth for which they should be desired that on the contrary it must be the universal wish of every rational being to be wholly free from them. Thus the worth of any object which is to be acquired by our action is always conditional. Beings whose existence depends not on our will but on nature's, have nevertheless, if they are irrational beings, only a relative value as means, and are therefore called things; rational beings, on the contrary, are called persons, because their very nature points them out as ends in themselves, that is as something which must not be used merely as means, and so far therefore restricts freedom of action (and is an object of respect). These, therefore, are not merely subjective ends whose existence has a worth for us as an effect of our action, but objective ends, that is, things whose existence is an end in itself; an end moreover for which no other can be substituted, which they should subserve merely as means, for otherwise nothing whatever would possess absolute worth; but if all worth were conditioned and therefore contingent, then there would be no supreme practical principle of reason whatever.

If then there is a supreme practical principle or, in respect of the human will, a categorical imperative, it must be one which, being drawn from the conception of that which is necessarily an end for everyone because it is an end in itself, constitutes an objective principle of will, and can therefore serve as a universal practical law. The foundation of this principle is: rational nature exists as an end in itself. Man necessarily conceives his own existence as being so; so far then this is a subjective principle of human actions. But every other rational being regards its existence similarly, just on the same rational principle that holds for me:[10] so that it is at the same time an objective principle, from which as a supreme practical law all laws of the will must be capable of being deduced. Accordingly the practical imperative will be as follows: So act as to treat humanity, whether in thine own person or in that of any other, in every case as an end withal, never as means only. We will now inquire whether this can be practically carried out.

To abide by the previous examples:

Firstly, under the head of necessary duty to oneself: He who contemplates suicide should ask himself whether his action can be consistent with the idea of humanity as an end in itself. If he destroys himself in order to escape from painful circumstances, he uses a person merely as a mean to maintain a tolerable condition up to the end of life. But a man is not a thing, that is to say, something which can be used merely as means, but must in all his actions be always considered as an end in himself. I cannot, therefore, dispose in any way of a man in my own person so as

---

10 This proposition is here stated as a postulate. The ground of it will be found in the concluding section.

to mutilate him, to damage or kill him. (It belongs to ethics proper to define this principle more precisely, so as to avoid all misunderstanding, e.g., as to the amputation of the limbs in order to preserve myself, as to exposing my life to danger with a view to preserve it, etc. This question is therefore omitted here.)

Secondly, as regards necessary duties, or those of strict obligation, towards others: He who is thinking of making a lying promise to others will see at once that he would be using another man merely as a mean, without the latter containing at the same time the end in himself. For he whom I propose by such a promise to use for my own purposes cannot possibly assent to my mode of acting towards him and, therefore, cannot himself contain the end of this action. This violation of the principle of humanity in other men is more obvious if we take in examples of attacks on the freedom and property of others. For then it is clear that he who transgresses the rights of men intends to use the person of others merely as a means, without considering that as rational beings they ought always to be esteemed also as ends, that is, as beings who must be capable of containing in themselves the end of the very same action.[11]

Thirdly, as regards contingent (meritorious) duties to oneself: It is not enough that the action does not violate humanity in our own person as an end in itself, it must also harmonize with it. Now there are in humanity capacities of greater perfection, which belong to the end that nature has in view in regard to humanity in ourselves as the subject: to neglect these might perhaps be consistent with the maintenance of humanity as an end in itself, but not with the advancement of this end.

Fourthly, as regards meritorious duties towards others: The natural end which all men have is their own happiness. Now humanity might indeed subsist, although no one should contribute anything to the happiness of others, provided he did not intentionally withdraw anything from it; but after all this would only harmonize negatively not positively with humanity as an end in itself, if every one does not also endeavour, as far as in him lies, to forward the ends of others. For the ends of any subject which is an end in himself ought as far as possible to be my ends also, if that conception is to have its full effect with me.

This principle, that humanity and generally every rational nature is an end in itself (which is the supreme limiting condition of every man's freedom of action), is not borrowed from experience, firstly, because it is universal, applying as it does to all rational beings whatever, and experience is not capable of determining anything about them; secondly, because it does not present humanity as an end to men (subjectively), that is as an object which men do of themselves actually adopt as an end; but as an objective end, which must as a law constitute the supreme limiting condition of all our subjective ends, let them be what we will; it must therefore spring from pure reason. In fact the objective principle of all practical legislation lies (according to the first principle) in the rule and its form of universality which makes it capable of being a law (say, e. g., a law of nature); but the subjective principle is in the end; now by the second principle the subject of all ends is each rational being, inasmuch as it is an end in itself. Hence follows the third practical principle of the will, which is the ultimate condition of its harmony with universal practical reason, viz.: the idea of the will of every rational being as a universally legislative will.

On this principle all maxims are rejected which are inconsistent with the will being itself universal legislator. Thus the will is not subject simply to the law, but so subject that it must be regarded as itself giving the law and, on this ground only, subject to the law (of which it can regard itself as the author).

In the previous imperatives, namely, that based on the conception of the conformity of actions to general laws, as in a physical system of nature, and that based on the universal prerogative of rational beings as ends in themselves—these imperatives, just because they were conceived as categorical, excluded from any share in their authority all admixture of any interest as a spring of action; they were, however, only assumed to be categorical, because such an assumption was necessary to explain the conception of duty. But we could not prove independently that there are practical propositions which command categorically, nor can it be proved in this section; one thing, however, could be done, namely, to indicate in the imperative itself, by some determinate expression, that in the case of volition from duty all interest is renounced, which is the specific criterion of categorical as distinguished from hypothetical

11 Let it not be thought that the common "quod tibi non vis fieri, etc." could serve here as the rule or principle. For it is only a deduction from the former, though with several limitations; it cannot be a universal law, for it does not contain the principle of duties to oneself, nor of the duties of benevolence to others ( for many a one would gladly consent that others should not benefit him, provided only that he might be excused from showing benevolence to them), nor finally that of duties of strict obligation to one another, for on this principle the criminal might argue against the judge who punishes him, and so on.

imperatives. This is done in the present (third) formula of the principle, namely, in the idea of the will of every rational being as a universally legislating will.

For although a will which is subject to laws may be attached to this law by means of an interest, yet a will which is itself a supreme lawgiver so far as it is such cannot possibly depend on any interest, since a will so dependent would itself still need another law restricting the interest of its self-love by the condition that it should be valid as universal law.

Thus the principle that every human will is a will which in all its maxims gives universal laws,[12] provided it be otherwise justified, would be very well adapted to be the categorical imperative, in this respect, namely, that just because of the idea of universal legislation it is not based on interest, and therefore it alone among all possible imperatives can be unconditional. Or still better, converting the proposition, if there is a categorical imperative (i.e., a law for the will of every rational being), it can only command that everything be done from maxims of one's will regarded as a will which could at the same time will that it should itself give universal laws, for in that case only the practical principle and the imperative which it obeys are unconditional, since they cannot be based on any interest.

Looking back now on all previous attempts to discover the principle of morality, we need not wonder why they all failed. It was seen that man was bound to laws by duty, but it was not observed that the laws to which he is subject are only those of his own giving, though at the same time they are universal, and that he is only bound to act in conformity with his own will; a will, however, which is designed by nature to give universal laws. For when one has conceived man only as subject to a law (no matter what), then this law required some interest, either by way of attraction or constraint, since it did not originate as a law from his own will, but this will was according to a law obliged by something else to act in a certain manner. Now by this necessary consequence all the labour spent in finding a supreme principle of duty was irrevocably lost. For men never elicited duty, but only a necessity of acting from a certain interest. Whether this interest was private or otherwise, in any case the imperative must be conditional and could not by any means be capable of being a moral command. I will therefore call this the principle of autonomy of the will, in contrast with every other which I accordingly reckon as heteronomy.

The conception of the will of every rational being as one which must consider itself as giving in all the maxims of its will universal laws, so as to judge itself and its actions from this point of view—this conception leads to another which depends on it and is very fruitful, namely that of a kingdom of ends.

By a kingdom I understand the union of different rational beings in a system by common laws. Now since it is by laws that ends are determined as regards their universal validity, hence, if we abstract from the personal differences of rational beings and likewise from all the content of their private ends, we shall be able to conceive all ends combined in a systematic whole (including both rational beings as ends in themselves, and also the special ends which each may propose to himself), that is to say, we can conceive a kingdom of ends, which on the preceding principles is possible.

For all rational beings come under the law that each of them must treat itself and all others never merely as means, but in every case at the same time as ends in themselves. Hence results a systematic union of rational being by common objective laws, i.e., a kingdom which may be called a kingdom of ends, since what these laws have in view is just the relation of these beings to one another as ends and means. It is certainly only an ideal.

A rational being belongs as a member to the kingdom of ends when, although giving universal laws in it, he is also himself subject to these laws. He belongs to it as sovereign when, while giving laws, he is not subject to the will of any other.

A rational being must always regard himself as giving laws either as member or as sovereign in a kingdom of ends which is rendered possible by the freedom of will. He cannot, however, maintain the latter position merely by the maxims of his will, but only in case he is a completely independent being without wants and with unrestricted power adequate to his will.

Morality consists then in the reference of all action to the legislation which alone can render a kingdom of ends possible. This legislation must be capable of existing in every rational being and of emanating from his will, so that the principle of this will is never to act on any maxim which could not without contradiction be also a universal law

12 I may be excused from adducing examples to elucidate this principle, as those which have already been used to elucidate the categorical imperative and its formula would all serve for the like purpose here.

and, accordingly, always so to act that the will could at the same time regard itself as giving in its maxims universal laws. If now the maxims of rational beings are not by their own nature coincident with this objective principle, then the necessity of acting on it is called practical necessitation, i.e., duty. Duty does not apply to the sovereign in the kingdom of ends, but it does to every member of it and to all in the same degree.

The practical necessity of acting on this principle, i.e., duty, does not rest at all on feelings, impulses, or inclinations, but solely on the relation of rational beings to one another, a relation in which the will of a rational being must always be regarded as legislative, since otherwise it could not be conceived as an end in itself. Reason then refers every maxim of the will, regarding it as legislating universally, to every other will and also to every action towards oneself; and this not on account of any other practical motive or any future advantage, but from the idea of the dignity of a rational being, obeying no law but that which he himself also gives.

In the kingdom of ends everything has either value or dignity. Whatever has a value can be replaced by something else which is equivalent; whatever, on the other hand, is above all value, and therefore admits of no equivalent, has a dignity.

Whatever has reference to the general inclinations and wants of mankind has a market value; whatever, without presupposing a want, corresponds to a certain taste, that is to a satisfaction in the mere purposeless play of our faculties, has a fancy value; but that which constitutes the condition under which alone anything can be an end in itself, this has not merely a relative worth, i.e., value, but an intrinsic worth, that is, dignity.

Now morality is the condition under which alone a rational being can be an end in himself, since by this alone is it possible that he should be a legislating member in the kingdom of ends. Thus morality, and humanity as capable of it, is that which alone has dignity. Skill and diligence in labour have a market value; wit, lively imagination, and humour, have fancy value; on the other hand, fidelity to promises, benevolence from principle (not from instinct), have an intrinsic worth. Neither nature nor art contains anything which in default of these it could put in their place, for their worth consists not in the effects which spring from them, not in the use and advantage which they secure, but in the disposition of mind, that is, the maxims of the will which are ready to manifest themselves in such actions, even though they should not have the desired effect. These actions also need no recommendation from any subjective taste or sentiment, that they may be looked on with immediate favour and satisfaction: they need no immediate propension or feeling for them; they exhibit the will that performs them as an object of an immediate respect, and nothing but reason is required to impose them on the will; not to flatter it into them, which, in the case of duties, would be a contradiction. This estimation therefore shows that the worth of such a disposition is dignity, and places it infinitely above all value, with which it cannot for a moment be brought into comparison or competition without as it were violating its sanctity.

What then is it which justifies virtue or the morally good disposition, in making such lofty claims? It is nothing less than the privilege it secures to the rational being of participating in the giving of universal laws, by which it qualifies him to be a member of a possible kingdom of ends, a privilege to which he was already destined by his own nature as being an end in himself and, on that account, legislating in the kingdom of ends; free as regards all laws of physical nature, and obeying those only which he himself gives, and by which his maxims can belong to a system of universal law, to which at the same time he submits himself. For nothing has any worth except what the law assigns it. Now the legislation itself which assigns the worth of everything must for that very reason possess dignity, that is an unconditional incomparable worth; and the word respect alone supplies a becoming expression for the esteem which a rational being must have for it. Autonomy then is the basis of the dignity of human and of every rational nature.

The three modes of presenting the principle of morality that have been adduced are at bottom only so many formulae of the very same law, and each of itself involves the other two. There is, however, a difference in them, but it is rather subjectively than objectively practical, intended namely to bring an idea of the reason nearer to intuition (by means of a certain analogy) and thereby nearer to feeling. All maxims, in fact, have:

1. A form, consisting in universality; and in this view the formula of the moral imperative is expressed thus, that the maxims must be so chosen as if they were to serve as universal laws of nature.
2. A matter, namely, an end, and here the formula says that the rational being, as it is an end by its own nature and therefore an end in itself, must in every maxim serve as the condition limiting all merely relative and arbitrary ends.

3. A complete characterization of all maxims by means of that formula, namely, that all maxims ought by their own legislation to harmonize with a possible kingdom of ends as with a kingdom of nature.[13] There is a progress here in the order of the categories of unity of the form of the will (its universality), plurality of the matter (the objects, i.e., the ends), and totality of the system of these. In forming our moral judgement of actions, it is better to proceed always on the strict method and start from the general formula of the categorical imperative: Act according to a maxim which can at the same time make itself a universal law. If, however, we wish to gain an entrance for the moral law, it is very useful to bring one and the same action under the three specified conceptions, and thereby as far as possible to bring it nearer to intuition.

We can now end where we started at the beginning, namely, with the conception of a will unconditionally good. That will is absolutely good which cannot be evil—in other words, whose maxim, if made a universal law, could never contradict itself. This principle, then, is its supreme law: "Act always on such a maxim as thou canst at the same time will to be a universal law"; this is the sole condition under which a will can never contradict itself; and such an imperative is categorical. Since the validity of the will as a universal law for possible actions is analogous to the universal connexion of the existence of things by general laws, which is the formal notion of nature in general, the categorical imperative can also be expressed thus: Act on maxims which can at the same time have for their object themselves as universal laws of nature. Such then is the formula of an absolutely good will.

Rational nature is distinguished from the rest of nature by this, that it sets before itself an end. This end would be the matter of every good will. But since in the idea of a will that is absolutely good without being limited by any condition (of attaining this or that end) we must abstract wholly from every end to be effected (since this would make every will only relatively good), it follows that in this case the end must be conceived, not as an end to be effected, but as an independently existing end. Consequently it is conceived only negatively, i.e., as that which we must never act against and which, therefore, must never be regarded merely as means, but must in every volition be esteemed as an end likewise. Now this end can be nothing but the subject of all possible ends, since this is also the subject of a possible absolutely good will; for such a will cannot without contradiction be postponed to any other object. The principle: "So act in regard to every rational being (thyself and others), that he may always have place in thy maxim as an end in himself," is accordingly essentially identical with this other: "Act upon a maxim which, at the same time, involves its own universal validity for every rational being." For that in using means for every end I should limit my maxim by the condition of its holding good as a law for every subject, this comes to the same thing as that the fundamental principle of all maxims of action must be that the subject of all ends, i.e., the rational being himself, be never employed merely as means, but as the supreme condition restricting the use of all means, that is in every case as an end likewise.

It follows incontestably that, to whatever laws any rational being may be subject, he being an end in himself must be able to regard himself as also legislating universally in respect of these same laws, since it is just this fitness of his maxims for universal legislation that distinguishes him as an end in himself; also it follows that this implies his dignity (prerogative) above all mere physical beings, that he must always take his maxims from the point of view which regards himself and, likewise, every other rational being as law-giving beings (on which account they are called persons). In this way a world of rational beings (mundus intelligibilis) is possible as a kingdom of ends, and this by virtue of the legislation proper to all persons as members. Therefore every rational being must so act as if he were by his maxims in every case a legislating member in the universal kingdom of ends. The formal principle of these maxims is: "So act as if thy maxim were to serve likewise as the universal law (of all rational beings)." A kingdom of ends is thus only possible on the analogy of a kingdom of nature, the former however only by maxims, that is self-imposed rules, the latter only by the laws of efficient causes acting under necessitation from without. Nevertheless, although the system of nature is looked upon as a machine, yet so far as it has reference to rational beings as its ends, it is given on this account the name of a kingdom of nature. Now such a kingdom of ends would be actually realized by means of maxims conforming to the canon which the categorical imperative prescribes to all rational beings, if they were universally followed. But although a rational being, even if he punctually follows this maxim himself, cannot reckon

13 Teleology considers nature as a kingdom of ends; ethics regards a possible kingdom of ends as a kingdom nature. In the first case, the kingdom of ends is a theoretical idea, adopted to explain what actually is. In the latter it is a practical idea, adopted to bring about that which is not yet, but which can be realized by our conduct, namely, if it conforms to this idea.

upon all others being therefore true to the same, nor expect that the kingdom of nature and its orderly arrangements shall be in harmony with him as a fitting member, so as to form a kingdom of ends to which he himself contributes, that is to say, that it shall favour his expectation of happiness, still that law: "Act according to the maxims of a member of a merely possible kingdom of ends legislating in it universally," remains in its full force, inasmuch as it commands categorically. And it is just in this that the paradox lies; that the mere dignity of man as a rational creature, without any other end or advantage to be attained thereby, in other words, respect for a mere idea, should yet serve as an inflexible precept of the will, and that it is precisely in this independence of the maxim on all such springs of action that its sublimity consists; and it is this that makes every rational subject worthy to be a legislative member in the kingdom of ends: for otherwise he would have to be conceived only as subject to the physical law of his wants. And although we should suppose the kingdom of nature and the kingdom of ends to be united under one sovereign, so that the latter kingdom thereby ceased to be a mere idea and acquired true reality, then it would no doubt gain the accession of a strong spring, but by no means any increase of its intrinsic worth. For this sole absolute lawgiver must, notwithstanding this, be always conceived as estimating the worth of rational beings only by their disinterested behaviour, as prescribed to themselves from that idea [the dignity of man] alone. The essence of things is not altered by their external relations, and that which, abstracting from these, alone constitutes the absolute worth of man, is also that by which he must be judged, whoever the judge may be, and even by the Supreme Being. Morality, then, is the relation of actions to the relation of actions will, that is, to the autonomy of potential universal legislation by its maxims. An action that is consistent with the autonomy of the will is permitted; one that does not agree therewith is forbidden. A will whose maxims necessarily coincide with the laws of autonomy is a holy will, good absolutely. The dependence of a will not absolutely good on the principle of autonomy (moral necessitation) is obligation. This, then, cannot be applied to a holy being. The objective necessity of actions from obligation is called duty.

From what has just been said, it is easy to see how it happens that, although the conception of duty implies subjection to the law, we yet ascribe a certain dignity and sublimity to the person who fulfils all his duties. There is not, indeed, any sublimity in him, so far as he is subject to the moral law; but inasmuch as in regard to that very law he is likewise a legislator, and on that account alone subject to it, he has sublimity. We have also shown above that neither fear nor inclination, but simply respect for the law, is the spring which can give actions a moral worth. Our own will, so far as we suppose it to act only under the condition that its maxims are potentially universal laws, this ideal will which is possible to us is the proper object of respect; and the dignity of humanity consists just in this capacity of being universally legislative, though with the condition that it is itself subject to this same legislation.

### The Autonomy of the Will as the Supreme Principle of Morality

Autonomy of the will is that property of it by which it is a law to itself (independently of any property of the objects of volition). The principle of autonomy then is: "Always so to choose that the same volition shall comprehend the maxims of our choice as a universal law." We cannot prove that this practical rule is an imperative, i.e., that the will of every rational being is necessarily bound to it as a condition, by a mere analysis of the conceptions which occur in it, since it is a synthetical proposition; we must advance beyond the cognition of the objects to a critical examination of the subject, that is, of the pure practical reason, for this synthetic proposition which commands apodeictically must be capable of being cognized wholly a priori. This matter, however, does not belong to the present section. But that the principle of autonomy in question is the sole principle of morals can be readily shown by mere analysis of the conceptions of morality. For by this analysis we find that its principle must be a categorical imperative and that what this commands is neither more nor less than this very autonomy.

### Heteronomy of the Will as the Source of all spurious Principles of Morality

If the will seeks the law which is to determine it anywhere else than in the fitness of its maxims to be universal laws of its own dictation, consequently if it goes out of itself and seeks this law in the character of any of its objects, there always results heteronomy. The will in that case does not give itself the law, but it is given by the object through its relation to the will. This relation, whether it rests on inclination or on conceptions of reason, only admits of hypothetical imperatives: "I ought to do something because I wish for something else." On the contrary, the moral, and therefore categorical, imperative says: "I ought to do so and so, even though I should not wish for anything else." E.g., the former says: "I ought not to lie, if I would retain my reputation"; the latter says: "I ought not to lie, although it should not bring me the least discredit." The latter therefore must so far abstract from all objects that they shall have no influence on the will, in order that practical reason (will) may not be restricted to administering an interest not belonging to it, but may simply show its own commanding authority as the supreme legislation. Thus, e.g., I ought to endeavour to promote the happiness of others, not as if its realization involved any concern of mine (whether by immediate inclination or by any satisfaction indirectly gained through reason), but simply because a maxim which excludes it cannot be comprehended as a universal law in one and the same volition.

### Classification of All Principles of Morality Which Can be Founded on the Conception of Heteronomy

Here as elsewhere human reason in its pure use, so long as it was not critically examined, has first tried all possible wrong ways before it succeeded in finding the one true way.

All principles which can be taken from this point of view are either empirical or rational. The former, drawn from the principle of happiness, are built on physical or moral feelings; the latter, drawn from the principle of perfection, are built either on the rational conception of perfection as a possible effect, or on that of an independent perfection (the will of God) as the determining cause of our will.

Empirical principles are wholly incapable of serving as a foundation for moral laws. For the universality with which these should hold for all rational beings without distinction, the unconditional practical necessity which is thereby imposed on them, is lost when their foundation is taken from the particular constitution of human nature, or the accidental circumstances in which it is placed. The principle of private happiness, however, is the most objectionable, not merely because it is false, and experience contradicts the supposition that prosperity is always proportioned to good conduct, nor yet merely because it contributes nothing to the establishment of morality—since it is quite a different thing to make a prosperous man and a good man, or to make one prudent and sharp-sighted for his own interests and to make him virtuous—but because the springs it provides for morality are such as rather undermine it and destroy its sublimity, since they put the motives to virtue and to vice in the same class and only teach us to make a better calculation, the specific difference between virtue and vice being entirely extinguished. On the other hand, as to moral feeling, this supposed special sense,[14] the appeal to it is indeed superficial when those who cannot think believe that feeling will help them out, even in what concerns general laws: and besides, feelings, which naturally differ infinitely in degree, cannot furnish a uniform standard of good and evil, nor has anyone a right to form judgements for others by his own feelings: nevertheless this moral feeling is nearer to morality and its dignity in this respect, that it pays virtue the honour of ascribing to her immediately the satisfaction and esteem we have for her and does not, as it were, tell her to her face that we are not attached to her by her beauty but by profit.

Amongst the rational principles of morality, the ontological conception of perfection, notwithstanding its defects, is better than the theological conception which derives morality from a Divine absolutely perfect will. The former is, no doubt, empty and indefinite and consequently useless for finding in the boundless field of possible reality the greatest amount suitable for us; moreover, in attempting to distinguish specifically the reality of which we are now speaking from every other, it inevitably tends to turn in a circle and cannot avoid tacitly presupposing the morality which it is to explain; it is nevertheless preferable to the theological view, first, because we have no intuition of the divine perfection and can only deduce it from our own conceptions, the most important of which is that of morality, and our explanation would thus be involved in a gross circle; and, in the next place, if we avoid this, the only notion of the Divine will remaining to us is a conception made up of the attributes of desire of glory and dominion, combined with the awful conceptions of might and vengeance, and any system of morals erected on this foundation would be directly opposed to morality.

However, if I had to choose between the notion of the moral sense and that of perfection in general (two systems which at least do not weaken morality, although they are totally incapable of serving as its foundation), then I should decide for the latter, because it at least withdraws the decision of the question from the sensibility and brings it to the court of pure reason; and although even here it decides nothing, it at all events preserves the indefinite idea (of a will good in itself free from corruption, until it shall be more precisely defined.

---

14 I class the principle of moral feeling under that of happiness, because every empirical interest promises to contribute to our well-being by the agreeableness that a thing affords, whether it be immediately and without a view to profit, or whether profit be regarded. We must likewise, with Hutcheson, class the principle of sympathy with the happiness of others under his assumed moral sense.

For the rest I think I may be excused here from a detailed refutation of all these doctrines; that would only be superfluous labour, since it is so easy, and is probably so well seen even by those whose office requires them to decide for one of these theories (because their hearers would not tolerate suspension of judgement). But what interests us more here is to know that the prime foundation of morality laid down by all these principles is nothing but heteronomy of the will, and for this reason they must necessarily miss their aim.

In every case where an object of the will has to be supposed, in order that the rule may be prescribed which is to determine the will, there the rule is simply heteronomy; the imperative is conditional, namely, if or because one wishes for this object, one should act so and so: hence it can never command morally, that is, categorically. Whether the object determines the will by means of inclination, as in the principle of private happiness, or by means of reason directed to objects of our possible volition generally, as in the principle of perfection, in either case the will never determines itself immediately by the conception of the action, but only by the influence which the foreseen effect of the action has on the will; I ought to do something, on this account, because I wish for something else; and here there must be yet another law assumed in me as its subject, by which I necessarily will this other thing, and this law again requires an imperative to restrict this maxim. For the influence which the conception of an object within the reach of our faculties can exercise on the will of the subject, in consequence of its natural properties, depends on the nature of the subject, either the sensibility (inclination and taste), or the understanding and reason, the employment of which is by the peculiar constitution of their nature attended with satisfaction. It follows that the law would be, properly speaking, given by nature, and, as such, it must be known and proved by experience and would consequently be contingent and therefore incapable of being an apodeictic practical rule, such as the moral rule must be. Not only so, but it is inevitably only heteronomy; the will does not give itself the law, but is given by a foreign impulse by means of a particular natural constitution of the subject adapted to receive it. An absolutely good will, then, the principle of which must be a categorical imperative, will be indeterminate as regards all objects and will contain merely the form of volition generally, and that as autonomy, that is to say, the capability of the maxims of every good will to make themselves a universal law, is itself the only law which the will of every rational being imposes on itself, without needing to assume any spring or interest as a foundation.

How such a synthetical practical a priori proposition is possible, and why it is necessary, is a problem whose solution does not lie within the bounds of the metaphysic of morals; and we have not here affirmed its truth, much less professed to have a proof of it in our power. We simply showed by the development of the universally received notion of morality that an autonomy of the will is inevitably connected with it, or rather is its foundation. Whoever then holds morality to be anything real, and not a chimerical idea without any truth, must likewise admit the principle of it that is here assigned. This section then, like the first, was merely analytical. Now to prove that morality is no creation of the brain, which it cannot be if the categorical imperative and with it the autonomy of the will is true, and as an a priori principle absolutely necessary, this supposes the possibility of a synthetic use of pure practical reason, which however we cannot venture on without first giving a critical examination of this faculty of reason. In the concluding section we shall give the principal outlines of this critical examination as far as is sufficient for our purpose.